ANTITRUST LAW AND ECONOMICS

ENCYCLOPEDIA OF LAW AND ECONOMICS, SECOND EDITION

General Editor: Gerrit De Geest
School of Law, Washington University, St Louis, MO, USA

1. Tort Law and Economics
   Edited by Michael Faure
2. Labor and Employment Law and Economics
   Edited by Kenneth G. Dau-Schmidt, Seth D. Harris and Orly Lobel
3. Criminal Law and Economics
   Edited by Nuno Garoupa
4. Antitrust Law and Economics
   Edited by Keith N. Hylton

Future titles will include:

Procedural Law and Economics
Edited by Chris William Sanchirico

Regulation and Economics
Edited by Roger Van den Bergh

Contract Law and Economics
Edited by Gerrit De Geest

Methodology of Law and Economics
Edited by Thomas S. Ulen

Property Law and Economics
Edited by Boudewijn Bouckaert

Corporate Law and Economics
Edited by Joseph A. McCahery and Erik P.M. Vermeulen

Production of Legal Rules
Edited by Francesco Parisi

Intellectual Property Law and Economics
Edited by Ben Depoorter

For a list of all Edward Elgar published titles visit our site on the World Wide Web at http://www.e-elgar.co.uk

Antitrust Law and Economics

Edited by

Keith N. Hylton

Honorable Paul J. Liacos Professor of Law, Boston University School of Law, USA

ENCYCLOPEDIA OF LAW AND ECONOMICS,
SECOND EDITION

Edward Elgar
Cheltenham, UK • Northampton, MA, USA

Published by
Edward Elgar Publishing Limited
The Lypiatts
15 Lansdown Road
Cheltenham
Glos GL50 2JA
UK

Edward Elgar Publishing, Inc.
William Pratt House
9 Dewey Court
Northampton
Massachusetts 01060
USA

Cased edition reprinted 2014

A catalogue record for this book
is available from the British Library

Library of Congress Control Number: 2009940635

FSC
www.fsc.org
MIX
Paper from
responsible sources
FSC® C013056

ISBN 978 1 84720 731 9

Printed and bound in Great Britain by T.J. International Ltd, Padstow

Contents

Figures and tables

Figures

Tables

Contributors

Alden F. Abbott rejoined the Federal Trade Commission (FTC) in 2001 from the Commerce Department where he had served since 1994, most recently as Acting General Counsel. His previous career highlights include serving as an attorney advisor in the FTC's Office of Policy Planning, senior positions in the Departments of Justice and Commerce, and Associate Dean for Technology Policy at George Mason University Law School. He received his JD from Harvard University Law School, his MA from Georgetown University, and his BA from the University of Virginia.

Jonathan B. Baker is Professor of Law at American University's Washington College of Law, where he teaches courses primarily in the areas of antitrust and economic regulation. From 1995 to 1998, Professor Baker served as the Director of the Bureau of Economics at the Federal Trade Commission. Previously, he worked as a Senior Economist at the President's Council of Economic Advisers, Special Assistant to the Deputy Assistant Attorney General for Economics in the Antitrust Division of the Department of Justice, an Assistant Professor at Dartmouth's Amos Tuck School of Business Administration, an Attorney Advisor to the Acting Chairman of the Federal Trade Commission, and an antitrust lawyer in private practice. He is the co-author of an antitrust casebook, a past Editorial Chair of *Antitrust Law Journal*, and a past member of the Council of the American Bar Association's Section of Antitrust Law. Professor Baker has published widely in the fields of antitrust law and policy and industrial organization economics. In 2004 he received American University's Faculty Award for Outstanding Scholarship, Research, and Other Professional Accomplishments, and in 1998 he received the Federal Trade Commission's Award for Distinguished Service.

Roger D. Blair is the Walter K. Matherly Professor of Economics at the University of Florida. He has written many journal articles dealing with antitrust matters and has co-authored *Antitrust Economics*, *Monopsony in Law & Economics*, *Law and Economics of Vertical Integration and Control*, *The Economics of Franchising*, and *Proving Antitrust Damages*. He received his PhD in Economics from Michigan State University in 1968 and has been on the faculty at the University of Florida since 1970.

Celeste K. Carruthers is an assistant professor in the Department of Economics at the University of Tennessee. She is an affiliated researcher with the Center for Business and Economic Research at the University of Tennessee and the National Center for Analysis of Longitudinal Data in Education Research at the Urban Institute in Washington, D.C. She holds a PhD in Economics from the University of Florida (2009), and her dissertation research on charter school teachers has won awards from the University of Florida Department of Economics and the American Education Finance Association. Her research interests include, broadly, the economics of education, public finance, antitrust economics, regulation, and intersections therein. She has written for the *Antitrust Bulletin* and taught antitrust economics and public expenditure analysis at the University of Florida and the University of Tennessee.

Thomas F. Cotter is the Briggs and Morgan Professor of Law at the University of Minnesota Law School. He received his BS and MS degrees in economics from the University of Wisconsin-Madison, and graduated magna cum laude from the University of Wisconsin Law School. His principal research and teaching interests are in the fields of domestic and international intellectual property law, antitrust, and law and economics. He is the co-author, with Roger D. Blair, of *Intellectual Property: Economic and Legal Dimensions of Rights and Remedies*. He has authored or co-authored more than 25 other scholarly publications, including articles in the *California Law Review*, *Georgetown Law Journal*, and *Minnesota Law Review*.

Daniel A. Crane, Professor of Law at the University of Michigan, teaches contracts, antitrust, and antitrust and intellectual property. His recent scholarship has focused primarily on antitrust and economic regulation, particularly the institutional structure of antitrust enforcement, predatory pricing, bundling, and the antitrust implications of various patent practices. His work has appeared in the *University of Chicago Law Review*, the *California Law Review*, the *Michigan Law Review*, and the *Cornell Law Review*, among other journals. He is the co-editor, with Eleanor Fox, of the Antitrust Stories volume of Foundation Press's Law Stories series, and has a book on the institutional structure of antitrust enforcement forthcoming from Oxford University Press. An editor of the *Antitrust Law Journal* since 2005 and a member of the American Antitrust Institute's Advisory Board, he also serves as counsel in the litigation department of Paul, Weiss, Rifkind, Wharton & Garrison of New York.

Shubha Ghosh is a Professor of Law and an Honorary Fellow, and Associate Director, INSITE, at the University of Wisconsin, Madison. He writes and teaches in the areas of intellectual property, competition law and policy, international intellectual property, tort law, and law and economics. He holds a JD from Stanford, a PhD (economics) from Michigan, and a BA from Amherst College.

Jeffrey L. Harrison holds the Stephen C. O'Connell Chair and is Professor of Law at the College of Law, Gainesville, Florida. He holds a JD degree from the University of North Carolina and a PhD in Economics from the University of Florida. He is the co-author of, with Jules Theeuwes, *Law and Economics*; with Roger Blair, *Monopsony Law and Economics*; and with E.T. Sullivan, *Understanding Antitrust and its Economic Implications*. His principal teaching interests are contract law, copyright law, antitrust and law and economics.

Keith N. Hylton is the Honorable Paul J. Liacos Professor of Law at Boston University, where he teaches courses in antitrust, torts, and employment law. He has published numerous articles in American law journals and peer-reviewed law and economics journals. His textbook, *Antitrust Law: Economic Theory and Common Law Evolution*, was published in 2003. He serves as Co-editor of *Competition Policy International* and Editor of the Social Science Research Network's *Torts, Products Liability and Insurance Law Abstracts*. He is a former chair of the Section on Antitrust and Economic Regulation of the American Association of Law Schools, a former director of the American Law and Economics Association, and a member of the American Law Institute.

Bruce H. Kobayashi is Professor of Law at George Mason University School of Law. He has previously served as a Senior Economist in the Division of Economic Policy Analysis of the Federal Trade Commission, and has served as a Senior Research Associate at the United States Sentencing Commission, and as an Economist for the Antitrust Division of the US Department of Justice. He received his PhD and MA in Economics, and his BS in Economics-System Science, all from the University of California, Los Angeles.

Michael J. Meurer is the Michaels Faculty Scholar and Professor of Law at Boston University. He researches and teaches patent law, law and economics, antitrust law, copyright law, contract law and regulation. Before joining BU Law he was an economics professor at Duke University and later a law professor at the University at Buffalo. He also taught short courses in American intellectual property law at the law faculties of the University of Victoria and the National University of Singapore. He received his PhD in economics and JD from the University of Minnesota. Professor Meurer has received numerous grants and fellowships, including the David Saul Smith Award from BU Law, a grant from the Kauffman Foundation, two grants from the Pew Charitable Trust, a Ford Foundation grant, an Olin Faculty Fellowship at Yale Law School and a postdoctoral fellowship at AT&T Bell Labs. His book, *Patent Failure* was written with Jim Bessen.

William H. Page is the Marshall M. Criser Eminent Scholar and Senior Associate Dean for Academic Affairs at the University of Florida Levin College of Law. He has authored over fifty articles and book chapters and is co-author (with John Lopatka) of *The Microsoft Case: Antitrust, High Technology, and Consumer Welfare*. He was a trial attorney with the Antitrust Division of the US Department of Justice and has taught at Boston University and at Mississippi College, where he was the J. Will Young Professor of Law. He received his JD summa cum laude from the University of New Mexico and his LLM from the University of Chicago.

Joshua D. Wright is Assistant Professor of Law at George Mason University School of Law. He received both a JD and a PhD in economics from UCLA, where he was managing editor of the *UCLA Law Review*, and a BA in economics with highest departmental honors at the University of California, San Diego. His research focuses on antitrust law and economics, empirical law and economics, the intersection of intellectual property and antitrust, and the law and economics of contracts. His research has appeared in several leading academic journals, including the *Journal of Law and Economics*, *Antitrust Law Journal*, *Competition Policy International*, *Supreme Court Economic Review*, *Yale Journal on Regulation*, the *Review of Law and Economics*, and the *UCLA Law Review*.

Preface

This collection of chapters on fundamental topics in antitrust was arranged with the goal of presenting the subject in a manner that reflects modern thinking in both the law and the economics of antitrust. That is not an easy task. Antitrust economics has become a very complicated field. It requires specialization, and as a result it is quite difficult to stay abreast of both the law and the modern economic treatments.

Any effort to provide a balance of legal and economic analysis, given the long history of the law and the level of sophistication in modern economic research, will necessarily involve some sacrifice of both approaches. I am not sure it is possible to present a book that offers the combination of everything an antitrust law specialist would like to see, as well as everything an antitrust economist would like to see. But I think it is better to sacrifice a bit from both of the endpoints to produce something that blends the two approaches, which is what this volume attempts to do.

The argument for incorporating economic analysis in any modern discussion of antitrust law is obvious today. American courts use economic reasoning to reach conclusions on the best policies to adopt in antitrust cases. American antitrust litigation relies heavily on the input of experts trained in economics and statistics. It would be educational malpractice to train any law student to practice antitrust without communicating the importance of economic analysis to the student.

In Europe, the importance of economic analysis to antitrust (competition law as it is known in Europe) is even greater than in the US. The European Commission (EC) tries to act as a scientific body on matters of competition law. It employs economists to develop the competition norms that the EC would like to enforce, and relies on economists to determine the soundness of its enforcement actions. Moreover, since the European courts tend to defer to the EC on matters of policy, economists have a much greater pull on the development of law in the EU than in the US. This has provided enormous incentives for European economists to examine industrial organization issues at the heart of competition law cases.

The argument for incorporating a sophisticated legal approach to the analysis of antitrust has become less obvious today. But its importance should not be discounted. Economic analyses of antitrust divorced from serious consideration of the law tend to meander off into issues that are of little relevance to the courts. More importantly, and especially in the

US, judges have to administer antitrust law, not economists. Judges have to craft rules that can be applied consistently and predictably within the courts. Judges have to consider the likelihood that any given rule will be applied erroneously by future courts, and the costs of those mistakes. The rules that have been developed by courts reflect these considerations. In order to apply economics in a manner that will be useful to courts, the analysis has to be guided by a sense of what will work in application. Lawyers tend to have the advantage on this question.

The authors who have contributed to this volume have the great advantage, in my view, of being familiar with both the law and the economics of antitrust. I hope that this effort to synthesize the two approaches to antitrust yields a sum greater than its parts.

1 The economics of antitrust enforcement

Daniel A. Crane[1]

Antitrust law is only as good as the mechanisms by which it is enforced. Substance and procedure are not distinct bodies, but part of a continuum of legal and institutional rules, practices, and mechanisms working conjunctively to advance consumer welfare and efficiency. It is impossible to understand the substantive rules without understanding the relevant enforcement mechanisms. Judges tend to formulate liability rules with an eye on enforcement mechanisms. For example, judges tend to be skeptical of the ability of lay juries to decide predatory pricing cases, so they formulate deliberately underinclusive liability rules to thin out the number of predation cases reaching trial.[2] Similarly, the Supreme Court has made it hard to plead conspiracy in cartel cases because trial courts have trouble preventing discovery costs from skyrocketing.[3] Evaluating liability rules in a vacuum, without understanding the institutional considerations that motivate judges, might lead to false impressions about the courts' views of the merits of various competitive practices.

Many of the procedural and enforcement rules that apply to antitrust cases were not designed for antitrust, but are general features of civil or criminal law. Sometimes, mismatches occur between procedure's generality and antitrust's specificity. Generic enforcement methods are not always well-suited to the peculiarities of antitrust.

In the US legal system, antitrust enforcement is decentralized and largely uncoordinated. There are two separate federal antitrust enforcement agencies, fifty state attorneys general with enforcement powers, liberal rules for private enforcement, and a treble damages bounty that draws private litigation entrepreneurs into the antitrust litigation market. Antitrust is enforced both civilly and criminally, publicly and privately, prospectively (for injunction) and retrospectively (for damages or other penalties), formally and informally, and administratively and adjudicatively.

Evaluating this crazy quilt of enforcement mechanisms requires defining the goals of antitrust enforcement, which is the subject of the first part of this chapter. The second part asks what forms of public enforcement are best calibrated to achieve these goals. The third part considers two of the leading issues in private enforcement – standing rules and damages.

I. Enforcement goals

The goals of antitrust enforcement are bound up with the goals of antitrust law itself. How antitrust is enforced depends substantially on what antitrust law is intended to achieve. For much of the history of US antitrust law, there was debate and disagreement over antitrust law's goals.[4] The differing views implied widely varying possibilities about the structure of enforcement. Today, there is broad consensus on the goals of antitrust law, which makes possible a broad consensus on the goals and structure of enforcement.

A. Deterrence, compensation, and any others?

The modern consensus among economists and antitrust practitioners is that antitrust law should exist primarily to achieve allocative efficiency and to advance consumer welfare.[5] Although these two goals sometimes conflict when it comes to the specification of liability rules,[6] they are generally in harmony when it comes to antitrust's enforcement goal.[7] Both allocative efficiency and consumer welfare are best served by an enforcement structure that makes the defendant fully internalize the external cost of the violation – the deadweight loss borne by consumers and monopoly transfer from consumers to producers.[8] Such an approach deters anticompetitive behavior by making socially harmful behavior a negative expected value event.

Deterrence is only one of the recognized goals of antitrust enforcement. The Supreme Court has held that compensation of injured parties is an additional goal, although the Court has seemingly made compensation subsidiary to deterrence.[9] From an economic perspective, it is not obvious why compensation should matter at all. Wealth transfers, whether from consumers to producers or from one business to another business, are an external cost of antitrust violations and can decrease social welfare in a variety of subtle ways. However, economic theory cannot predict with great certainty the social welfare consequences of returning overcharges to the victims of the violation. For example, one might think that wealth transfers from consumers to producers would cause a diminution in net social welfare because producers tend to be wealthier than consumers and money begins to bring diminishing marginal utility returns at higher wealth levels. Hence, compensating the consumers would seem to increase social welfare.[10] But the assumption that producers are wealthier than shareholders is far from universalizable. Consider, for example, a cartel among publicly traded yacht manufacturers whose stock is owned in large portion by employees, small investors, and union pension funds. Compensation cannot be justified as a goal of antitrust enforcement on economic terms, although it may have moral or political justifications.

An additional enforcement goal is prevention through *ex ante*, firm-specific control. Instead of discentivizing anticompetitive behavior (as in the deterrence model), the prevention model involves *ex ante* scrutiny of specific commercial practices by identified actors. Merger control is a leading example of where antitrust works primarily on an *ex ante* approval basis. Instead of punishing firms that have entered into anticompetitive mergers or seeking to break them up after the fact, the Hart-Scott-Rodino Act requires firms that plan to merge to file a notification with the enforcement agencies, enabling the agencies to scrutinize the mergers before they occur. An issue that will be discussed further below is whether it would be preferable to rely more on such an administrative model of antitrust rather than on the adjudicative model that seeks to ascertain and punish past bad acts.

Deterrence and *ex ante* control are the two primary economic goals of antitrust enforcement. Most other goals (in addition to compensation, discussed above) cannot be justified on primarily economic terms. Although political considerations sometimes enter into enforcement decisions,[11] such considerations are largely outside of the jurisdiction of economics.

B. *Overdeterrence and underdeterrence*

In an ideal world, antitrust decision-makers would simply 'aim to get it right' and not worry about whether they were tending more toward overinclusion or underinclusion. But it is unrealistic to expect that bodies of law are free from systematic tilts toward false positives (erroneous findings of liability) or false negatives (erroneous findings of non-liability). For example, free speech law may be oriented toward false negatives. First Amendment law protects a good deal of speech that has little social value because the costs of disallowing socially useful speech are generally thought to be higher than the costs of protecting socially harmful speech. On the other hand, securities regulation may be oriented toward false positives. Publicly traded companies may be required to disclose more than the optimal amount of information – and pay penalties if they do not – because it is thought that the costs of overdisclosure are less than the costs of underdisclosure.

Whether antitrust should err in the direction of overdeterrence or underdeterrence is a question for both antitrust substance and antitrust procedure. Adjudicatory errors may occur in both directions – false positive and false negative – and at both the liability rule-framing level (through underinclusion or overinclusion) and at enforcement level (through factfinder error). A tendency in one direction in substantive rules can be counteracted by a tendency in the opposite direction in procedural rules. For example, a tendency toward false positives at the substantive level can be counteracted by the framing of procedural rules (such as evidentiary exclusion rules), stringency in the requirements for expert testimony, or heightened burdens of proof, that make a finding of liability less probable.[12]

As noted at the outset, courts tend to frame liability rules in a deliberately underinclusive manner.[13] They also tend to frame stringent procedural rules that weed out before trial all but the strongest antitrust cases. At both the motion to dismiss and summary judgment stages, courts scrutinize the economic plausibility of antitrust claims and dismiss those cases that lack a sufficiently rigorous foundation in economic theory.[14] The use of these procedural screens necessarily strains out some cases that might be found meritorious if allowed to proceed to discovery or trial. Thus, the recent tendency in US antitrust law has been to tilt both the procedural rules and sustentative liability rules toward underinclusion.

There are several possible explanations and justifications for attitudinal tilts toward false negatives in both liability rules and procedural rules. I will suggest three possibilities.

First, the costs of false positives tend to be greater than the costs of false negatives. In an economy characterized by low regulatory entry barriers, a high rate of innovation, and efficient capital markets, privately acquired market power may be fragile and perpetually contestable – which makes the need for antitrust intervention comparatively low. This would suggest that false negatives are likely to cost relatively little. On the other hand, false positives in antitrust cases may impose costly constraints on otherwise well-functioning capital and industrial markets.

Second, courts may err in the direction of false negatives over those facets of the legal system that they control because those aspects of the legal system that they do not control tilt toward false positives. In particular, the false-negative orientation of antitrust's procedural and substantive rules may be explained by judges' beliefs that jurors tend to err in the direction of overinclusion or false positives. This tendency may occur because jurors misunderstand the complex substance of antitrust law and manifest populist bias against large corporations that use cut-throat – although not necessarily exclusionary – competitive tactics.[15] If jury avoidance explains a least a portion of the judiciary's false-negative orientation, one would expect – or hope – to see judges tilting back toward equilibrium in equitable or administrative actions brought by the government, which do not entail juries. In fact, we observe relatively little difference in judicial attitude toward public and private antitrust cases.[16]

Finally, contemporary judges may be tilting toward false negatives in reaction to a history of perceived error in the opposite direction. The Chicago School critique of the interventionist antitrust precedents of the Warren Court and earlier eras has exerted a profound influence on the courts. Judicial pendulums sometimes swing to the opposite extreme before coming to rest in the middle. Antitrust enforcement may presently be biased toward underinclusion simply because it was formerly biased toward overinclusion.

II. Public enforcement

US public enforcement is comparatively decentralized. Two different federal departments or agencies enforce federal antitrust law, as do each state's attorney general. The Sherman Act is enforced both criminally and civilly. On the civil side, the Justice Department can seek both civil penalties and injunctions, and the injunctions may be simple or complex. These various enforcement mechanisms interact in complex ways.

A. Executive or agency

Both the Antitrust Division of the Department of Justice (and the regional United States Attorneys offices, which are subsets of the Justice Department) and the Federal Trade Commission (FTC) enforce the antitrust laws. The Justice Department and FTC enjoy concurrent enforcement authority over some statutes and exclusive authority over others.[17] However, the two agencies effectively exercise co-extensive authority over all antitrust (with the exception of criminal enforcement, which is the exclusive prerogative of the Justice Department).

In theory, one might justify the existence of two federal agencies on the grounds of comparative advantage over different kinds of matters. The FTC is set up to be politically independent and technocratic. It enjoys rule-making powers and can try matters before specialized administrative law judges, rather than generalist Article III judges. Power is dispersed among five commissioners, no more than three of whom can be of the same political party. By contrast, the Department of Justice enjoys the advantages of unitary executive control, which can accelerate and streamline decision-making.

Unfortunately, there is very little correspondence between the agencies' comparative advantages based on institutional structure and their division of labor.[18] For example, in 2002 the Antitrust Division and the FTC entered into a formal clearance agreement in order to avoid duplication of investigations.[19] The agreement divided antitrust enforcement responsibility based on the agencies' comparative expertise and experience with different industry sectors, not the institutional structure of the agencies. Thus, for example, the FTC was to investigate computer hardware, energy, healthcare, retail stores, pharmaceuticals, and professional services and the Antitrust Division agriculture, computer software, financial services, media and entertainment, telecommunications, and travel.[20] That the Justice Department was to handle computer software while the FTC handled computer hardware had nothing to do with hardware being better suited to the institutional capabilities of the FTC. It was simply a convenient division of labor based on what the two agencies had done in the past. Although the clearance agreement quickly folded due to political pressure from Congress, it exemplifies the essential fungibility of the two agencies.

Not surprisingly, calls have been made to consolidate enforcement in a single agency. For example, this might be accomplished by taking away the FTC's antitrust enforcement powers and leaving it only a consumer protection/anti-fraud mission. Nonetheless, the institutional status quo seems secure for the foreseeable future. Although very few people would draw up the institutional status quo if working on a blank slate, *tabula rasa* design is a very different question from whether to dismantle a system that, whatever its quirks, seems to be working reasonably well.

B. Federal or state

State attorneys general can enforce federal antitrust law in three ways: (1) as 'persons' qualified to seek injunctive relief under Section 16 of the Clayton Act; (2) as persons injured in their business or property when the antitrust violation has harmed the state in its proprietary capacity (*i.e.*, the state government has purchased software from Microsoft); and (3) as *parens patriae* on behalf of their residents.[21] The states attorneys general can also sue in various capacities to enforce their respective state antitrust laws.

State antitrust enforcers have been perceived as being increasingly active in the last two decades, perhaps in response to less aggressive enforcement in Washington. Some commentators have viewed state enforcers through a public choice lens and accused them of pursuing parochial and localist business interests instead of consumer welfare.[22] Others have complained that state enforcers have interfered with federal antitrust enforcement. Richard Posner, who attempted to mediate a settlement in the *Microsoft* case, later complained that the participation of the states made it more difficult to coordinate a settlement and interfered with the federal government's efforts to resolve the matter.[23] Posner has proposed that the federal enforcers should have the authority to preempt state antitrust enforcement in particular cases.[24]

Despite such criticisms, there is no doubt that state enforcement of antitrust law can be a valuable complement to federal enforcement, particularly when it is focused on local market conditions over which the states have a comparative advantage. In recent years, the National Association of Attorneys General (NAAG) has made increasing efforts to coordinate enforcement among the states, to systematize and regularize state enforcement protocols, and to achieve greater transparency by making publicly available a database describing the states' enforcement activities.[25] Some commentators have viewed state enforcement as a valuable counterweight to periodic variations in the vigor of federal enforcement, due to changes in administration.

C. Criminal or civil

Sections 1, 2, and 3 of the Sherman Act, Section 3 of the Robinson-Patman Act, and Section 14 of the Clayton Act provide for criminal penalties. Yet, while a wide range of antitrust activity could potentially subject individual defendants and corporations to criminal fines and (in the case of individuals) imprisonment, the Justice Department today prosecutes criminally only against hard-core cartel behavior such as covert price fixing, bid rigging, and market division.

Figure 1.1 shows the level of Antitrust Division case filings, adjusted for the amount of economic activity in the country.[26] The figure shows raw civil and criminal case filing numbers and antitrust filings as a percentage of real GDP, which allows a historical comparison of agency filings adjusted for overall economic activity. Two aspects of the data are significant. First, overall Department of Justice enforcement – at least measured by case filings – has declined significantly as a percentage of the economy in the last two decades.[27] Second, the ratio of civil to criminal enforcement has varied much more historically than the overall ratio of enforcement to economic activity. Thus, for example, during the Reagan administration criminal enforcement increased considerably even while civil enforcement declined considerably.

The ratio of civil to criminal enforcement depends in large part on the administration's enforcement priorities. Criminal enforcement will rise when the administration views covert behavior, such as price fixing, as a relatively greater menace than publicly disclosed behavior, such as exclusionary joint venture bylaws. Criminal enforcement is justified by the need to make covert collusive behavior an *ex ante* negative expected value activity. If a cartel believes that there is only a 10 per cent chance that it will be caught, the penalty for being caught must be at least ten times the cartel's expected profits from the collusion. If it is less, it will make economic sense for the cartel to proceed. Since the treble damages available in private cases are probably not enough to make collusion a negative expected value event (more on this below), some stronger deterrent may be needed.

There are two ways to take the expected profitability out of collusion. One, just discussed, is to increase the penalty. Another way is to increase the probability of detection. In the past decade, the Justice Department

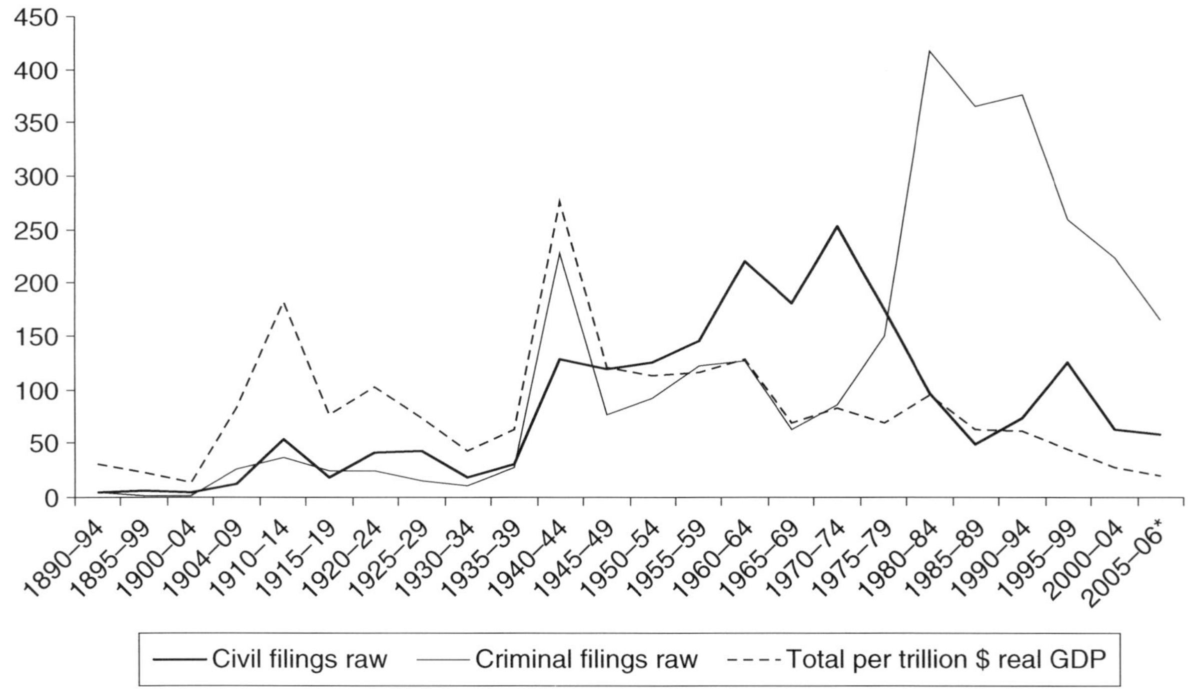

Source: Department of Justice Antitrust Division and Posner (1970), 'A Statistical Study of Antitrust Enforcement', Table 5.5.

Figure 1.1 DOJ cases filed per five-year period

has found a highly effective means of increasing the probability of detection – offering leniency to members of the cartel who disclose the cartel's existence before it is otherwise detected.[28] Such leniency effectively exploits the prisoners' dilemma facing cartels – sticking together is optimal, cheating first is next best, finding out that another member cheated first is pessimal.

Despite government claims that criminal enforcement is increasing in effectiveness, it is hard to know just how effective anti-cartel enforcement is. Between 1997 and 2006, 156 antitrust defendants were sentenced to incarceration for a total of 64,852 days, an average of 416 days per defendant.[29] Thus, the average defendant faces just a little bit more than a year in prison for price fixing. One is tempted to compare the marginal costs and benefit of this expectation of prison to the marginal costs and benefit of adding an additional factor to the damages multiplier – for example, increasing the damages multiplier from three to four for cartels – but the trade-offs between criminal and civil enforcement are never that simple. The individual corporate managers who engage in price fixing may be impervious to further increases in the monetary penalty since their own ability to pay a judgment individually was surpassed long before the multiplier reached three. Hence, criminal liability and civil damages liability may be sending incentives to very different entities – criminal to individual managers and civil to the shareholders, who should respond by engaging in more effective monitoring of their managers.

D. Injunctions and administrative solutions

Antitrust injunctions can take various forms, from short, simple and modest to long and complicated. The simplest form – 'cease and desist' orders – require only the defendant to refrain from doing a specified anticompetitive act. Often, however, the enforcement agencies opt for open-ended consent decrees with elaborate protocols for future judicial supervision of the defendant's behavior. The 'Paramount decrees', which impose a variety of complex restrictions on vertical integration and horizontal practices in the movie business, have remained in place (albeit with some relaxations) since 1948.[30] In a recent study, Richard Epstein makes a compelling case for less ambitious, less intrusive, and shorter-lasting consent decrees.[31] Epstein sensibly argues that consent decrees work best when the decree's prohibitions are tied directly to the underlying antitrust violations and have a predetermined sun-down, as in the provision terminating the Microsoft consent decree after five years.[32]

On the other hand, consent decrees may in some circumstances replace antitrust liability with a quasi-contractual and privately enforceable regime that may be cheaper to administer and more effective at regulating market power than the threat of antitrust liability. A leading example of public–private antitrust is the rate-setting mechanism under the BMI and ASCAP consent decrees, which is now codified in a federal statute.[33] BMI and ASCAP are music performance rights clearing houses that aggregate and license millions of individual artists' performance rights.[34] The transactions costs of individual licensing negotiations between each artist and each potential licensee make the clearing houses very economically efficient.[35] At the same time, the aggregation of millions of licenses in the hands of large collective bargaining agents creates a substantial amount of market power and the potential for anticompetitive abuse. The solution has been a long-term consent decree resulting from an antitrust action brought by the Justice Department. Under the consent decrees, BMI and ASCAP must make through-to-the-listener licenses available for public performances of their music repertoires and provide applicants with proposed license fees upon request. If the clearing houses and the applicant cannot agree on a fee, either party may apply to the rate court for the determination of a reasonable fee.[36]

It is uncertain whether the rate-setting court solution to the market power problem is effective. There have been relatively few rate-setting proceedings under the BMI and ASCAP consent decrees and virtually none under other rate-setting provisions for intellectual property in antitrust consent decrees.[37] Just as business firms often bargain in the shadow of antitrust law, so too do they bargain in the shadow of rate-setting courts.

Another form of antitrust enforcement that is largely informal and administrative in character is merger review, under the Hart-Scott-Rodino Antitrust Improvements Act of 1976.[38] Hart-Scott specifies that, as to certain classes of stock and asset acquisitions, the acquiring and/or acquired person must file a premerger notification with the Department of Justice and FTC.[39] Unless the agencies give early termination, the merger or acquisition cannot close for 30 days following the filing.[40] Prior to the termination of the 30-day waiting period, the agencies can issue a 'second request', a species of subpoena for categories of documents and information additional to those that must automatically accompany the initial filing.[41] The agencies can then extend the waiting period for 30 days following satisfaction of the second request.[42] Formally, compliance with Hart-Scott does not mean that a merger is approved or that the merger is deemed legal.[43] But the effect of Hart-Scott has been to create a *de facto* administrative regime of merger approval by government economists and antitrust lawyers who consider, *ex ante*, the likely structural consequences of a merger and negotiate with the merging parties for divestiture packages or conduct commitments sufficient to alleviate competitive concerns.[44] Merger practice has become an administrative enterprise conducted by federal industrial policy experts with wide powers to specify the structure and competitive behavior of merging corporations.[45]

Administrative solutions have many potential advantages over conventional adjudication in furthering antitrust values. Conventional adjudication is largely binary – *i.e.*, the merger is lawful or it is not; the defendant did or did not monopolize. Administrative processes can come up with more fine-tuned solutions to the problem of market power. Conventional adjudication tends to delegate decision-making to generalist judges and lay jurors. Administrative solutions tend to be more technocratic and involve decisions by experts. Conventional adjudication tends to be backward-looking (damages, deterrence) while administrative solutions are often forward-looking (rate-setting, merger-structuring).

It is conventional to juxtapose antitrust adjudication and regulation as competing modalities of economic control, but administrative solutions need not be conventionally regulatory or entail centralized command-and-control regulation. As noted, enforcement of the BMI and ASCAP consent decrees is initiated privately. Similarly, in recent years a number of patent pools adjacent to standard-setting organizations have created private administrative mechanisms to set patent royalty rates and other licensing terms in an effort to replace antitrust litigation with a quasi-contractual solution to the problem of market power.[46]

III. Private enforcement

For every antitrust case filed by the US government (whether the Department of Justice or the FTC), there are approximately ten private cases filed in the federal courts.[47] The United States is unique in this regard. In most other jurisdictions with serious antitrust laws, public enforcement is the norm and private enforcement the rare exception. Given the volume of private cases, two enforcement issues become critical: *who* can sue and *how much* can they recover?

A. Standing rules

Although antitrust law exists supposedly for the benefit of consumers, consumers do not make up a majority of the plaintiffs who file private antitrust cases. The Georgetown Study of Private Antitrust Litigation, conducted on a sample of 2,500 antitrust cases from 1973–1983, found that one-third of private plaintiffs were defendants' competitors, another 30 per cent were dealers or distributors, and less than 20 per cent were customers or otherwise consumers.[48] The high number of suits by competitors and other business interests is worrisome. Antitrust lawsuits are themselves powerful vehicles for raising rivals' costs and excluding competition.[49]

One solution would be to bar competitor suits and limit standing to injured consumers. But that solution has its own problems. First, some anticompetitive violations never succeed in harming consumers because the defendant fails to achieve monopoly power. Yet, there is much sense in allowing a claim for attempted monopolization and not only the completed act.[50] Second, the injury to consumers is often too diffuse to make consumer suits cost effective. Each purchaser may have only pennies at stake, while the monopoly gains to the defendant, and losses to its rivals and other vertically related businesses, are enormous. Class action treatment, which has its own problems, provides only a partial solution. Rivals of the defendant and other business interests may have informational advantages over consumers in identifying and fighting anticompetitive conduct. Consumers may be unaware of how a dominant firm's conduct is keeping new competitors from coming to market but the potential new competitors will know.

So, if private litigation is going to remain an integral part of the enforcement system, it is probably not wise to limit standing to consumers. There are other ways to limit abusive suits by rivals or other disadvantaged business interests. I will mention two of them briefly.[51] First, the Supreme Court has vigorously pressed an 'antitrust injury' doctrine which requires a plaintiff to show not merely that the defendant committed an antitrust violation but also that the harm to the plaintiff was of the kind with which the antitrust laws are concerned. Thus, for example, in *Brunswick Corp v. Pueblo Bowl-O-Mat, Inc.*[52] the Court confronted a claim by a bowling center operator who alleged that it was anticompetitive for a bowling equipment maker to integrate vertically and acquire a bowling center chain that was otherwise going into bankruptcy. The plaintiff's alleged injury was based on the fact that competition continued when, but for the allegedly anticompetitive acquisition, competition would have diminished. Thus, the injury was not the kind that antitrust law was intended to prevent, even if the acquisition itself was anticompetitive. This 'antitrust injury' rule has facilitated the dismissal of competitor suits that raise hypothetical antitrust violations but have not resulted in real consumer harm.

A second antitrust doctrine that has weeded out a number of lawsuits is the 'direct injury' rule.[53] In a moment, we shall consider this rule in the context of claims by purchasers (the 'direct purchaser' issue), but the rule is also invoked to limit suits by rivals and other business interests. The rule is similar to the proximate cause rule of tort law, although it adds some extra wrinkles. The basic intuition is that antitrust violations often cause injury in a falling domino pattern. The defendant organizes a boycott of its rival which harms the rival, the rival's shareholders (and the shareholders of the rival's shareholders, and so on), and the rival's suppliers (and the suppliers of the rival's suppliers, and so on). All of these actors may be able to say that they were injured by the antitrust violation, but not all of them should be able to sue. For one thing, there would be a good deal of duplication of damages and windfalls if both the injured rival and its shareholders could sue.[54] This is less obviously true of the supplier, but if we allowed the rival's direct supplier to sue, then why not allow the supplier's supplier to sue, and so forth up and down the economic chain? The direct injury rule tries to cut off standing at the most immediate level of harm, which is often the rival firm. The strong intuition is that the most direct victims of the antitrust violation will also be the best motivated and informed parties to file the antitrust suit and more than capable of performing the deterrence function. Even if some damages from the violation are not incurred by the direct victims and hence not recoverable from the defendant, the automatic trebling should more than make up for any such slippage.

Similar 'directness' issues are raised with respect to customer standing to sue. Suppose that a price-fixing cartel raises prices $100 above the competitive level. Ultimately, buyers of the defendants' product will pay $100 more, but which buyers? If the defendants are manufacturers, the goods may be sold first to a wholesaler, then to a retailer, and then to an initial consumer, and then resold (used, but still reflecting a monopoly mark-up) to a second consumer. If each of these purchasers sued for the full overcharge paid by that person, the recoverable damages would total far more than $100.

The US Supreme Court addressed these concerns in a trilogy of cases. In the first case, *Hanover Shoe Inc. v. United Shoe Machinery Corp.*,[55] the Court held that the direct purchaser (the wholesaler in our example who buys directly from the price-fixer) has standing to sue for the full amount of the overcharge to him, even though he may have passed on the overcharge downstream and suffered no economic damage as a result. In the second case, *Illinois Brick Co. v. Illinois*,[56] the Court held, conversely, that an indirect purchaser (the retailer or customer in our example) cannot sue even though he may have been the party that actually absorbed the overcharge and suffered economic harm. In the trilogy's third case, *California v. ARC America Corp.*,[57] the Court held that federal antitrust law does not preempt state antitrust laws that allow indirect purchaser suits.

These three cases, while not illogical individually, have made quite a mess of things. First, it is not always easy to determine who is or isn't a 'direct' purchaser so the direct purchaser rule's chief justification – ease of administration – is often eroded by the creation of exceptions to the rule and extensive litigation over its meaning and application. Second, even if the simplicity and symmetry of the *Hanover Shoe–Illinois Brick* regime has efficiency and deterrence justifications, it also creates the morally unappealing result of economically uninjured large businesses reaping windfall damages recoveries while economically injured consumers take nothing. A number of states have reacted by effectively repealing *Illinois Brick* (either judicially or legislatively) under their own antitrust statutes and allowing indirect purchasers to sue. But this only creates more havoc, since there are now *Illinois Brick* repealer states, non-repealer states, and states somewhere between. This leads to extreme complexity, choice of law gamesmanship, and forum shopping in antitrust cases concerning national markets.

The congressionally appointed Antitrust Modernization Commission recently made a recommendation for legislative reforms that would overrule both *Hanover Shoe* and *Illinois Brick* and allow for removal of state cases to federal court and consolidation of all damages claims as to a particular violation.[58] The court would then make a determination of what the total monopoly overcharge was, treble the overcharge, and allocate the damages pot to the different plaintiffs based on the proportion of their individual injuries to the total. While this system would entail its own complications, it would provide a strong improvement over the status quo.

B. Damages rules

From a deterrence perspective, the goal of antitrust damages is to make antitrust violations a negative expected value event and, hence, to discourage anyone from committing an antitrust violation. This much private antitrust enforcement shares with public antitrust enforcement. Defendants are relatively (although not completely) indifferent to the payee of their penalty – whether it be the government or a private party.[59] Thus, an increase in the amount of public penalties can offset a decrease in the amount of private penalties, and vice versa.

As noted earlier, the probability of detection is a crucial input into ascertaining the optimal penalty. If the penalty were set at just the social cost of the violation – roughly, the overcharge from consumers to the defendant, the deadweight costs of forgone transactions, and the costs of enforcement – then there would be suboptimal deterrence, because violations might remain positive expected value events. Thus, the optimal penalty, including both private damages and government fines, is equal to the monopoly overcharge, plus the wealth transfer from consumers to the defendant, plus the costs of enforcement, times the probability of detection.[60] For example, if the social cost of the violation is $100 and it was 20 per cent likely that the violation was going to be detected, the optimal penalty is $500.

Under US antitrust law, private damages recoveries are automatically trebled (juries are not told about this, so unless one of the jurors knows independently about trebling, it is unlikely that the jury will discount the damages award knowing that it will be trebled). The trebling rule could be justified partially by the fact that not all of the social cost of the antitrust violation is recoverable as damages. In a cartel case, for example, the usual plaintiffs will be purchasers of the price-fixed good or service who paid more as a result of the conspiracy. But those plaintiffs' loss represents merely the wealth transfer consequence of the violation. Consumers who considered purchasing the defendants' goods or service but found the price too high and therefore substituted to some second-best solution are the core victims – their injury is the inefficient deadweight loss. But it is very hard to make plaintiffs out of people who did not purchase the defendants' goods. There are no transactions to be identified and the claim 'I would have purchased' is often highly speculative. So most purchaser–victim classes consist of plaintiffs who did transact and paid a higher price, not of the core antitrust victims who are usually unidentifiable.

The trebling rule could reflect a rough intuition that only one of out every three antitrust violations is detected and that most are not publicly prosecuted in any event. Even assuming that this intuition is correct on average, it is very unlikely that probability of detection in antitrust cases clusters toward the mean. To the contrary, there appear to be classes of antitrust cases where detection is highly likely and other classes where it is highly unlikely. According to one study, a cartel's probability of detection is between 13 and 17 per cent.[61] Although the estimates vary considerably, most put the probability of detection below 20 per cent.[62] On the other hand, certain types of predation strategies rely heavily on signaling long-term predatory commitments to rivals, and thus are only likely to work if they are detected.[63] Some anticompetitive schemes work only by stealth, others only by loud announcement, and yet the undifferentiated treble damages multiplier treats them all as if they operated by the same degree of stealth.

One potential solution is to tailor the damages multiplier to the degree of the concealment. For example, a jury might be asked an initial binary question – did the defendant conceal its anticompetitive behavior – and then, if the answer is yes, make a further decision as to what number – say 25, 50, or 75 per cent – is closest to the likelihood of detection.[64] The judge would then multiply the actual damages award by an amount corresponding to the number selected sufficient to make the antitrust violation a negative expected value event.[65] Whether this would improve over the status quo is subject to some doubt – introducing more complexity into already complex antitrust trials might just increase the overall error rate.

Although trebling receives the lion's share of attention on the question of private remedy, an equally important question concerns what to do with uncertainty about the amount of damages. Antitrust violations disrupt markets and recovering the 'but for' world is highly problematic. This problem is particularly acute in claims by would-be new entrants that were excluded from the market by the defendant's anticompetitive conduct. At common law, plaintiffs who were denied a new business opportunity by some wrongful act of the defendant – say a breach of contract or tort – faced denial of their damages claim under a 'new business rule' that denied lost profits to firms that did not have an established track record.[66] Even where the 'new business rule' was not applied in rule-like form, the plaintiff still bore the burden of proving its lost profits with reasonable certainty. This effectively meant that the costs of the uncertainty created by the defendant's wrong were borne by the injured party rather than the wrongdoer.

Antitrust law treats the frustrated new entrant's claim quite differently. As a threshold matter, the plaintiff must prove that it was 'prepared' to enter the market – that it had the intention and capability of entering and that it took material, affirmative steps toward entry.[67] But once the plaintiff establishes standing, the law effectively shifts the costs of uncertainty about the amount of damages to the defendant.[68] In a case where there was damage but the amount is quite speculative, the plaintiff is given considerable leeway in creating a model of lost profits.

In combination leniency in proof of the amount of damages and trebling create the possibility of overdeterrence – that is to say, that the law will deter socially beneficial conduct. This is particularly a concern given that many of the cases where damages are most speculative are lost profits claims by allegedly foreclosed new entrants – cases where, unlike cartel cases, the probability of detection is very high because the harm is concentrated in a single entity and the conduct is visible.

There is no formulaic solution to the problem of uncertainty over damages awards. Verbal formulations – 'reasonable certainty', 'malfeasant should bear the costs of the uncertainty', and so on – fail to provide meaningful guidelines for courts. Perhaps the best that can be suggested is that courts should play a rigorous gatekeeping role on expert testimony about damages, ensuring that damages estimates are based on reliable benchmarks and credible economic theories.

Notes

1. Professor of Law, University of Michigan.
2. *See* Crane, D. (2007), 'Antitrust Anitfederalism', *Cal. L. Rev.*, **96**, 1.
3. *Bell Atlantic Corp. v. Twombly*, 127 S.Ct. 1955, 1966–67 (2007) (justifying restrictive pleading rule in part because of expense of discovery and inability of trial judges to control overflow of discovery).

4. Hovenkamp, H. (2005), *The Antitrust Enterprise: Principle and Execution*, Cambridge, MA and London, UK: Harvard University Press, 1–2.
5. *See* Hovenkamp, *supra* n. 4 at 1. The reasons that antitrust actually exist may be quite different. As George Stigler has pointed out, the actual purposes of antitrust can only be derived from its effects. Stigler, G. (1975) 'Supplementary Note on Economic Theories of Regulation', in *The Citizen and the State*, Chicago, IL and London, UK: University of Chicago Press. In many cases, the effect of antitrust enforcement has been to shift wealth to politically advantaged interest groups rather than to advance the welfare of consumers. *See* generally McChesney, F. & W. Shughart (eds) (1995), *The Causes and Consequences of Antitrust: The Public Choice Perspective*, Chicago, IL and London, UK: University of Chicago Press.
6. *See* Williamson, E. (1968), 'Economies as an Antitrust Defense: The Welfare Tradeoffs', *Am. Econ. Rev.*, 58, 18 (discussing trade-offs between consumer welfare and overall allocative efficiency).
7. Divergences between total welfare and consumer welfare standards may be more significant in theory than in practice. Tom Barnett, who is currently the Assistant Attorney General in charge of the Antitrust Division, reports that from his perspective as an enforcer, 'the consumer welfare and total welfare standards can diverge, although I think it is a rare case in practice'. Barnett, T. (2005), 'Substantial Lessening of Competition – The Section 7 Standard', *Colum. Bus. L. Rev.*, 2005, 293, 297.
8. *See generally* Hylton, K. (2003), *Antitrust Law: Economic Theory & Common Law Evolution*, Cambridge, UK and New York, NY: Cambridge University Press, 43–4; Landes, W. (1983), 'Optimal Sanctions for Antitrust Violations', *U. Chi. L. Rev.*, 50, 652; Becker, G. (1968), 'Crime & Punishment: An Economic Approach', *J. Pol. Econ.*, 76, 169–217.
9. *Illinois Brick Co. v. Illinois*, 431 U.S. 720, 746 (1977). In *Illinois Brick*, the Court held that only 'direct purchasers' have standing to sue for overcharges resulting from anticompetitive behavior, a holding that may be satisfactory from a deterrence perspective but not from a compensation perspective since the 'direct purchasers' are often wholesalers or retailers who simply pass on the overcharge to the consumer.
10. On the diminishing marginal utility of money, see generally Blum, W. & H. Kalven, Jr. (1953), *The Uneasy Case for Progressive Taxation*, Chicago, IL and London, UK: University of Chicago Press, 40–1, 45–6, 51–4, 56–63 and Posner, R. (1981), *The Economics of Justice*, Cambridge, MA and London, UK: Harvard University Press, 55–6, 80.
11. Pitofsky, R. (1979), 'The Political Content of Antitrust', *U. Pa. L. Rev.*, 127, 1051; *but see* Crane, D. (2008), 'Technocracy and Antitrust', *Tex. L. Rev.*, 86, 1159 (arguing that antitrust law has become increasingly depoliticized and advocating further movement in a technocratic direction).
12. Bierschback, R. & A. Stein (2005), 'Overenforcement', *Geo. L.J.* 93, 1743, 1758.
13. Kovacic, W. (2007), 'The Intellectual DNA of Modern U.S. Competition Law for Dominant Firm Conduct: The Chicago/Harvard Double Helix', *Colum. Bus. L. Rev.*, 2007, 1, 72 (noting that both the Chicago and Harvard schools of antitrust have contributed to underinclusive liability norms for dominant firm behavior); Schoen, D. (2005), 'Exclusionary Conduct After Trinko', *N.Y.U. L. Rev.*, 80, 1625, 1647 (noting that the Supreme Court has created deliberately underinclusive liability norms for refusals to deal by dominant firms); Brodley, J. (1995), 'Antitrust Standing in Private Merger Cases: Reconciling Private Incentives and Public Enforcement Goals', *Mich. L. Rev.*, 94, 1, 23 n. 88 (noting that predatory pricing plaintiffs 'must overcome deliberately underinclusive liability rules').
14. *See Bell Atlantic Corp. v. Twombly*, 127 S. Ct. 1955, 1965–6 (2007) (requiring dismissal of antitrust conspiracy claim that lacked plausible basis); *Matsushita Elec. Industrial Co. v. Zenith Radio Corp.*, 475 U.S. 574, 596–7 (1986) (requiring grant of summary judgment against conspiracy and predatory pricing theory that was economically implausible).

15. *See* Crane, *Technocracy*, *supra* n. 11 at 1217.
16. *Id.* at 1187–8.
17. In general, the Department of Justice enforces the Sherman Act, the FTC enforces the FTC Act (which means basically the same thing as the Sherman Act), and both agencies enforce the Clayton and Robinson-Patman Acts.
18. Some of the FTC's potential comparative advantages are not exploited. For example, the FTC does not engage in rule-making on issues of antitrust substance even though a statute gives it that power.
19. Memorandum of Agreement Between the Federal Trade Commission and the United States Department of Justice Concerning Clearance Procedures for Investigations (March 5, 2002), available at http://www.ftc.gov/opa/2002/02/clearance/ftcdojagree.pdf.
20. *Id.* at Appendix A.
21. *Hawaii v. Standard Oil Co.*, 405 U.S. 251 (1972).
22. *See, e.g.*, Greve, M. (2005), 'Cartel Federalism? Antitrust Enforcement by State Attorneys General', *U. Chi. L. Rev.* 72, 99.
23. References to Judge Posner's complaints are collected in DeBow, M. 'State Antitrust Enforcement: Empirical Evidence and a Modest Reform Proposal' (2004), in M. Greve and R. Epstein (eds), *Competition Laws in Conflict: Antitrust Jurisdiction in the Global Economy*, Washington, DC: AEI Press, 267, at 282. *See also* Hahn, R. & A. Layne-Farrar (2003), 'Antitrust in Federalism', *Harv. J.L. & Pub. Pol'y*, 26, 877, 878 (arguing that the involvement of the state attorneys general in the Microsoft litigation 'lengthened the lawsuit, complicated the settlement process, and increased both legal uncertainty and litigation costs'); Posner, R. (2004), 'Federalism and the Enforcement of Antitrust Laws by State Attorneys General', in M. Greve and R. Epstein (eds), *Competition Laws in Conflict: Antitrust Jurisdiction in the Global Economy*, Washington, DC: AEI Press, 252.
24. *See* Posner, R. (2001), *Antitrust Law*, Chicago, IL: University of Chicago Press, 281–2 (proposing that federal government should be given a preemptive right of first refusal over state and private suits).
25. *See* 'NAAG State Antitrust Ligitation Database', available at http://www.naag.org/antitrust/search/.
26. The underlying data are pooled from two sources. For 1938–2006, the data were provided to the author by the Department of Justice Antitrust Division. For earlier years, the data were drawn from Posner (1970), 'A Statistical Study of Antitrust Enforcement', at 82, Table 5.5. Posner's data were compiled from the Commerce Clearing House ('CCH'). For the years in which there was overlap between Posner's CCH data and the data provided by the Department of Justice, there were slight but relatively insignificant differences. Real GDP numbers are chained 2000. Numbers from 1929 forward are collected from Bureau of Economic Analysis, http://www.bea.gov/national/xls/gdplev.xls. Pre-1929 numbers are collected from http://eh.net/hmit/gdp/.
27. A fuller discussion of these data and their meaning appears in Crane, *Technocracy*, *supra* n. 11 at 1175–6.
28. Spratling, G. *Making Companies an Offer They Shouldn't Refuse: The Antitrust Division's Corporate Leniency Policy – An Update*, Address Before the Bar Association of the District of Columbia's 35th Annual Symposium on Associations and Antitrust 1–2 (Feb. 16, 1999) (noting greater success in criminal enforcement against international cartels since the adoption of the amnesty policy), *available at* http://www.usdoj.gov/atr/public/speeches/2247.pdf.
29. 'Antitrust Division Workload Statistics: FY 1998 – 2007' (2007), available at http://www.usdoj.gov/atr/public/workstats.htm.
30. Epstein, R. (2007), *Antitrust Consent Decrees in Theory and Practice: Why Less Is More*, Washington, DC: AEI Press, 20–21.
31. *Id.*
32. *Id.* at 112–15. *But see* Hovenkamp, H. (2005), *The Antitrust Enterprise: Principle and*

Execution, Cambridge, MA and London, UK: Harvard University Press, 298–304 (sharply criticizing the Microsoft consent decree as weak and ineffective).
33. *See* Cardi, W. J. (2007), 'Über-Middlemen: Reshaping the Broken Landscape of U.S. Copyright', *Iowa L. Rev.*, 92, 835, 846–7; Wu, T. (2004), 'Copyright's Communications Policy', *Mich. L. Rev.* 103, 278, 304–11. The essential mechanisms of the BMI decree are discussed in *United States v. Broadcast Music, Inc.*, 426 F.3d 91, 95 (2nd Cir. 2005). The rate-setting provision is codified in 17 U.S.C.A. § 513 (2007).
34. The economic justifications for the *BMI* and *ASCAP* system are discussed in *Broadcast Music, Inc. v. Columbia Broadcasting System, Inc.*, 441 U.S. 1 (1979).
35. *Id.*
36. *Broadcast Music*, 426 F.3d at 95.
37. *See* Crane, D., 'Bargaining in the Shadow of Rate-Setting Courts', *Antitrust L. J.*, forthcoming.
38. Pub. L. No. 94–435, 90 Stat. 1383 (1976) (codified in relevant part at 15 U.S.C. § 18a).
39. 15 U.S.C. § 18a(a).
40. *Id.* at § 18a(b)(1).
41. *Id.* at § 18a(e).
42. *Id.* at § 18a(e)(2).
43. Nor does the agency's negotiation of a divestiture package preclude private parties from arguing that the agencies did not go far enough to ensure a competitive market. *See Six West Retail Acquisition, Inc. v. Sony Theatre Management Corp.*, No. 97 CIV. 5499(DNE), 2000 WL 264295, at *23 (S.D.N.Y. Mar. 09, 2000).
44. *See* Sullivan, E.T. (1986), 'The Antitrust Division as a Regulatory Agency: An Enforcement Policy in Transition', *Wash. U. L. Q.*, 64, 997, 1025–42.
45. *See* Crane, *Antitrust Antifederalism*, *supra* n. 2 at 52–3.
46. *See* Crane, D. (2009), 'Patent Pools, RAND Commitments, and the Problematics of Price Discrimination', *Antitrust L. J.* 76, 307.
47. *See* Crane, *Technocracy*, *supra* n. 11 at 1178, 1182.
48. White, L. (1985), 'The Georgetown Study of Private Antitrust Litigation', *Antitrust L. J.* 54, 59, 62.
49. McAfee, P. & N. Vakkur (2005), 'The Strategic Abuse of the Antitrust Laws', *J. Strategic Mgmt. Educ.*, 2, 37, 37–8; Snyder, E. & T. Kauper (1991), 'Misuses of the Antitrust Laws: The Competitor Plaintiff', *Mich. L. Rev.*, 90, 551; Baumol, W. & J. Ordover (1984), 'Use of Antitrust to Subvert Competition', *J. L. & Econ.*, 28, 247; Easterbook, F. (1984), 'The Limits of Antitrust', *Tex. L. Rev.* 63, 1.
50. The classic articulation of the existence of a separate category of attempted monopolization is Justice Holmes's opinion in *Swift & Co. v. United States*, 196 U.S. 375 (1905).
51. For a more general discussion of standing issues, *see* Page, W., 'The Scope of Liability for Antitrust Violations', *Stan. L. Rev.* 37, 1445 (1985).
52. *Brunswick Corp. v. Pueblo Bowl-O-Mat, Inc.* 429 U.S. 477 (1977).
53. The leading antitrust case in this area is *Associated Gen. Contractors of Cal., Inc. v. Carpenters,* 459 U.S. 519 (1983), where the Court denied standing to union that alleged that a contractor's association had coerced third parties to do business with non-unionized labor suppliers. The Supreme Court has reinforced the direct injury rule in several more recent Racketeering Influenced Corrupt Organizations Act (RICO) decisions. *See Anza v. Ideal Steel Supply Corp.*, 547 U.S. 451 (2006); *Holmes v. Securities Investor Protection Corporation,* 503 U.S. 258 (1992).
54. It is also the case that some shareholders will be made whole by the rival's damages recovery, although the present shareholders may not be ones who suffered the original loss and the securities markets may not have fully valued the rival's antitrust lawsuit.
55. *Hanover Shoe Inc. v. United Shoe Machinery Corp.*, 392 U.S. 481 (1968).
56. *Illinois Brick Co. v. Illinois*, 431 U.S. 720 (1977).
57. *California v. ARC America Corp.*, 490 U.S. 93 (1989).
58. Report and Recommendation of the Antitrust Modernization Commission Chapter

Two (April 2007), available at http://www.amc.gov/report_recommendation/.chapter3.pdf.

59. The reason for the 'although not completely' caveat is that firms would rather not pay their competitors damages, since such payments entail not merely reducing the defendant's own funds but also (potentially) weakening its market position as a competitor is strengthened.
60. *See* Hylton, *supra* n. 8 at 43–7.
61. Bryant, P. and W. Eckhard (1991), 'Price Fixing: The Probability of Getting Caught', *Rev. Econ. & Stat.*, 73, 531.
62. *See, e.g.*, Sentencing Options: Hearing Before the United States Sentencing Commission (1986), available in United States Sentencing Commission: Unpublished Public Hearings 1986, at 15 (1988) (Statement of Assistant Attorney General Douglas Ginsburg) (estimating that only one in ten cartels is discovered).
63. *See* Crane, D. (2005), 'The Paradox of Predatory Pricing', *Cornell L. Rev.*, 91, 1, 40.
64. It would seem silly to include the number zero, since the conduct necessarily *was* detected if it is now in litigation.
65. For example, if the violation were only 25 per cent likely to be detected, it would be necessary to quadruple the actual damages – plus a little bit – to make the violation a negative expected value activity.
66. *See, e.g., MindGames, Inc. v. Western Publ'g Co.*, 218 F.3d 652, 656–7 (7th Cir. 2000) (explaining common law rule).
67. *E.g.*, *Ashley Creek Phosphate Co. v. Chevron USA, Inc.*, 315 F.3d 1245, 1254–5 (10th Cir. 2003).
68. *Bigelow v. RKO Radio Pictures*, 327 U.S. 251, 265–6 (1946) (the most elementary conceptions of justice and public policy require that the wrongdoer shall bear the risk of the uncertainty which his own wrong has created).

References

'Antitrust Division Workload Statistics: FY 1998 – 2007' (2007), available at http://www.usdoj.gov/atr/public/workstats.htm.

Barnett, T. (2005), 'Substantial Lessening of Competition – The Section 7 Standard', *Colum. Bus. L. Rev.*, 2005, 293.

Baumol, W. & J. Ordover (1984), 'Use of Antitrust to Subvert Competition', *J. L. & Econ.*, 28, 247.

Becker, G. (1968), 'Crime & Punishment: An Economic Approach', *J. Pol. Econ.*, 76, 169.

Bierschback, R. & A. Stein (2005), 'Overenforcement', *Geo. L.J.*, 93, 1743.

Blum, W. & H. Kalven, Jr. (1953), *The Uneasy Case for Progressive Taxation*, Chicago, IL and London, UK: University of Chicago Press.

Brodley, J. (1995), 'Antitrust Standing in Private Merger Cases: Reconciling Private Incentives and Public Enforcement Goals', *Mich. L. Rev.*, 94, 1.

Bryant, P. and W. Eckhard (1991), 'Price Fixing: The Probability of Getting Caught', *Rev. Econ. & Stat.*, 73, 531.

Cardi, W. J. (2007), 'Über-Middlemen: Reshaping the Broken Landscape of U.S. Copyright', *Iowa L. Rev.*, 92, 835.

Crane, D. (forthcoming), 'Bargaining in the Shadow of Rate-Setting Courts', *Antitrust L. Journal.*

Crane, D. (2009), 'Patent Pools, RAND Commitments, and the Problematics of Price Discrimination', *Antitrust L. J.*, 76, 307.

Crane, D. (2008), 'Technocracy and Antitrust', *Tex. L. Rev.*, 86, 1159.

Crane, D. (2007), 'Antitrust Antifederalism', *Cal. L. Rev.*, 96, 1.

Crane, D. (2005), 'The Paradox of Predatory Pricing', *Cornell L. Rev.*, 91, 1.

Current–Dollar and 'Real' Gross Domestic Product (2008), available at http://www.bea.gov/national/xls/gdplev.xls.

DeBow, M. 'State Antitrust Enforcement: Empirical Evidence and a Modest Reform

Proposal' (2004), in M. Greve and R. Epstein (eds), *Competition Laws in Conflict: Antitrust Jurisdiction in the Global Economy*, Washington, DC: AEI Press.
Easterbook, F. (1984), 'The Limits of Antitrust', *Tex. L. Rev.*, 63, 1.
Epstein, R. (2007), *Antitrust Consent Decrees in Theory and Practice: Why Less Is More*, Washington, DC: AEI Press.
Greve, M. (2005), 'Cartel Federalism? Antitrust Enforcement by State Attorneys General', *U. Chi. L. Rev.*, 72, 99.
Hahn, R. & A. Layne-Farrar (2003), 'Antitrust in Federalism', *Harv. J.L. & Pub. Pol'y*, 26, 877.
Hovenkamp, H. (2005), *The Antitrust Enterprise: Principle and Execution*, Cambridge, MA and London, UK: Harvard University Press.
Hylton, K. (2003), *Antitrust Law: Economic Theory & Common Law Evolution*, Cambridge, UK and New York, NY: Cambridge University Press.
Kovacic, W. (2007), 'The Intellectual DNA of Modern U.S. Competition Law for Dominant Firm Conduct: The Chicago/Harvard Double Helix', *Colum. Bus. L. Rev.*, 2007, 1.
Landes, W. (1983), 'Optimal Sanctions for Antitrust Violations', *U. Chi. L. Rev.*, 50, 652.
McAfee, P. & N. Vakkur (2005), 'The Strategic Abuse of the Antitrust Laws', *J. Strategic Mgmt. Educ.*, 2, 37.
McChesney, F. & W. Shughart (eds.) (1995), *The Causes and Consequences of Antitrust: The Public Choice Perspective*, Chicago, IL and London, UK: University of Chicago Press.
Memorandum of Agreement Between the Federal Trade Commission and the United States Department of Justice Concerning Clearance Procedures for Investigations (2002), available at http://www.ftc.gov/opa/2002/02/clearance/ftcdojagree.pdf.
'NAAG State Antitrust Ligitation Database', available at http://www.naag.org/antitrust/search/.
Page, W. (1985), 'The Scope of Liability for Antitrust Violations', *Stan. L. Rev.*, 37, 1445.
Pitofsky, R. (1979), 'The Political Content of Antitrust', *U. Pa. L. Rev.*, 127, 1051.
Posner, R. (2004) 'Federalism and the Enforcement of Antitrust Laws by State Attorneys General', in M. Greve and R. Epstein (eds), *Competition Laws in Conflict: Antitrust Jurisdiction in the Global Economy*, Washington, DC: AEI Press, 252.
Posner, R. (1981), *The Economics of Justice*, Cambridge, MA and London, UK: Harvard University Press.
Posner, R. (1970), 'A Statistical Study of Antitrust Enforcement', *J. L. & Econ.*, 13, 365, reprinted in Fred S. McChesney and William F. Shughart II (eds) (1995), *The Causes and Consequences of Antitrust: The Public–Choice Perspective*, Chicago, IL and London, UK: University of Chicago Press, 73.
Report and Recommendation of the Antitrust Modernization Commission Chapter Two (2007), available at http://www.amc.gov/report_recommendation/.chapter3.pdf.
Schoen, D. (2005), 'Exclusionary Conduct After Trinko', *N.Y.U. L. Rev.*, 80, 1625.
'Sentencing Options: Hearing Before the United States Sentencing Commission' (1986), available in United States Sentencing Commission: Unpublished Public Hearings 1986, at 15 (1988) (Statement of Assistant Attorney General Douglas Ginsburg).
Snyder, E. & T. Kauper (1991), 'Misuses of the Antitrust Laws: The Competitor Plaintiff', *Mich. L. Rev.*, 90, 551.
Spratling, G. (1999), *Making Companies an Offer They Shouldn't Refuse: The Antitrust Division's Corporate Leniency Policy – An Update*, Address Before the Bar Association of the District of Columbia's 35th Annual Symposium on Associations and Antitrust 1–2 (Feb. 16, 1999), available at http://www.usdoj.gov/atr/public/speeches/2247.pdf.
Stigler, G. (1975) 'Supplementary Note on Economic Theories of Regulation', in *The Citizen and the State*, Chicago, IL and London, UK: University of Chicago Press.
Sullivan, E.T. (1986), 'The Antitrust Division as a Regulatory Agency: An Enforcement Policy in Transition', *Wash. U. L. Q.*, 64, 997.
White, L. (1985), 'The Georgetown Study of Private Antitrust Litigation', *Antitrust L. J.* 54, 59.

Williamson, E. (1968), 'Economies as an Antitrust Defense: The Welfare Tradeoffs', *Am. Econ. Rev.*, 58, 18.
Wu, T. (2004), 'Copyright's Communications Policy', *Mich. L. Rev.*, 103, 278.

Cases

Anza v. Ideal Steel Supply Corp., 547 U.S. 451 (2006).
Ashley Creek Phosphate Co. v. Chevron USA, Inc., 315 F.3d 1245 (10th Cir. 2003).
Associated Gen. Contractors of Cal., Inc. v. Carpenters, 459 U.S. 519 (1983).
Bell Atlantic Corp. v. Twombly, 127 S.Ct. 1955 (2007).
Bigelow v. RKO Radio Pictures, 327 U.S. 251 (1946).
Broadcast Music, Inc. v. Columbia Broadcasting System, Inc., 441 U.S. 1 (1979).
Brunswick Corp. v. Pueblo Bowl-O-Mat Inc., 429 U.S. 477 (1977).
California v. ARC America Corp., 490 U.S. 93 (1989).
Hanover Shoe Inc. v. United Shoe Machinery Corp., 392 U.S. 481 (1968).
Hawaii v. Standard Oil Co., 405 U.S. 251 (1972).
Holmes v. Securities Investor Protection Corporation, 503 U.S. 258 (1992).
Illinois Brick Co. v. Illinois, 431 U.S. 720 (1977).
Matsushita Elec. Industrial Co. v. Zenith Radio Corp., 475 U.S. 574 (1986).
MindGames, Inc. v. Western Publ'g Co., 218 F.3d 652 (7th Cir. 2000).
Swift & Co. v. United States, 196 U.S. 375 (1905).
Six West Retail Acquisition, Inc. v. Sony Theatre Management Corp., No. 97 CIV. 5499(DNE), 2000 WL 264295, at *23 (S.D.N.Y. Mar. 09, 2000).
United States v. Broadcast Music, Inc., 426 F.3d 91 (2nd Cir. 2005).

Statutes

15 U.S.C. § 18a(a).
15 U.S.C. § 18a(b)(1).
15 U.S.C. § 18a(e).
15 U.S.C. § 18a(e)(2).
17 U.S.C.A. § 513 (2007).

2 Facilitating practices and concerted action under Section 1 of the Sherman Act

*William H. Page**

I. Introduction

Collusion, tacit or express, is the 'joint determination of outputs and prices by ostensibly independent firms'.[1] Successful collusion requires that rivals reach consensus on the key terms and deploy some means of detecting and penalizing cheaters, usually by tracking rivals' transaction prices.[2] 'Facilitating practices' are mechanisms that enhance rival firms' ability to police such an arrangement.[3] Examples include price reporting systems,[4] preannouncements of price changes,[5] most favored customer clauses,[6] meeting competition clauses,[7] delivered or basing-point pricing[8] and industry-wide resale price maintenance.[9] Whatever else they may do, facilitating practices make list or transaction pricing more transparent and thus make it easier for firms to check whether their rivals are adhering to a tacit or explicit understanding to maintain a price level. Antitrust lawyers and economists often use the term (or a variant of it) to refer to the theory underlying a famous public enforcement campaign that began in the late 1970s.[10] But the kinds of market phenomena that the term describes were matters of antitrust concern long before then and remain relevant subjects of study in both antitrust law and industrial organization economics.

Facilitating practices are a species of oligopoly behavior, and therefore relevant to the analysis of a variety of practices under the antitrust laws. The enforcement agencies' *1992 Merger Guidelines*, for example, observe that 'reaching terms of coordination may be facilitated . . . by existing practices among firms, practices not necessarily themselves antitrust violations, such as standardization of pricing or product variables on which firms could compete'.[11] The presence of facilitating practices thus might increase the chances that a horizontal merger would be found anticompetitive under Section 7 of the Clayton Act on the grounds that it would increase the probability of 'coordinated interaction that harms consumers'.[12] This role of facilitating practices is examined in Chapter 10. In this chapter, I will consider the role of facilitating practices in the analysis of collusion under Section 1 of the Sherman Act.

Section 1 prohibits every 'contract, combination . . . , or conspiracy' in restraint of trade. Although these three words have different meanings in other contexts, in antitrust law they mean the same thing: an agreement. As the Supreme Court has emphasized, the agreement element of Section 1 is designed to limit the category restraints of trade to those that are more likely to be harmful:

> Concerted activity inherently is fraught with anticompetitive risk. It deprives the marketplace of the independent centers of decision-making that competition assumes and demands. In any conspiracy, two or more entities that previously pursued their own interests separately are combining to act as one for their common benefit. This not only reduces the diverse directions in which economic power is aimed but suddenly increases the economic power moving in one particular direction. Of course, such mergings of resources may well lead to efficiencies that benefit consumers, but their anticompetitive potential is sufficient to warrant scrutiny even in the absence of incipient monopoly.[13]

The framers of the Act evidently believed that, in cases other than monopolization, firms could ordinarily reduce competition only by engaging in some sort of agreement. The prototypical agreement in restraint of trade is the cartel. The early cases that condemned cartels under Section 1 involved express, usually written agreements that the statutory language obviously encompassed.[14] No one contested the applicability of the agreement requirement to these arrangements; any problems of interpretation in these cases lay in other areas, such as whether Section 1 prohibited all restraints of trade or only unreasonable ones.[15]

The interpretive conundrum concerning the meaning of agreement arises when informal patterns of conduct in oligopoly mimic the effects of an express cartel.[16] At least since the 1930s, economists have shown that firms in an oligopoly can, in certain conditions, achieve noncompetitive prices and outputs without a formal agreement by making choices that anticipate each others' likely responses[17] – what courts have called oligopolistic interdependence,[18] conscious parallelism,[19] or tacit collusion.[20] In game theory, behavior like this can allow firms to achieve noncompetitive prices.[21] The pristine case often hypothesized involves rival gas stations at the same street corner in a remote town: by publicly posting a price increase, one station might invite similar actions by rivals, who may comply[22] if they see that they will all profit if they all follow the first firm's price and stick to it, rather than keep prices down in order to increase output temporarily.[23]

It was not always clear whether this sort of conduct violates Section 1. The language of the statute is not decisive, because one might characterize the initial price increase as an 'offer' that the rivals then 'accept' by following suit.[24] Donald Turner argued decades ago, however, that conscious parallelism, without more, cannot be an agreement, or at least an illegal agreement under Section 1, because the rivals are only acting rationally based on available information, like competitive firms.[25] Moreover, Turner argued, it would be vain to try to prevent this sort of conduct, because the remedy would require firms to act irrationally or to submit to direct price regulation.[26] Richard Posner famously responded (and still responds) that, because tacit collusion requires conscious choices, it should be viewed as 'a form of concerted action'[27] that the law could remedy without 'telling oligopolists to behave irrationally'.[28] To make a very long story short, courts have sided with Turner in this dispute.[29] The Supreme Court has recently observed that parallel conduct is 'consistent with conspiracy, but just as much in line with a wide swath of rational and competitive business strategy unilaterally prompted by common perceptions of the market'.[30] Thus, modern courts would certainly hold that the firms in the gas station scenario have not done anything culpable or at least not anything the courts could sensibly penalize or enjoin without doing more harm than good.

The presence of facilitating practices complicates the Section 1 treatment of parallel conduct. The simple gas station scenario rarely occurs in real-world markets, because firms are typically not able to coordinate their actions simply by publicly posting prices.[31] Successful coordination, as I have already noted, requires detection and punishment of deviators. In many markets, firms' list prices may be difficult for their rivals to discover from public information. The list prices may also differ from transaction prices, because firms offer selective, secret discounts. Heterogeneous products and power buyers can multiply the problems of coordination.[32] In these circumstances, cheating might quickly undermine the tacitly arranged price. Thus, firms may adopt a facilitating practice to keep tabs on each other's prices.[33]

As I will show in Part III below, if firms expressly agree to adopt one of these facilitating practices, for example as a trade association rule, and the effect of the practice is to reduce competition, then that agreement may be independently illegal under Section 1. Moreover, the Sherman Act may preempt a state law that requires rivals to use a facilitating practice. A more difficult question arises, however, where the firms each adopt the same facilitating practice without any express agreement: does parallel pricing together with parallel adoption of facilitating practices allow a court to infer the requisite agreement? Both Turner and Posner believed that, unlike simple parallel pricing, the parallel adoption of a facilitating practice that permits noncompetitive pricing should be unlawful, because the problem of remedy is mitigated.[34] Where the market is behaving noncompetitively and facilitating practices make that possible, so the argument goes, courts may characterize the circumstances as a Section 1 agreement and enjoin the use of the practices.

But conduct is not evidence of an agreement simply because it can be enjoined; it must also have no benign, independent justification. Facilitating practices may do more than simply facilitate rivals' efforts to achieve an inefficient oligopoly price. They also may provide certain immediate benefits to consumers by, among other things, reducing search or transaction costs (for example, by disseminating price information to consumers). In these circumstances, the firms' adoption of the practice might well be for the benign rather than the malign, collusive reason. The lesson of the public enforcement campaign against facilitating practices is that courts will not easily infer an agreement from the parallel adoption of facilitating practices where the practices have beneficial functions apart from facilitating price coordination. Courts evaluate facilitating practices as one type of circumstantial evidence that may but usually does not warrant an inference of a Section 1 agreement.

Unfortunately, the stated legal standards of agreement under which courts evaluate circumstantial evidence, including facilitating practices, are inadequate. In the next Part, I review the deficiencies of the present law governing the definition and proof of agreement under Section 1 and propose that the law should recognize that communication among rivals is necessary for concerted action. In Part III, I examine cases involving facilitating practices in a variety of Section 1 contexts, and suggest that the courts have come to recognize the importance of communications among rivals in evaluating whether the evidence warrants an inference of agreement.

II. The definition and proof of agreement

Courts have traditionally evaluated price-fixing claims under two legal standards: a definition of agreement, and a standard of sufficiency of the evidence to raise a jury question. The first of these standards, which jurors are expected to apply if the issue of agreement reaches them, is deficient, because the terms used to define agreement are too ambiguous to make the essential distinctions. The Supreme Court has said that a Sherman Act agreement need not be 'explicit',[35] 'express',[36] or 'formal',[37] so long as the firms have 'a unity of purpose, a common design and understanding, or a meeting of the minds'[38] or 'a conscious commitment to a common scheme'.[39] The Court repeated the 'meeting of the minds' shibboleth in its recent *Twombly* decision.[40] Interpreted charitably, these phrases seem to suggest that rivals agree if they act in the same way, thinking they share a common goal. But those conditions are met by consciously parallel pricing, which we now know is lawful.[41] Thus, the law's definition of agreement offers no basis for making the most difficult distinction courts and juries must make under Section 1.

Nor has antitrust law borrowed a useful definition of agreement from ordinary usage, the law of contracts, or economics. The courts recognize that agreement under the Sherman Act is a 'term of art' whose meaning differs from its usage in 'ordinary parlance'.[42] An agreement under the Sherman Act also cannot be the same as an enforceable agreement in the law of contracts, because Sherman Act agreements, if they restrain trade, are necessarily illegal and unenforceable.[43] Finally, agreement has no technical meaning in economics. Economists distinguish between competitive and noncompetitive outcomes, but they do not formally distinguish between noncompetitive outcomes achieved by consciously parallel action and those achieved by an informal agreement.[44] Thus, economists are typically not permitted to testify whether circumstantial evidence raises an inference of an agreement, because that issue lies outside of their expertise.[45] Consequently, if a case alleging horizontal agreement goes to trial, the jurors that decide the case will not be permitted to apply their common understanding of agreement, yet they will not be given a meaningful definition of agreement by the court or by the expert witnesses.

Most cases based on circumstantial evidence do not go to trial, however, because of the second standard, which defines the sufficiency of evidence to raise a jury question. Under *Matsushita*, 'to survive a motion for summary judgment or for a directed verdict, a plaintiff seeking damages for a violation of § 1 must present evidence "that tends to exclude the possibility" that the alleged conspirators acted independently'.[46] Alternatively, courts require evidence that 'tend[s] to exclude the possibility that the defendants merely were engaged in lawful conscious parallelism'.[47] Another way courts express this standard is by requiring the plaintiff to produce evidence amounting to a 'plus factor'.[48] Although this latter term has a long history and has been used in a variety of ways,[49] courts now use it almost exclusively as a label to characterize evidence that tends to exclude the possibility of independent action, and thus creates a jury issue of agreement.[50] Several pieces of evidence viewed as whole may raise the necessary inference.[51] The Supreme Court's recent decision in *Twombly*[52] on pleading standards for conspiracy cases is a logical outgrowth of this rule: it is not enough for the plaintiff to allege parallel conduct; it must also allege some plausible ground for thinking the parallel conduct is the result of a conspiracy.[53]

This criterion is significant, because it prohibits an inference of agreement in cases in which each defendant's actions are in its individual self-interest, regardless of whether the other defendants act in the same way. In such circumstances, the evidence is fully consistent with independent action; it is certainly not consistent only with collusion. For example, in the classic *Theatre Enterprises* case, the defendant film distributors refused to license first-run films to a suburban theater.[54] Although the actions were parallel and uniform, each firm had an independent justification for the action, because downtown theaters offered more profitable venues.

Although consciously parallel conduct does not raise an inference that the firms in the market have agreed, it remains unclear what sort of evidence does. Courts often suggest that evidence of actions contrary to the defendants' individual self-interest can amount to a plus factor.[55] But this observation must be qualified: it does not mean that parallel conduct is evidence of agreement if the conduct is profitable only if all firms act in the same way. In such a case, each firm may be acting against its short-run self-interest, because it could profit immediately by breaking with the group and increasing sales. But the firms may be acting in their long-run self-interest by, for example, maintaining the higher price by conscious parallelism. Because courts have recognized that simple conscious parallelism is lawful, 'individual self-interest' must also include the interest in gaining the benefits of consciously parallel action.[56] It is, in other words, legitimately in the self-interest of a firm to anticipate the actions of one's rivals and to act accordingly, even if it means sacrificing short-run profits in hopes of long-term noncompetitive pricing. Thus, if a customer were to sue our hypothetical rural gas stations who coordinated a price increase by interdependent actions, the customer would suffer summary judgment. Even if the first station might have lost $100 in profit to the others had they chosen to abjure the price increase and to sell more gasoline (at the first station's expense) at a lower price, the stations do not act against their self-interest by matching the price increase and selling less, if they split $200 in profit by doing so.[57] Consequently, the plaintiff must produce something more than evidence that the defendants have acted against their short-run self-interest.

The uncertainty about what sort of evidence amounts to a plus factor is attributable mainly to the vacuity of the Supreme Court's definitions of agreement and the absence of a coherent economic definition that might fill the void. If we knew better what a Section 1 agreement was, we could be more certain about what sort of evidence makes it reasonable to infer the agreement, and what role facilitating practices might play in that inference. We would also be more certain what sorts of allegations raise a plausible inference of conspiracy under *Twombly*'s pleading standard.

I have argued elsewhere,[58] building on the work of Oliver Black,[59] that US law should frankly acknowledge that communication is an element of agreement. According to Black, parties' parallel actions can be arranged along a spectrum of degrees of 'correlation'.[60] In the most highly correlated conduct that US law would call conscious parallelism, the firms act in reliance of their belief that their rivals will act in a certain way; the firms have the same goal; and all have knowledge that these conditions have been met. The firms' actions become concerted if the conditions of conscious parallelism are met in part because the firms have communicated their reliance and goals to each other.[61] Notice that, in this formulation, concerted action does not require the sort of exchange of promises or assurances that would be necessary for a completed verbal agreement, because the parallel action itself supplies an element of the offense.

Although Black formulates this conception of agreement using the tools of analytical philosophy, his account bears a close resemblance to economists' stated beliefs, if not their formal theories, about the role of communication in cartels. As we have seen, economic theory does not recognize informal agreement as a category distinct from conscious parallelism. It also has not conclusively shown the role of communication of various sorts, especially 'cheap' or nonbinding talk, in achieving noncompetitive outcomes.[62] Nevertheless, many economists, including those with extensive experience in antitrust litigation, believe that communication is necessary to coordinate pricing in complex markets, even if it may not be in desert-island hypotheticals like our gas station example.[63] Studies of the functioning of real-world cartels invariably show extensive communications to coordinate 'price, volume allocation, production quotas, and, in the case of bid-rigging, who wins any given bid and what that winning bid will be'.[64]

Not all communications among rivals are suspicious. Carlton, Gertner, and Rosenfield suggest that communications are most likely to be anticompetitive if they are private rather than public, if they relate to current and future prices rather than historical prices, and if they are repeated rather than isolated.[65] Although these authors do not propose these categories of communications as a definition of agreement, the categories are consistent with Black's definition, which requires that the communications convey the firms' intended actions and their mutual reliance. More important, as I have argued elsewhere, US courts, although still citing the decades-old meaningless definitions, have implicitly adopted a definition of concerted action that requires communication of intent and reliance.[66] This understanding of the nature of concerted action has important implications for the evaluation of facilitating practices.

III. Facilitating practices

Facilitating practices raise issues under Section 1 in two primary contexts: where rivals adopt the practices by express agreement (or, analogously, pursuant to a state mandate), and where they adopt the practices by parallel action. Both contexts require analysis of the effects of the practice on the rivals' ability to coordinate prices. In the first context, however, the fact that rivals have found it necessary to agree to adopt the practice (or the state has found it necessary to compel it) simplifies the analysis, not only satisfying the agreement element, but by eliminating many of the possible independent and beneficial explanations for the practices. As we see in the next section, the legality of practices in this first category may hinge on whether the facilitating practice consists of an agreement to adhere to particular terms of dealing or an agreement to share information. Both types of agreement may facilitate price coordination, but courts view the agreements on terms of dealing with greater suspicion.

The more difficult cases are those in the second category: parallel adoption of the facilitating practices, which I address in the final section of this Part. These cases raise the issue of whether the practice permits inference of an agreement. Some have argued that the presence of facilitating practices makes oligopoly pricing illegal. As I noted in the introduction, both Posner and Turner agreed that the existence of facilitating practices would justify a finding of Section 1 liability for consciously parallel action, because that would avoid the problem of remedy: enjoining the practice would eliminate the noncompetitive pricing. But the presence of facilitating practices does not avoid the antecedent problem of inferring an agreement. Applying the *Matsushita* standard, courts have recognized that '"facilitating devices" are not necessarily sufficient under the law to constitute a "plus factor"'.[67] The same principles that prevent courts from inferring an agreement based on parallel pricing, also often prevent them from inferring an agreement from parallel pricing accompanied by facilitating practices. I suggest below that cases involving facilitating practices are best understood if they are evaluated under a definition of agreement that requires communication of reliance and intent. Since facilitating practices may themselves involve communications, they can meet the clarified definition, particularly if other evidence supports the necessary inferences concerning the nature and content of the communications.

A. Agreements on (or state mandates of) terms of dealing that increase pricing transparency

Agreements that facilitate price coordination by fixing rivals' terms of dealing are likely to be held illegal per se.[68] In *Catalano*,[69] for example, the Court condemned an agreement among beer distributors not to offer short-term credit. The agreement eliminated a common type of discount equal to the time value of the money owed. Although the agreement made transaction prices more transparent, it did so by limiting the rivals' 'action with respect to the published prices'.[70] Indeed, the arrangement was a facilitating practice primarily because it inhibited firms from engaging in secret discounting, which might have undermined any understanding on prices. The express agreement in *Catalano* was crucial to the result. Had the evidence shown only that the defendants individually declined to offer short-term credit, there would have been no inference of an agreement under *Matsushita*, because each firm could offer independent reasons for its actions. The fact that the firms found it necessary to agree on the practice, however, shows that any independent reasons for adopting it were not the decisive ones.

Earlier cases reached similar results. In *Sugar Institute*,[71] the Court held unlawful an agreement among rivals to adhere to publicly announced prices. Again, the agreement to abide by particular terms of dealing was the decisive factor. An industry-wide practice of announcing list prices and adhering to them would have been no more than conscious parallelism. An agreement to announce list prices, without the agreement to adhere to them, would place the practice in the more benign category of data dissemination. But an agreement by each firm to adhere to list prices, like the agreement in *Catalano*, amounted to an agreement to eliminate secret discounting.[72] Similar reasoning would apply to agreements to adopt other practices, like resale pricc maintenance or basing-point or delivered pricing,[73] that enhance price transparency by restricting terms of dealing.[74]

An analogous line of decisions extends the reasoning of these cases to invalidate state-mandated facilitating practices.[75] Federal antitrust law preempts state economic legislation that mandates or authorizes private conduct that violates the antitrust laws, unless the regulatory scheme meets the requirements of state-action immunity, particularly 'clear articulation' of the policy and 'active supervision' by state regulators.[76] The Supreme Court has invalidated state laws that authorized private firms to restrain trade in ways that closely resemble antitrust violations, even where the restraints did not technically involve a private agreement. Thus, the Supreme Court has struck down state laws that authorized a manufacturer or wholesaler to dictate the prices at which its products could be resold by downstream firms.[77] The Court reasoned that the restraints amounted to state-mandated resale price maintenance, even though the state law did not require a vertical agreement, only compliance with terms laid down by the upstream firm. One of the grounds the Court offered for these results was that this sort of resale price maintenance is a facilitating practice:

> We have noted that industrywide resale price maintenance also may facilitate cartelization. Mandatory industrywide resale price fixing is virtually certain to reduce interbrand competition as well as intrabrand competition, because it prevents manufacturers and wholesalers from allowing or requiring retail price competition. The New York statute specifically forbids retailers to reduce the minimum prices set by wholesalers.[78]

On similar grounds, lower courts have condemned 'post and hold' statutes, which require liquor distributors to announce price lists and to charge only those prices for as long as the list is in effect.[79] The Fourth Circuit characterized the statute as 'a hybrid restraint that amounts to a per se violation of § 1'.[80] The arrangement differs from a purely private cartel, because nothing in the statute requires distributors to agree with each other. Nevertheless, the statute mandates a facilitating practice, and thus is closely analogous to cases, like *Sugar Institute*, in which firms agree to adopt a facilitating practice that limits their ability to discount. In effect, the statutory mandate serves the function of the trade association rule. The restraint is hybrid, and, because there is no active supervision of the private actors, it does not qualify for state action immunity.[81]

B. Agreements to exchange information

Horizontal agreements to exchange information, like those at issue in the trade association cases of the 1920s[82] and in *Container*,[83] are also facilitating practices, because they make it easier for rivals to coordinate prices. Unlike the restraints in *Catalano* and *Sugar Institute*, however, the terms of an information-exchange agreement do not control how the information will affect the rivals' terms of dealing. In some instances, they can benefit consumers by spreading information in the market.[84] Thus, courts must weigh the likely anticompetitive and procompetitive effects.[85] The legality of these sorts of agreements thus depends on the nature of the information exchanged and the likely (and actual) effects of the practice, given the characteristics of the market. The cases suggest that exchanges of information are more likely to be unlawful if they include present and future prices, relate to specific transactions, and rely upon a central authority which interprets the data and makes recommendations.[86] These criteria closely resemble those proposed by Carlton, et al.[87], for identification of anticompetitive communications.

An information exchange may be unlawful if it is found to have an unreasonable effect on prices, or if it is found to be a plus factor permitting an inference of a per se illegal agreement to fix prices.[88] Interestingly, the inquiries for these issues are similar. The existence of an agreement in cases alleging price fixing is the dividing line between lawful and unlawful behavior, and thus involves policy choices about the legitimacy of various types of interactions among rivals. Thus, inference of a per se illegal agreement to fix prices requires a balancing of procompetitive and anticompetitive effects that resembles a rule of reason analysis of the express agreement to exchange information.

Eastern States Retail Lumber Dealers' Association v. United States[89] illustrates this point, although it involved an agreement to exclude competition rather than to fix prices. The retailers' association had gathered and evaluated complaints from members about wholesalers that sold directly to the retailers' customers. The association distributed a 'blacklist' of the direct-selling wholesalers to its members, who then generally refused to deal with those on the list. The Supreme Court held that the evident purpose and 'natural consequence' of the 'concerted action' of circulating the list was to induce the refusals to deal.[90] The arrangement 'tend[ed] to prevent other retailers who [had] no personal grievance against' the wholesaler from trading with it 'solely because of the influence of the report circulated among the members of the associations'.[91] The Court might have condemned the agreement to distribute the list because of its effects, but instead relied on the same evidence to infer the existence of a per se illegal boycott. The agreement's tendency to induce refusals to deal by retailers unaffected by direct selling suggested that those refusals had no independent justification, and thus justified an inference of an agreement.

The key element in this inference was communication through the mechanism of data collection and dissemination. Retailers refused to deal because of the blacklist, which was assembled from their rivals' reports and presumably in reliance on their rivals doing the same. The case is thus distinguishable from *Cement Manufacturers*, in which an association circulated a list of firms engaged in fraud,[92] because that was information a retailer would find sufficient as a reason to refuse to deal regardless of the actions of its rivals.

C. *Parallel adoption of facilitating practices*

Finally, we are in a position to consider the legality of parallel pricing accompanied by parallel use of facilitating practices. It now seems clear that rivals' parallel use of a facilitating practice does not, by itself, raise an inference of agreement. One court stated, for example, that '"facilitating devices" are not necessarily sufficient under the law to constitute a "plus factor"'.[93] There is often an independent justification for a firm to adopt a practice that might facilitate price coordination. For example, in *Ethyl*, the court refused to condemn industry-wide use of advance notification of price changes, price protection clauses, and delivered pricing, even though they facilitated price uniformity, because the practices had been adopted when there was only a single seller in the market and thus evidently served non-collusive purposes that consumers wanted.[94] Thus, under the *Matsushita* standard, the parallel adoption of a facilitating practice typically cannot exclude the possibility that the rivals were acting independently.

The Supreme Court's recent *Leegin* decision,[95] which abandoned the per se illegality of resale price maintenance, provides another useful illustration of the issues. That case held that resale price maintenance was not invariably anticompetitive, and so should be judged under the rule of reason. Manufacturers might use the practice in various ways to induce retailers to provide point-of-sale services and thus enhance interbrand competition.[96] On the other hand, the practice would be anticompetitive if manufacturers used it to police a cartel by 'identifying price-cutting manufacturers'.[97] Such a cartel would be per se illegal and any 'vertical agreement setting minimum resale prices' that the members adopted to 'facilitate' the cartel would be 'unlawful under the rule of reason'.[98] This passage states the uncontroversial point that any resale price maintenance scheme that cartel members adopted to enable more effective enforcement of the cartel's price terms would be illegal along with the horizontal price fixing agreement itself. Indeed, it would be illegal, under *Catalano*, for rivals to agree to adopt resale price maintenance, even if they did not agree on prices.

But what if there were no express, horizontal agreement? Turner, writing in 1962, concluded that it was 'an unlawful agreement for oligopolists to make interdependent decisions to adopt fair trade, regardless of the means employed'.[99] *Leegin,* however, states only that resale price maintenance agreement might be 'useful evidence for a plaintiff attempting to prove the existence of a horizontal cartel'[100] and 'should be subject to more careful scrutiny . . . if many competing manufacturers adopt the practice'.[101] This language strongly implies that industry-wide resale price maintenance alone would not constitute a plus factor. 'Additional scrutiny' would be necessary, first, to determine whether the vertical agreements were anti-competitive. If the vertical agreements benefited consumers by inducing retailers to provide point-of-sale services, the agreements would each be lawful, and the parallel adoption of them would not permit the inference of a horizontal agreement under *Matsushita*, because each manufacturer would have legitimate reason for adopting the practice. If the vertical agreements were anticompetitive because they facilitated noncompetitive oligopolistic behavior without inducing retailers to provide beneficial services, then they might be illegal under the rule of reason.[102] Even in that case, however, the industry-wide adoption of the practice alone would likely not justify an inference of a horizontal agreement, because the pattern would be consistent with lawful oligopolistic interdependence.

Of course, the widespread adoption of resale price maintenance, or any other facilitating practice, combined with other evidence might justify inference of a horizontal agreement. In Part III.C, I suggested that, while courts continue to quote the Supreme Court's vague definitions, they have in recent years begun to apply a more specific definition of concerted action, one that closely resembles the communication model I have advanced here. Under that model, concerted action under Section 1 of the Sherman Act requires, beyond evidence of parallel conduct, evidence that rivals have communicated their intentions to act in a certain way and their reliance on each other to follow suit. To convey the requisite information, the communications must ordinarily be private and repeated, and must relate to present or future prices. These considerations apply in the case of facilitating practices as well.

In the hypothetical rural gas station, for example, coordination of prices would be more difficult if the stations did not post their prices on signs as well as at the pump. Thus, public price posting is literally a facilitating practice that involves price communication. But courts would certainly not find that posting prices on signs amounted to a plus factor, because it also has the legitimate purpose of informing consumers of rivals' prices. Public 'signaling' and 'monitoring' of prices are too ambiguous in their effects to amount to plus factors, because they cannot convey the necessary intent and reliance.[103] If the information communicated is private, however, a court might infer that the communication conveyed the necessary message of intent to act in a particular way in reliance of the expectation that others would do the same. In *Container*, for example, the Supreme Court reasoned:

> Here all that was present was a request by each defendant of its competitor for information as to the most recent price charged or quoted, whenever it needed such information and whenever it was not available from another source. Each defendant on receiving that request usually furnished the data with the expectation that it would be furnished reciprocal information when it wanted it. That concerted action is of course sufficient to establish the combination or conspiracy, the initial ingredient of a violation of Section 1 of the Sherman Act.[104]

The Court thus inferred the agreement to exchange current price information from the private, repeated practice of providing current pricing information when requested. The Court emphasized that this conduct was 'obviously quite different from the parallel business behavior condoned in' *Theatre Enterprises*.[105] In this case, the inference was that the parties had agreed to exchange information, but similar evidence, in different circumstances, might imply an agreement to fix prices.

Petroleum Products, which appeared to condemn a kind of public price signaling, is not to the contrary. There, the court suggested in dicta[106] that firms' announcements of increases in wholesale prices and withdrawals of dealer discounts would support an inference of conspiracy, because the actions made it easier for firms to coordinate price increases.[107] The court pointed out, however, that because the defendants sold through franchised dealers, publishing *wholesale* prices would not give consumers useable information; the evidence indicated that the publication of wholesale prices was intended to inform rivals.[108] In a footnote, the court emphasized that its 'conclusion would necessarily be different were the appellants' inference of a price-fixing conspiracy based on the dissemination or advertising of *retail* prices; permitting an inference of conspiracy from such evidence would make it more difficult for retail consumers to get the information they need to make efficient market decisions'.[109]

In some circumstances, the court may infer that the requisite communications have occurred even without direct proof of the communications themselves. In *Cement Institute*, for example, the Court affirmed the FTC's inference of an agreement to engage in basing-point pricing.[110] Like an agreement to adhere to announced prices, an agreement among rivals to calculate freight from basing points greatly reduces the complexity of coordinating prices. Because basing-point pricing might provide benefits, however, parallel adoption of the practice would not alone justify the inference of an agreement to adopt it. In *Cement Institute*, however, the FTC inferred an agreement from evidence that the defendants not only quoted delivered prices from standard basing points, but also coordinated efforts to punish deviators from the practice.[111] These methods included the imposition of punitive basing points at the locations of cement dealers that did not follow the system. These and other practices made it reasonable for the FTC to infer the agreement, even in the absence of testimony about specific communications.

IV. Conclusion

Facilitating practices are of continuing interest to antitrust courts and scholars because they may enable noncompetitive pricing. This characteristic of the practices is especially relevant to the characterization and proof of agreements under Section 1 of the Sherman Act. Express agreements among rivals (for example by adoption of a trade association rule) to adopt facilitating practices that limit terms of dealing in ways that make it easier to detect secret discounting are generally illegal per se. Analogously, when a state enacts a statute that requires rivals in an industry to adopt a facilitating practice, the courts usually hold the arrangement an invalid hybrid restraint. Where rivals adopt facilitating practices without an express agreement, however, the conduct is lawful, absent additional evidence that the adoption and maintenance of the practice was made possible by communication.

Notes

* Marshall M. Criser Eminent Scholar, University of Florida, Levin College of Law.

1. George J. Stigler, *A Theory of Oligopoly*, 72 J. Pol. Econ. 44, 44–61 (1964); *reprinted* in

GEORGE J. STIGLER, THE ORGANIZATION OF INDUSTRY 39–63 (Homewood, Ill.; Richard D. Irwin, 1968).

2. *Id.* at 42–3.
3. The term is a variant of 'facilitating devices', a phrase then assistant AG John Shenefield used to propose a legal strategy for challenging some forms of oligopolistic conduct under Section 1 of the Sherman Act. Memorandum from John H. Shenefield, Assistant Attorney General, Antitrust Division, on Shared Monopolies, *reprinted* in 874 ANTITRUST & TRADE REG. REP. (BNA) F-1 (1978). *See generally* K.N. HYLTON, ANTITRUST LAW: ECONOMIC THEORY AND COMMON LAW EVOLUTION 144–65 (Cambridge University Press, 2003); Salop, S.C., *Practices that (Credibly) Facilitate Oligopoly Coordination*, in NEW DEVELOPMENTS IN THE ANALYSIS OF MARKET STRUCTURE 265–90 (J.E. Stiglitz & G. Frank Mathewson eds, 1986); Shapiro, C., *Theories of Oligopoly Behavior*, in 1 HANDBOOK OF INDUSTRIAL ORGANIZATION 329, 329–414 (Richard Schemalensee & Robert D. Willig eds, 1989).
4. Christopher R. Leslie, *Trust, Distrust, and Antitrust*, 82 TEX. L. REV. 515, 575–6 (2004).
5. Blechman, M.D., *Conscious Parallelism. Signaling and Facilitating Devices: The Problem of Tacit Collusion Under the Antitrust Laws*, 24 N.Y.L. SCH. L. REV. 881, 881–906 (1979); Holt, C.A. & D.T. Scheffman, *Facilitating Practices: The Effects of Advance Notice and Best-Price Policies*, 18 RAND J. ECON. 187, 187–97 (1987); Kestenbaum, L., *What Is "Price Signalling" and Does It Violate the Law?*, 49 ANTITRUST L.J. 911, 911–23 (1980); Kattan, J., *Beyond Facilitating Practices: Price Signaling and Price Protection Clauses in the New Antitrust Environment*, 63 ANTITRUST L.J. 133, 133–52 (1994).
6. Besanko, D. & T.P. Lyon, *Equilibrium Incentives for Most-Favored Customer Clauses in an Oligopolistic Industry*, 11 INT'L J. INDUS. ORG. 347, 347–67 (1993); Cooper, T.E., *Most-Favored-Customer Pricing and Tacit Collusion*, 17 RAND J. ECON. 377, 377–88 (1986); Kattan, J. & S.A. Stempel, *Antitrust Enforcement and Most Favored Nation Clauses*, ANTITRUST 20, 20–24 (1996, Summer).
7. Salop, *supra* note 3, at 277–82.
8. Carlton, D.W., *A Reexamination of Delivered Pricing Systems*, 26 J.L. & ECON. 51 (1983); Haddock, D.D., *Basing-Point Pricing: Competitive v. Collusive Theories*, 72 AM. ECON. REV. 289 (1982); RICHARD A. POSNER, ANTITRUST LAW: AN ECONOMIC PERSPECTIVE 91–93 (University of Chicago Press, 2001); George J. Stigler, *A Theory of Delivered Price Systems*, in THE ORGANIZATION OF INDUSTRY 147–64 (University of Chicago Press. 1968).
9. Posner, *supra* note 8, at 88–9; Telser, L.G. (1960), *Why Should Manufacturers Want Fair Trade?*, 3 J.L. & ECON. 86, 99–104 (1960).
10. Goldman, L., *Oligopoly Policy and the Ethyl Corp. Case*, 65 OR. L. REV. 73, 73–121 (1986); Hay, G.A., *Facilitating Practices: The Ethyl Case* (1984), in THE ANTITRUST REVOLUTION: ECONOMICS, COMPETITION AND POLICY 182–201 (John E. Kwoka, Jr. & Lawrence J. White eds, Oxford University Press 3rd edn, 1999); Vita, M.G., *Fifteen Years After Ethyl: The Past and Future of Facilitating Practices*, 68 ANTITRUST L.J. 991, 991–1006 (2001). The enforcement campaign also used the term 'shared monopoly'. Hay, G.A., *Oligopoly, Shared Monopoly, and Antitrust Law*, 67 CORNELL L. REV. 439, 453 (1982).
11. *See* Department of Justice and Federal Trade Commission Horizontal Merger Guidelines § 2.11 (1992, revised 1997), available at http://www.usdoj.gov/atr/public/guidelines/horiz_book/hmg1.html.
12. *Id.* at § 2.10. *See generally* Gurrea, S.D. & B.M. Owen, *Coordinated Interaction and Clayton § 7 Enforcement*, 12 GEO. MASON L. REV. 89, 101–02 (2003).
13. *Copperweld Corp. v. Independence Tube Corp.*, 467 U.S. 752, 768–9 (1984).
14. For terms of formal cartel agreements, *see United States v. Trans-Missouri Freight Ass'n*, 166 U.S. 290, 292–7 (1897); *United States v. Addyston Pipe & Steel Co.*, 85 F. 271, 273–5 (6th Cir. 1898), *aff'd* 175 U.S. 211 (1899). For discussion of an early price-fixing

arrangement that avoided explicit agreement, see Page, W. H., *The Gary Dinners and the Meaning of Concerted Action*, 62 SMU L. REV. 597 (2009)

15. Compare *Trans-Missouri, supra* note 14, at 341 (condemning 'all agreements which are a restraint of trade' with *id.* at 371 (White, J., dissenting) (arguing only unreasonable restraints should be unlawful).
16. For a recent examination of the history of this conundrum, *see* Piraino, T.A., Jr., *Regulating Oligopoly Conduct Under the Antitrust Laws*, 89 MINN. L. REV. 9, 9–70 (2004).
17. *See, e.g.*, E.H. CHAMBERLIN, THE THEORY OF MONOPOLISTIC COMPETITION: A RE-ORIENTATION OF THE THEORY OF VALUE ch. 3 (Cambridge; Harvard University Press 6th. edn, 1948).
18. *JTC Petroleum Co. v. Piasa Motor Fuels, Inc.*, 190 F.3d 775, 780 (7th Cir. 1999).
19. *Bell Atlantic Corp. v. Twombly*, 127 S.Ct. 1955, 1963 (2007).
20. *Brooke Group Ltd. v. Brown & Williamson Tobacco Corp.*, 509 U.S. 209, 227 (1993).
21. Jaquemin, A. & M.E. Slade, *Cartels, Collusion, and Horizontal Merger*, in 1 HANDBOOK OF INDUSTRIAL ORGANIZATION 415, 415–73 (Richard Schmalensee & Robert D. Willig eds, 1989).
22. There are, of course, many other outcomes of this scenario.
23. Carlton, D.W., R.H. Gertner & A.M. Rosenfield, *Communication Among Competitors: Game Theory and Antitrust*, 5 GEO. MASON L. REV. 423, 428–9 (1997). *See also* Page, W.H., *Communication and Concerted Action*, 37 LOYOLA UNIV. CHI. L.J. 405, 411–12 (2007); Piraino, *supra* note 16, at 19–20.
24. *In re High Fructose Corn Syrup Antitrust Litig.*, 295 F.3d 651, 654 (7th Cir. 2002) (Posner, J.) ('If a firm raises price in the expectation that its competitors will do likewise, and they do, the firm's behavior can be conceptualized as the offer of a unilateral contract that the offerees accept by raising their prices.'). Judge Posner recognized, however, that courts have not accepted this reasoning. *Id. See also* Devlin, A., *Note, A Proposed Solution to the Problem of Parallel Pricing in Oligopolistic Markets*, 59 STAN. L. REV. 1111, 1121–2 (2007).
25. Turner, D.F., *The Definition of Agreement Under the Sherman Act: Conscious Parallelism and Refusals to Deal*, 75 HARV. L. REV. 655, 666 (1962).
26. *See id.* at 669–70; *see also JTC Petroleum Co. v. Piasa Motor Fuels, Inc.*, 190 F.3d 775, 780 (7th Cir. 1999) (reasoning that it would be impractical to frame relief for tacit collusion); *Clamp-All Corp. v. Cast Iron Soil Pipe Inst.*, 851 F.2d 478, 484 (1st Cir. 1988) (same).
27. Posner, *supra* note 8, at 94. Posner acknowledges that 'most other economically minded students of antitrust policy' disagree. *Id.*
28. *Id.* at 97–8.
29. Some still argue that tacit collusion should be unlawful. *See, e.g.*, *Devlin, supra* note 24; Piraino, *supra* note 16.
30. *Bell Atlantic Corp. v. Twombly*, 127 S.Ct. 1955, 1964 (2007).
31. *See, e.g.*, 1992 Merger Guidelines, *supra* note 11, at § 2.11 ('[R]eaching terms of coordination may be limited or impeded by product heterogeneity or by firms having substantially incomplete information about the conditions and prospects of their rivals' businesses, perhaps because of important differences among their current business operations.').
32. Stigler, ORGANIZATION, *supra* note 1, at 41; Dick, A.R., *Identifying Contracts, Combinations and Conspiracies in Restraint of Trade*, 17 MANAGERIAL & DECISION ECON. 203, 209 (1996).
33. DeSanti, S.S. & E.A. Nagata, *Competitor Communications: Facilitating Practices or Invitations To Collude?*, 63 ANTITRUST L.J. 93, 121 (1994).
34. Posner, *supra* note 8, at 98–9; Turner, *supra* note 25, at 675–6.
35. *United States v. Gen. Motors Corp.*, 384 U.S. 127, 142–3 (1966).
36. *United States v. Paramount Pictures, Inc.*, 334 U.S. 131, 142 (1948) (noting that '[i]t is enough that a concert of action is contemplated and that the defendants conformed to the arrangement').

37. *Am. Tobacco Co. v. United States*, 328 U.S. 781, 809–10 (1946) (adding that evidence of a violation 'may be found in a course of dealings or other circumstances as well as in any exchange of words'). The Supreme Court has also stated that an agreement need not involve 'letters, agreements, or other testimonials to a conspiracy'. *Norfolk Monument Co. v. Woodlawn Mem'l Gardens, Inc.*, 394 U.S. 700, 703–4 (1969).
38. *Am. Tobacco, supra* note 37, at 810.
39. *Monsanto Co. v. Spray-Rite Serv. Corp.*, 465 U.S. 752, 768 (1984); *In re Flat Glass*, 385 F.3d at 357 (citations and internal quotations omitted).
40. *Twombly, supra* note 30, at 1966.
41. Other scholars have observed this deficiency in the definition. *See* Baker, J.B., *Identifying Horizontal Price Fixing in the Electronic Marketplace*, 65 ANTITRUST L.J. 41, 47 (1996); Kovacic, W.E., *The Identification and Proof of Horizontal Agreements Under the Antitrust Laws*, 38 ANTITRUST BULL. 5, 24–5 (1993); Werden, G.J. *Economic Eudence on the Existence of Collusion: Reconciling Antitrust Law with Oligopoly Theory*, 71 ANTITRUST L.J. 719, 777–8 (2004).
42. *Virginia Vermiculite, Ltd. v. Historic Green Springs, Inc.*, 307 F.3d 277, 281–2 (4th Cir. 2002).
43. Carlton et al., *supra* note 23, at 424.
44. M.D. WHINSTON, LECTURES ON ANTITRUST ECONOMICS 20 (Cambridge; MIT Press 2006); Stigler, G.J., *What Does an Economist Know?*, 33 J. LEGAL EDUC. 311, 311–12 (1983). Economists do distinguish between cooperative and noncooperative equilibria. But cooperation, in this sense, means that the parties have formed an enforceable contract: D.M. KREPS, GAME THEORY AND ECONOMIC MODELING 9 (1990). Since the sort of agreements prohibited by the Sherman Act are unenforceable, they would all be considered noncooperative.
45. Milne, R.A. & J.E. Pace, *Conspiratologists at the Gate: The Scope of Expert Testimony on the Subject of Conspiracy in a Sherman Act Case*, 17 ANTITRUST 36, 39–42 (2003).
46. *Matsushita Elec. Indus. Co. v. Zenith Radio Corp.*, 475 U.S. 574, 588 (1986).
47. *City of Tuscaloosa v. Harcros Chems., Inc.*, 158 F.3d 548, 571 n.35 (11th Cir. 1998).
48. *See, e.g., Blomkest Fertilizer, Inc. v. Potash Corp. of Sask.*, 203 F.3d 1028, 1032–4 (8th Cir. 2000) (holding that the plaintiff 'has the burden to present evidence of consciously paralleled pricing supplemented with one or more plus factors').
49. *See, e.g.*, Kovacic, *supra* note 41, 35 (observing that courts rarely rank plus factors or 'specify the minimum critical mass of plus factors that must be established to sustain an inference' of collusion). Kovacic identifies as plus factors in this broader sense a motive for collective action; the absence of an independent motive; actions that are inexplicable unless collective; a history of collusion; meetings and communications among the defendants; facilitating practices; and industry structure and performance consistent with collusion. *Id.* at 37–55. *See also Todd v. Exxon Corp.*, 275 F.3d 191, 198 (2d Cir. 2001) (describing 'defendant's use of facilitating practices' as a plus factor in this more general sense).
50. *City of Tuscaloosa supra* note 47, at 571 n.35, 572 (holding plaintiff must produce plus factors 'tending to exclude the possibility of lawful action'). *See also In re Baby Food Antitrust Litig.*, 166 F.3d 112, 122 (3d Cir. 1999) ('The simple term "plus factors" refers to "the additional facts or factors required to be proved as a prerequisite to finding that parallel action amounts to a conspiracy".' (citation omitted)); cf. *Blomkest, supra* note 48, (dissenting opinion) ('[I]t is useful to distinguish between "plus factors" that establish a background making conspiracy likely and "plus factors" that tend to exclude the possibility that the defendants acted without agreement.').
51. *Continental Ore Co. v. Union Carbide & Carbon Corp.*, 370 U.S. 690, 699 (1962) (courts should not 'compartmentaliz[e] the various factual components [of the plaintiffs case] and wip[e] the slate clean of scrutiny of each').
52. *Bell Atl. Corp. v. Twombly*, 127 S. Ct. 1955 (2007).
53. *Id.* at 1966 (holding that allegations must 'be placed in a context that raises a

suggestion of a preceding agreement, not merely parallel conduct that could just as well be independent action').

54. *Theatre Enterprises, Inc. v. Paramount Film Distributing Corp.*, 346 U.S. 537, 541–2 (1954).
55. Kovacic, *supra* note 41, at 38–42; Piraino, *supra* note 16, at 37.
56. *City of Tuscaloosa*, *supra* note 47, at 570 n. 33 (describing an act is against the defendants' self-interest if 'each defendant would have acted unreasonably in a business sense if it had engaged in the challenged conduct unless that defendant had received assurances from the other defendants that they would take the same action') (citation omitted).
57. In real cases, pricing involves uncertainties that make a choice to follow the price increase more ambiguous. *Williamson Oil Co. v. Philip Morris USA*, 346 F.3d 1287, 1311 (11th Cir. 2003) (observing that not matching a rival's price increase 'likely would have resulted in little if any market share gain [and] would have minimized profits, given that lower prices generate smaller revenues').
58. Page, *supra* note 23.
59. BLACK, O., CONCEPTUAL FOUNDATIONS OF ANTITRUST (New York; Cambridge University Press, 2005).
60. *Id.* at 185–7.
61. *Id.* at 187. Cf. Hay, G.H., *The Meaning of 'Agreement' under the Sherman Act: Thoughts from the 'Facilitating Practices' Experience*, 16 REV. INDUS. ORG. 113, 128 (2000) ('[I]f there is to be a category of unlawful tacit collusion which is to be distinguished from classic oligopoly, the difference must lie, not in the state of mind of the competitors, but on the specific elements of behavior that brought about the state of mind.').
62. Jaquemin & Slade, *supra* note 21, at 447–8; Whinston, *supra* note 44, at 46.
63. Baker, J.B., *Identifying Horizontal Price Fixing in the Electronic Marketplace*, 65 ANTITRUST L.J. 41, 48 (1996); Elzinga, K.G., *New Developments on the Cartel Front*, 29 ANTITRUST BULL. 3, 25 (1984); VIVES, X., OLIGOPOLY PRICING: OLD IDEAS AND NEW TOOLS 320 (Cambridge; MIT Press 1999); Werden, *supra* note 41, at 763; Whinston, *supra* note 44, at 321.
64. *See also* Leslie, *supra* note 4, at 580. Leslie adds that communication is also necessary to 'build trust' in the representations cartel members make to each other. *Id.* He also summarizes the results of economic experiments that tend to show that communication is necessary for effective cooperation. *Id.* at 538–9.
65. Carlton, et al., *supra* note 23, at 431–3.
66. Page, *supra* note 23, at 446–59.
67. *Holiday Wholesale Grocery Co. v. Philip Morris Inc.*, 231 F.Supp.2d 1253, 1274–5 (N.D. Ga.), *aff'd sub nom. Williamson Oil Co., Inc. v. Philip Morris USA*, 346 F.3d 1287 (11th Cir. 2003).
68. Lande, R.H. & H.P. Marvel, *The Three Types of Collusion: Fixing Prices, Rivals, and Rules*, WIS. L. REV. 941, 945–6 (2000).
69. *Catalano, Inc. v. Target Sales, Inc.*, 446 U.S. 643 (1980).
70. *Id.* at 649–50.
71. *Sugar Inst., Inc. v. United States*, 297 U.S. 553 (1936).
72. Genesove, D. & W.P. Mullin, *Rules, Communication, and Collusion: Narrative Evidence from the Sugar Institute Case*, 91 AM. ECON. REV. 379, 380–4 (2001).
73. *FTC v. Cement Institute*, 333 U.S. 683, 690–93 (1948). In *Catalano*, *supra* note 69, the Court confirmed that the agreement condemned in *Cement Institute* under Section 5 of the FTC Act conduct 'would also violate § 1 of the Sherman Act'. 44 U.S. at 648 n.10. *See also Clamp-All Corp. v. Cast Iron Soil Pipe Inst.*, 851 F.2d 478, 484–5 (1st Cir. 1988).
74. Leslie, *supra* note 4, at 577–8.
75. Lopatka, J.E. & W.H. Page, *State Action and the Meaning of Agreement Under the Sherman Act: An Approach to Hybrid Restraints*, 20 YALE J. ON REG. 269, 294–7 (2003).

76. *California Retail Liquor Dealers Ass'n v. Midcal Aluminum, Inc.*, 445 U.S. 97, 105 (1980).
77. *324 Liquor Corp. v. Duffy*, 479 U.S. 335, 344–5 (1987).
78. *Id.* at 342.
79. *Costco Wholesale Corp. v. Maleng*, Nos. 06-35538, 2008 WL 223121 (9th Cir. Jan. 29, 2008); *TFWS, Inc. v. Schaefer*, 242 F.3d 198 (4th Cir. 2001); *Miller v. Hedlund*, 813 F.2d 1344, 1350 (9th Cir. 1986); *Beer & Pop Warehouse v. Jones*, 41 F. Supp. 2d 552, 560–2 (M.D. Pa. 1999); *Canterbury Liquors & Pantry v. Sullivan*, 16 F. Supp. 2d 41, 47–8 (D. Mass. 1998); *Anheuser-Busch, Inc. v. Goodman*, 745 F. Supp. 1048, 1056 (M.D. Pa. 1990). But *see Battipaglia v. N. Y. State Liquor Auth.*, 745 F.2d 166 (2d Cir. 1984).
80. *TFWS v. Schaefer*, *supra* note 79, at 206.
81. The Ninth Circuit in *Maleng* correctly struck down Washington's post-and-hold statute as a hybrid restraint, accepting the argument that it closely resembled an agreement to adhere to posted prices. *Costco Wholesale Corp. v. Maleng*, 2008 WL 223121, at 12–15. The court, again correctly, noted that an 'adherence requirement effectively removes a market uncertainty by making pricing behavior transparent and discouraging variance'. *Id.* at 14. But the court went on to uphold Washington's 'volume discount ban, the delivered pricing ban, and the ban on credit sales' on the grounds that, apart from the post-and-hold requirement, they are 'unilateral restraints imposed by the State, with no degree of discretion delegated to private individuals'. *Id.* at 16. The court reasoned that:

    > any anticompetitive effect arising out of these restraints is the result not of private discretion, but of the sovereign's command. There is no 'meeting of the minds' to determine how much discounts will be, whether territorial variations in price will be allowed, or whether credit may be extended over a certain period of time. The State of Washington commands that no discounts be given, no credit be extended, and no transportation allowances be factored in; that the wholesalers comply with these commands is not enough to deem the restraints hybrid.

    Id. This reasoning fails to recognize that each of the challenged restraints is as much a facilitating practice as the post-and-hold requirement. None involves an agreement or a 'meeting of the minds' among retailers in the usual Section 1 sense. Yet all involve state mandates to use a term of dealing that prevents secret discounting, while preserving individual discretion to establish prices. Thus all of the mandated practices should be preempted for facilitating noncompetitive price coordination by means closely analogous to a trade association rule imposing the same requirements.
82. *Am. Column & Lumber Co. v. United States*, 257 U.S. 377 (1921); *United States v. Am. Linseed Oil Co.*, 262 U.S. 371 (1923); *Maple Flooring Mfg. Assn. v. United States*, 268 U.S. 563 (1925); *Cement Mfrs. Protective Assn. v. United States*, 268 U.S. 588 (1925).
83. *United States v. Container Corp. of Am.*, 393 U.S. 333, 334–5 (1969).
84. *United States v. Citizen & S. Nat'l Bank*, 422 U.S. 86, 113 (1975).
85. Pearlstein, D.J. et al., 1 ABA Section of Antitrust Law, Antitrust Law Developments 95 (5th. ed. 2002) (exchanges are lawful if 'a legitimate business reason for the exchange offsets any likely anticompetitive effect').
86. *Id.* at 98.
87. Carlton, et al., *supra* note 23 at 431–3.
88. *Cf. Todd v. Exxon Corp.*, 275 F.3d 191, 198 (2d Cir. 2001) (distinguishing between information exchange as plus factor in establishing per se illegal price fixing agreement and independent violation under rule of reason).
89. 234 U.S. 600 (1914).
90. *Id.* at 612.
91. *Id.*
92. *See Cement Mfrs. Protective Ass'n v. United States*, 268 U.S. 588, 601–6 (1925).
93. *Holiday Wholesale Grocery Co. v. Philip Morris Inc.*, 231 F.Supp.2d 1253, 1274–5 (N.D.

Ga.), *aff'd sub nom. Williamson Oil Co., Inc. v. Philip Morris* USA, 346 F.3d 1287 (11th Cir. 2003).

94. *E.I. du Pont de Nemours & Co. v. FTC (Ethyl)*, 729 F.2d 128, 133–4, 140–42 (2d Cir. 1984). Although the claim in *Ethyl* was under Section 5 of the Federal Trade Commission Act, which does not facially require proof of agreement, the court imposed requirements evidently drawn from Section 1 of the Sherman Act. The court's analyses under the two statutes would likely be identical.
95. *Leegin Creative Leather Products, Inc. v. PSKS, Inc.*, 127 S.Ct. 2705 (2007).
96. *Id.* at 2715.
97. *Id.* at 2716.
98. *Id.* at 2717.
99. Turner, *supra* note 25, at 681.
100. *Leegin, supra* note 95, at 2717.
101. *Id.* at 2719.
102. For analysis of resale price maintenance as a facilitating practice, *see* Greg Shaffer, *Slotting Allowances and Resale Price Maintenance: A Comparison of Facilitating Practices*, 22 RAND J. ECON. 120, 120–55 (1991).
103. *Holiday Wholesale Grocery, supra* note 93, at 1275–96. *See also In re Flat Glass Antitrust Litig.*, 385 F.3d 350, 360, 369–70 (3rd Cir. 2004) (holding no inference of conspiracy where an independent entity collected truckload prices for replacement glass, selected one as a benchmark to calculate a suggested retail price, and where glass manufacturers each matched the selected, implicit truckload price).
104. *United States v. Container Corp.*, 393 U.S. 333, 335 (1969).
105. *Id.* at 335 n. 2.
106. The case also included direct evidence of agreement. *In re Citric Acid Litig.*, 191 F.3d 1090, 1096 (9th Cir. 1999).
107. *In re Coordinated Pretrial Proceedings in Petroleum Prods. Antitrust Litig.*, 906 F.2d 432, 445–50 (9th Cir. 1990).
108. *Id.* at 448 (stating that 'the public dissemination of such information served little purpose other than to facilitate interdependent or collusive price coordination').
109. *Id.* at 448 n.14.
110. *See, e.g., FTC v. Cement Institute*, 333 U.S. 683, 714 (1948) (citing evidence of boycotts against 'dealers who persisted in selling foreign cement' and efforts by Institute officials to 'secur[e] pledges by producers not to permit sales f.o.b. mill to purchasers who furnished their own trucks, a practice regarded as seriously disruptive of the entire delivered price structure of the industry'. The Court also pointed to unexplained, precisely identical bids by numerous rivals. *Id.* at 713, n.15.
111. *Id.* at 714.

References

ABA Section of Antitrust Law (2002), *Antitrust Law Developments (Fifth)*, Chicago: American Bar Association Section of Antitrust Law.

Baker, J.B. (1996), 'Identifying Horizontal Price Fixing in the Electronic Marketplace', *Antitrust Law Journal*, 65, 41–55.

Besanko, D. & T.P. Lyon (1993), 'Equilibrium Incentives for Most-Favored Customer Clauses in an Oligopolistic Industry', *International Journal of Industrial Organization*, 11, 347–67.

Black, O. (2005), *Conceptual Foundations of Antitrust*, New York: Cambridge University Press.

Blechman, M.D. (1979), 'Conscious Parallelism. Signaling and Facilitating Devices: The Problem of Tacit Collusion Under the Antitrust Laws', *New York Law School Law Review*, 24, 881–906.

Carlton, D.W. (1983), 'A Reexamination of Delivered Pricing Systems', *Journal of Law & Economics*, 26, 51–70.

Carlton, D.W., R.H. Gertner & A.M. Rosenfield (1997), 'Communication Among Competitors: Game Theory and Antitrust', *George Mason Law Review*, 5, 423–40.

Chamberlin, E.H. (1948), *The Theory of Monopolistic Competition: A Re-orientation of the Theory of Value* (6th ed), Cambridge, MA: Harvard University Press.

Cooper, T.E. (1986), 'Most-Favored-Customer Pricing and Tacit Collusion', *The RAND Journal of Economics*, 17, 377–88.

Department of Justice and Federal Trade Commission Horizontal Merger Guidelines § 2.11 (1992, revised 1997), http://www.usdoj.gov/atr/public/guidelines/horiz_book/hmg1.html.

DeSanti, S.S. & E.A. Nagata (1994), 'Competitor Communications: Facilitating Practices or Invitations To Collude?', *Antitrust Law Journal*, 63, 93–132.

Devlin, A. (2007), Note, 'A Proposed Solution to the Problem of Parallel Pricing in Oligopolistic Markets', *Stanford Law Review*, 59, 1111–51.

Dick, A.R. (1996), 'Identifying Contracts, Combinations and Conspiracies in Restraint of Trade', *Managerial and Decision Economics*, 17, 203–16.

Elzinga, K.G. (1984), 'New Developments on the Cartel Front', *Antitrust Bulletin*, 29, 3–26.

Genesove, D. & W.P. Mullin (2001), 'Rules, Communication, and Collusion: Narrative Evidence from the Sugar Institute Case', *American Economic Review*, 91, 379–98.

Goldman, L. (1986), 'Oligopoly Policy and the Ethyl Corp. Case', *Or. L. Rev.*, 65, 73–121.

Gurrea, S.D. & B.M. Owen (2003), 'Coordinated Interaction and Clayton § 7 Enforcement', *George Mason Law Review*, 12, 89–118.

Haddock, D.D. (1982), 'Basing-Point Pricing: Competitive v. Collusive Theories', *American Economic Review*, 72, 289–306.

Hay, G.A. (1982), 'Oligopoly, Shared Monopoly, and Antitrust Law', *Cornell Law Review*, 67, 439–81.

Hay, G.A. (1984), 'Facilitating Practices: The Ethyl Case', in Kwoka, J.E. and L.J. White, eds. (1999), *The Antitrust Revolution* (3d ed), New York: Oxford University Press, pp. 182–201.

Hay, G.A. (2000), 'The Meaning of "Agreement" under the Sherman Act: Thoughts from the "Facilitating Practices" Experience', *16 Rev. Indus. Org.* 113–29.

Holt, C.A. & D.T. Scheffman (1987), 'Facilitating Practices: The Effects of Advance Notice and Best-Price Policies', *The RAND Journal of Economics*, 18, 187–97.

Hylton, K.N. (2003), *Antitrust Law: Economic Theory and Common Law Evolution*, Cambridge: Cambridge University Press, pp. 144–65.

Jaquemin, A. & M.E. Slade, 'Cartels, Collusion, and Horizontal Merger', in Schmalensee, R. and R.D. Willig (eds.) (1989), *Handbook of Industrial Organization*, vol. I, Amsterdam: North Holland, pp. 415–73.

Kattan, J. (1994), 'Beyond Facilitating Practices: Price Signaling and Price Protection Clauses in the New Antitrust Environment', *Antitrust Law Journal*, 63, 133–52.

Kattan, J. & S.A. Stempel (1996, Summer), 'Antitrust Enforcement and Most Favored Nation Clauses', *Antitrust*, 20–24.

Kestenbaum, L. (1980), 'What Is "Price Signaling" and Does It Violate the Law?', *Antitrust Law Journal*, 49, 911–23.

Kovacic, W.E. (1993), 'The Identification and Proof of Horizontal Agreements Under the Antitrust Laws', *Antitrust Bulletin*, 38 (1), 5–81.

Kreps, D.M. (1990), *Game Theory and Economic Modeling*, Oxford: Oxford University Press.

Lande, R.H. & H.P. Marvel (2000), 'The Three Types of Collusion: Fixing Prices, Rivals, and Rules', *Wisconsin Law Review*, 2000, 941–1000.

Leslie, C.R. (2004), 'Trust, Distrust, and Antitrust', *Texas Law Review*, 82, 515–680.

Lopatka, J.E. & W.H. Page (2003), 'State Action and the Meaning of Agreement Under the Sherman Act: An Approach to Hybrid Restraints', *Yale Journal on Regulation*, 20, 269–323.

Milne, R.A. & J.E. Pace (2003, Spring), 'Conspiratologists at the Gate: The Scope of Expert Testimony on the Subject of Conspiracy in a Sherman Act Case', *Antitrust*, 17, 36–44.

Page, W.H. (2007), 'Communication and Concerted Action', *Loyola University of Chicago Law Journal*, 37, 405–60.
Page, W.H. (2009), 'The Gary Dinners and the Meaning of Concerted Action', *SMU Law Review*, 62, 567–619.
Pearlstein, D.J. et al. (2002), *1 ABA Section of Antitrust Law, Antitrust Law Developments* (5th edn), Chicago: ABA.
Piraino, T.A., Jr. (2004), 'Regulating Oligopoly Conduct Under the Antitrust Laws', *Minnesota Law Review*, 89, 9–70.
Posner, R.A. (2001), *Antitrust Law: An Economic Perspective* (2d ed), Chicago: University of Chicago Press.
Salop, S.C., 'Practices that (Credibly) Facilitate Oligopoly Coordination', in Stiglitz, J.E. (1986), *New Developments in the Analysis of Market Structure*, pp. 265–90.
Shaffer, G. (1991), 'Slotting Allowances and Resale Price Maintenance: A Comparison of Facilitating Practices', *The RAND Journal of Economics*, 22, 120–55.
Shapiro, C., 'Theories of Oligopoly Behavior', in Schmalensee, R. and R.D.Willig (eds.) (1989), *Handbook of Industrial Organization*, vol. I, Amsterdam: North Holland, pp. 329–414.
Shenefield, J. H. (1978), Assistant Attorney General, Antitrust Division, 'Memorandum', in *Antitrust & Trade Regulation Report (BNA)*, 874, F-1.
Stigler, G. (1964, February), 'A Theory of Oligopoly', *Journal of Political Economy* 72 (1), 44–61; reprinted in Stigler, George J. (1968), *The Organization of Industry*, pp. 39–63, Chicago: University of Chicago Press.
Stigler, G.J. (1968), 'A Theory of Delivered Price Systems', *The Organization of Industry*, Chicago: University of Chicago Press, pp. 147–64.
Stigler, G.J. (1983), 'What Does an Economist Know?', *Journal of Legal Education*, 33, 311–13.
Telser, L.G. (1960), 'Why Should Manufacturers Want Fair Trade?', *Journal of Law & Economics*, 3, 86–104.
Turner, D.F. (1962), 'The Definition of Agreement Under the Sherman Act: Conscious Parallelism and Refusals to Deal', *Harvard Law Review*, 75, 655–706.
Vita, M.G. (2001), 'Fifteen Years After Ethyl: The Past and Future of Facilitating Practices', *Antitrust Law Journal*, 68, 991–1006.
Vives, X. (1999), *Oligopoly Pricing: Old Ideas and New Tools*, Cambridge, MA: MIT Press.
Whinston, M.D. (2006), *Lectures on Antitrust Economics*, Cambridge, MA: MIT Press.

Cases

324 Liquor Corp. v. Duffy, 479 U.S. 335 (1987).
Am. Column & Lumber Co. v. United States, 257 U.S. 377 (1921).
Am. Tobacco Co. v. United States, 328 U.S. 781 (1946).
Anheuser-Busch, Inc. v. Goodman, 745 F. Supp. 1048 (M.D. Pa. 1990).
Battipaglia v. N.Y. State Liquor Auth., 745 F.2d 166 (2d Cir. 1984).
Beer & Pop Warehouse v. Jones, 41 F. Supp. 2d 552 (M.D. Pa. 1999).
Bell Atlantic Corp. v. Twombly, 127 S.Ct. 1955 (2007).
Blomkest Fertilizer, Inc. v. Potash Corp. of Sask., 203 F.3d 1028 (8th Cir. 2000).
Brooke Group Ltd. v. Brown & Williamson Tobacco Corp., 509 U.S. 209 (1993).
California Retail Liquor Dealers Ass'n v. Midcal Aluminum, Inc., 445 U.S. 97 (1980).
Canterbury Liquors & Pantry v. Sullivan, 16 F. Supp. 2d 41 (D. Mass. 1998).
Catalano, Inc. v. Target Sales, Inc., 446 U.S. 643 (1980).
Cement Mfrs. Protective Assn. v. United States, 268 U.S. 588 (1925).
City of Tuscaloosa v. Harcros Chems., Inc., 158 F.3d 548 (11th Cir. 1998).
Clamp-All Corp. v. Cast Iron Soil Pipe Inst., 851 F.2d 478 (1st Cir. 1988).
Continental Ore Co. v. Union Carbide & Carbon Corp., 370 U.S. 690 (1962).
Copperweld Corp. v. Independence Tube Corp., 467 U.S. 752 (1984).
Costco Wholesale Corp. v. Maleng, Nos. 06-35538, 2008 WL 223121 (9th Cir. Jan. 29, 2008).

Eastern States Retail Lumber Dealers' Ass'n v. U.S., 234 U.S. 600 (1914).
E.I. du Pont de Nemours & Co. v. FTC, 729 F.2d 128 (2d Cir. 1984).
FTC v. Cement Institute, 333 U.S. 683 (1948).
Holiday Wholesale Grocery Co. v. Philip Morris Inc., 231 F.Supp.2d 1253 (N.D. Ga.), aff'd sub nom. *Williamson Oil Co.* (see *infra*).
In re Baby Food Antitrust Litig., 166 F.3d 112 (3d Cir. 1999).
In re Citric Acid Litig., 191 F.3d 1090, 1096 (9th Cir. 1999).
In re Coordinated Pretrial Proceedings in Petroleum Prods. Antitrust Litig., 906 F.2d 432 (9th Cir. 1990).
In re Flat Glass Antitrust Litig., 385 F.3d 350 (3rd Cir. 2004).
In re High Fructose Corn Syrup Antitrust Litig., 295 F.3d 651 (7th Cir. 2002).
JTC Petroleum Co. v. Piasa Motor Fuels, Inc., 190 F.3d 775 (7th Cir. 1999).
Leegin Creative Leather Products, Inc. v. PSKS, Inc., 127 S.Ct. 2705 (2007).
Maple Flooring Mfg. Assn. v. United States, 268 U.S. 563 (1925).
Matsushita Elec. Indus. Co. v. Zenith Radio Corp., 475 U.S. 574 (1986).
Miller v. Hedlund, 813 F.2d 1344 (9th Cir. 1986).
Monsanto Co. v. Spray-Rite Serv. Corp., 465 U.S. 752 (1984).
Norfolk Monument Co. v. Woodlawn Mem'l Gardens, Inc., 394 U.S. 700 (1969).
Sugar Inst., Inc. v. United States, 297 U.S. 553 (1936).
TFWS, Inc. v. Schaefer, 242 F.3d 198 (4th Cir. 2001).
Theatre Enterprises, Inc. v. Paramount Film Distributing Corp., 346 U.S. 537 (1954).
Todd v. Exxon Corp., 275 F.3d 191 (2d Cir. 2001).
United States v. Addyston Pipe & Steel Co., 85 F. 271 (6th Cir. 1898), aff'd 175 U.S. 211 (1899).
United States v. Am. Linseed Oil Co., 262 U.S. 371 (1923).
United States v. Citizen & S. Nat'l Bank, 422 U.S. 86 (1975).
United States v. Container Corp. of Am., 393 U.S. 333 (1969).
United States v. Gen. Motors Corp., 384 U.S. 127 (1966).
United States v. Paramount Pictures, Inc., 334 U.S. 131 (1948).
United States v. Trans-Missouri Freight Ass'n, 166 U.S. 290 (1897).
Virginia Vermiculite, Ltd. v. Historic Green Springs, Inc., 307 F.3d 277 (4th Cir. 2002).
Williamson Oil Co., Inc. v. Philip Morris USA, 346 F.3d 1287 (11th Cir. 2003).

Statute

15 U.S.C. 1.

3 The law of group boycotts and related economic considerations

Jeffrey L. Harrison[1]

The terms 'group boycott' and 'refusal to deal' do not have precise definitions. The meanings range from what is called a classic boycott – whereby competitors join to deny other actual or potential competitors access to upstream suppliers or downstream customers[2] – to simple horizontal agreements pertaining to terms of an exchange.[3] In between are arrangements among competitors to regulate some aspect of trade. For the most part, horizontal agreements about terms of exchange are economically indistinguishable from price fixing and are not considered here. For example, one of the classic refusal to deal cases involved a horizontal agreement to enter into contracts with arbitration clauses.[4] In that type of case, the agreement on terms is a risk allocation device that could be substituted for by a price allowance.

For purposes of this chapter, whether labeled a group boycott or a refusal to deal, the focus is on concerted activity that targets specific firms, suppliers, or customers. 'Concerted' denotes an agreement between or among competitors and, thus, is reviewed under Section 1 of the Sherman Act.[5] Much of the analysis of boycotts can be applied to single firm behavior as well and, consequently, is examined under Section 2 of the Sherman Act.[6]

In general, the boycotts considered here have one of two relatively distinct goals. One is to regulate competition among participating firms. For example, the organizers of a golf tournament may disqualify a golfer who has been caught cheating.[7] In these instances, from an economic standpoint, although not necessarily from the standpoint of antitrust law, the critical issue is not whether firms have formed an agreement to engage in a boycott but whether the purpose and effect of the boycott is likely to be anticompetitive. In this sense, a regulatory boycott can be distinguished from price fixing, horizontal divisions of territory, or even a 'classic boycott' as defined below. In the case of regulatory boycotts the agreement and the purpose are separate matters. In the case of a classic boycott the two issues merge.

The classic boycott is designed to damage a direct competitor by denying access to suppliers or customers. For example, a group of retailers may horizontally agree not to purchase from a wholesaler who is operating at retail or threatening to do so. Alternatively, a single powerful buyer (or seller) may pressure its suppliers (or customers) in order to deny a new entrant access to suppliers (or customers). As already indicated, like price fixing and horizontal territorial divisions, the agreement and the practice are inseparable. These two types of boycotts will be considered in turn. First, we turn to a brief examination of the relevant economic considerations when examining boycotts.

A. Economic perspectives on boycotts

Concerted action that may be regarded as a boycott can increase or decrease consumer welfare. Increases in consumer welfare from boycotts result from three possible effects: increases in efficiency, the introduction of new products, or a decrease in consumer transaction or search costs. Decreases in consumer welfare result from higher prices, lower output, or few choices. When a boycott decreases consumer welfare, the loss in welfare or most of it, will accrue as gain to the boycotters. Ideally, antitrust law distinguishes between consumer-welfare-increasing and consumer-welfare-decreasing boycotts. The costs of extended assessment of these practices by enforcement agencies should also be factored in and it makes sense to develop rules that minimize enforcement costs. In antitrust this means the application of a rule of per se illegality to actions that seem very unlikely to enhance consumer welfare and per se legality to those that rarely decrease consumer welfare.[8]

There are at least two approaches to the economic issues raised by boycotts. A boycott that decreases consumer welfare will rarely be one in which the boycotters gain as much as the consumers lose. Thus, a Coasian-like analysis can be applied.[9] If the practice is seen as a 'right', which party would attribute the greater value to the right? Put differently, in a transaction-cost free environment, who would own the right to engage in a boycott or prevent others from engaging in one? Unless one of the three consumer benefits listed above occurs and outweighs anticompetitive effects, consumers would value the right to block the boycott more than boycotting firms value the right to engage in the boycott.[10] When one of these three benefits do occur, consumers will lower their bids for the right to prohibit the boycott accordingly. Thus, the question comes down not to whether boycotters are better off but whether they can make consumers better off as well.

For example, take the case of *Neeld v. National Hockey League*[11] in which the National Hockey League (NHL) was sued by a potential player because the league enforced a rule barring one-eyed players. Now view that right to play or not to play as a right. The NHL will value the right to the extent it increases profits either by lowering costs or increasing the attractiveness of the product so that higher prices may be charged. On the other hand, one-eyed players would pay up to the difference between an expected salary and their opportunity costs. Their 'demand' for a no boycott rule would be strengthened by any consumer who would like to see them play or who places a value on their right to play. If these two interests face off in a Coasian-style auction, which would bid more for the right?

Consumers would (unless they are receiving benefits that would decrease the maximum they would be willing to pay to buy the boycott right from potential boycotters under conditions of zero transaction cost). The most likely possibility is that the elimination of one-eyed hockey players increases safety and lowers liability costs for owners who, in turn, lower consumer prices. Given that the existence of one-eyed players means higher ticket prices, one would expect the willingness of one-eyed players to pay off consumers for the 'no boycott' rule would be less than their willingness to pay off owners for such a rule. This is not to say that the agreement by owners not to employ one-eyed hockey players is not technically anticompetitive. It does mean that if NHL owners value the right more than those who are 'harmed' in any way by the restriction, it makes little sense to view the boycott as 'anticompetitive'.[12] Put differently, from an economic perspective, the term 'anticompetitive' would be misused if applied to prevent wealth maximizing outcomes.

The 'production' of consumer benefits can be viewed as a form of intellectual property. Thus, the economics of intellectual property provides a useful analogy.[13] In the context of intellectual property, exclusion is the price of encouraging consumer welfare-increasing creativity. The inventor or composer is permitted to internalize the gains from his or her works, but this is only a means to an end of promoting welfare more generally. In theory, if the value of a work is exceeded by the cost of exclusion, the work should not be protected.[14] Moreover, any work should be produced at the lowest possible exclusion cost. For example, copyrighted work that would be produced if the copyright duration were only 20 years need not be protected beyond that period.[15]

In the case of the economies traced to boycott-type activities, the analogy is clear. There is no incentive to engage in activities that lead to productive or buying efficiencies if some portion of the gains cannot be internalized by members of the group. The same applies to the creation of a new product. For example, a group of physicians who join to offer an array of services to patients must be permitted to gain by virtue of the arrangement. The economics of information-related costs is even more on point. It is generally felt that information is produced and disseminated in suboptimal qualities. The principal reason is that information is very susceptible to free riding. For example, suppose the manufacturer of housing insulation realizes that for buyers to understand the quality of the product there must be a rating system and instructions on what the ratings mean. Any individual manufacturer that provided that information could expect other manufacturers to free ride. Consequently, for the information to be produced and disseminated at all, it may be necessary to allow competitors to develop a rating system while excluding some other manufacturers.[16]

In intellectual property law, protection from infringement is the means to an end of a generally beneficial activity. In antitrust the most similar concept is the ancillary restraints doctrine. The ancillary restraints doctrine was originated by the Supreme Court in *United States v. Addyston Pipe*,[17] an 1898 case, as a way to reconcile business realities with the broad language of the relatively new Sherman Act prohibiting all restraints. The development of the rule of reason standard made the ancillary restraints doctrine less important but it underwent something of a rebirth with the Supreme Court's decision in *Broadcast Music, Inc. v. Columbia Broadcast System*[18] which is viewed as applying a product necessity defense. Applied to boycotts, the ancillary restraints question is whether the restraint is necessary for a consumer-benefiting result and, ideally, whether the restraint is as narrow as possible and does not offset the procompetitive effects.[19]

Three points in particular should be noted. Part of the analysis is the question of whether the procompetitive effects necessitate collective action. The argument, sometimes made in the context of professionals, that a boycott is necessary to assure product quality, seems somewhat hollow.[20] First, individuals who provide high quality output will survive in the market without colluding. Second, although the economic ideal would be to examine each of these instances to determine that the restraint is no broader (anticompetitive) than necessary, that analysis in itself can be time consuming, expensive, and inexact. Finally, there is a fundamental paradox in the examination of boycotts. Given that participants are obviously self-interested, they are not likely to engage in a boycott that does not increase profit. Often the source of the profit is the exclusivity itself. Consequently, in most instances legality cannot hinge on exclusivity alone. Put differently, boycotts are by their nature anticompetitive. That anticompetitive effect and some level of internalization are necessary for increases in consumer welfare. In short, as in the intellectual property context, the boycotter must be permitted to retain some of the gain traceable to exclusivity.

B. Regulatory boycotts

As noted, some boycotts regulate competition among the participants. To the extent firms simply agree to adhere to the same contract term, the analogy to price fixing is obvious and not considered here. This analysis examines boycotts that are devoted to regulating the relationship between the boycotting competitors and individuals, groups of suppliers, or groups of customers. The boycotts considered here are not, therefore, aimed at the exclusion of competitors by exerting leverage on suppliers or customers.

The prototypical case in which consumer welfare is enhanced is one in which the group boycott amounts to an ancillary restraint that is necessary to produce a new product or perhaps a new brand. Excellent examples come from sports leagues. For example, in *Deesen v. Professional Golfers' Association* (PGA), [21] a case decided during a period of little judicial tolerance for boycotts, the PGA's eligibility requirements were challenged. In effect, golfers who had not been successful at shooting low scores were not permitted to compete in tournaments. The court applied a rule of reason analysis and approved the PGA's practice, reasoning that the 'purpose is to insure that professional golf tournaments are not bogged down with great numbers of players of inferior ability. The purpose is thus not to destroy competition but to foster it by maintaining a high quality of competition'.[22] The court did not expressly invoke the ancillary restraints approach but applied it implicitly with the view that the restraint was a means of increasing competition.

Dreesen was distinguished in *Blalock v. Ladies Professional Golf Association*.[23] There Jane Blalock, a professional golfer, was suspended from a tournament, put on probation, and fined $500 by the executive board of the Ladies Professional Golf Association (LPGA) after she was observed moving her ball closer to the hole. After it announced her punishment, the LPGA held another meeting and invited Blalock's competitors. After that meeting, Blalock's punishment was extended to a one-year suspension. In her antitrust action Blalock claimed that the suspension was a violation of Section 1 of the Sherman Act. The court held that the one-year suspension was a per se unlawful boycott.[24] *Dreesen* was distinguished because Dreesen could take steps that would enable him to play in tournaments. In addition, in *Dreesen* player-competitors were less directly involved in the suspension decision. Although here again the court did not expressly apply the ancillary restraints doctrine, the theme was one of allowing a restraint in order to produce greater competition by virtue of the existence of a superior product. The ultimate result was that the PGA did what was necessary to preserve competition while the LPGA had gone too far.[25]

The analysis of regulatory boycotts, thus, begins with the question of whether the choices available to consumers would diminish in the absence of the boycott. The same analysis has been applied to other professional sports leagues that limit the number of teams. The theory is that more teams in a league would mean lower quality and a less attractive product when compared to substitute forms of entertainment. It has also been invoked in the context of the National Football League (NFL) draft. In *Smith v. Pro Football, Inc.*,[26] the court examined the NFL draft from the perspective of whether it was a per se unlawful group boycott. In the NFL draft, if a player is drafted by a specific team, no other team will compete for the player's services. The 1968 draft considered by the court had 16 rounds. The court first addressed whether the draft would be assessed under the per se standard or the rule of reason. It applied the rule of reason and distinguished per se boycotts from rule of reason boycotts. The distinction, described by the Supreme Court years later in *Northwest Wholesale Stationers v. Pacific Stationery and Printing Co.*,[27] largely turned on whether the goal of the boycott was to deny competitors access to needed business relationships.[28] Not only was this element missing, but the teams were not, according to the court, competitors in an economic sense.[29] Additionally, they were not attempting to block access of another team. Most importantly, some restraint was necessary for the competitive balance required to make professional football an attractive product in the entertainment market. Having taken the draft out of the per se category, the court went on express doubts that the draft was essential for competitive balance. In effect, it required a showing of a connection between the procompetitive end and the restriction. It also noted the existence of less anticompetitive alternatives.[30]

This is not to say that every joint venture/product necessity boycott should be regarded as legal or even subjected to the rule of reason. Again, the crucial consideration is not whether the boycott has some anticompetitive characteristics but whether those characteristics are necessary to produce offsetting procompetitive effects. There is no reason to regard as legal or even to examine very closely so-called product necessity boycotts that employ means that are not the least anticompetitive possible. For example, a decision by the sponsors of golf tournaments not to allow the use of golf balls produced by a specific supplier would not be necessary to hold a successful tournament. On the other hand, a decision to require all golfers to use balls, regardless of the manufacturer, that meet uniform specifications would be consistent with advancing a competitive product.

When there is no plausible procompetitive outcome that necessitates collective action, it is unnecessary to seriously consider the ancillary restraint. For example, in *Federal Trade Commission v. Indiana Federation of Dentists*,[31] the Supreme Court rejected out of hand an agreement among dentists not to submit X-rays to insurance companies that would assess the necessity and, consequently, the coverage of treatment indicated by the X-rays. Dentists argued that not submitting X-rays would enhance the quality of dental care. Precisely why each dentist would not offer the highest quality of care feasible in the absence of the joint effort was not clear.

The area of professional qualifications is one in which procompetitive, boycott-like actions are often found. For example, the Supreme Court has recognized that professional associations may enforce ethical requirements.[32] These actions may lower information costs for consumers and allow the profession to compete more effectively with other suppliers. Similarly, physicians practicing as a group may offer a greater variety of services with easier referrals and coordination than they could individually. This increases competition in the market and lowers patient search costs. Similar justifications exist for exclusive panels of physicians on hospital staffs.[33] Again, at least some of the benefits of the arrangements must be captured by the participants themselves and this would be unlikely or impossible without some level of exclusivity.[34]

These cases, like their intellectual property counterparts, are characterized by the importance of curtailing free riding in order that something beneficial to the general public be created. Three Supreme Court cases, in particular, separated in time and by judicial philosophy, are indicative of this process. In *Silver v. New York Stock Exchange*,[35] the plaintiff was an over the counter municipal bond brokerage firm with a private phone link to the Stock Exchange. This link was evidently essential for the continued operation of the firm, because the plaintiff went out of business when the link was discontinued. The Supreme Court, in 1963, noted that unless the Stock Exchange was viewed as enjoying some form of immunity, the exclusion would be per se unlawful. This automatically illegal approach left little or no room to assess the actual competitive impact of the exclusion or the set of rules that led to the exclusion.

When competition is eliminated as it was in *Silver*, an approach that allows a procompetitive justification is appropriate to remove the practice from the per se category to the rule of reason category. This requires a showing that the procompetitive purpose necessitates the anticompetitive action. Judge Bork has written about *Silver*, 'The NYSE is a joint economic endeavor, and there must be *some* circumstance under which it can order its member not to refuse to deal . . .'.[36] While Bork is correct, permitting the *possibility* of some justification for refusing to deal to result in a rule of reason approach without first requiring the defendants to offer a plausible procompetitive justification makes little sense. More specifically, what benefits does the refusal to deal allow defendants to internalize and how are consumers, therefore, better off? If Silver were a free rider, the exclusion could be a net benefit to consumers. Instead Silver's exclusion was the result of not reporting certain information in its application and engaging in practices that were seen as 'derogatory' in nature.[37] Similarly, there is little indication that Silver's exclusion lowered costs – production or transaction. Unless the questions about Silver's prior practices could have been translated into generalized harm to the operation of the Stock Exchange, the principal impact was to reduce output. In short, *Silver* represents a case in which no plausible procompetitive necessity was offered.

The second case is *Associated Press v. United States*.[38] Here again the Court applied a per se standard to prohibit the news gathering coop from denying non-member newspapers access to the news items gathered by members of the coop. More specifically, members were not permitted to sell AP stories to other newspapers. According to the Court:

> . . . the fact that an agreement to restrain trade does not inhibit competition in all of the objects of that trade cannot save it from the condemnation of the Sherman Act. It is apparent that the exclusive right to publish news in a given field, furnished by AP and all of its members, gives many newspapers a competitive advantage over their rivals.[39]

In this case, almost certainly the Court could have refined its analysis in order to examine the possible impact. The Associated Press is, in effect, a joint venture among newspapers. Each took from and contributed to the whole. In effect, the cost of access to news of others is the contribution of news stories. The collected news had an intellectual property-like quality in that selling it to non members could undercut the incentive to share news with the rest of the coop. For example, newspaper A may be a member of Associated Press in competition with newspaper B, a non-member. What A is able to do is publish news about events in relatively remote locations without having a reporter present in those locations. If other members of the coop sell stories to newspaper B, the return on A's investment (of making stories available to other members of the coop) diminishes. At least some degree of exclusivity was a necessary part of the coop. A more discerning analysis would have examined whether the restriction on selling stories was the least restrictive measure necessary to preserve the coop.[40]

More troublesome in terms of determining the appropriate treatment is a more recent case, *Northwest Wholesale Stationers v. Pacific Stationery and Printing Co*.[41] Northwest was a buying coop composed of retail sellers of office supplies. It also acted as a wholesaler. The coop members, but not other customers of the coop, received rebates at the end of the year. In effect, coop members acquired inventory at lower prices than non-members. Pacific, both a wholesaler and a retailer, was a member of the coop before its suspension for reasons allegedly connected to a failure to report an ownership change.[42] For the most part it appears the Court used *Northwest Wholesale Stationers* as an opportunity to modernize its position on boycotts. It held that the expulsion of a coop member was to be assessed under the rule of reason. In one of the more difficult passages in antitrust case law to interpret, the Court noted that it had 'generally' applied the per se standard in the case of classic boycotts (efforts to deny a competitor access to suppliers or customers). In addition, the firms involved 'frequently' possessed dominant market power and were unable to produce a convincing procompetitive justification.[43] The Court then noted that not all of these conditions were necessary for an action to be labeled per se unlawful.

The obvious message was that the per se standard would be applied sparingly and, probably only in the case of classic boycotts. In its haste to bring the notion of 'boycotts' in line with its post-Chicago approach to previously per se offenses, the Court may have missed an opportunity to announce a more economically-oriented approach. To understand why, it is important to note that there was no question that an agreement existed among competitors and that the outcome of the expulsion was to raise the costs of a party that threatened to compete both as a wholesaler and as a retailer. This would be enough to conclude that the agreement and the expulsion were more likely than not to make a relevant market less competitive. In short, a horizontal agreement that injures a competitor whose membership was once unobjectionable, is enough to require the defendants to explain why the action was ultimately beneficial to consumers. Instead, the Court's approach seems to be the opposite – one that asks whether there is any possible procompetitive reason for the expulsion. Thus:

> the act of expulsion from a wholesale cooperative does not necessarily imply anticompetitive animus and thereby raise a probability of anticompetitive effect. Wholesale purchasing cooperatives must establish and enforce reasonable rules in order to function effectively. Disclosure rules, such as the one on which *Northwest* relies, may well provide the cooperative with a needed means for monitoring the creditworthiness of its members.[44]

The Court applies something that is close to the rational relationship test from constitutional law.

As already noted, this is not to say that the Court's decision is economically incorrect. For example, using the approach suggested here, the questions would have been: (1) What does a buying coop deliver for consumers? and (2) Is a policy that requires expulsion of a member who does not report an ownership change necessary to protect those consumer benefits? In short, what is the connection between expulsion and possible free riding by a coop member?

Specifically, a broader examination of the facts of the case illustrates how the methodology suggested here would have likely led to the same outcome while setting forth a more economically rational approach. Pacific Stationery, the plaintiff in the case, was operating at both the wholesale and retail level. In fact, the coop passed a rule, evidently after Pacific Stationery became a member, prohibiting wholesale operations by members. Pacific Stationery was grandfathered in and shortly thereafter was expelled for failing to report the change in membership. In fact, Pacific Stationery argued that the expulsion based on the reporting problem was a pretense[45] and that the actual motivation for expulsion was the wholesale operation. The Court's response was:

> [s]uch a motive might be more troubling. If *Northwest's* action were not substantially related to the efficiency-enhancing or procompetitive purposes that otherwise justify the cooperative's practices, an inference of anticompetitive animus might be appropriate. But such an argument is appropriately evaluated under the rule-of-reason analysis.[46]

Given these facts, a more promising analysis would have asked whether it was anticompetitive to suspend a coop member for operating at the wholesale level in competition with the coop. First, the Court could have recognized the procompetitive effects of the coop.[47] Second, the Court could determine whether expulsion of wholesale competitors was necessary to achieve these gains. Almost certainly an expulsion would be necessary. In effect, whatever consumer-benefiting effects are generated will only exist if members of the coop are permitted to internalize some portion of the gain. A coop member who enters into competition with the coop at the wholesale level is likely to be a free rider with the capacity to undercut the necessary internalization.

C. Non-regulatory boycotts

When a group of competitors combines and communicates to suppliers or to customers that they will lose the business of the group if the suppliers or customers deal with a competitor or potential competitor, the term 'classic boycott' is applied. The law on these types of boycotts was both relatively clear and economically rational until the early 1980s. These types of boycotts were per se unlawful. Since that time, due to reinterpretation of the early cases[48] and confusing language,[49] the status of these types of boycotts is in doubt. The question here is whether movement of classic boycotts from a per se status to either a rule of reason or a 'quick look' approach is consistent with an economic approach to boycotts as set out at the beginning of this chapter.

Three cases are generally regarded as establishing the rule of per se illegality for group boycotts. In *Eastern States Retail Lumber Dealers' Association v. United States*,[50] retail sellers of lumber agreed to keep track of wholesalers that were selling to retail customers. The defendants argued that the arrangement was 'promotive of the public welfare in providing retail facilities'.[51] In short, for the retail level to survive, wholesalers' access to retail customers had to be inhibited. Obviously, this was a weak argument even in 1914. There was no connection between consumer welfare and an independent layer of 'retailers' in the chain of distribution. Although the case was decided in advance of the development of the per se rules, the Court dealt with the issue without any serious examination of the impact on the market. This treatment was obviously consistent with the approach suggested here – the exclusion of new competitors in sales to consumers was hardly a procompetitive end that justified the boycott.

In *Fashion Originators' Guild v. Federal Trade Commission*,[52] the designers and manufacturers of women's clothing agreed not to sell to retailers who purchased clothing from so-called 'style pirates'. Style pirates manufactured 'knock-offs' – clothing based on the original designs of defendants. The procompetitive justification was that the style pirates were free riders and the consequence of the free riding was that designers of originals were unable to internalize the benefits of their efforts and creativity. They were, in effect, attempting to create through a form of self-help an outcome comparable to that enjoyed by authors and inventors under federal copyright and patent law. Although not using the term 'per se', the Court's analysis left no doubt that an inquiry into actual impact was not necessary. The 'purpose and object' of the defendants was enough to fall within the prohibitions of the antitrust laws.[53]

The public benefit justification of the defendants fell on deaf ears as it probably should have. First, the Constitutional provisions allowing Congress to pass laws to protect intellectual property are broad enough to authorize the protection of clothing design, but Congress has not so acted. In effect, the defendants attempted to create and protect a property right that Congress seems to have specifically declined to create. Second, as the Court noted,[54] the means by which the defendant manufacturers sought to survive was the elimination of competing manufacturers. Just as the retailers in *Eastern States* attempted to survive by eliminating potential retailers, the defendants here attempted to eliminate their most powerful competitors. The argument of a competitor that it could survive if simply permitted to eliminate another competitor is not likely to be one the antitrust laws endorse.

Judge Bork offers another possible procompetitive justification.[55] Suppose a manufacturer of originals attempted to compete through advertising and other means. That advertising might result in visits to the store but if competing, less expensive knock-offs are available, consumers would choose them and, perhaps, even be steered to them. The manufacturer could avoid these problems if it became the exclusive supplier to the retailer. The manufacturer could threaten to pull his products without a promise of exclusivity. According to Judge Bork, the promise of exclusivity is unlikely to be made if the manufacturer demanding it could not offer a complete product line. An agreement among several manufacturers may be a means of offering a complete product line. Thus, the combination 'may be nothing more than an attempt to gain efficiencies of advertising and promotion that lead to exclusive dealing in many industries'.[56] This would permit the manufacturers of original fashions to compete with other manufacturers free of the free riding problem. Judge Bork's analysis has the flavor of a product necessity defense. It is similar to the theory that it may make sense to limit intrabrand competition as a means of increasing interbrand competition.[57]

In effect, Judge Bork offers this as a possible procompetitive rationale for what amounts to a demand by one set of competitors that they be dealt with exclusively at the expense of other competitors who have not similarly combined. This was essentially what the Fashion Originators did. His point seems to be that a per se rule eliminates an exploration of this possibility. It is important to note that Judge Bork is not proposing limiting intrabrand competition in order to increase interbrand competition. Instead it is the more difficult case of weighing restrictions on interbrand competition as a means to increase competition among a different set of interbrand competitors.[58] Moreover, it is not clear that the procompetitive end will be produced at all; in terms of free riding, it has little impact. If a buyer can visit one store to examine designer clothing and buy a substitute at a store three doors down, the anticompetitive act does not achieve what Judge Bork is looking for. In fact, what may be more likely to achieve Bork's desired end are designer-only stores that demand a cover charge. Prohibiting photography within those stores would also raise the cost of producing knock-offs.

The third key classic boycott case is (or for reasons explained below, was) *Klor's Inc. v. Broadway-Hale Stores, Inc.*[59] There, Broadway Hale, a retailer, pressured its suppliers not to sell to Klor's, a retail level competitor. The defendant offered to demonstrate that there was no actual anticompetitive effects since both Klor's and Broadway-Hale had many nearby competitors. The Court clearly applied the per se standard by indicating the boycott fell into the 'forbidden category' of cases that could not be saved by arguments that they are reasonable.[60]

The application of *Klor's* to classic boycott cases was undermined in *Business Electronics Corporations v. Sharp Electronics Corporation*,[61] a resale price maintenance case. There the Court suggested that a critical element in *Klor's* was the existence of horizontal agreements among manufacturers and distributors.[62] In effect, Broadway-Hale acted alone in facilitating an agreement, but there was no agreement among firms at the level at which the boycotted firm operated.

The legal position of classic boycotts was, as described earlier, further scrambled by the Court in *Northwest Wholesale Stationers*. There, in a non-classic boycott case, the Court described its prior use of the per se standard as involving boycotts in which some combination of three factors were involved: an agreement to deny access to suppliers or customers; a dominant market share; and the absence of a procompetitive justification. No further clarification has been offered. Still, to some extent, *Northwest Wholesale Stationers* could have revitalized at least one element of the rule applied in *Klor's*. Specifically, in describing past boycotts that were deemed to be per se unlawful, the Court refers to 'joint efforts by a firm or firms to disadvantage competitors'.[63] The term 'joint efforts' suggests an agreement is necessary at the level where competition is decreased. On the other hand, the word 'firm' suggests that a *Klor's*-like arrangement would also qualify for the per se rule. In other words, a single firm could orchestrate a boycott if it had enough power to coerce suppliers or customers. In addition, after *Northwest Wholesale Stationers*, it seems clear the Court has indicated its receptiveness to an ancillary restraints analysis of boycotts in the same manner that it has indicated that willingness in the context of other cases involving horizontal restraints.

If this is the case, an argument like that put forth by Justice Bork in the context of *Fashion Originators* would likely be the type of restraint that a court might be expected to consider. Unfortunately, in *Northwest Wholesale Stationers* the Court does not offer examples of the possible procompetitive effects of classic boycotts. It is doubtful that many such procompetitive justifications exist in part because they ultimately are based on the premise that the market will be more competitive if one interbrand competitor is, or a group of interbrand competitors are replaced by another group of interbrand competitors.

One useful exploration of the status of group boycotts in the post *Northwest Wholesale Stationers* era is *Toys 'R' Us v. Federal Trade Commission*.[64] The case takes the form of *Klor's*. Toys 'R' Us, a retailer of toys, formed vertical agreements with manufacturers and helped facilitate agreements among manufacturers designed to prevent the sale of toys to large discount clubs or warehouse stores. Evidently, the vertical agreements alone were not sufficient to achieve Toys 'R' Us's ends because manufacturers were concerned that other manufacturers would 'cheat' and continue making the sales to the warehouse stores.[65] Notably, there was no agreement at one distribution to eliminate competition at that level.

The Federal Trade Commission regarded the network of agreements as per se unlawful and was affirmed by the Seventh Circuit Court of Appeals. The court followed the *Northwest Wholesale Stationers* roadmap. Toys 'R' Us had acted to eliminate competition at its level by coercing its suppliers not to sell to Toys 'R' Us's competitors. Toys 'R' Us possessed dominant power as a buyer of toys and, although it offered an 'avoidance of free riding defense', the court properly rejected it. The court stressed the importance of the horizontal agreement among manufacturers. The implication is if Toys 'R' Us, as a powerful buyer, had simply entered into a series of vertical agreements with each manufacturer then a per se analysis would not have been appropriate. Then the question would have been whether a series of exclusive dealing arrangements would violate the Act. This would involve applying a rule of reason analysis.

The position of classic boycotts, like other violations that were once per se unlawful, is less predictable than it once was. The term 'per se' may still be used but the language in *Northwest Wholesale Stationers* seems to require a horizontal agreement at either the pressuring level or the pressured level. In addition, the firm or firms at the level benefitting from the boycott may need to possess market power. Finally, the Court will consider procompetitive justifications. This modern rule sacrifices the economies inherent in the per se rule. It is not clear that it makes a great deal of sense from an economic point of view. The consistent procompetitive argument in a classic boycott is that one competitor or a group of cooperating competitors is somehow superior to another competitor or group of competitors and that the superiority cannot be established through market forces alone. If one returns to the intellectual property analogy, the argument should be pressed at least to the point of asking what anticompetitive free riding would take place in the absence of the boycott. A plausible argument to this effect seems unlikely. In fact, in the context of the classic boycott, it does not appear that the Supreme Court has yet found such a case.

D. Conclusion

Although all boycotts do not fall neatly into one category or the other, for the most part they are designed either to regulate competition among a group of competitors or to eliminate actual or potential competitors. In both cases, as in every other antitrust question, the ideal distinction is between those agreements that leave consumers better off and those that leave them worse off. Complexity arises because in order for even procompetitive boycotts to exist, there must be some gain to those engaged in the boycott. In short, there must be some internalized benefit.

This chapter proposes the use of an intellectual property analogy. The question is whether the costs of exclusion and internalization by the boycotters is offset by the gain to others. It also suggests that regulatory and classic boycotts be treated slightly differently and finds that, with some exceptions, judicial treatment of boycotts has evolved to the point of recognizing this difference. In the case of regulatory boycotts, the goal is not to eliminate competitors. Consumer choices still determine the end result. In this context, defendants should be able fairly easily to escape per se condemnation by indicating: (1) A plausible procompetitive end and (2) That the horizontal agreement represents the least restrictive means of achieving that end.

Classic boycotts are different. Here the goal is to eliminate actual competitors. In effect, the agreeing firms want to bypass the market and consumer choice. A court's approval of these agreements represents a decision that one group of competitors is competent to determine that another group of competitors is to be eliminated and that this is in the interest of consumer welfare. This type of economic paternalism is worrisome and there appear to be few cases in which such authority should be vested with competitors. A per se rule is probably still warranted in these cases. If not, it should be avoided only by a clear showing of a not merely plausible, but likely, procompetitive justification.

Notes

1. Stephen C. O'Connell Chair and Professor of Law, University of Florida College of Law.
2. See e.g., *Eastern States Retail Lumber Dealers' Ass'n. v. United States*, 234 U.S. 600 (1914).
3. See e.g., *Paramount Famous Lasky Corp. v. United States*, 282 U.S. 30 (1930).
4. *Id.*
5. 15 U.S.C. 1.
6. 15 U.S.C. 2. Enforcement is also possible by the Federal Trade Commission under Section 5 of the Federal Trade Commission Act.
7. Ronald Coase, 'The Problem of Social Cost', 3 J. L. & Econ. 1 (1960); Jeffrey L. Harrison, 'An Instrumental Approach to Market Power and Antitrust Policy', 59 S.M.U. L. Rev. 1673 (2006).
8. In practice, if a practice is not per se unlawful it will be assessed under the rule of reason. This typically means the defendant prevails.
9. For an application of the same analysis to market power questions see Coase, *supra* note 7.
10. This is because consumers will lose not simple consumer surplus that is captured by the boycotters but the deadweight loss associated with all deviation from conditions of perfect competition. The question for a court becomes how to allocate the right in a manner that is consistent with wealth maximizing principles.
11. 594 F.2d 1297 (C.A. Cal. 1979).
12. The idea of viewing the issue in the context of a market emphasizes the wealth maximizing or Kaldor-Hicks approach to the issue. The Kaldor-Hicks or wealth maximizing concept to efficiency requires that resources be allocated to those who value them the most. The outcome is sometimes called potential Pareto Superior because in a transaction cost free context the parties would have voluntarily bargained for the exchange.

13. See William M. Landes & Richard A. Posner, 'An Economic Analysis of Copyright Law', 18 Journal of Legal Studies 325 (1989).
14. The narrow case-by-case cost benefit analysis is hardly reflected in statutory patent law or copyright law although certain elements of both these areas of law can be squared with an economic approach.
15. See generally, Jeffrey L. Harrison, 'A Positive Externalites Approach to Copyright: Theory and Practice', 13 Journal of Intellectual Property Law 1 (2005). Duration is one of the major ways in which copyright law deviates from economic efficiency.
16. See for example, Trade Regulation Rules; Labeling and Advertising of Home Insulation, 44 Fed. Reg. 50218, Federal Trade Commission, 1979.
17. *United States v. Addyston Pipe*, 85 F. 271 (6th Cir, 1898), aff'd., 175 U.S. 211 (1899).
18. 441 U.S. 1 (1979).
19. The connection to the treatment of covenants not to compete under the common law is obvious. In that context, the covenant must be appropriate with respect to the activity, the time period and the geographic area affected.
20. This justification was offered in *FTC v. Indiana Federation of Dentists*, 476 U.S. 447 (1986).
21. *Herbert C. Deesen v. Professional Golfers' Assoc*. 358 F.2d 165 (C.A.Cal 1966).
22. *Id.* at 170.
23. 359 F.Supp. 1260 (D.C. Georgia, 1973).
24. *Id.* at 1266.
25. See also *Molinas v. National Basketball Association*, 190 F.Supp. 241 (D.C.N.Y., 1961).
26. 593 F.2d 1173 (D.C. Cir. 1978).
27. 472 U.S. 284 (1985).
28. 593 F.2d at 1178.
29. The court did not address the economic competition on the buying side of the market and the monopsony power of the League.
30. Id. at 1187. Subsequently, in *Powell v. National Football League*, 711 F. Supp. 959 (D. Minn. 1989) the draft was held to fall within the nonstatutory labor exemption for collective bargaining agreements.
31. 476 U.S. 447 (1986).
32. *Goldfarb et al. v. Virginia State Bar*, 421 U.S. 773 (1975).
33. A description is found in *Jefferson Parish Hospital District No. 2 v. Hyde*, 466 U.S. 2, 43–5 (1984)(J. O'Conner, concurring).
34. See generally, Robert Heidt, 'Industry Self-Regulation and the Useless Concept of "Group Boycott"', 39 Vand. L. Rev. 1507 (1986). For some period of time between *Silver v. New York Stock Exchange*, 373 U.S. 341 (1963) and *Northwest Wholesale Stationers v. Pacific Stationery and Printing Co.*, 472 U.S. 284 (1985) the analysis of these agreements often concerned the issue of whether the excluded competitor had been afforded due process. In *Northwest Wholesale Stationers*, however the Supreme Court announced:

    > In any event, the absence of procedural safeguards can in no sense determine the antitrust analysis. If the challenged concerted activity of Northwest's members would amount to a *per se* violation of § 1 of the Sherman Act, no amount of procedural protection would save it. If the challenged action would not amount to a violation of § 1, no lack of procedural protections would convert it into a *per se* violation because the antitrust laws do not themselves impose on joint ventures a requirement of process. (*Id.* at 293.)

35. 373 U.S. 341 (1963).
36. Robert H. Bork, *The Antitrust Paradox*, 343 (1978) (emphasis in original). Interestingly, in his 1978 book Judge Bork identifies a number instances in which the per se rule against boycotts was applied. In addition to *Silver*, the list includes *Fashion Originators' Guild of America v. Federal Trade Commission*, 312 U. S. 457 (1941) and *Associated*

Press v. United States, 326 U.S. 1 (1945). He writes that it is impossible to know whether application of the per se rule did more harm than good. R. Bork at 338. This is an odd question given that we would not know whether any course of action would have done more harm than good. What we do know is that whatever impact those decisions had, the New York Stock Exchange and the Associated Press remain robust enterprises. Although the Fashion Originators' Guild of America did cease operation, one would be hard pressed to show that the development of fashion has been slowed.

37. *Silver v. New York Stock Exchange*, 302 F.2d 714, 716. (2d Cir, 1963).
38. 326 U.S. 1 (1945).
39. *Id.* at 17 (notes deleted).
40. In theory, if the impact of exclusivity is extreme, access could be regarded as an essential facility. This is not to suggest that the essential facilities doctrine is a promising one for plaintiffs.
41. 427 U.S. 284 (1985).
42. *Id.* at 287.
43. *Id.* at 294.
44. *Id.* at 296.
45. *Id.* at 287 n.7.
46. 472 U.S. 296 n.7.
47. This would be aside from agreeing in order to exert monopsony power. This is a distinction the Court seems to make. *Id.* at 295.
48. See discussion at text to notes 61–3, *supra*.
49. See the crucial language of *Northwest Wholesale Stationers* discussed at text to notes 42–5, *supra*.
50. 234 U.S. 600 (1914).
51. *Id.* at 613.
52. 312 U.S. 457 (1941).
53. *Id.* at 468.
54. *Id.* at 467–8.
55. Robert Bork, note 36 *supra*, at 339.
56. *Id.*
57. See *Continental T.V. v. GTE Sylvania*, 433 U.S. 36 (1977).
58. This is the standard issue in any exclusive dealing arrangements.
59. 359 U.S. 207 (1959).
60. *Id.* at 212.
61. 108 S.Ct. 1515 (1988).
62. *Id.* at 1525.
63. *Id.* at 294.
64. 221 F.3d 928 (7th Cir. 2000).
65. *Id.* at 932.

References

Bork, R. (1978), *The Antitrust Paradox*, New York, Basic Books.

Coase, R. (1960), The Problem of Social Cost, *Journal of Law & Economics*, 3, 1–44.

Federal Trade Commission (1979), Trade Regulation Rules; Labeling and Advertising of Home Insulation, 44 Fed. Reg. 50218.

Harrison, J. (2005), A Positive Externalites Approach to Copyright: Theory and Practice, 13 *Journal of Intellectual Property Law*, 13 (1), 1–59.

Harrison, J. (2006), An Instrumental Approach to Market Power and Antitrust Policy, *SMU Law Review*, 59 (4), 1673–715.

Heidt, R. (1986), Industry Self-Regulation and the Useless Concept of 'Group Boycott', *Vanderbilt Law Review*, 39 (7), 1507–8.

Landes, W. and R. Posner (1989), An Economic Analysis of Copyright Law, *Journal of Legal Studies*, 18 (2), 325–63.

Cases and statutes

15 U.S.C. 1.
15 U.S.C. 2.
Addyston Pipe & Steel Co. v. United States, 175 U.S. 211 (1899).
Associated Press v. United States, 326 U.S. 1 (1945).
Blalock v. Ladies Prof'l Golf Ass'n, 359 F.Supp. 1260 (D.C. Ga, 1973).
Broad. Music, Inc. v. Columbia Broad. System, Inc., 441 U.S. 1 (1979).
Business Electronics Corp. v. Sharp Electronics Corp., 485 U.S. 717 (1988).
Continental T.V. v. GTE Sylvania, 433 U.S. 36 (1977).
Deesen v. Prof'l Golfers' Ass'n., 358 F.2d 165 (C.A.Cal 1966).
E. States Retail Lumber Dealers' Ass'n v. United States, 234 U.S. 600 (1914).
Fashion Originators' Guild of America v. FTC, 312 U.S. 457 (1941).
F.T.C. v. Indiana Fed'n of Dentists, 476 U.S. 447 (1986).
Goldfarb et. al. v. Virginia State Bar, 421 U.S. 773 (1975).
Jefferson Parish Hosp. Dist. No. 2 v. Hyde, 466 U.S. 2 (1984).
Klor's, Inc. v. Broadway-Hale Stores, Inc., 359 U.S. 207 (1959).
Molinas v. Nat'l Basketball Association, 190 F.Supp. 241 (D.C.N.Y., 1961).
Neeld v. Nat'l Hockey League, 594 F.2d 1297 (C.A. Cal. 1979).
Northwest Wholesale Stationers, Inc. v. Pacific Stationery and Printing Co., 472 U.S. 284 (1985).
Paramount Famous Lasky Corp. v. United States, 282 U.S. 30 (1930).
Powell v. Nat'l Football League, 711 F. Supp. 959 (D. Minn. 1989).
Silver v. New York Stock Exchange, 302 F.2d 714 (2d Cir. 1963).
Silver v. New York Stock Exchange, 373 U.S. 341 (1963).
Smith v. Pro Football, Inc., 593 F.2d 1173 (D.C. Cir. 1978).
Toys 'R' Us, Inc. v. F.T.C., 221 F.3d 928 (7th Cir. 2000).
United States v. Addyston Pipe & Steel Co., 85 F. 271 (6th Cir, 1898).

4 The economics of monopoly power in antitrust

*Roger D. Blair and Celeste K. Carruthers**

I. Introduction

Section 2 of the Sherman Act condemns monopolizing conduct, stating that '[e]very person who shall monopolize . . . any part of the trade or commerce among the several states, or with foreign nations, shall be deemed guilty of a felony . . . '.[1] This language suggests, and the judicial interpretation confirms, that not all monopolies are unlawful. This, of course, is sensible antitrust policy since we do not want to punish success achieved through honest means.[2] In order to avoid creating perverse incentives, it is only *unreasonable* monopolies that are condemned by the Sherman Act. This is recognized in the Supreme Court's two-pronged *Grinnell* test for unlawful monopoly. The test involves both structure and conduct:

> The offense of monopolization under §2 of the Sherman Act has two elements: (1) the possession of monopoly power in the relevant market and (2) the willful acquisition or maintenance of that power as distinguished from growth or development as a consequence of a superior product, business acumen, or historic accident.[3]

Thus, an essential element of unlawful monopolization is proof of monopoly power in the relevant market. But it is not just §2 cases that require proof of monopoly power. In fact, there can be no doubt that monopoly power is a critical element in all areas of antitrust except for horizontal conspiracies under §1 of the Sherman Act.[4]

In its recent *Leegin*[5] decision, the Court explained that vertical restraints are subject to rule of reason treatment. Under the rule of reason, one important factor to consider is market power.[6] Merger enforcement under §7 of the Clayton Act is also influenced – if not determined – by considerations of monopoly power that may result from a merger.[7]

In this chapter, we explore monopoly power from an economic perspective. We also try to demonstrate the extent to which the law and economics are aligned with respect to monopoly power. The chapter is organized as follows. In Section II, we outline the economics of single-firm monopolies and present measures that capture the economic consequences of monopoly power. Section III illustrates monopoly power in the case of a dominant firm. Section IV discusses some complications and practical problems with the identification of monopoly power, and Section V concludes.

II. Monopoly power in economics

Before illustrating a stylized model of monopoly, it will be useful to review a benchmark case of what monopoly is *not*: perfect competition. In a perfectly competitive industry, there are many relatively small firms and many relatively small buyers of a homogeneous product. Competitive firms are price takers, meaning that they have no control over the market price; they take the market price as given in their profit-maximizing calculus. A profit maximizing firm will produce a quantity of goods (call it q^*) such that the marginal cost of producing the last unit is exactly equal to the marginal revenue, or in this case, price.[8] Anything less than q^* would leave profit on the table, and anything more would cut into profit (assuming that marginal cost is increasing in q, as would typically be the case in a competitive industry).[9]

Perfectly competitive firms can easily enter and exit the market. If there are economic (as opposed to accounting) profits to be had in a particular market, firms will enter and drive the price down until each firm earns zero economic profit.[10] If there are losses, some firms will exit and drive the market price up until the remaining firms earn zero economic profit.

There are three major results in a model of perfect competition, and the zero profit condition is one of them. The other two are market equilibrium and social welfare maximization. Competitive markets tend toward equilibrium, where the quantity supplied equals the quantity demanded. This is Adam Smith's 'invisible hand' at work.[11] Competitive markets are characterized by economic efficiency, or social welfare maximization. Social welfare, in the economic context, quantifies the total surplus that consumers and producers enjoy when the market price is different from their reservation prices. For most consumers, the market price for a good is less than their perception of the product's inherent value. A good quantification of that value is consumers' maximum willingness to pay, as described by the demand curve. Consumer surplus is the difference between the total value that consumers receive from a good and the price they pay. Similarly, producer surplus is the aggregate difference between market price and the minimum price at which a given quantity would be produced. Social welfare is the sum of consumer and producer surplus, and it is maximized under perfect competition. This is a consequence of the assumptions that led to market equilibrium: price-taking sellers and buyers, free entry and free exit, homogenous goods, and full information.

Figure 4.1 illustrates a perfectly competitive market, where *D* represents

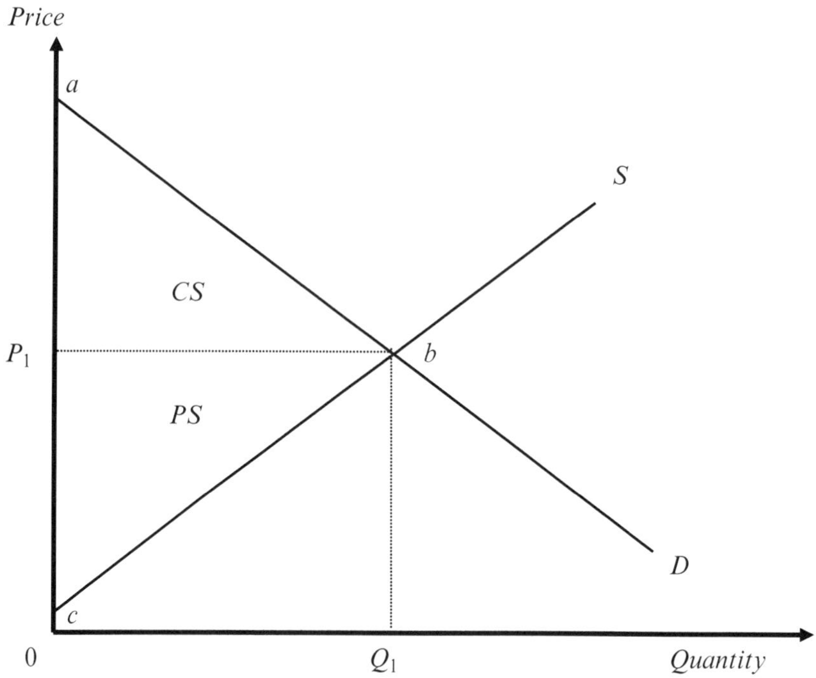

Figure 4.1 *Social welfare under perfect competition*

market demand and *S* represents market supply. At a price of P_1 and a quantity of Q_1, the market is in equilibrium. At a price of P_1, the quantity demanded is precisely equal to the quantity supplied. As a result, there will be no market forces pushing price above or below P_1. Consumer surplus, the value of Q_1 to consumers net of what they have to pay, is represented by the triangular area abP_1. Producer surplus, the difference between the price received and the sellers' reservation prices, is measured by the triangular area P_1bc. Social welfare – the sum of consumer and producer surplus – is the triangular area *abc*. Given the demand and supply curves shown, social welfare is maximized at the competitive equilibrium. Any deviation will reduce social welfare.

A monopolized industry is at the opposite end of the competitive spectrum from a perfectly competitive industry. Instead of many small sellers, a pure monopoly exists when there is only one seller. Monopolies may or may not earn positive profits, but their efforts to maximize profit lead to output decisions that are inconsistent with welfare maximization. A pure monopolist is *not* a price-taker. The firm can choose to produce any quantity along the market demand curve and charge the corresponding price. Much like a competitive firm, a monopolist will seek to maximize profits by expanding production until marginal cost equals marginal revenue. But since a monopolist is not a price taker, marginal revenue is not a fixed market price. Formally, marginal revenue is the change in total revenue resulting from a small increase in output.[12] The monopolist aims to maximize profit. Consider the following profit function:

$$\Pi = P(Q)Q - C(Q)$$

$P(Q)$ is the price at which a given quantity Q is demanded, $C(Q)$ is the monopolist's total cost of producing that quantity, and Π is monopolist's profit. The monopolist will expand output until the incremental profit from expansion goes to zero:

$$\frac{d\Pi}{dQ} = P + Q\frac{dP}{dQ} - \frac{dC}{dQ} = 0$$

The term $P + Q(dP/dQ)$ is marginal revenue (MR) and dC/dQ is marginal cost (MC). Then the monopolist's profit maximizing rule is to produce such that:

$$MR = MC$$

Figure 4.2 illustrates a monopolist's profit-maximizing price and output. Graphically, MR has the same intercept as demand, but a steeper, more negative slope.[13] Profit is maximized by producing Q_2, corresponding to the intersection of MR and MC. The monopoly price is P_2, which is the maximum price that the monopolist can charge for an output of Q_2. As long as average cost is less than P_2, the monopolist will earn a positive *economic* profit. In this illustration, the profit is indicated by the rectangular shaded area in Figure 4.2. Note that the monopolist's price is higher than P_1, which is the competitive price. Moreover, the monopolist's output is lower than the economically efficient output Q_1. These are the economic symptoms of monopoly. A monopolist will produce less than the socially efficient quantity of output and charge a supra-competitive price. As a consequence, society incurs a deadweight social welfare loss in the form of forgone surplus. Graphically, this forgone surplus is the triangular area *abc*. Inefficiency, illustrated in Figure 4.2 by the area of deadweight loss, is the major economic case against monopolization.[14] The monopolist will forfeit economic efficiency and social welfare in its pursuit of greater profit for itself. This is not sinister; it is simply the natural result of profit maximization in the absence of any competition.

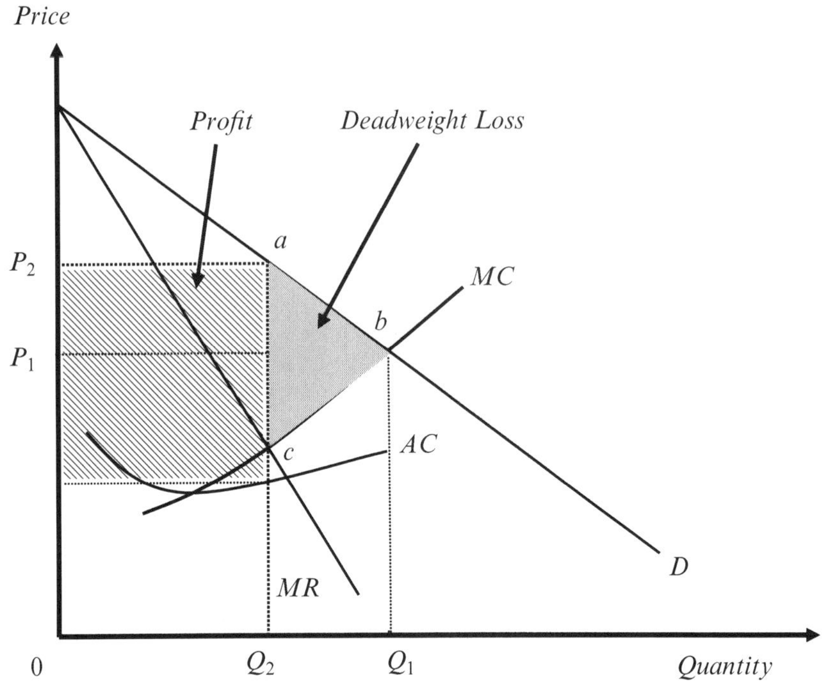

Note: The monopolist produces Q_2 where $MR = MC$, and sets price (P_2) according to the maximum willingness to pay. There is a social welfare loss equal to the triangular area *abc*.

Figure 4.2 Monopoly price and output

In practice, firms which are accused of exploiting monopoly power look very different from the firm in Figure 4.2. But even in more complex industrial settings, the exercise of monopoly power typically results in supra-competitive prices and suboptimal output. The ability to exercise monopoly power relies on high barriers to entry and a well-defined product (one with few close substitutes). These market features were taken for granted in Figure 4.2, but monopoly power is considerably weakened in their absence. Section IV describes briefly the importance of entry barriers and market definition in assessing the viability of antitrust claims.

Measuring monopoly power: the Lerner Index

A monopolist differs from a perfectly competitive firm in its ability to raise price above marginal cost by restricting output. This is the essence of monopoly power: the ability to deviate from the competitive price (i.e., marginal cost) by restricting the quantity produced. Abba Lerner proposed a measure of monopoly power, which now bears his name – the Lerner Index.[15] For Lerner, the degree of monopoly power is the margin by which a monopolist's price exceeds marginal cost, which is the competitive price. The Lerner Index is then defined as:

$$\lambda = \frac{P - MC}{P}$$

where P is price and MC is marginal cost, evaluated at the monopolist's profit-maximizing price and output. It is easily shown that the Lerner Index is closely related to another economic concept: the elasticity of demand (η).[16]

For a pure profit maximizing monopoly, the Lerner Index is equal to the inverse of the absolute value of η:[17]

$$\lambda = \frac{P - MC}{P} = \frac{1}{|\eta|}$$

The price-cost margin will be smaller if demand is more elastic. This makes sense because a high elasticity of demand indicates that consumers are very sensitive to price changes. As a result, a monopolist will not find it profitable to impose a high markup when demand is relatively elastic. In contrast, when demand is less elastic, consumers are less responsive to price changes, and the monopolist's markup will be larger, as seen in Figure 4.3. Demand functions D_1 and D_2 equal marginal cost at the same output, Q_1. The corresponding marginal revenues (MR_1 and MR_2) equal marginal cost at a quantity of Q_2. The profit maximizing prices, however, are quite different: P_1 is considerably higher than P_2. This is because D_1 is less elastic than D_2 at Q_2.[18]

The Lerner Index is a misnomer, in that it fails as a monotonic measure of monopoly power. The value of λ depends on underlying costs and consumer preferences, not the degree to which one firm can exclude others from competing. An ideal index of monopoly power would have a ceiling, equal to some unique value for any pure monopoly. By contrast, the Lerner Index will vary even among pure monopolies. For example, a pure monopolist facing a relatively flat demand may find it optimal to operate where $\eta = -5$ while another may find it optimal to produce where $\eta = -2$. Even though both firms produce 100 per cent of the output in their respective markets, and therefore, are pure monopolists, the Lerner Index for the first firm is 0.2 while it is 0.5 for the second. This can lead to some confusion.

A related source of confusion stems from the fact that monopolists with very different price-cost margins may have the same Lerner Index. This can be shown with a simple example. Suppose that the profit

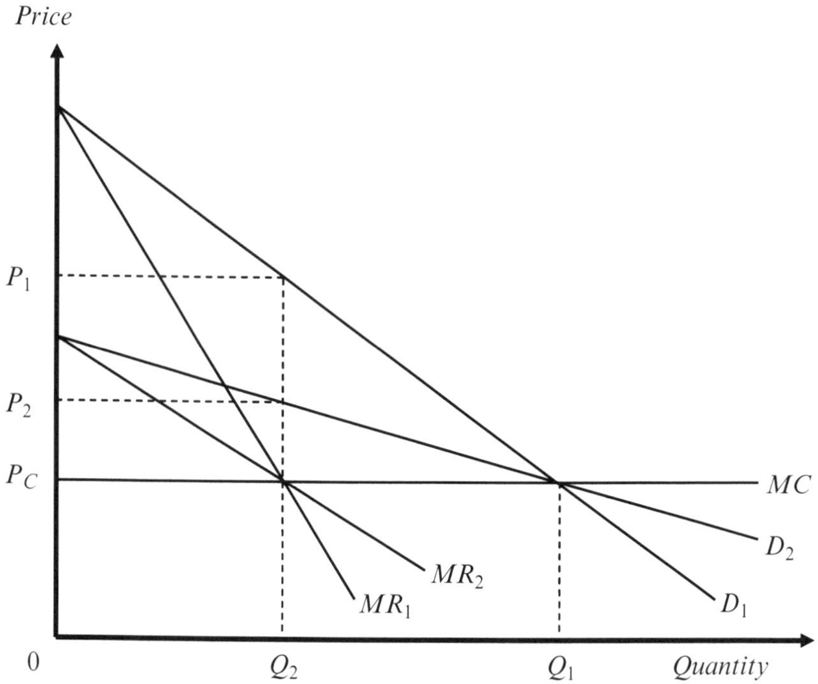

Note: The monopolist produces Q_2 where $MR = MC$, and sets price (P_2) according to the maximum willingness to pay. There is a social welfare loss equal to the triangular area *abc*.

Figure 4.3 Monopoly pricing, by elasticity of demand

maximizing price of a souvenir t-shirt is \$15 while the marginal cost is \$5. Then the price-cost margin is \$10. Suppose a monopolist of marble bookends finds the optimal price to be \$90 while the marginal cost is \$30. The price-cost margin is \$60. Both monopolists have the same Lerner Index since:

$$\lambda = \frac{15 - 5}{15} = \frac{90 - 30}{90} = 0.67$$

Despite its shortcomings, the Lerner Index is a useful tool for showing the *existence* of monopoly power, if not the degree. In this sense, the Lerner Index can be used to complement other types of antitrust evidence, like evidence of entry barriers. But one must recognize the ambiguities associated with measuring the magnitude of monopoly power once existence *per se* has been established.

III. Dominant firms

A well-defined industry with only one unregulated firm is rare. There are, however, situations that are near monopolies. These usually involve a dominant firm that has the lion's share of the market and a so-called competitive fringe, which comprises small firms that respond to price announcements of the dominant firm just as competitive firms respond to market-determined prices. A dominant firm will act like a monopolist, choosing output such that marginal cost equals marginal revenue, but with respect to *residual demand* rather than market demand. Residual demand is the difference between the market demand and the competitive fringe supply at any given price. This can be seen with the help of Figure 4.4.

In Figure 4.4, the market demand curve is represented by D and the supply curve of the competitive fringe is denoted S_{CF}. Note that S_{CF} is the horizontal sum of the marginal cost curves of all fringe firms. Absent the competitive fringe, the dominant firm would be a pure monopolist and would therefore face the market demand (D) and be able to determine the optimal quantity it would produce and the corresponding price it would charge. Given the presence of the competitive fringe, however, the dominant firm must consider how the fringe producers will respond to its price announcement. Thus, the demand that a dominant firm faces is not the market demand, but the residual demand (d), which is the difference between the market demand and the supply of the competitive fringe. In short:

$$d = D - S_{CF}$$

The marginal revenue associated with the residual demand is denoted as mr in Figure 4.4. Now, the dominant firm proceeds to maximize its profits in the usual way; it produces that output where its marginal cost (MC) equals residual marginal revenue (mr) and sells it for the market clearing price, which is found on the *residual* demand curve. This output and price are shown in Figure 4.4 as Q_{DF} and P, respectively. The competitive fringe will respond to this price in a predictable way – by producing Q_{CF}, which is the quantity on S_{CF} that corresponds to a price of P. Together, the dominant firm and the competitive fringe supply Q, which is precisely the amount that the market demands at a price of P, i.e., $Q = Q_{DF} + Q_{CF}$.

A dominant firm sets a lower price than a pure monopolist would have set, and accordingly, the Lerner Index will be lower for a dominant firm than it would have been absent the competitive fringe. This makes sense, since we would expect the residual demand to be more elastic than the market demand. Let η_r represent the elasticity of residual demand, η_m the elasticity of market demand, and ε the elasticity of fringe supply. Let S and $(1 - S)$ represent the market shares for the dominant firm and fringe

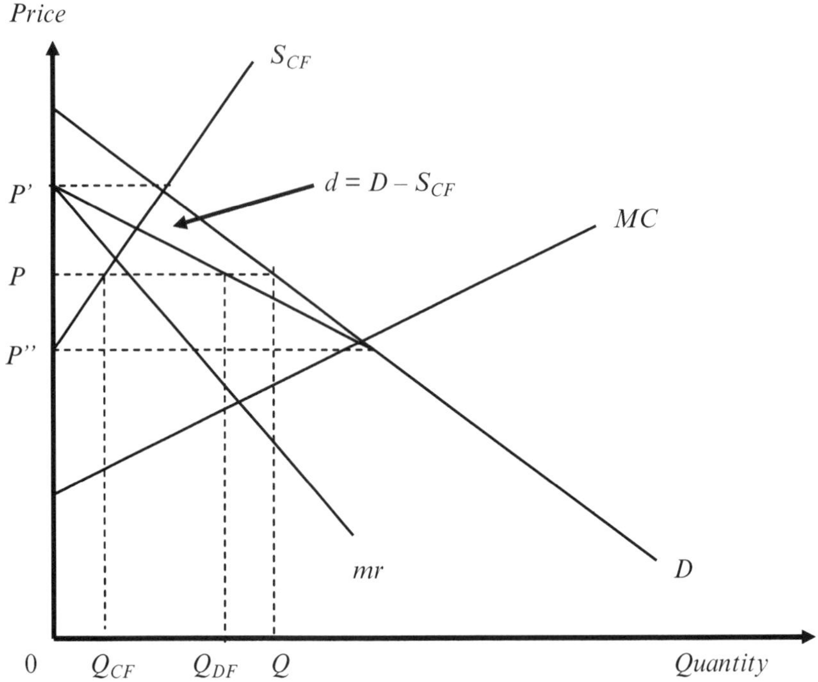

Figure 4.4 *Profit maximization for a dominant firm*

firms, respectively. In the context of the dominant firm model, the Lerner Index becomes:

$$\lambda = \frac{P - MC}{P} = -\frac{1}{\eta_r}$$

The elasticity of residual demand (η_r) is a function of the elasticity of the market demand (η_m), the elasticity of the fringe supply (ε), and the share of the market controlled by the dominant firm. It can be shown algebraically that η_r is related to η_m, ε, and S as follows:[19]

$$\eta_r = \frac{\eta_m - (1 - S)\varepsilon}{S}$$

Substitute η_r into the dominant firm's Lerner Index to get,

$$\lambda = \frac{S}{|\eta_m| + (1 - S)\varepsilon}.$$

The Lerner Index for a dominant firm facing a competitive fringe is decreasing with ε and the absolute value of η_m. That is, for more elastic fringe supply or market demand, the Index is smaller. The Index is increasing with the market share of the dominant firm. As S increases, so does λ. As the above equation illustrates, however, market share is not the only determinant of market power. As in a model of pure monopoly, the Lerner Index will not measure the degree of power that a dominant firm exerts over the consumers and the fringe firms. Instead, it measures the monopolist's relative markup taking into account the presence of the fringe. The next section examines how the courts have tried to resolve this and other discrepancies between theoretical and practical understandings of monopoly power.

IV. Monopoly power in antitrust law

The Supreme Court held in *du Pont* (the *Cellophane* case) that '[m]onopoly power is the power to control prices or exclude competition'.[20] The Court's use of 'or' rather than 'and' has caused some confusion in practice. Based on this single sentence, which is taken out of context, some may believe that one can establish the fact of monopoly power by simply showing that a dominant firm can exclude some competition or exert some control over price. This belief is misguided. Over the last half century, the courts have become increasingly sophisticated in their understanding of what constitutes monopoly power.

From an economic perspective, monopoly power refers to the ability of a firm to raise prices above the competitive level and thereby earn more profit. For antitrust purposes, however, a successful plaintiff will have to *prove* that monopoly power exists. This, of course, can be accomplished with direct or circumstantial evidence.

Direct evidence

A plaintiff can prove the existence of monopoly power by showing that the defendant raised price substantially above the competitive level or actually excluded some of its competitors. This is often hard to do. For example, showing that price is above the competitive level may be ambiguous. A perfectly competitive market that is in disequilibrium will have prices that exceed the long-run competitive equilibrium price. Prices will equal short-run marginal cost, but may far exceed average cost. Even in equilibrium, infra-marginal firms will enjoy excess profits due to their superior efficiency, better location, or more astute management.

The exclusion of rivals as evidence of monopoly power is often problematic as well. Some rivals exclude themselves because they are less efficient or otherwise poorly managed. As a policy matter, we are concerned with the exclusion of equally efficient firms. Inefficient firms should be on their own.

Circumstantial evidence

Over the years, the most prominent piece of circumstantial evidence has been market share. In *Alcoa*, the Court found that a share of 90 per cent was conclusive proof of monopoly.[21] Although market share may not be dispositive, it has been relied upon by many courts and endorsed by the Supreme Court. In *Grinnell*,[22] for example, the Court found it reasonable to infer monopoly power from a predominant share of the market. In the *Cellophane* case, the Court noted that a market share of 75 per cent constituted monopoly.[23] Somewhat more recently, the Supreme Court found that an 80 per cent market share provided an adequate foundation for an inference of monopoly power.[24] This, of course, raises the question of thresholds. As a general proposition, a market share above 70 per cent creates a rebuttable presumption of monopoly power, while a market share below 50 per cent usually precludes an inference of monopoly power.[25] For cases involving a dominant firm with market share between 50 and 70 per cent, there have been varying judicial decisions.[26]

The problem with relying solely on market share is easy to show. Suppose a firm has a market share of 70 per cent and, therefore, is presumed to have monopoly power. At first blush, this does not seem unreasonable. After all, a firm wields monopoly power by reducing output and thereby increasing price. But suppose that the absolute value of the elasticity of demand (η^m) equals 2 and the elasticity of fringe supply (ε^f) is also equal to 2. In that event, the Lerner Index will be:

$$\lambda = \frac{0.70}{2 + 2(0.30)} = 0.27$$

In other words, by unilaterally reducing output, the dominant firm will be able to elevate price until marginal cost is 27 per cent below price.

Suppose another firm has a market share of 40 per cent and, therefore, is presumed to have no monopoly power. If the absolute value of the demand elasticity is 1.25 and the fringe supply elasticity is 0.25, the Lerner Index will be:

$$\lambda = \frac{0.40}{1.25 + 0.25(0.60)} = 0.29$$

In this case, the firm with a 40 per cent market share has more monopoly power than the firm with a 70 per cent market share.

The problem of product differentiation

According to the *Department of Justice and Federal Trade Commission Merger Guidelines*,[27] if a firm can profitably raise its price by 5 per cent above the competitive level, that product constitutes a relevant antitrust market. If it is the only producer, presumably that firm would be a monopolist. The problem is that this may characterize a wide array of firms in industries marked by product differentiation and substantial rivalry. In monopolistically competitive industries, equilibrium market prices may be equal to average cost, but they will be above marginal cost.[28] Since competitive prices are equal to marginal cost, equilibrium involves supracompetitive pricing. Generally, however, this is of no antitrust significance.[29] Restructuring such markets would be futile because these results are the natural consequences of product differentiation, which provides choice to consumers.

Importance of entry barriers

Responsible managers act in the interest of the shareholders who own the company. In doing so, they will maximize the firm's profits on behalf of those shareholders who will benefit from higher dividends and appreciation in the market value of their shares.[30] In order to maximize profit, the manager must exercise the market power that the firm possesses.[31] The economic profit that the firm earns will attract the interest of those outside the industry as they would like to dip into that pot of gold. Entry by those firms will lead to competition and an erosion of monopoly power. Consequently, for monopoly power to be more than a temporary bump in an otherwise competitive road, there must be some barriers to entry.[32]

As a general proposition, an entry barrier can be defined as a cost that new entrants must bear that the incumbent did not (or does not) have to bear.[33] Alternatively, we may define an entry barrier as an advantage that an incumbent firm enjoys over potential entrants.[34] There is some disagreement among economists about which definition is most useful. For our purposes, we only want to point out that low entry barriers, however defined, will shorten a monopolist's tenure. In contrast, high entry barriers mean that monopoly (or market) power will persist, as will its exercise and its effect on social welfare.

Courts consider evidence of barriers to entry in determining the existence of monopoly power. If there are no substantial barriers to entry, courts are apt to find no monopoly power. This, of course, is suitable from an economic perspective; prices and profits above the competitive level will attract entry, and the resulting competition will reduce both. Conversely, substantial entry barriers support an inference of monopoly power based on market share because they will insulate the firm from competition.

Many things have been characterized as entry barriers. These include high capital costs, limited supplies of critical inputs, long-term supply contracts, legal licenses, network effects, intellectual property,[35] and brand names, among others. The problem with some of these so-called entry barriers is that they were earned by the incumbent. For example, any consumer preference for computers with 'Intel Inside' was earned by Intel through years of producing high-quality microprocessors. Rivals can compete with an established brand by offering high quality products, pricing aggressively, and being a reliable source of supply. Similarly, high capital costs are not unique to the entrant. The incumbent also incurred high capital costs along with the associated risks of its investments. Capital costs are only an entry barrier if potential entrants cannot get access to the necessary capital due to some form of market imperfection. Otherwise, entrants must incur those costs just as the incumbent did. In some industries, network effects may be pronounced. Entry may be difficult if an incumbent has substantial market penetration; in that case, an entrant's product will not have much value until it has been accepted by a critical mass of consumers. This creates a chicken-and-egg situation. A firm will not find entry attractive unless it expects a large customer base, but potential customers will not purchase the entrant's product unless it has a large customer base.

In some instances, courts have considered the presence of supra-competitive prices and profits as proof of monopoly power. The most prominent problem with this inference is that price and profit data come from accounting records, which do not reflect the economic concept of cost. The accounting costs found in financial statements only tell part of the story, leaving out the implicit opportunity costs of a firm's assets and investments.[36]

Importance of market definition

Monopoly power does not exist in a vacuum. Rather, it exists in a sensibly defined relevant market. If a market is defined too narrowly, a firm without a meaningful monopoly will be seen as a monopolist. For example, if one examined the 'market' for Burger King's Whopper sandwiches, Burger King would appear to be a monopolist since no one else sells Whoppers. But such a market makes no economic sense because it ignores reasonably close substitutes that are supplied by McDonald's, Wendy's, Hardee's, What-a-Burger, and others. On the other hand, if a market is defined too broadly, a firm with substantial monopoly power will be seen to have none. For example, if ready-to-eat breakfast cereal, which has been defined as a relevant market,[37] were produced by a single firm, that firm would be a monopolist. If the relevant market were defined as all foods that people eat for breakfast, the breakfast cereal monopolist would be seen as competing with the producers of hot cereals, donuts and other pastries, eggs and various breakfast meats, potatoes, pancakes, French toast, cold pizza, apple pie, and a host of other products.

For antitrust purposes, the courts have recognized that market definition is critical in proving monopoly power. In *Walker Process*, for example, the Supreme Court observed that '[w]ithout a definition of [the relevant] market, there is no way to measure [a firm's] ability to lessen or destroy competition'.[38] The Supreme Court's *Grinnell* standard clearly requires proof of the relevant market.[39] The Supreme Court's ruling in *Spectrum Sports* also makes it very clear that market definition is an essential element in § 2 cases.[40]

V. Concluding remarks

The power a monopolist wields resides in its ability to raise price above the competitive level, which it accomplishes by producing a suboptimal quantity of output. A natural signal of monopoly power, then, is the Lerner Index. The Lerner Index demonstrates the extent to which a monopolist can increase price above the competitive level and thereby earn greater profit. The Lerner Index alone, however, cannot communicate the degree of monopoly power enjoyed by a firm. Monopoly power will be influenced by the existence of reasonable substitutes, which is why market definition is important. Another important consideration is the height of entry barriers, since the durability of a monopolist's power critically depends on the likelihood that new rivals will enter the market. A rigorous economic analysis of monopoly power will look for factors that maintain monopoly power, like thinly distributed substitutes and high entry barriers, in addition to symptoms of monopoly power, like supra-competitive prices.

Notes

* Blair: Department of Economics, University of Florida; Carruthers: Department of Economics, University of Tennessee. We appreciate the financial support of the Warrington College of Business Administration. We also appreciate Keith Hylton's invitation to participate in this venture. For past collaboration, we thank Amanda Esquibel.

1. 15 U.S.C. §2.
2. If a firm's product is so superior to that of its rivals, for example, it would not make much sense to punish the resulting monopolist even though it 'monopolized' that part of the trade or commerce.
3. *United States v. Grinnell Corp.*, 384 U.S. 563, 570–1 (1966). See Chapter 5 for a thorough analysis of monopolization.
4. 15 U.S.C. §1: 'Every contract, combination . . . or conspiracy, in restraint of trade or commerce . . . is declared to be illegal.' Horizontal conspiracies, i.e., those among competitors, that fix prices, rig bids, allocate markets, withdraw credit, or otherwise tamper with the price mechanism have been deemed illegal per se. Since the act is illegal, there is no need to show monopoly power.

5. *Leegin Creative Leather Products, Inc. v. PSKS, Inc.*, 127 S. Ct. 2705 (2007).
6. *Id.* at 2712 ('. . .market power is a further, significant consideration'.) From an economic perspective, monopoly power and market power are the same thing; see, Thomas G. Krattenmaker, Robert H. Lande & Steven C. Salop, *Monopoly Power and Market Power in Antitrust Law*, 76 Georgetown Law Journal 241 (1987).
7. See §0.1 of the *1992 Department of Justice and Federal Trade Commission Horizontal Merger Guidelines*.
8. Profit can be written as:

$$\Pi = Pq - C(q)$$

where P is the market-determined price, q is the quantity of output, and $C(q)$ is the firm's cost function. Profit maximization requires producing the quantity where:

$$\frac{d\Pi}{dq} = P - \frac{dC(q)}{dq} = 0$$

Since dC/dq is marginal cost, we have the result that $P = MC$.
9. For a review of the competitive model, see Roger D. Blair & David L. Kaserman, *Antitrust Economics*, Chapter 2 (2nd edn, 2008). Also, see Michael Parkin, *Economics*, Chapter 11 (7th edn, 2005).
10. Economic profits are not the same as accounting profits. The former account for all opportunity costs, which represent the value of the next-best venture that a firm's resources could be pursuing. When a firm earns zero economic profits, its accounting profits may be positive, but this will not induce entry.
11. Adam Smith, *An Inquiry into the Nature and Causes of the Wealth of Nations* 423 (Modern Library, 1937), qtd. in F.M. Scherer, *Industrial Market Structure and Economic Performance*, 9 (2nd edn, 1980).
12. Since price declines as quantity increases along the demand curve, total revenue is:

$$TR = P(Q)Q$$

and marginal revenue is by definition given by

$$\frac{dTR}{dQ} = P + Q\frac{dP}{dQ}$$

Since dP/dQ is negative (i.e., demand curves are negatively sloped), marginal revenue is less than price: $MR < P$.
13. For a linear demand, $P = a - bQ$, total revenue is $PQ = aQ - bQ^2$, and marginal revenue is $dPQ/dQ = a - 2bQ$. Thus, the marginal revenue curve is twice as steep as the demand curve, with the same intercept.
14. Richard A. Posner, *The Social Cost of Monopoly and Regulation*, 83 Journal of Political Economy 807 (1975), warns us that the pursuit of monopoly may involve rent seeking activity that is not socially productive. The resources used in this pursuit are wasted as they could have been used to produce something of value to society.
15. Abba Lerner, *The Concept of Monopoly and the Measurement of Monopoly Power*, 1 Review of Economic Studies 157 (1934).
16. Elasticity (η) is a unit-free metric that describes the per cent by which the quantity demanded will change for a given per cent change in price:

$$\eta = \frac{\%\Delta Q}{\%\Delta P}$$

where Δ denotes an arbitrarily small change. More precisely, the elasticity of demand at any point on the demand curve is given by:

$$\eta = \frac{dQ}{dP} * \frac{P}{Q}$$

where the specific values of P and Q are the coordinates of a point on the demand curve.

For some price and quantity, an elasticity less than minus one ($\eta < -1$) means that in response to an x percentage decrease in price, the quantity demanded will increase by a percentage greater than x. Conversely, when η is between -1 and 0, an x percentage decrease in price yields an increase in the quantity demanded by a percentage less than x. The elasticity of demand is negative for all goods except Giffen goods, which are a theoretical exception rarely (if ever) encountered in practice.

17. The profit a maximizing monopolist will produce where:

$$P + Q\frac{dP}{dQ} - MC = 0$$

or

$$P - MC = -Q\frac{dP}{dQ}$$

Dividing both sides by P yields the Lerner Index:

$$\lambda = \frac{P - MC}{P} = -\frac{1}{\eta}$$

Since $\eta = (dQ)/(dP)(P)/(Q)$ by definition.

18. Marginal revenue is $P + Q(dP/dQ)$ and can be written as $P[1 + (Q/P)(dP/dQ)]$. By definition of the elasticity of demand, this can be written as $P[1 + (1/\eta)]$. In Figure 3, $MR_1 = MR_2$ at Q_2 and, therefore, $P_1[1 + (1/\eta_1)] = P_2[1 + (1/\eta_2)]$. Since $P_1 > P_2$, η_1 must be less than η_2.
19. See Thomas R. Saving, *Concentration Ratios and the Degree of Monopoly*, 11 International Economic Review 139, 146 (1970). For an antitrust application, see William M. Landes & Richard A. Posner, *Market Power in Antitrust Cases*, 94 Harvard Law Review 937 (1981). For an empirical application, see Simran K. Kahai, David L. Kaserman & John W. Mayo, *Is the 'Dominant Firm' Dominant? An Empirical Analysis of AT&T's Market*, 39 Journal of Law and Economics 499 (1996).
20. *United States v. E.I. du Pont de Nemours & Co.*, 351 U.S. 377 (1956).
21. *United States v. Aluminum Company of America*, 148 F. 2d 416 (2nd Cir. 1945).
22. *Grinnell, supra* n. 3.
23. *United States v. E.I. du Pont de Nemours, supra* n. 20, at 379.
24. *Eastman Kodak Co. v. Image Technical Services*, 504 U.S. 451, 481 (1992).
25. ABA Section of Antitrust Law, *Antitrust Law Developments* 231–2 (6th ed. 2007).
26. *Id.*
27. United States Department of Justice and Federal Trade Commission (1997), *Horizontal Merger Guidelines*.
28. See Parkin, *supra* n. 9, at Chapter 13.
29. See, e.g., Richard A. Posner, *Antitrust Law* 22 (2nd edn, 2001): '. . . to infer that every seller who faces a downward-sloping demand curve has market power in a sense interesting to antitrust law would be a profound mistake.'
30. The managers are rewarded for maximizing profit in the form of bonuses, promotions, stock option plans, and so on.
31. In *American Tobacco Co. v. United States*, 328 U.S. 781, 811 (1946), the Court held that monopoly power could be found even if it were unexercised. But a plaintiff should have to explain why a for-profit firm would not exercise monopoly power.
32. *Barriers to entry* is used in several ways, which does not aid our understanding. See Dennis W. Carlton & Jeffrey M. Perloff, *Modern Industrial Organization* 76–7 (4th edn, 2005).
33. This definition can be traced to George J. Stigler, *The Organization of Industry* 67 (1968).
34. This advantage may be in the form of 'absolute capital requirements' which have

already been paid by the incumbent. See Joe S. Bain, *Barriers to New Competition* 55 (1956).

35. Patents alone are not sufficient for an inference of monopoly power; see *Illinois Tool Works v. Independent Ink*, 547 U.S. 28 (2006). For an excellent analysis, see Bruce Kobayashi, *Spilled Ink or Economic Progress: The Supreme Court's Decision in* Illinois Tool Works v. Independent Ink, 53 Antitrust Bulletin, 5 (2008).
36. For a thorough analysis, see Franklin M. Fisher & John J. McGowan, *On the Misuse of Accounting Rates of Return to Infer Monopoly Profits*, 73 American Economic Review 82 (1983). In a similar vein, see Franklin M. Fisher, *On the Misuse of the Profit-Sales Ratio to Infer Monopoly Power*, 18 RAND Journal of Economics 384 (1987).
37. See *Kellogg*, 99 FTC 8 (1982). For an economic analysis, see Richard M. Schmalensee, *Entry Deterrence in the Ready-to-Eat Breakfast Cereal Industry*, 9 Bell Journal of Economics 305 (1978).
38. *Walker Process Equip. v. Food Mach. & Chem. Corp.*, 382 U.S. 172, 177 (1965).
39. *United States v. Grinnell Corp.*, 384 U.S. 563, 570–1 (1966).
40. *Spectrum Sports v. McQuillian*, 506 U.S. 447, 459 (1992).

References

ABA Section of Antitrust Law (2007), *Antitrust Law Developments* (6th edn), Chicago: American Bar Association.

Bain, J. (1956), *Barriers to New Competition*, Cambridge, MA: Harvard University Press.

Blair, R. and D. Kaserman (2008), *Antitrust Economics* (2nd edn), New York: Oxford University Press.

Carlton, D. and J. Perloff (2005), *Modern Industrial Organization* (4th edn), Boston: Addison Wesley.

Fisher, F. (1987), 'On the Misuse of the Profit-Sales Ratio to Infer Monopoly Power', *RAND Journal of Economics*, 18 (3), 384–96.

Fisher, F. and J. McGowan (1983), 'On the Misuse of Accounting Rates of Return to Infer Monopoly Profits', *American Economic Rev*iew, 73 (1), 82–97.

Kahai, S., D. Kaserman and J. Mayo (1996), 'Is the 'Dominant Firm' Dominant? An Empirical Analysis of AT&T's Market', *Journal of Law & Economics* 39 (2), 499–517.

Kobayashi, B. (2008), 'Spilled Ink or Economic Progress: The Supreme Court's Decision in *Illinois Tool Works v. Independent Ink*', *Antitrust Bulletin*, 53, 5–33.

Krattenmaker, T., Lande, R. and S. Salop (1987), 'Monopoly Power and Market Power in Antitrust Law', *Georgetown Law Journal*, 76 (2), 241–69.

Landes, W. and R. Posner (1981), 'Market Power in Antitrust Cases', *Harvard Law Review*, 94 (5), 937–96.

Lerner, A. (1934), 'The Concept of Monopoly and the Measurement of Monopoly Power', *Review of Economic Studies* 1 (3), 157–75.

Parkin, M. (2005), *Economics* (7th edn), Boston: Addison Wesley.

Posner, R. (2001), *Antitrust Law* (2nd edn), Chicago: University of Chicago Press.

Posner, R. (1975), 'The Social Cost of Monopoly and Regulation', *Journal of Political Economy*, 83 (4), 807–27.

Saving, T. (1970), 'Concentration Ratios and the Degree of Monopoly', *International Economic Review*, 11 (1), 139–46.

Schmalensee, R. (1978), 'Entry Deterrence in the Ready-to-Eat Breakfast Cereal Industry', *Bell Journal of Economics*, 9 (2), 305–27.

Smith, A. *An Inquiry into the Nature and Causes of the Wealth of Nations* (Modern Library, 1937), quoted in Scherer, F. (1980), *Industrial Market Structure and Economic Performance*, (2nd edn), Boston: Houghton Mifflin.

Stigler, G. (1968), *The Organization of Industry*, Homewood, Ill.: R.D. Irwin.

United States Department of Justice and Federal Trade Commission (1997), *Horizontal Merger Guidelines*, available at http://www.usdoj.gov/atr/public/guidelines/horiz_book/hmg1.html.

Cases

American Tobacco Co. v. United States, 328 U.S. 781 (1946).
Eastman Kodak Co. v. Image Technical Services, 504 U.S. 451 (1992).
Illinois Tool Works v. Independent Ink, 547 U.S. 28 (2006).
Kellogg Co, 99 F.T.C. 8 (1982).
Leegin Creative Leather Products, Inc. v. PSKS, Inc., 127 S. Ct. 2705 (2007).
Spectrum Sports v. McQuillian, 506 U.S. 447 (1992).
United States v. Aluminum Co. of America, 148 F. 2nd 416 (2d Cir. 1945).
United States v. E.I. du Pont de Nemours & Co., 351 U.S. 377 (1956).
United States v. Grinnell Corp., 384 U.S. 563 (1966).
Walker Process Equip. v. Food Mach. & Chem. Corp., 382 U.S. 172 (1965).

Statutes

15 U.S.C. §1.
15 U.S.C. §2.

5 The law and economics of monopolization standards

*Keith N. Hylton**

I Introduction

Monopolization, the restriction of competition by a dominant firm, is regulated in roughly half of the world's nations.[1] The two most famous laws regulating monopolization are Section 2 of the Sherman Act,[2] in the United States, and Article 82 of the European Community Treaty.[3] Both laws have been understood as prohibiting 'abuses' of monopoly power.

In this chapter I will review the law on monopolization in the US, with a view toward identifying the legal tests for monopolization. I will also review the literature on monopolization standards. Since both the law and literature on monopolization are older and more developed in the US, it is no serious drawback to focus only on the Sherman Act and related literature. The issues addressed here apply equally well to monopolization law outside of the US.

In general, two approaches to distinguishing lawful from unlawful monopolization have appeared in the law and in the literature: a specific intent approach and welfare balancing approach. These are general categories that contain several specific versions.[4] The key difference is that the specific intent approach condemns monopolizing acts when it appears that the dominant firm's sole purpose was to destroy competition. The welfare balancing approach condemns monopolizing acts after balancing anticompetitive effects against some notion of procompetitive benefits.

I set out models of the various monopolization tests in an effort to clarify the distinctions and to raise questions about the underlying goals of the tests. I argue that the traditional specific intent approach is equivalent to the 'no economic sense' and 'profit sacrifice' tests recently proposed. Within the model, the profit sacrifice test (appropriately generalized), the no-economic-sense test, and the equally-efficient-competitor test are alternative statements of the same standard. The welfare balancing tests have been described in two versions: a consumer harm test and general welfare balancing test.

Although the general welfare balancing test comes closest to mimicking a cost-benefit standard, it is not necessarily the most desirable test when error costs are taken into account. If false convictions are more costly then false acquittals, the specific intent test is best as a default rule. Conversely, if false acquittals are more costly than false convictions, the consumer harm test may be preferable. Several propositions in the literature on monopolization suggest that false convictions are generally more costly than false acquittals. In light of these propositions, I argue that the specific intent test is optimal as a general default standard in monopolization cases.

However, one important message of this chapter is that instead of there being a single monopolization test that is appropriate for all cases, the optimal test depends on the distribution of error costs. Of course, there is a need for default rules, to provide clarity under the competition laws. But if with respect to a certain category of activities, false acquittals are more costly than false convictions, a test that is biased toward false convictions, such as the consumer harm test, may be appropriate. For example, where dominance is secured through state support, a monopolization test biased toward false convictions may be preferable to one biased toward false acquittals.

Part II provides a brief history of monopolization law in the US. Part III surveys the literature on monopolization standards. Part IV models monopolization standards, in an effort to clarify the relationships among proposed tests. Part V examines monopolization standards in light of error costs. The appendix elaborates on the model of monopolization standards and examines the welfare tradeoff analysis of Williamson when value as well as cost efficiencies are present. Unsurprisingly, Williamson's argument for taking efficiencies into account in antitrust analysis becomes stronger when both value and cost efficiencies are present. In each part of this chapter I have tried to identify the key insights from the literature, and to expand upon those insights where possible.

II A brief history of monopolization law

This part provides a brief overview of the development of Section 2 law.[5] Section 2, like Section 1, is a relatively short provision stating its prohibition in general terms. However, while the two key provisions of the Sherman Act are alike in terms of brevity and generality, they are quite different in terms of the interpretations that could have been given to those provisions at the time of enactment. Section 1 could be interpreted in terms of a long history of case law on contracts in restraint of trade. Section 2, on the other hand, had little to draw on as a source of interpretive norms from prior case law.

Even if we start with an acceptance of the commonplace observation that statutes are invitations to develop common law, Section 2 of the Sherman Act is a surprisingly broad invitation. Congress invited courts to develop a common law of monopolization. What existed before then as common law on monopolization was scant and unlikely to be of much use to courts in interpreting the Sherman Act.

A Common law background

Some scholars have questioned the existence of a pre-Sherman Act common law of monopolization.[6] Perhaps the best evidence of such a body of common law is a single English case, *Darcy v. Allen*.[7] The Queen had granted Darcy a patent to manufacture and import playing cards. The court rejected the patent on the ground that it was against the common law. The court held that the Queen had been deceived because patents were designed to enhance social welfare, but this one served no purpose other than to allow Darcy to extract wealth from consumers.

If *Darcy v. Allen* is the best evidence of the existence of pre-Sherman Act common law on monopoly, it immediately suggests that judges would have a difficult time developing common law based on Section 2 of the Sherman Act. The obvious difference is that *Darcy v. Allen* invalidates efforts by the government to cordon off certain markets and hand them over to monopolists, while Section 2 of the Sherman Act aims at private efforts to monopolize markets. There were legislative and common law efforts here and there (e.g., the market-interference statutes governing 'forestalling' and other acts[8]) to control specific instances of advantage taking based on temporary monopoly status, but no general prohibition of private monopolization on the scale of Section 2.[9]

B Early development of Section 2 law: specific intent approach

Probably because of the absence of useful common law on the monopoly problem, courts took a conservative approach initially to Section 2. With virtually no case law other than that based on Section 1 to draw on for guidance, they extended the reach of Section 2 only to conduct that seemed most clearly to violate it.[10] The most comprehensive early effort to interpret Section 2 appears in the *Standard Oil* decision of 1911.[11] Areeda described *Standard Oil* as 'remarkable for its cloudy prolixity',[12] and that is a fair and perhaps charitable summary. It is a singular example of poor writing from the bench; repetitive, vague, and in some parts an almost impenetrable jungle of big words.

In spite of these weaknesses, *Standard Oil* does manage to deliver a few basic lessons about the early understanding of Section 2. It adopts the 'abuse standard' of monopolization.[13] Under that standard, a firm can be found guilty of violating Section 2 if it engages in conduct that would violate Section 1 if engaged in by a combination of firms. Moreover, the abuse standard requires a finding of specific intent to monopolize.[14]

Specific intent to monopolize, in turn, is inferred by conduct that cannot be justified on the basis of legitimate competitive goals, conduct that can be understood only as an effort to destroy competition from rivals. The early opinions, including *Standard Oil*, suggest that it is an objective inquiry based on facts.[15] In other words, the intent inquiry is not described in the early opinions as an effort to discover intent by searching the words of the defendant. It is described as an inference based on the defendant's conduct.

The early cases also made clear that monopoly status by itself is not unlawful.[16] The statute was interpreted to prohibit efforts to monopolize, say by destroying competitors. However, the statute was not interpreted to prohibit the setting of the monopoly price or the monopoly quantity.

This conservative approach to Section 2 was not without controversy. Proponents of strong antitrust enforcement wanted a more aggressive interpretation and found their position vindicated, in their eyes, by the government's loss in the *United States Steel* case of 1920.[17] On the other hand, the conservative approach discouraged judges from attempting to conduct their own consumer-welfare tests of dominant firm conduct. The specific intent approach originally taken with respect to Section 2 asked courts to determine whether there were plausible pro-efficiency or competitive bases for the defendant's conduct. If so, the specific intent test implied that the defendant should not be found guilty of unlawful monopolization.

C Modern Section 2 law: balancing test approach

The conservative approach came to an end in 1945 with Judge Learned Hand's decision in *Alcoa*.[18] The *Alcoa* opinion is a marvel in clarity in comparison to *Standard Oil*. However, its statement of the new monopolization standard leaves room for alternative interpretations.[19] One point appears to be absolutely clear: the specific intent test is no longer required under Section 2.[20] Beyond that unambiguous point, Judge Hand's decision suggests that, as a general rule, violations of Section 2 will be determined by a balancing of the procompetitive and anticompetitive effects of the defendant's conduct. In other words, under Hand's test, the defendant may have substantial efficiency justifications for its conduct, yet it may still be found in violation of Section 2 because the anticompetitive effects were deemed too severe by the court.

Judge Hand's approach to Section 2 law remains valid as a general description of the law today. Courts continue to refer to it as a starting point in discussions of the monopolization test.[21] But a more detailed look reveals that the standard for monopolization has been altered in practice since *Alcoa*, and largely in a direction that favors dominant firm defendants. The date at which the change in Section 2 law began appears to be 1975, with the publication of the Areeda and Turner article on predatory pricing.[22] Areeda and Turner noted the uncertainty surrounding predation charges and the costs of error, and proposed a cost-based test to screen out predation claims with high error costs. Following their article, courts began to adopt their cost-based screen and to take seriously the costs of false convictions.

The changes in Section 2 case law have not occurred across the board, but in specific pockets. One pocket in which the law has changed is predatory pricing. The *Matsushita*[23] and *Brooke Group*[24] line of cases require, in order to hold a firm guilty of predatory pricing under Section 2, a price below some measure of cost (average variable cost usually) and objective evidence that the defendant would be able to recoup the losses incurred in the predatory (low-price) period.[25] The *Brooke Group* test is equivalent to a specific intent test.[26] The reason is that if the requirements of the *Brooke Group* test are satisfied, then one can say that the objective evidence implies that the defendant's intent could only have been predatory.

As this example suggests, the choice between the pre-*Alcoa* and post-*Alcoa* monopolization standards may not be terribly important in the end. Whether the monopolization test is framed, as in the pre-1945 period, in terms of specific intent, or, as in the post-1945 period, as a consumer welfare balancing test, the underlying question is the evidentiary burden placed on plaintiffs in a monopolization case. In general, the specific intent test, as historically applied, puts the greatest evidentiary burden on the plaintiff. The consumer welfare test, by its terms, places a much lighter burden on the plaintiff. But if the consumer welfare test were coupled with additional evidentiary burdens – e.g., standards requiring proof by clear and convincing evidence – it could present roughly the same obstacles to plaintiffs as the specific intent test. Conversely, if the specific intent test were applied in a way that put too little weight on defendants' evidence and too much weight on plaintiffs' anticompetitive theories, the results might be indistinguishable from a consumer welfare balancing test applied with a pro-plaintiff bias. The issue at bottom is one of evidentiary burden.

Another pocket of Section 2 case law in which courts seem to have drifted back to the specific intent formulation is that involving 'essential facilities'.[27] The holding in *Aspen*,[28] which suggested that the defendant lost solely because it failed to provide a credible competitive justification for its conduct, carried the implication that the mere provision of such a justification would immunize a defendant from liability in an essential facilities case.

That implication appeared to receive confirmation with the Court's opinion in *Trinko*.[29] Justice Scalia's opinion for the Court, expressing skepticism toward the essential facilities doctrine, described *Aspen* as a case 'at or near the outer boundary of Section 2 liability'.[30] Scalia described the defendant's conduct in *Aspen* as refusing, without a competitive justification, to supply a product at retail price to one's competitor,[31] which suggested an intent to harm. The defendant in *Trinko*, like that in *Aspen*, failed to provide a pro-competitive justification for its actions. However, the Court refused to find an antitrust violation based solely on the defendant's failure to embrace a statutory burden to support rivals. Thus, *Trinko* implies that a sufficient justification for denying access to an essential facility is the desire to avoid providing a benefit to a rival. If that is a sufficient justification for denying liability, then it follows that a plaintiff, in order to prevail in an essential facilities case, has to present evidence indicating that the defendant had an intention to harm its rival.[32]

Recent decisions and commentary have recommended that a profit-sacrifice test be used to determine violations of Section 2.[33] The profit-sacrifice test asks whether the dominant firm conduct in question would be profitable but for its tendency to eliminate or lessen competition.[34] The profit-sacrifice test has the appeal, to some observers, of being able to operate in a manner similar to the specific intent test. Indeed, the aim of the profit-sacrifice test is the same as the more general specific intent test: to limit findings of guilt under Section 2 to those instances in which the evidence suggests that the dominant firm's conduct could only have been motivated by an intent to monopolize and not to benefit consumers.

The most celebrated non-Supreme Court Section 2 case of recent history, *Microsoft*,[35] suggests a broader shift toward the specific intent approach. The DC Circuit's opinion initially states the monopolization test as a consumer welfare balancing test.[36] Then, when it gets around to actually applying the test to Microsoft's conduct, it moves into a specific intent analysis. The court repeatedly condemns Microsoft's conduct because it appeared to the court to have no credible pro-efficiency or competitive rationale.[37]

Of the 117 years that the Sherman Act has been in effect, courts applied a specific intent test under Section 2 for 55 of those years – from 1890 to 1945, the date of *Alcoa*. *Alcoa* introduced a balancing test in 1945 and scrapped the specific intent test. However, since roughly 1975 and beginning with the predatory pricing cases, the specific intent approach has re-emerged within specific pockets of monopolization law.

III Literature: proposed monopolization standards

Given the ambiguity of Learned Hand's description of the monopolization standard in *Alcoa*[38] and the recent splintering of the standard in specific subject matters such as predation, antitrust scholars have proposed several approaches for determining violations of Section 2. Some of the new proposals mirror those offered by an earlier generation of scholars. Still, in view of its importance for the law, surprisingly few scholars have attempted to provide either a positive or normative theory of monopolization law. In this part I will review the proposed approaches.

The proposed approaches hew closely to the two dominant standards in the Section 2 case law – the specific intent test and the consumer welfare test. I will review the literature chronologically in each of these categories. The chronological approach may seem artificial, but it is based on the premise that ideas run free, and as a consequence later authors may have been influenced by earlier authors even if there is no direct acknowledgment in their work.

A Specific intent approaches

1 Kahn (1953) Perhaps the earliest article to attempt to explain and to provide a normative approach to the legal test for monopolization is Alfred Kahn's, *Standards for Antitrust Policy*.[39] Kahn distinguished three potential approaches to monopolization under the Sherman Act: a per se approach based on structural evidence, an objective consumer welfare test, and an intent-based approach. Without delving seriously into the case law history, Kahn argued that the specific intent approach was both the traditional and the prevailing approach; and that it was the best approach. Kahn viewed *Alcoa* as an exceptional case in which the court appeared to adopt a more restrictive effects-based test because of the unusually high level of market power.[40] However, Kahn argued that evidence of intent still appeared to be an important factor in the *Alcoa* decision.[41]

Kahn's argument consists largely of four propositions. First, that a per se approach based on structure would be undesirable because it would eliminate a good deal of conduct that benefits consumers. Second, that a true consumer welfare test would fail to generate predictable rules, require an intrusive level of government intervention, and largely be unworkable. Third, that a legal test for monopolization devoid of any inquiry into intent would have to involve per se elements, which would generate undesirable outcomes. Kahn's fourth claim was that in light of the first three propositions, some inquiry into intent would have to be a feature of any useful legal test for monopolization.

Kahn argued that the objective welfare approach, to be workable, would have to develop per se rules. But this would be undesirable because it would discourage some procompetitive conduct.

While Kahn's approach is quite consistent with that of modern proponents of the specific intent test, it reflects a somewhat dated skepticism toward the capacity of courts to rigorously apply the consumer welfare test. Kahn noted that 'there are no scientific standards for drawing the line between desirable and undesirable consequences, even when they are traceable'.[42] Antitrust scholars and practitioners probably would reject such an assessment today, given the advances in econometrics and economic theory, and their inroads into the litigation process.

2 Cass and Hylton (2001) Cass and Hylton offered a positive and normative theory of the monopolization test and case law, based on the specific intent approach.[43] The normative theory builds on Easterbrook's error-cost argument.[44] Cass and Hylton provided a typology of the factors that influence the likelihood of error and its costs in monopolization cases. They argued that error probabilities in antitrust are determined by the competence of courts to determine whether conduct is welfare enhancing and the distribution of private information among litigants. Error costs are determined largely by the presence of market constraints (Easterbrook's point) and rent seeking. Relying on Tullock's analysis of the costs of monopolization,[45] Cass and Hylton argued that rent seeking would put upward pressure on false conviction costs. This upward pressure, in combination with the downward pressure on false acquittal costs due to market constraints, implies that the specific intent test is preferable to the consumer welfare approach. The defense of the specific intent approach in Cass and Hylton does not rely on any notion of the welfare test being scientifically standardless as suggested by Kahn.

Cass and Hylton did not specify a precise approach to applying the specific intent test. They describe the specific intent test as requiring objective evidence that the sole or overwhelming purpose of the defendant's conduct is to reduce competition. In particular, conduct should not be condemned when it involves a mixture of potentially procompetitive (pro-consumer or efficiency-enhancing) and potentially anticompetitive actions.

3 Posner (2001) Posner proposed as a general test for monopolization the equally-efficient-competitor standard. Under this standard, the defendant's conduct would not be deemed unlawful monopolization unless the evidence proved that the conduct was likely under the circumstances to exclude from the market an equally efficient competitor.[46]

Although the equally-efficient-competitor test generates interpretive issues,[47] it does not appear to be a balancing test. If the exclusionary effect of the defendant's conduct is entirely attributable to its efficiency, then the equally-efficient-competitor test shields the defendant from antitrust liability.

4 Elhauge (2003) Elhauge argued that the monopolization standard should focus on whether the exclusionary conduct succeeds in furthering monopoly power only if the monopolist has improved its own efficiency or by impairing rival efficiency whether or not it enhances monopolist efficiency.[48] While it is not immediately clear whether this is designed to be an intent-based test, it is clearly not a welfare-balancing test.[49]

Unless Elhauge's proposed standard is designed to be a per se test (which would be undesirable as explained by Kahn), any attempt to determine whether an exclusionary act is designed to improve the monopoly firm's efficiency or to impair the efficiency of rivals will inevitably involve some assessment of facts in order to determine the objectives of the monopolist. The reason for this is that there are likely to be cases in which it will not be clear whether the monopolist's conduct was designed to take advantage of its own efficiency or impair the efficiency of rival firms. For example, a firm may enter into an exclusive dealing contract, which has the potential to improve its own efficiency and to impair the efficiency of rivals. A per se test based on the eventual outcome would effectively discourage such contracts. An approach that attempted ex post to assess the objectives of the firm would avoid the per se approach. However, it would also be equivalent to the specific intent test.

One major focus of the Elhauge article is a critique of the profit-sacrifice standard. Elhauge argued that the standard was ineffective because the sacrifice of profit is neither necessary nor sufficient for conduct to have an anticompetitive effect.

5 Melamed (2005) Melamed argued that the profit-sacrifice standard is the best approach to distinguishing lawful from unlawful monopolization.[50] Melamed defines the profit-sacrifice test as asking whether anticompetitive conduct would be profitable for the defendant and would make good business sense even if it did not exclude rivals and thereby create or preserve market power for the defendant. As Melamed notes, this is not a welfare balancing test, and it raises the likelihood of a false acquittal in comparison to the welfare balancing test.

Melamed's definition of the profit-sacrifice test, which has now become standard (see Vickers[51]), is useful because it distinguishes the general profit-sacrifice test from its more specific version in the predatory pricing context – specifically, the recoupment test of *Brooke Group*. The profit-sacrifice test has been criticized because the more specific version used in the context of predatory pricing is not easily generalized to other settings.[52] In addition, Elhauge's critique of the profit-sacrifice standard is easily applied in the case of the specific sacrifice-plus-recoupment version. A firm could take a decision that involves the sacrifice of profits in anticipation of recoupment without having an anticompetitive effect; and conversely an anticompetitive act might not require the sacrifice of profits. Melamed's generalization of the profit-sacrifice test avoids these criticisms.

6 Werden (2006) Werden suggested a 'no-economic-sense' test as the best formulation of a specific intent standard.[53] Werden offered the test as a definition for exclusionary conduct, which makes the test a necessary rather than sufficient condition for liability under his formulation. Although the notion that one could define both necessary and sufficient conditions for characterizing the conduct of a dominant firm as unlawful monopolization opens up new questions, the Werden paper, beyond mentioning safe harbors, does not specify the precise differences between these conditions. To simplify matters, I will treat the no-economic-sense formulation as a description of the test for unlawful monopolization.

The no-economic-sense test condemns exclusionary conduct when the conduct would make no economic sense but for its tendency to eliminate or lessen competition. Werden argued that this formulation is superior to the profit-sacrifice standard – because the sacrifice of profits with anticipation of recoupment is neither necessary nor sufficient for an anticompetitive effect. However, the more general statement of the profit-sacrifice test offered by Melamed appears to be immune from this critique and, as I will argue below, is equivalent to the no-economic-sense test.

Although the general profit-sacrifice test articulated by Melamed and the no-economic-sense test of Werden appear to be immune to the criticisms that apply to the sacrifice-plus-recoupment test, it remains true that both tests are neither necessary nor sufficient to define conduct that has an anticompetitive effect.[54] I will explore this distinction below in the course of modeling monopolization standards.

B Consumer welfare approaches

The consumer welfare approach has recently been promoted by Steven Salop.[55] However, the welfare approach had been urged by an earlier generation of scholars advocating a market performance test.

1 Market performance test The earlier generation of scholars that considered the ideal standard for monopolization – among them Edward Mason,[56] Clare E. Griffin,[57] and S. Chesterfield Oppenheim[58] – provided arguments in favor of the consumer welfare approach as the appropriate legal test for monopolization. Rather than referring to this approach as welfare balancing, the labels that they used were 'market performance' test and 'workable competition'. However, since the test that they envisioned required an objective assessment of the benefits to consumers as well as the efficiency gains from firm conduct,[59] it is equivalent to the approach modern scholars refer to as welfare balancing. The market performance test advocates drew heavily on the work of economists such as J. M. Clark[60] and George Stigler,[61] who had written extensively on how to determine whether an industry was sufficiently competitive that the prospects for successful government intervention to enhance consumer welfare were slim.

The market performance scholars argued that the law should move away from its traditional focus on anticompetitive intent and focus on the actual performance of firms and industries. Edward Mason suggested the following questions as part of an assessment of market performance:

> 1. Progressiveness: are the firms in the industry actively and effectively engaged in product and process innovation? 2. Cost-price relationships: are reductions in cost, whether due to falling wages or material prices, technical improvements, discovery of new sources of supply, passed on promptly to buyers in the form of price reductions? 3. Capacity-output relationships: is investment excessive in relation to output? 4. The level of profits: are profits continually and substantially higher than in other industries exhibiting similar trends in sales, costs, innovations, etc.? 5. Selling expenditures: is competitive effort chiefly indicated by selling expenditures rather than by service and product improvements and price reductions?[62]

2 Salop (2006) The market performance approach has been resuscitated recently in the work of Steven Salop. Salop and Romaine suggested that the proper approach to monopolization cases is one that balances consumer benefits from improved product performance or efficiency against potential harms from anticompetitive conduct.[63] Later, Salop elaborated that the proper test should focus largely on consumer welfare.[64] The consumer welfare test urged by Salop would not involve Williamsonian balancing of efficiency gains against consumer harms, but would focus largely on consumers.[65] The test would condemn conduct as exclusionary whenever the net effect on consumers is harmful. In other words, Salop argues in favor of a consumer harm standard.

Thus, there are two approaches in the literature on balancing tests for monopolization. One is the overall welfare balancing test, which involves a comparison of anticompetitive harms and efficiency gains. The other, due to Salop, focuses on a comparison of the direct consumer benefits from product performance and the consumer harms from the erection of anticompetitive barriers.

IV Modeling monopolization standards

I will offer a simple model of the monopolization standards proposed in an attempt to provide clarity. Suppose a dominant firm takes an action that improves the quality of its product in a manner that benefits consumers by the amount Δv. Suppose the same action permits the firm to erect barriers to competition, allowing the firm to increase its price by Δp. Lastly, suppose that the same action causes the firm's cost to change by Δc.

As an illustration, suppose a dominant firm enters into an exclusivity contract with a supplier. The exclusivity contract has the consequence of foreclosing access to the supplier to the firm's competitor. As a result, the competitor's costs rise, because it has to seek inferior sources of supply, forcing the competitor to increase its price. The exclusivity contract permits the dominant firm to enhance the reliability of its own product and also reduce production costs. However, since it also raises the costs of the dominant firm's competitor, it permits the dominant firm to increase its price. Suppose the price increase is $25 and the value of reliability enhancement is $5.

A Welfare balancing approaches

Consumers are harmed by the dominant firm's conduct if the conduct involves an increase in price that exceeds the value increment to consumers; that is, if $\Delta p > \Delta v$. The consumer harm standard of Salop condemns exclusionary conduct when:

$$\Delta p - \Delta v > 0 \tag{5.1}$$

In the preceding example in which the exclusivity contract enables the dominant firm to increase its price by $25 ($\Delta p$ = $25) and also enhances value by $5 ($\Delta v$ = $5), the consumer harm test leads to the conclusion that the exclusivity contract violates the Sherman Act.

The consumer harm test proposed by Salop is a general description of factors that should be considered in examining consumer harm. As a test, it has to be understood as approximate and conservative. It understates the level of consumer harm because it does not take into account the forgone consumer surplus from restriction of supply.[66]

The general welfare balancing test suggested by the market performance advocates involves a comparison of efficiency gains to consumer harms. The simplest description of such a test would declare the dominant firm's conduct lawful if the net harm to consumers is less than the efficiency gain to the firm:

$$\Delta p - \Delta v < -\Delta c \tag{5.2}$$

This approach is closest to Williamsonian balancing of efficiency gains against consumer harms.[67] In the exclusivity contract example considered earlier, assessing whether the contract constitutes unlawful monopolization requires information on the productive efficiency gain. If the price increase is \$25 and the value increment is only \$5, consumers suffer a net harm – because they are paying more for the value increment than it is worth to them. The reason this occurs is because competition barriers have restricted the consumers' options to purchase substitutes at a cheaper price. If the productive efficiency gain is only \$1 ($\Delta c = -\$1$), then the general welfare balancing test implies that the conduct constitutes unlawful monopolization – because the efficiency gain of \$1 is insufficient to offset the consumer harm of \$20. However, if the productive efficiency gain is \$50, the welfare balancing test excuses the dominant firm's conduct.

The general welfare balancing test overstates the weight that should be put on the harm to consumers due to the price increase. In a precise balancing test for overall welfare, much of the price increase would be treated as a transfer between the consumer and the firm, not affecting overall welfare. Only the portion of the price increase reflected in the deadweight loss (i.e., the social value of forgone output) from monopolization would be counted in such an evaluation. To elaborate, suppose the output level before the monopolizing act was Q_0 and the output level after the monopolizing act is Q_1. A welfare evaluation would condemn the monopolizing act when:[68]

$$\Delta p(Q_0 - Q_1) < (\Delta v - \Delta c)Q_1 \tag{5.3}$$

Since the ratio of the output change to the initial output level – i.e., of $(Q_0 - Q_1)$ to Q_1 – will be less than one in most cases, the general welfare test, by giving the price increase the same weight as the efficiency gain, will overweight the consumer harm by treating a substantial part of the transfer as a reduction in social welfare.[69] Indeed, this is a key point of Williamson's welfare tradeoff analysis. Williamson's analysis provides a relatively precise formula for analysing the welfare effects in the context of this model:

$$\frac{\Delta v}{v} - \frac{\Delta c}{c} > \frac{\eta}{2}\left(\frac{\Delta p}{p}\right)^2 \tag{5.4}$$

where η is the elasticity of demand and Δp is the price increase, both measured along the original (pre-value enhancement) demand schedule. Because Williamson's analysis avoids overweighting the consumer harm, it implies that relatively modest efficiency gains will be sufficient to justify the firm's conduct in an overall welfare analysis.

There is, however, a counterargument to the claim that the general welfare test overweights consumer harm. If, as Tullock argued,[70] firms invest into the creation of barriers to competition, perhaps all of the consumer harm can be treated as a reduction in social welfare. In this case, the transfer from consumers will serve as an upper-bound approximation of the directly unproductive investments into monopolization. This argument should have a rather limited application, though. If a firm's investment has the dual payoff of enhancing efficiency and creating a barrier to competition, then those investments cannot be viewed as directly unproductive. The argument has a better fit to investments into state-granted competition barriers, such as licenses or taxi medallions. Investments into state-granted competition barriers do not enhance efficiency and are likely to be more durable as competition barriers than is the typical efficiency-motivated investment. This suggests that in the case of state-granted competition barriers, the general welfare test does not necessarily overweight the consumer harm component.

The decision maker could assign different weights to the components of the welfare balancing test,[71] based on his preferences for consumer welfare versus productive efficiency. A general welfare balancing test would take the form:

$$(1 - \alpha)(\Delta p - \Delta v) < - \alpha \Delta c \tag{5.5}$$

where the weight on efficiency is given by the parameter α $(0 \leq \alpha \leq 1)$. Setting the efficiency weight α equal to ½ leads to the Williamsonian welfare balancing approach, which reflects an assumption that a dollar given to shareholders is just as productive of social welfare as a dollar given to consumers. Hence there is no reason to prefer the welfare of consumers over the welfare of firm owners. In a setting in which ownership stakes are widely dispersed, and the class of owners is indistinguishable from the class of consumers, the general welfare balancing approach would have the appeal of treating equal increments in social welfare equally.

Setting the efficiency weight at close to one, in the general welfare balancing test, would be defensible when the increment to social welfare is greater when firm owners are given a dollar than when consumers are given an extra dollar. Suppose, for example, the dominant firm is owned by its workers and produces a luxury product (e.g., yachts) consumed by a small number of wealthy clients. In this setting it may be appropriate to treat a dollar going to workers as more productive of social welfare than one hundred dollars going to the consumers. A consumer injury of $100 might be excused under the monopolization test if the underlying conduct generates $1 in productive efficiency gains.

Setting the efficiency weight at zero, or close to it, yields the consumer harm test, which reflects the assumption that $1 additional consumer surplus is more productive of social welfare than $100 of efficiency gains. This reflects the traditional view of the firm owner as a lone robber baron, while the consumers are a large class reflecting the average wealth status of the population. If marginal utility is diminishing in income, a dollar in additional consumer surplus will enhance social welfare more than would an additional dollar of efficiency gain – unless the efficiency gain generates higher wages. This view is increasingly anachronistic as stock ownership becomes more widely dispersed. Moreover, it is not clear why society should prefer the consumer harm test over the general welfare balancing test in light of dynamic considerations. There are many settings in which a small efficiency gain today will be followed by more substantial efficiency gains later, as the dominant firm works its way down the learning curve.[72]

B Specific intent inquiries

The specific intent test asks whether the sole purpose of the dominant firm's conduct is to harm competition. This is equivalent to asking whether the conduct would have made economic sense even if it did not have an exclusionary effect. Clearly, if the firm's conduct leads to an increase in value or a reduction in cost, it would make sense even in a competitive setting. Thus, one way of defining the specific intent approach is to say that in order to find a dominant firm guilty of monopolization in violation of the law:

$$\Delta v - \Delta c < 0 \tag{5.6}$$

If this condition holds, the overall welfare effect of the firm's conduct is negative, even if the conduct did not create a barrier to competition. A competitive market would not support such conduct.

An alternative and equivalent approach to modeling the specific intent test would ask whether $\Delta v > 0$ and c is unaffected ($\Delta c = 0$), or whether $\Delta c < 0$ and v is unaffected ($\Delta v = 0$). If either of these is true, the difference $\Delta v - \Delta c > 0$, so the firm's conduct would be supported by a competitive environment.

Return to the exclusive contract example mentioned earlier. Suppose, as a consequence of entering into an exclusivity relationship with a supplier, the dominant-firm price increase is \$25, the value increase is \$5, and the productive efficiency gain is \$1. The dominant firm's decision to enter the contract would be condemned under the consumer harm test and under the general welfare balancing test. However, it would not be condemned under the specific intent test since

$$\Delta v - \Delta c = \$5 - (-\$1) = \$6$$

The formulations of the specific intent test in the Cass and Hylton article and in Werden's article are consistent with this approach. Both the Cass and Hylton and Werden articles suggest that the test should excuse dominant firm conduct that is based in efficiency.[73] However, this approach could be too lenient. Suppose the firm degrades its product and at the same time reduces production costs. Although part of its conduct is efficient, that should not immunize the firm from a finding of unlawful monopolization. For example, suppose the productive efficiency gain is \$5 and the loss in the consumer's valuation from product degradation is \$6. Even though there is an efficiency justification that the dominant firm could point to as a defense (e.g., cost reduction), that should not be sufficient to avoid liability. Even though there is an efficiency gain in the form of lower production costs, the firm's conduct would be inefficient overall. A competitive market would not support the conduct.

It follows that the specific intent test should not be understood as excusing the dominant firm's conduct as long as there is any plausible efficiency basis for it whatsoever.[74] The specific intent test should require an examination of the overall efficiency of the firm's conduct. If the productive efficiency gain is \$5 and the consumer valuation loss from product degradation is only \$1, the conduct is efficient overall and should be excused under the specific intent test. However, if the efficiency gain is \$5 and the consumer valuation loss from product degradation is \$10, the conduct should not be excused under the specific intent test.

The profit-sacrifice test (appropriately generalized, as described by Melamed) can be shown to be equivalent to the preceding formulations of the specific intent test. Let Π represent the unit profit of the dominant firm. The profit decomposition of the firm's action can be expressed as follows:

$$\Delta\Pi = \Delta p - \Delta c = (\Delta p - \Delta v) + (\Delta v - \Delta c) \tag{5.7}$$

This expression decomposes the firm's incremental unit profit into two components, the gain from creating barriers to competition and the overall efficiency gain. If the overall efficiency gain is zero or negative, then the only way that the firm could profit from its conduct is by harming consumers. Thus, if the firm's conduct is profitable only because of the harmful effect on competition, the net consumer harm $(\Delta p - \Delta v)$ will be positive while the overall efficiency gain $(\Delta v - \Delta c)$ is either zero or negative.

What if the firm's conduct is profitable because it is both efficient and creates barriers to competition? This is excused under the profit-sacrifice test, because the test condemns conduct only when limiting competition is necessary for the conduct to be profitable. Suppose the dominant firm enters into an exclusivity contract that effectively impairs the efficiency of rivals, forcing them to cut back and raise their prices. If the exclusive contract is efficient overall in the sense that it reduces costs without hurting product quality, then it is excused under the profit-sacrifice test.

As an alternative illustration, consider the following example offered by Salop.[75] Suppose a firm changes its product design, leading to an increase in value of \$5, and increase in unit cost of \$3. If the design change also makes the dominant firm's product incompatible with similar products, it may effectively raise competition barriers to the point that the dominant firm can increase its price by \$50. The firm's change in profit can be decomposed as:

$$\$50 - \$3 = (\$50 - \$5) + (\$5 - \$3)$$

The firm's per-unit profit of \$47 consists of a \$45 gain from the raising of entry barriers and a \$2 gain from overall efficiency. Since the design change would have been carried out even if it had no impact on competition barriers, the profit-sacrifice test does not condemn it.

It should be clear, in this profit-decomposition analysis, that a firm's conduct may have an anticompetitive effect, in the sense of imposing a net harm on consumers, even though it does not require a sacrifice in overall efficiency. In other words, the specific intent (or profit-sacrifice or no-economic-sense) test is neither necessary nor sufficient to define an anticompetitive act. However, this analysis leads into the deeper question of how to define an anticompetitive act. The theoretical monopolization standards discussed to this point propose tests for determining a violation of the law, but these tests do not necessarily provide a definition of anticompetitive conduct.

Elhauge's proposed efficiency test, which focuses on improvement of own efficiency versus impairment of rival efficiency, is best examined within this profit decomposition analysis. If the firm's own efficiency is the basis for its conduct, $\Delta v - \Delta c$ will be positive. On the other hand, if the basis of the conduct is to impair the efficiency of a rival, $\Delta p - \Delta v$ will be positive. If Elhauge's test is interpreted as an inquiry into the intent of the dominant firm – whether it sought to improve its own efficiency or impair its rivals' efficiency – then evidence that it sought to improve its own efficiency should immunize the firm from liability. However, if Elhauge's test is based on outcomes, then it is distinguishable from the specific intent test, and is indeed an alternative statement of the consumer harm test. The reason is that if the test is based on outcomes, then a finding that there is net consumer harm due to the impairment of rival efficiency is sufficient to find unlawful monopolization under the test.

The profit decomposition approach is also useful in examining Posner's equally-efficient-competitor test as a version of the specific intent standard. If the overall efficiency of the defendant's conduct is negative or neutral, $\Delta v - \Delta c$ will be less than or equal to zero. The defendant's conduct will be profitable then, only because of its exclusionary effects. Since rivals are clearly equally efficient in this scenario, the defendant will be in violation of the standard because the conduct excluded equally efficient rivals.

Suppose the defendant's conduct is efficient and simultaneously creates barriers to competition. Consider, for example, the design standard change analysed above. If the competition barriers derive solely from the effect of the efficient design modification, then the equally-efficient-competitor standard should immunize the firm's conduct. In other words, the equally-efficient-competitor standard should preclude a finding of liability under Section 2 when the exclusion results from the dominant firm's efficiency and its collateral effects. This analysis suggests that the equally-efficient-competitor standard is equivalent to the other versions of specific intent tests, such as the profit-sacrifice and no-economic-sense tests.

The equally-efficient-competitor test has some advantages over the other specific intent tests. Consider, for example, the news-sharing network in *Associated Press v. United States*.[76] Under the profit decomposition analysis the gain to the defendants from setting up a news-sharing network can be divided into a portion due to the overall efficiency gain ($\Delta v - \Delta c$), and a portion due to the creation of competition barriers ($\Delta p - \Delta v$). There are two cases to consider. Suppose, first, that the competition barriers are all incidental to the development of the news-sharing network. For example, if the network employs the lion's share of available talent in the industry, the creation of the network will unavoidably impair the efficiency of potential rivals, at least in the short run. However, the impairment that results from natural monopoly features of the market should not be considered a violation of the equally-efficient competitor test. Second, suppose the competition barriers are in part the result of a second category of acts, unrelated to the efficiency of the network, that directly obstruct competition from rivals. Under the equally-efficient-competitor test, this second category of acts could violate the law. The acts in the second category, that directly create competition barriers and have no relation to the efficiency-enhancing conduct, could exclude an equally efficient competitor. If the acts in the second category are sufficiently powerful in effect that they could exclude an equally efficient rival, then the equally-efficient-competitor test does not suggest that the defendant should be immunized from a finding of liability.[77] This example suggests that the equally-efficient-competitor test, though equivalent to other specific intent tests, makes it easier for a court to analyze cases in which the defendant's conduct involves a combination of efficient and entry-blocking actions.

V Assessment of monopolization standards in light of error

There has been little effort in the literature to define a standard by which errors should be determined in antitrust. In the criminal law, a false conviction can be determined largely by reference to the law. If someone is convicted for murder even though his conduct does not satisfy the statutory elements of the crime, then the judgment is most likely erroneous. In antitrust, at least in the US, the prohibition against unlawful monopolization cannot easily be captured in simple statutory provisions. The underlying prohibition is determined, more or less, by the objective of the statute.

Although most commentators would say 'consumer welfare' is the objective of the statute, that approach is probably too narrow.[78] If the statute aims to enhance consumer welfare alone, then an act that in the short run enhances efficiency by $100 and harms consumers by $1 has to be condemned. However, in the long run, such a large efficiency gain will probably benefit consumers, as entry and competition force firms to share the efficiency gains with consumers. By taking efficiency defenses into account in mergers, antitrust law has already conceded that efficiency deserves to be counted as one of the objectives of the statute.

In an ideal world in which courts made no mistakes, the optimal test would be the welfare balancing test. The reason is that the welfare balancing test comes closest to a test for maximizing social welfare (equivalently, total wealth). Any desired allocation of welfare among economic agents could be arranged through transfers among them (e.g., between firm owners and consumers). Moreover, if the social welfare function requires putting more weight on the avoidance of harm to consumers, the general welfare balancing test could be designed to replicate the concerns reflected in the social welfare function by choosing the appropriate weights to put on efficiency gains and net consumer harm.

Given that society should prefer the test that maximizes welfare, we can define mistakes in terms of the general welfare norm. If a test condemns conduct that enhances social welfare, we can call such judgments 'false convictions'. Similarly, if a test approves, or declares as lawful, conduct that reduces social welfare, we can call such judgments 'false acquittals'.

A Types of errors and biases

The types of errors generated by the monopolization tests are easy to assess in this framework. Consider first the consumer harm test. The consumer harm test puts no weight at all on productive efficiency gains.

The consumer harm test is biased in the direction of committing false convictions, because it condemns monopolizing acts even when those acts enhance social welfare because of their contribution to productive efficiency. This type of error is costly because it discourages incentives to invest in efficiency. Another reason that there is a tendency toward false convictions in the consumer harm test is that it treats much of the price increase as a reduction in welfare rather than a transfer.

As an illustration, suppose the dominant firm enters into an exclusivity contract that has the effect of raising competition barriers. As a result, price increases by $30. Because of the promotional advantages of the exclusivity deal, product value (through enhanced consumer education) increases by $5. The exclusivity deal also results in more efficient distribution, reducing cost by $40. Under the consumer harm test, the exclusivity arrangement should be condemned, because the $5 value increase is insufficient to offset the $30 price increase. However, social welfare is enhanced. The supply-side efficiency gain, $40, is larger than the net harm to consumers, $25. Discouraging such conduct reduces society's welfare. The consumer harm test generates a false conviction in this case.[79]

Next, consider the specific intent test. This test puts no weight on the consumer harm portion. It is biased toward false acquittals because it will excuse some acts of monopolization even when society loses more in the short run from the monopolizing act than from the overall efficiency gains (cost reductions and product performance improvements).

To illustrate, return to the incompatible design change example (due to Salop). The firm's conduct leads to an increase in value of $5, and an increase in unit cost of $3. It also leads to an increase in price of $50, due to new competition barriers. Since the overall efficiency gain is positive ($\$5 - \$3 > 0$), the specific intent test approves the conduct. However, consumers are harmed (consumer welfare changes by $-\$45$). And under the general welfare test, the design change is harmful to social welfare because there is no efficiency gain to offset the reduction in consumer welfare ($\$50 - \$5 > -\$3$). Thus, application of the specific intent test results in a false acquittal in this case.

I have already noted that the general welfare balancing test appears to be the least biased of the three tests, in the sense that it does not totally ignore some substantial component of welfare analysis. In spite of this, it shares the same tendency of the consumer harm test to overstate the social harm of monopoly pricing. However, totally ignoring a component of welfare analysis is probably a more serious error than over- or under-weighting that component.

For this reason, it is plausible to assume that the general welfare test would be the best if the costs of false convictions and false acquittals were symmetrical. However, the costs of false convictions and false acquittals are unlikely to be symmetrical.

B False acquittal versus false conviction costs

That the general welfare balancing test is not clearly biased toward false convictions or false acquittals is not a sufficient reason for preferring it, because one needs to also consider the aggregate (or expected) costs of both types of error. Suppose false acquittals and false convictions both occur at a rate of 5 per cent under the general welfare balancing test. If false convictions are substantially more costly than false convictions, it may be socially preferable to have a test that is biased toward false acquittals.

There are four reasons offered in the literature to believe that false convictions tend to be more costly than false acquittals. The first is the existence of market constraints that limit the social costs of efforts to create barriers to competition. Another is the Williamson tradeoff model. The third is the problem of rent seeking. The fourth, more of an empirical observation than a theoretical account of the ratio of error costs, focuses on baseline probabilities and the ex post distribution of errors.

1 Market constraints and error costs Easterbrook argued that market constraints limit the extent to which a firm will be able to exploit anti-competitive barriers.[80] A firm that takes an action that raises barriers to competition will obviously attempt to exploit those barriers by increasing its price. But the profits that would result from the firm's action would also attract new entrants and encourage existing competitors to steal business from the dominant firm. In addition, consumers would seek substitutes. In the long run, firms would enter to compete until economic profits are driven to zero.

The costs of false acquittals will be kept in check by entry of new rivals, competition from existing rivals, and the substitution efforts of downstream purchasers. False conviction costs, however, are not policed by the same market forces. Easterbrook's argument implies that the costs of false convictions are greater than false acquittals in the long run.

As an illustration, consider again the example of a dominant firm that changes the design of its product in a manner that enhances competition barriers because of incompatibility. Recall that the consumer valuation increases by \$5, cost increases by \$3, and price increases by \$50. Of the overall unit profit enhancement of \$47, \$45 can be attributed to the new competition barriers (i.e., $\Delta p - \Delta v = \$45$) and \$2 can be attributed to efficiency (i.e., $\Delta v - \Delta c = \$2$). With such a large share of revenue due to temporary competition barriers created by product design, the market will provide a strong inducement to existing competitors and new entrants to compete for a share of the profits. Suppose, for example, competitors will suffer a cost increase of $6 in order to redesign to become competitive with the dominant firm. As long as the unit profit, to the dominant firm, attributable to competition barriers is greater than $1, competitors will find redesign for entry purposes profitable. Entry will continue until the dominant firm's price (market price) falls by $44, at which point its unit profits are attributable entirely to its efficiency advantage over rivals.

2 *Welfare tradeoff considerations* Return to the welfare tradeoff model of Williamson,[81] though applying it in reverse order. Under the welfare tradeoff model, relatively modest price increases due to the erection of competition barriers are likely to be offset by efficiency gains. This is plausible in a scenario in which the dominant firm faces a risk of especially vigorous competition if it raises its price above a certain level, perhaps determined by the cost of transportation for foreign competitors. In such a scenario, the dominant firm will be able to exploit competition barriers, but only up to a point. If the same conduct that generates competition barriers also generates efficiency gains, the outcome is likely to be one in which the efficiency gains swamp the net consumer harm.

Now reverse the argument: Williamson's model suggests that the costs of discouraging investments in efficiency are likely to be larger than the social costs of monopoly pricing. This suggests that false acquittal costs (exploitation of constrained market power) are generally smaller than false conviction costs (discouraged investment).

Return to the case of the exclusivity contract that enables the dominant firm to erect a barrier to competition. Suppose the contract enables the firm to increase its price by 5 per cent. If the elasticity of demand is 2, the firm's output falls by (at most) 10 per cent. That leaves 90 per cent of the sales base still intact. It is over this 90 per cent sales base that the efficiency cost of discouraged investment should be assessed. On the other hand, it is only over the 10 per cent output reduction that the cost of monopolization should be assessed. A modest (less than 5 per cent) per-unit efficiency cost, spread over 90 per cent of the original sales base, will be greater than the 5 per cent price increase spread over 10 per cent of the sales base.

3 *Rent seeking* Recall that Tullock stressed the importance of directly unproductive, rent seeking investments in the evaluation of the social costs of monopoly.[82] Such investments could provide a defense for the overweighting of the consumer harm component in the general welfare test.

Directly unproductive investments should also be taken into account in comparing false acquittal and false conviction costs in monopolization law. False convictions send the signal that monopolization law can be used as a tool in competition. Firms may interpret the law as providing a strategic weapon against competitors that cut prices or make investments in efficiency. And once it becomes clear that the law can be used as a weapon in competition, the same competitive pressures that drive firms to cut prices will also drive them to file monopolization lawsuits against aggressive competitors.

How much will firms invest into directly unproductive litigation? If the dominant firm's efficiency gain resulting from its action can be taken as a measure of the long run threat to the profits of rival firms, those rivals will have a stronger incentive to invest in litigation as the efficiency gain increases. In other words, investment into monopolization lawsuits will vary with the efficiency of the defendant's conduct rather than the consumer harm. This implies both larger investments into litigation than warranted and poorly targeted litigation. Such unproductive investments put upward pressure on the false conviction costs of monopolization law.

4 Baseline probabilities and ex post error rates The foregoing arguments focus on costs and ignore the issue of error rates. Examining error rates is a bit more complicated because it introduces empirical questions that have not been resolved. Still, if one takes error rates into account, there is a powerful case that error rates will tend toward false convictions, even under the welfare balancing test.[83]

First, one must distinguish between ex ante and ex post error rates. Ex ante, a monopolization standard, such as the welfare balancing test, may have a predictable rate of error. If courts are equally likely to make mistakes in acquitting or convicting, false acquittals and false convictions will be equally probable ex ante. However, the ex post rate of error depends on the underlying base rates of anticompetitive and procompetitive conduct challenged by the test.

Much of the conduct that is the subject of monopolization lawsuits consists of standard competitive practices – price cutting, exclusive dealing, product tying. In other words, much of the conduct targeted in litigation is observed in competitive markets. If the conduct is generally procompetitive, which is plausible in the case of conduct that is frequently observed in competitive markets, then even a modest error rate would imply a large share of false convictions within the pool of guilty verdicts. This suggests that even a slight differential putting the false conviction cost greater than the false acquittal cost translates into large aggregate difference between the two types of cost.

Suppose ex ante error rates (false convictions and false acquittals) under the general welfare balancing test are both equal to 5 per cent. Operating on a random assortment of 200 cases involving procompetitive and anti-competitive conduct, this would lead to five false convictions and five false acquittals. But if the balance of the sample is shifted so that there are 160 cases involving procompetitive conduct, then there will be eight false convictions and two false acquittals. With a total of 46 convictions, the ex post rate of false convictions will be 17 per cent. The ex post rate of false acquittals will be 1 per cent. Now let the cost of a false conviction be \$105 and the cost of false acquittal be \$100. The total cost of false convictions would be \$840 and the total cost of false acquittals \$200.

C Summing up and moving forward

These arguments suggest that the specific intent test is the best on error-cost grounds, the general welfare balancing test comes in second, and the consumer harm test third. This provides a justification for the pre-1945 legal standard on monopolization, and some of the recent decisions, such as *Brooke Group* and *Trinko*, effectively returning to that standard. However, it does not provide a justification for using the standard of *Alcoa* as a default standard for monopolization.

A broader message from this analysis is that monopolization standards should be shaped in view of the expected costs of errors. If courts adopted a general welfare balancing test as the default standard, as the *Alcoa* opinion appears to do, that test should be applied in a manner that is sensitive to error costs. Thus, as a general rule the default standard should be applied in a manner that minimizes the risk of false convictions. The lesson here, then, is not that *Alcoa* is impossible to justify in an error cost framework: it is that the issue at bottom is evidentiary burden. The *Alcoa* standard could be applied in a manner that is consistent with the implications of this analysis, as long as the burdens of proof are allocated in a way that puts greater weight on avoiding false convictions than false acquittals.

An even broader message is suggested. The optimal monopolization standard depends on the balance of error costs. Although the specific intent rule appears best as a default rule in this analysis, the most desirable rule in any setting will depend on the likelihood and cost of error. In some settings, the balance of error costs may indicate that either the welfare balancing test or the consumer harm test would be preferable to the specific intent standard.

For example, in the case of state-sponsored barriers to competition, much of the error cost analysis considered previously in this chapter would have to be modified. First, the incentive to invest in such barriers for anti-competitive purposes will be stronger than usual, given the more durable nature of state-supported competition barriers. Second, the market constraints that ordinarily put downward pressure on false acquittal costs would no longer be present. The reason is that state-erected barriers, backed by the state's coercive power, are more effective at barring competition than most privately-created barriers. This suggests that in a setting of state-sponsored protection from competition, the consumer harm test is probably preferable to the specific intent test.

Another example in which the standard error cost analysis might be reversed is in the case of some types of essential facilities. One of the key reasons that the Court in *Trinko* suggested support for the specific intent test was the concern that an alternative test would discourage capital investment. Firms that invest in essential facilities, such as telecommunications networks or electricity transmission grids, would have a diminished incentive to do so under a legal rule that required them to share the efficiency gains from those investments with rivals. However, suppose that instead of investing on the usual terms in a risky infrastructure, the dominant firm acquires the essential facility from the state in a rigged auction. In this case, a legal rule requiring the sharing of the facility's benefits would not necessarily discourage productive investment. If appropriately limited, the rule could discourage wealth transfers from the state, such as corrupt privatizations.

The characteristics of the type of essential facility case in which an access sharing rule has a greater than ordinary procompetitive potential are easy to describe. They would involve the state transferring, without a competitive auction, control over some market portal (or essential entry path) to a private firm or a group of firms. Another characteristic is the absence of a significant scope for efficiency enhancing investments on the part of the possessor of the facility. For example, in *American Federation of Tobacco Growers v. Neal*,[84] the state of Virginia handed the power to regulate warehouse sales of tobacco to the defendant trade association, and the association used that power to exclude a new entrant. *Tobacco Growers* is an example of the state handing control over entry to a private group.

In a setting like *Tobacco Growers*, the likelihood of false acquittal costs being checked by competition is a lot lower than in the case of a free-entry market. Moreover, the prospect of gaining the power to block entry will encourage efforts by private parties to seek control over market portals. The error cost balance in this setting is not clearly in favor of a specific intent test, and may be closer to favoring the consumer harm test.

Although I have argued that the specific intent test appears best as a default rule on error cost grounds, the error cost approach to monopolization standards suggests a great deal of flexibility. One could argue that there is no need for default rules under the error cost approach; that the optimal monopolization test can be decided on a case-by-case basis by an assessment of error cost considerations specific to each case. Similarly, one could argue, as I have suggested, that a general balancing test could be adopted and evidentiary burdens could be used to strike the right balance in terms of error costs. Indeed, one could argue that each case should be decided on an empirical assessment of the relative costs of false acquittals and false convictions.

The flaw in this line of reasoning is that it ignores the need for clear rules in antitrust. Firms have to make investment decisions on the basis of the monopolization test in force. If there is a risk that they will be required under antitrust law to share the efficiency gains from those investments, they will be discouraged from investing. Using the error cost framework as a general set of norms that each court would apply in fashioning a particular result fails to provide firms with clear signals from the law.

Because the law affects investment decisions, there is a need for clear default rules in antitrust. The error cost framework should be used to identify broad categories in which various monopolization tests would be applied. The specific intent test has reemerged in specific pockets of American antitrust law, and the argument of this chapter is that it is an especially appealing default rule for monopolization cases. However, the error cost framework does not rule out alternative tests for specific pockets of monopolization law.

VI Conclusion

Lack of clarity has been a long running problem in monopolization law.[85] Part of the problem is a failure to develop a theory of monopolization tests that is capable of application to the case law. I have tried to improve matters a little on that score in this chapter.

The default rule tests for monopolization can be stated with clarity: consumer harm, general welfare balancing, and specific intent. Over time, the law will probably contain all three of these tests, though allocated to the types of monopolization cases for which they are optimal in light of error costs.

Notes

* Honorable Paul J. Liacos Professor of Law, Boston University, knhylton@bu.edu.

1. Of the roughly 200 nations in the world, slightly over 100 have competition laws. Hylton, K.N. & F. Deng, *Antitrust Around the World: An Empirical Analysis of the Scope of Competition Laws and Their Effects*, 74 Antitrust L. J. 271, 272 (2007). The vast majority of the competition statutes have provisions governing monopolization. For a survey of competition laws around the world, see Hylton, K.N. et al., *Antitrust World Reports*, http://antitrustworldwiki.com.
2. For an overview and discussion of statute and case law on monopolization, see Areeda, P. et al., Antitrust Analysis: Problems, Text, Cases 368–442 (New York; Aspen lishers 2004).

3. For an overview, see FAULL, J. & A. NIKPAY (EDS), FAULL & NIKPAY: THE EC LAW OF COMPETITION (New York; Oxford University Press 1999).
4. These versions have been presented by several authors, and will be examined in the text below. For an economic analysis of several specific versions, see Salop, S.C., *Exclusionary Conduct, Effect on Consumers, and the Flawed Profit-Sacrifice Standard,* 73 ANTITRUST L.J. 311, 311–74 (2006). For an analysis that focuses on the law, see Lao, M., Defining Exclusionary Conduct Under Section 2: The Case for Non-Universal Standards, Fordham International Antitrust Law & Policy, 433–68 (Barry Hawk ed., 2006).
5. This history of the law borrows heavily from remarks I delivered at a conference on antitrust, see Hylton, K.N., *Section 2 and Article 82: A Comparison of American and European Approaches to Monopolization Law*, Boston University School of Law Working Paper No. 06–11, http://ssrn.com/abstract=902655.
6. LETWIN, W., LAW AND ECONOMIC POLICY IN AMERICA: THE EVOLUTION OF THE SHERMAN ANTITRUST ACT 19 (Chicago; The University of Chicago 1965).
7. *Darcy v. Allen*, 77 Eng. Rep. 1260 (KB 1603).
8. HYLTON, K.N., ANTITRUST LAW: ECONOMIC THEORY AND COMMON LAW EVOLUTION 31–3 (New York; Cambridge University Press 2003).
9. For example, admiralty law prevented hard bargains in the course of rescuing distressed ships at sea. *See, e.g.*, EPSTEIN, R.A., CASES AND MATERIALS ON TORTS 55 (New York: Aspen 8th ed. 2004). This was an effort by the law to prohibit an especially brutal form of monopoly exploitation.
10. *See, e.g.*, Hylton, *supra* n. 8, at 186–8 (discussing early Section 2 case law).
11. *Standard Oil Co. v. United States*, 221 US 1 (1911).
12. AREEDA, P., ANTITRUST ANALYSIS: PROBLEMS, TEXT, AND CASES 148 (3rd ed., Boston; Little Brown 1981).
13. *E.g.*, Hylton, *supra* n. 8, at 187.
14. *Id.* This is also clear from perusing the early opinions. *See, e.g.*, Areeda et al., *supra* n. 2, 369–72 (providing excerpts from *Standard Oil*, 221 US at 58, 61, 67, 75, and *United States v. American Tobacco Co.*, 221 US 106, 181–3 (1911), stating that the defendant was found guilty of violating Section 2 because its conduct indicated an intent to monopolize by excluding or destroying rivals).
15. *See, e.g.*, Areeda et al., *supra* n. 2, at 369–72 (excerpts from *Standard Oil*, 221 US at 61, 62, 75 and *American Tobacco*, 221 US at 181–3).
16. *See e.g.*, *Standard Oil*, 221 US at 62 ('[T]he statute . . . *by the omission of any direct prohibition against monopoly* in the concrete . . . indicates a consciousness that the freedom of the individual right to contract. . .was the most efficient means for the prevention of monopoly') (emphasis added).
17. *United States v. US Steel Corp.*, 251 US 417 (1920).
18. *United States v. Alum. Co. of America*, 148 F.2d 416 (2d Cir. 1945) (hereinafter *Alcoa*).
19. *See, e.g.*, Salop, S.C. & R. C. Romaine, *Preserving Monopoly: Economic Analysis, Legal Standards and Microsoft*, 7 GEO. MASON L. REV. 617, 617–72 (1998) (interpreting *Alcoa* as a 'no fault' or strict liability standard), versus Cass, R.A. & K.N. Hylton, *Preserving Competition: Economic Analysis, Legal Standards, and Microsoft*, 8 GEO. MASON L. REV. 1, 1–40 (1999) (interpreting *Alcoa* as a balancing test).
20. *Alcoa*, 148 F.2d at 432 ('no monopolist monopolizes unconscious of what he is doing').
21. *See, e.g., F. Hoffman-La Roche Ltd. v. Empagram S.A.*, 542 US 155, 165 (2004); *Eastman Kodak Co. v. Image Tech. Svces.*, 504 US 451, 483 (1992); *Aspen Skiing Co. v. Aspen Highland Skiing Corp.*, 472 US 585 (1985); *United States v. Microsoft Corp.*, 253 F.3d 34, 44 (D.C. Cir. 2001), *cert. denied*, 534 US 952 (2001).
22. Areeda, P. & D. Turner, *Predatory Pricing and Related Practices under Section 2 of the Sherman Act*, 88 HARV. L. REV. 697, 697–733 (1975).
23. *Matsushita Elec. Indus. Co. v. Zenith Radio Corp.*, 475 US 574 (1986).
24. *Brooke Group, Ltd. v. Brown & Williamson Tobacco Corp.*, 509 US 209, 226 (1993)

(evidence of below-cost pricing is not alone sufficient to permit an inference of probable recoupment and injury to competition).

25. *Id.*, at 240–42; *Matsushita*, 475 US at 595–8.
26. Salop & Romaine, *supra* n. 19, at 17, 24, 35; Cass & Hylton, *supra* n. 19, at 639, 671.
27. *See generally* Areeda, P.E., *Essential Facilities: An Epithet in Need of Limiting Principles*, 58 ANTITRUST L.J. 841, 841–54 (1990); Cotter, T.F., *Intellectual Property and the Essential Facilities Doctrine*, 44 ANTITRUST BULL. 211, 211–50 (1999); Hylton, K.N., *Economic Rents and Essential Facilities*, 1991 BYU. L. REV. 1243, 1243–84 (1991); Lipsky, A.B., Jr. & J.G. Sidak, *Essential Facilities*, 51 STAN. L. REV. 1187, 1187–248 (1999); Robinson, G.O., *On Refusing to Deal with Rivals*, 87 CORNELL L. REV. 1177, 1177–1232 (2002).
28. *Aspen Skiing Co. v. Aspen Highlands Skiing Corp.*, 472 US 585 (1985).
29. *Verizon Communications Inc. v. Law Offices of V. Trinko, LLP.*, 540 US 398 (2004).
30. *Trinko*, 540 US at 409.
31. *Id.*, at 408–9.
32. The link between the specific intent standard and essential facility cases is also suggested by Judge Ginsburg's opinion in *Covad Communications Co. v. Bell Atlantic Corp.*, 398 F.3d 666 (D.C. Cir. 2005). Judge Ginsburg applies the predation doctrine of *Brooke Group* to *Bell Atlantic's* refusal to deal, suggesting that the two types of claim (predation and essential facilities) should be treated under the same legal test, see *Covad Communications*, 398 F.3d at 675–6.
33. The profit-sacrifice test is suggested by the language of *Aspen*, 472 US at 608–10, and *Trinko*, 540 US at 409. For arguments in favor of the profit sacrifice test see Melamed, A.D., *Exclusionary Conduct Under the Antitrust Laws: Balancing, Sacrifice, and Refusals to Deal*, 20 BERKELEY TECH. L.J. 1247, 1247–68 (2005).
34. Vickers, J., *Abuse of Market Power*, 115 ECONOMIC JOURNAL F244, F253 (June 2005).
35. *Microsoft*, 253 F.3d at 34.
36. *Id.*, at 58.
37. *Id.*, at 72, 74, 76, 77. The opinion is confusing because the D.C. Circuit's application of the specific intent test was arguably equivalent to a balancing test conducted with a pro-plaintiff bias. In examining the complaints concerning Microsoft's integration of Internet Explorer with its Windows operating system, the court found that two of the three complaints (excluding Internet Explorer from the Add/Remove Programs function and commingling browser and operating system code) were violations of the Sherman Act, because Microsoft offered no credible procompetitive justification, while one (overriding the choice of an alternative default browser in certain circumstances) was not a violation because Microsoft's justification was sufficient. *Id.*, at 66–7. Yet it seems that the technical justifications offered by Microsoft, and accepted by the court, in response to the complaint that was rejected should apply just as well to the other two complaints.
38. The ambiguity of Hand's standard, from the perspective of a judge who had to apply it, was at least suggested by Judge Wyzanski's discussion in *United Shoe* of different approaches to the monopolization standard. Wyzanski described three approaches to the monopolization test and argued that United Shoe's conduct could be held unlawful under any one of the tests. *U.S. v. United Shoe Machinery Corp.*, 110 F.Supp. 295, 341–3 (D. Mass. 1953).
39. Kahn, A.E., *Standards for Antitrust Policy*, 67 HARV. L. REV. 28, 28–54 (1953).
40. *Id.*, at 30–1.
41. *Id.*, at 31.
42. Kahn, *supra* n. 39, at 51–2.
43. Cass, R.A. & K.N. Hylton, *Antitrust Intent*, 74 S. CAL. L. REV. 657, 657–746 (2001).
44. Easterbrook, F.H., *The Limits of Antitrust*, 63 TEX. L. REV. 1, 1–40 (1984).
45. Tullock, G., *The Welfare Costs of Tariffs, Monopolies, and Theft*, 5 W. ECON. J. 224, 224–32 (1967).
46. POSNER, R.A., ANTITRUST LAW: AN ECONOMIC PERSPECTIVE 194–5, (2nd ed., Chicago; University of Chicago Press 2001).

47. For example, some commentators have argued that the equally-efficient-competitor standard is flawed because it immunizes the defendant when he excludes a less efficient rival, *see, e.g.*, Salop, *supra* n. 4, at 328–9. But this is not clear. If the defendant's conduct would exclude an equally efficient rival, then the equally-efficient-competitor standard probably would not immunize his conduct, even if the complainant is a less efficient competitor.
48. Elhauge, E., *Defining Better Monopolization Standards*, 56 STAN. L. REV. 253, 253–344 (2003). By impairing rival efficiency, Elhauge means taking actions that raise the short run costs of rivals. On impairing efficiency in this sense, see Salop, S. & D. Scheffman, *Raising Rivals' Costs*, 73 AM. ECON .REV. 267, 267–71 (1983); Krattenmaker, T. & S.C. Salop, *Anticompetitive Exclusion: Raising Rivals' Costs to Achieve Power over Price*, 96 YALE L. J. 209, 209–94 (1986).
49. Elhauge argues against using an open-ended balancing approach because it would create 'massive business uncertainty'. *Supra* n. 48, at 315. He also argues that an open-ended balancing inquiry 'would often be inaccurate, hard to predict years in advance when the business decisions must be made, and too costly to litigate'. *Id.*, at 317.
50. Melamed, *supra* n. 33.
51. Vickers, *supra* n. 34.
52. Salop, *supra* n. 4, at 314–19.
53. Werden, G.J., *Identifying Exclusionary Conduct Under Section 2: The 'No Economic Sense' Test*, 73 ANTITRUST L. J. 413, 413–34 (2006).
54. Salop, *supra* n. 4, at 318–26.
55. *Id.*
56. Mason, E.S., *The Current Status of the Monopoly Problem in the United States*, 62 HARV. L. REV. 1265, 1265–85 (1949).
57. Griffin, C.E., *An Economic Approach to Antitrust Problems (*New York; American Enterprise Association 1951).
58. Oppenheim, S.C., *Federal Antitrust Legislation: Guideposts to a Revised National Antitrust Policy*, 50 MICH. L. REV. 1139, 1139–244 (1952).
59. Mason, *supra* n. 56, at 1280.
60. Clark, J.M., *Toward a Concept of Workable Competition*, 30(2) AM. ECON. REV. 241, 241-56 (1940).
61. Stigler, G.J., *The Extent and Bases of Monopoly*, 32 (2) AM. ECON. REV. 1 (Supplement), 1–22 (1942).
62. Mason, *supra* n. 56, at 1281–2.
63. Salop, S.C. & C. Romaine, *Preserving Monopoly: Economic Analysis, Legal Standards, and Microsoft*, 7 GEO. MASON L. REV. 617, 617–72 (1999).
64. Salop, *supra* n. 4.
65. Williamson, O.E., *Economies as an Antitrust Defense: The Welfare Tradeoffs*, 58 AM. ECON. REV. 18, 18–36 (1968).
66. See Appendix.
67. Williamson, *supra* n. 65. See the Appendix for a detailed presentation of the tradeoff analysis. The Appendix shows that in the presence of value and cost efficiency gains, Williamson's argument for taking efficiencies into account in antitrust analysis becomes stronger.
68. This is not a precise formulation. The left hand term overstates the forgone consumer welfare. See Figure 5.A1 in the Appendix.
69. The overweighting point might be made clearer by rewriting the welfare evaluation as $\Delta p\beta$ $(\Delta v - \Delta c)$, where $\beta = (Q_0 - Q_1)/Q_1$. In the case of linear demand and cost schedules, and the firm's barriers permit it to move from perfect competition to absolute monopoly, $\beta = 1$. But this extreme will not be observed in general.
70. Tullock, *supra* n. 45; see also Posner, R.A., *The Social Cost of Monopoly and Regulation*, 83(4) J. POL. ECON. 807, 807–28 (1975).
71. *See* Mason, *supra* n. 56, at 1283. Williamson notes that weights could reflect concerns over income distribution, or the asymmetric effects of price increases and productive

efficiency gains. For example, while productive efficiency gains are product specific, price increases might weaken competition across markets that include substitute goods. Williamson, *supra* n. 65, at 27–8.

72. On learning curve effects and monopolization, see Spence, A.M., *The Learning Curve and Competition*, 12(1) Bell J. Econ. 49, 49–70 (1981).
73. Werden suggests that efficient (e.g., cost-reducing) conduct should serve as a 'safe harbor' for monopolization defendants, see Werden, *supra* n. 53, at 418.
74. In this narrow sense, the framework provided here agrees with Andrew Gavil's criticism of the no-economic-sense test on the ground that it might immunize conduct that produces any efficiency gain, see Gavil, A.I., *Exclusionary Distribution Strategies by Dominant Firms: Striking a Better Balance*, 72 Antitrust L. J. 3, 53 (2005). The test should require an examination of overall efficiency. In addition, there is the question of proof. For the test to have some ability to reject weak defenses, it should require credible evidence of efficiency gains rather than mere speculation, see Cass & Hylton, *supra* n. 43, at 677.
75. Salop, *supra* n. 4, at 345–6.
76. *Associated Press v. United States*, 326 US 1 (1945).
77. This raises a causation issue that has not been adequately analysed in court opinions. When the equally-efficient-competitor standard is applied to a mixture of conduct, it would appear to be necessary to find that the anticompetitive conduct, rather than the efficient conduct, caused the exclusionary injuries to rival firms. The causation issue was considered in *United States v. Microsoft*, 253 US F.3d 34 (D.C. Cir. 2001), but the causation requirement was set so low that virtually any allegedly anticompetitive act could meet it. If courts continue to apply such a light causation requirement, it would be preferable to let efficiency serve as a safe harbor, as suggested by Werden, *supra* n. 53, at 418.
78. Williamson, *supra* n. 65; Bork, R.H., The Antitrust Paradox: A Policy at War with Itself, 107–15 (New York; Basic Books, Inc. 1978).
79. As suggested earlier, the result could be made to depend on the welfare weights assigned to consumer welfare and supply-side efficiency. The analysis in the text assumes equal weights. If the weight on supply-side efficiency is zero, then the consumer harm test generates no errors. Suppose, instead, the weight on efficiency is 40%. Then under the welfare test one would have to compare 60% of the net consumer harm, which is $15, to 40% of the supply-side efficiency gain, which is $16. Thus, even if we give supply-side efficiency a weight of only 40%, the consumer harm test still generates a false conviction. For the consumer harm test to avoid generating a false conviction in this example, the welfare weight on supply-side efficiency must be less than 38.5%.
80. Easterbrook, *supra* n. 44.
81. Williamson, *supra* n. 65.
82. Tullock, *supra* n. 45.
83. Hylton, K.N. & M.A. Salinger, *Tying Law and Policy: A Decision-Theoretic Approach*, 69 Antitrust L. J. 469, 469–526 (2001); Evans, D.S. & A.J. Padilla, *Designing Antitrust Rules for Assessing Unilateral Practices: A Neo-Chicago Approach*, 72 U. Chi. L. Rev. 73, 73–98 (2005); Cooper, J.C., L.M. Froeb, D. O'Brien, and M. Vita, *Vertical Antitrust Policy as a Problem of Inference*, 23 Intn'l. J. Indus. Org. 639, 639–64 (2005).
84. *American Fed'n of Tobacco Growers, Inc. v. Neal*, 183 F.2d 869 (1950).
85. Kahn, *supra* n. 39, at 40–41; Elhauge, *supra* n. 48, at 253.

References

Areeda, P. (1981), *Antitrust Analysis: Problems, Text, and Cases* (3d edn), Boston; Little, Brown.

Areeda, P. (1990), 'Essential Facilities: An Epithet in Need of Limiting Principles', *Antitrust L.J.*, 58, 841–54.

Areeda, P. & D. Turner (1975), 'Predatory Pricing and Related Practices under Section 2 of the Sherman Act', *Harv. L. Rev.* 88, 697–733.

Areeda, P. et al. (2004), *Antitrust Analysis: Problems, Text, Cases* (6th edn), New York; Aspen Publishers.

Bork, R.H. (1978), *The Antitrust Paradox: A Policy at War with Itself*, New York; Basic Books, Inc.

Cass, R.A. & K.N. Hylton (1999), 'Preserving Competition: Economic Analysis, Legal Standards, and Microsoft', *Geo. Mason L. Rev.*, 8, 1–40.

Cass, R.A. & K.N. Hylton (2001), 'Antitrust Intent', *S. Cal. L. Rev.*, 74, 657–746.

Clark, J.M. (1940, June), 'Toward a Concept of Workable Competition', *Am. Econ. Rev.*, 30 (2), 241–56.

Cooper, J.C., L.M. Froeb, D. O'Brien, and M. Vita (2005), 'Vertical Antitrust Policy as a Problem of Inference', *Intn'l. J. Indus. Org.*, 23 (7–8), 639–64.

Cotter, T.F. (1999), 'Intellectual Property and the Essential Facilities Doctrine', *Antitrust Bull.*, 44, 211–50.

Easterbrook, F.H. (1984), The Limits of Antitrust, *Tex. L. Rev.*, 63, 1–40.

Elhauge, E. (2003), 'Defining Better Monopolization Standards', *Stan. L. Rev.*, 56, 253–344.

Epstein, R.A. (2004), *Cases and Materials on Torts* (8th edn), New York: Aspen.

Evans, D.S. & A.J. Padilla (2005), 'Designing Antitrust Rules for Assessing Unilateral Practices: A Neo-Chicago Approach', *U. Chi. L. Rev.*, 72, 73–98.

Faull, J. & A. Nikpay (eds) (1999), *Faull & Nikpay: The EC Law of Competition*, New York; Oxford University Press.

Gavil, A.I. (2005), 'Exclusionary Distribution Strategies by Dominant Firms: Striking a Better Balance', *Antitrust L. J.*, 72, 3–83, 53.

Griffin, C.E. (1951), *An Economic Approach to Antitrust Problems*, New York; American Enterprise Association.

Hylton, K.N. (1991), 'Economic Rents and Essential Facilities', *BYU. L. Rev.*, 1991 (3), 1243–1284.

Hylton, K.N. (2003), *Antitrust Law: Economic Theory and Common Law Evolution*, New York; Cambridge University Press.

Hylton, K.N. (2005), 'Section 2 and Article 82: A Comparison of American and European Approaches to Monopolization Law', Boston University School of Law Working Paper No. 06-11, http://ssrn.com/abstract=902655.

Hylton, K.N. & M.A. Salinger (2001), 'Tying Law and Policy: A Decision-Theoretic Approach', *Antitrust L. J.*, 69, 469–526.

Hylton, K.N. & F. Deng (2007), 'Antitrust Around the World: An Empirical Analysis of the Scope of Competition Laws and Their Effects', *Antitrust L. J.*, 74, 271–341.

Hylton, K.N. et al. (2007), 'Antitrust World Reports', http://antitrustworldwiki.com.

Kahn, A.E. (1953), 'Standards for Antitrust Policy', *Harv. L. Rev.*, 67, 28–54.

Krattenmaker, T. & S.C. Salop (1986), 'Anticompetitive Exclusion: Raising Rivals' Costs to Achieve Power over Price', *Yale L. J.*, 96 (2), 209–94.

Lao, M. (2006), 'Defining Exclusionary Conduct under Section 2: The Case for Non-Universal Standards', *Fordham International Antitrust Law & Policy*, 433–68 (Barry Hawk ed.).

Letwin, W. (1965), *Law and Economic Policy in America: The Evolution of the Sherman Antitrust Act*, Chicago; The University of Chicago, 19.

Lipsky, A.B., Jr. & J.G. Sidak (1999), 'Essential Facilities', *Stan. L. Rev.*, 51, 1187–248.

Mason, E.S. (1949), 'The Current Status of the Monopoly Problem in the United States', *Harv. L. Rev.*, 62, 1265–85.

Melamed, A.D. (2005), 'Exclusionary Conduct Under the Antitrust Laws: Balancing, Sacrifice, and Refusals to Deal', *Berkeley Tech. L.J.*, 20, 1247–68.

Oppenheim, S.C. (1952), 'Federal Antitrust Legislation: Guideposts to a Revised National Antitrust Policy', *Mich. L. Rev.*, 50, 1139–244.

Posner, R.A. (1975, August), 'The Social Cost of Monopoly and Regulation', *J. Pol. Econ.*, 83 (4), 807–28.

Posner, R.A. (2001), *Antitrust Law: An Economic Perspective* (2nd edn), Chicago; University of Chicago Press.

Robinson, G.O. (2002), 'On Refusing to Deal with Rivals', *Cornell L. Rev.*, 87, 1177–232.
Salop, S.C. (2006), 'Exclusionary Conduct, Effect on Consumers, and the Flawed Profit-Sacrifice Standard', *Antitrust L.J.*, 73 (2), 311–74.
Salop, S.C. & R.C. Romaine (1999), 'Preserving Monopoly: Economic Analysis, Legal Standards and Microsoft', *Geo. Mason L. Rev.*, 7, 617–72
Salop, S.C. & D. Scheffman (1983, May), 'Raising Rivals' Costs', *Am. Econ. Rev.*, 73 (2), 267–71.
Spence, A.M. (1981, Spring), 'The Learning Curve and Competition', *Bell J. Econ.*, 12 (1), 49–70.
Stigler, G.J. (1942, June), 'The Extent and Bases of Monopoly', *Am. Econ. Rev.*, 32 (2) (Supplement), 1–22.
Tullock, G. (1967), 'The Welfare Costs of Tariffs, Monopolies, and Theft', *W. Econ. J.*, 5, 224–32.
Vickers, J. (2005, June), 'Abuse of Market Power', *The Economic Journal*, 115, F244–F262.
Werden, G.J. (2006), 'Identifying Exclusionary Conduct Under Section 2: The "No Economic Sense" Test', *Antitrust L. J.*, 73, 413–34.
Williamson, O.E. (1968), 'Economies as an Antitrust Defense: The Welfare Tradeoffs', *Am. Econ. Rev.*, 58, 18–36.

Cases

American Fed'n of Tobacco Growers, Inc. v. Neal, 183 F.2d 869 (1950).
Aspen Skiing Co. v. Aspen Highland Skiing Corp., 472 US 585 (1985).
Associated Press v. United States, 326 US 1 (1945).
Brooke Group, Ltd. v. Brown & Williamson Tobacco Corp., 509 US 209, 226 (1993).
Covad Communications Co. v. Bell Atlantic Corp., 398 F.3d 666 (D.C. Cir. 2005).
Darcy v. Allen, 77 Eng. Rep. 1260 (KB 1603).
Eastman Kodak Co. v. Image Tech. Svces., 504 US 451, 483 (1992).
F. Hoffman-La Roche Ltd. v. Empagram S.A., 542 US 155, 165 (2004).
Matsushita Elec. Indus. Co. v. Zenith Radio Corp., 475 US 574 (1986).
Standard Oil Co. v. United States, 221 US 1 (1911).
United States v. Alum. Co. of America, 148 F.2d 416 (2d Cir. 1945).
United States v. American Tobacco Co., 221 US 106, 181-3 (1911).
United States v. Microsoft Corp., 253 F.3d 34, 44 (D.C. Cir. 2001), *cert. denied*, 534 US 952 (2001).
United States v. United Shoe Machinery Corp., 110 F.Supp. 295, 341-3 (D. Mass. 1953).
United States v. U.S. Steel Corp., 251 US 417 (1920).
Verizon Communications Inc. v. Law Offices of V. Trinko, LLP., 540 US 398 (2004).

Appendix: monopolization tests and welfare tradeoffs

ABCD = Productive efficiency gain
CEF = Deadweight loss (forgone consumer surplus)
IFGJ = Welfare gain from product enhancement
HGJ = Recaptured welfare gain from enhancement

Figure 5.A1 presents the welfare effects of conduct that enhances barriers to competition and simultaneously generates productive efficiency gains ($\Delta c < 0$) and product quality gains ($\Delta v > 0$). If the price increase is less than or equal to the valuation gain, there is no deadweight loss resulting from the dominant firm's conduct. In other words, no deadweight loss results unless $\Delta p > \Delta v$.

The consumer harm is equal to area DEHK, which is the sum of the original consumer surplus transferred to the monopolist and the forgone original consumer surplus.

The monopolist's conduct is socially desirable if the sum of the welfare gains from enhancement and productive efficiency exceed the deadweight

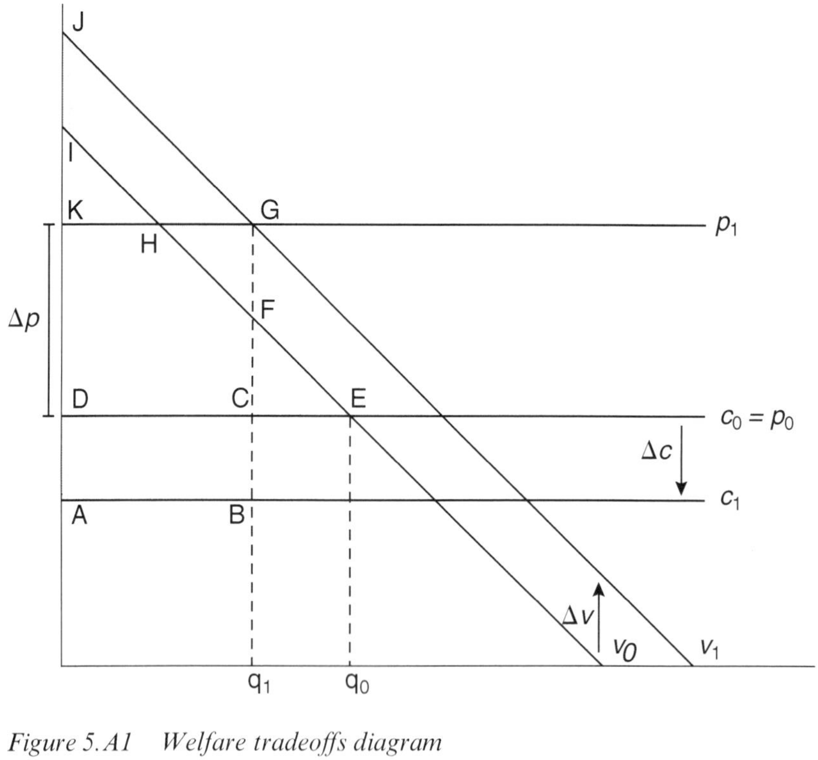

Figure 5.A1 Welfare tradeoffs diagram

loss. In terms of Figure 5.A1, the conduct is desirable if the sum of area ABCD and area IFGJ exceed area CEF. If ABCD + IFGJ > CEF, the firm's conduct is permissible under the consumer welfare test for monopolization. It should be clear that Williamson's argument that modest efficiency gains will often outweigh the harmful effects of price increases is stronger in this model.

The consumer harm due to competition barriers is represented by the area KDEH, which is the sum of the portion of the original consumer surplus transferred to the monopolist (KDCFH) and the deadweight loss portion (CEF). The gain to consumers from product enhancement is represented by IHGJ. Thus, consumers are harmed if KDEH − IHGJ > 0. Since the deadweight loss component is difficult to determine, we can refer to the 'measurable consumer harm' as the difference KDCFH − IHGJ. The consumer harm test proposed by Salop is equivalent to determining whether KDCG − IFGJ > 0. This is equivalent to the measurable consumer harm. However, it understates the real consumer harm by excluding the deadweight loss portion CEF.

The specific intent test declares the monopolist's act unlawful only if IFGJ + ABCD < 0. Obviously, this requires either a productive efficiency loss or degradation of product quality.

6 The law and economics of predatory pricing

Bruce H. Kobayashi[1]

I Introduction

Predatory pricing is a specific form of exclusionary pricing conduct in which the predatory firm sacrifices short term profits in order to achieve long term gains. The most general definition of predation would be 'any action taken by a firm with market power which causes a rival to exit and in doing so reduces social welfare' (Scheffman (1981)). Antitrust regulation of predatory pricing is limited, however, by the challenges of differentiating potentially anticompetitive predatory pricing from procompetitive price competition. As a result, antitrust rules aimed at regulating predatory pricing have paid special attention to the administrability of the rule, as well as the potential deterrent effect such rules may have on procompetitive price competition. Thus, despite recent articles showing that predation is both theoretically possible and may occur in the marketplace, the courts have adopted and generally maintained permissive rules to regulate predatory pricing under the antitrust laws.

This chapter focuses on and is organized around two primary issues relating to the economics of predatory pricing: the economic analysis of predatory pricing as a form of anticompetitive exclusion and the economics of optimal antitrust rules. Section II of this chapter reviews both the theoretical and empirical literature on predatory pricing then examines the economics of optimal antitrust rules. Section III sets out the optimal theory of antitrust rules, and examines definitions and tests of predatory pricing.

Section IV examines the antitrust regulation of predatory pricing, tracing the Supreme Court's consideration of the economic analysis of predatory pricing and its application of this knowledge in choosing to set out a bright line and administrable test in *Brooke Group.* It then examines some of the issues faced in administering such a rule, including the relevant measure of costs and the extension of the *Brooke Group* rule to issues such as multiproduct pricing, market share and other loyalty discounts and predatory buying. Section V concludes.

II The economics of predation

This section reviews the economic literature on predation. Part (a) reviews the pre-1980s theoretical and empirical literature on price predation that resulted in widespread skepticism regarding the rationality and frequency of predatory pricing. Reviewing the literature and evidence to date in his influential 1978 book, *The Antitrust Paradox*, Bork noted that while '[t]hese considerations do not demonstrate that price cutting could never under any circumstances be a successful method of predation', it was nonetheless 'unwise, therefore, to construct rules about a phenomenon that probably does not exist'. Easterbrook (1981a) concluded that, while predation was possible, 'there is no sufficient reason for antitrust law or the courts to take predation seriously' and that if there is 'any room in antitrust law for rules of *per se* legality, one should be created to encompass predatory conduct'. Moreover, this literature was cited by the US Supreme Court in its recent decisions on price predation. The Court, in addressing predatory pricing in *Matsushita*, cited the literature discussed in Part (a) of this section as evidence that 'there is a consensus that predatory pricing schemes are rarely tried, and even more rarely successful'.[2] The Court repeated this passage in its decision in *Brooke Group*.[3]

Part (b) examines the post-1980 theoretical literature that responded to the literature discussed in Part (a). Part (c) examines the post-1980s empirical literature on predation. In sum, the models of rational predation and the empirical papers reviewed in this section demonstrate that the academic conclusions reached in the early 1980s regarding the rationality and rarity of predatory pricing, and accepted by the Supreme Court in its *Matsushita* and *Brooke Group* decisions may not tell the whole story. Many have noted and criticized the Court's failure to date to incorporate this new learning into the antitrust treatment of predation (*see, for example*, Hemphill (2001), Bolton, et al. (2000), Klevorick (1993)). However, it is far from clear that this is a mistake. The models showing rational predation can exist and the evidence consistent with episodes of predation does not demonstrate that predation is either ubiquitous or frequent. Moreover, many of these models do not consider the welfare effects of predation, and those that do generally find the welfare effects ambiguous. Furthermore, this line of research does not suggest easy to administer tests for predatory pricing. As a result, while the literature usefully questions one of the premises underlying the Court's recent predatory pricing holdings, it has not conclusively shown that the Court's approach to predatory pricing in *Brooke Group*, which stresses the costs of erroneous condemnations of price competition as well as the benefits of having an administrable predation rule, should be replaced.

a Price theory and predation – 1958–1980

A natural starting point to review the economics of predation is John McGee's (1958) influential article on the *Standard Oil* case. In this article, McGee challenged the conventional wisdom that predatory price discrimination was used by John Rockefeller to create an oil refining monopoly. The *Standard Oil* case was long thought to be a classic case where predation was achieved through local price cutting. However, McGee's review of the record found that there was little or no evidence that Standard Oil systematically used local price cutting to monopolize the oil refining industry.[4]

In addition to analyzing the Standard Oil record, McGee examined the use of predatory price cutting as a method to monopolize. McGee criticized the logic of the standard predatory pricing theory, noting that the usual argument involves a firm with existing monopoly power using its monopoly profits to outlast its less capitalized rivals. McGee noted that such an argument presupposes market power without explaining how market power is obtained. He also questioned whether predation would be successful. Any limits on internal financing would be made irrelevant by infusions of outside capital which would allow the rival firm to either survive until or re-enter the market when prices rose above predatory levels.

Moreover, McGee noted that unless there are legal constraints, it would be more profitable and permanent for a potential predator to acquire a rival than to incur losses in driving it from the market through price predation. Rather than dissipate profits through price cutting, the predator could instead offer the rival a premium to induce him to sell his assets. McGee also found it unlikely that predatory pricing could be used to depress the price of the acquisition. He questioned whether the purchase price would be significantly affected by price cutting that was not permanent. Because the predatory firm must expand output in order to depress the price, the losses incurred by the prey, which can limit its losses by limiting sales at predatory prices or even temporarily shutting down, are likely to be smaller than those incurred by the predator. This would make it unlikely that the savings from a lower acquisition price would outweigh the direct losses incurred by the predator.

McGee's article was followed by numerous articles that also cast doubt on both the theoretical and empirical relevance of price predation. McGee (1980) revisited his earlier work, and noted in particular that his skepticism regarding the viability of predatory pricing was not based on the absence of antimerger laws. Easterbrook (1981a) extended McGee's theoretical arguments. In the single market predation case, Easterbrook notes that many factors, including the ability of potential victims and their customers to respond to predation, make successful predatory pricing uncertain and unattractive. Easterbrook also examines multi-market theories of predation and the use of credible commitments to support predation. He notes that models showing how credible commitments are used to support predation do not take into account the fact that credible commitments also can be used to defeat predation. With respect to multi-market predation, Easterbrook notes that the success of such strategies could be thwarted through the use of counterstrategies by the entrant. Easterbrook also observes that under the logic of backwards induction, multi-market predation in the finitely repeated setting suffers from the same problems as single market predation. This is the 'chain store paradox' (Selten (1978)). If there are a finite number of markets, predation in the final market would not be rational for the same reasons it is not rational in the single market setting. Knowing this, predation would not be rational in the period proceeding the last period, and given this, the period before.

In addition to addressing the theoretical arguments, scholars also re-examined other cases where predation was alleged. As with McGee's findings with respect to Standard Oil, scholars found little evidence of profitable predation. Koller (1971), in an influential and often cited work, examined 31 alleged incidents of predation, and found few instances of successful predation. Following McGee's methodology, Elzinga (1970) reexamined the history of the gunpowder trust, and found that many of the alleged victims were not victims of predatory pricing, and that there was no conclusive evidence that any of the victims were subjected to predatory pricing. Adelman (1966) found little evidence of predatory pricing by A&P despite the government's successful prosecution for predatory pricing. McGee (1964) examined the Spanish sugar industry, and found that predatory threats failed even in the absence of antitrust laws.

b Predation and strategic theory

One reason for the widespread skepticism of the rationality of predatory pricing was the absence of a coherent theory of rational predation prior to the 1980s (Ordover (1988)). The absence of a coherent theory of predatory pricing spurred work by economists challenging the McGee hypothesis that predation was irrational. Their work generally concentrated on examining theoretical conditions under which predation is a rational and profitable strategy. Ordover and Saloner (1989) usefully categorize this literature into three primary classes of models of predation based upon asymmetric information: asymmetric financial constraints, reputation based models, and signaling models. There are also recent models of rational predation not based on asymmetric information. This section briefly reviews these articles (see Ordover and Saloner (1989) for a more in-depth description of these models).

i Financial predation and the long purse The first category of asymmetric information models, those with asymmetric financial constraints, was addressed early on by Telser (1966). Telser set out a model of the 'long purse' in which predation occurs because the predator, with superior resources, can outlast the prey. In Telser's model the interest rate at which a firm can borrow increases as the firm's reserves decrease, which in turn constrains the amount a firm can borrow. In order to remain viable, firms must incur per period fixed costs even if they do not produce any output. Because this is common knowledge, the predatory firm can calculate the number of periods its prey could last given predatory prices. Under these conditions, a firm with greater resources can successfully deplete the reserves of the less capitalized victim, thus limiting the victim's ability to borrow and eventually driving him from the market. If the additional monopoly profits outweigh the predator's reduced profits that result from predatory pricing, predation is a rational strategy vis-à-vis a policy of entry accommodation.

However, because all information is common knowledge, predation would not be observed in equilibrium. Because predation is costly to both firms, Telser suggests that the threat of predation should either deter entry in the first place or result in the parties agreeing to merge, with the terms determined by the relative costs of predation in the absence of an agreement. Moreover, if potential victims anticipate this, they can alter their capital structure to increase the cost of successful predation, and thus favorably alter the buyout price.

Beniot (1984) also modeled predation with a financially constrained entrant. Beniot first presents an infinitely repeated extensive form game where the entrant has resources to survive a finite number of price wars. Under complete and perfect information, Beniot derives a 'reverse chain store paradox' result, where entry is deterred as long as the entrant's ability to survive is finite. He then examines a game with incomplete information where the predator knows the maximum number of periods the entrant can stay in, but only knows with probability $1 - p$ whether the entrant is committed to stay in the industry until bankrupt. Beniot derives a mixed strategy equilibrium where entry occurs, with entry being an increasing function of the entrant's financial staying power.

These models do not explain why the firms are financially constrained, and thus are subject to the criticism noted above that predation will be thwarted in well-functioning capital markets. Indeed, in Beniot's complete information model, the *incumbent* will be driven from the market if the entrant can acquire capital sufficient to outlast it. More generally, greater resources increase the probability of entry in the incomplete information model, and favorably alter the buyout price in Telser's model.

This critique was addressed through models of financial constraints based on asymmetric information. Fudenberg and Tirole (1986) created a model where the entrant is uncertain about his per period fixed costs and uses current profits to decide whether to remain in the market. Given this, the incumbent has an incentive to use predation to reduce the entrant's profits in order to cause the entrant to infer that he has high costs and should exit. Their 'signal jamming' model can also be applied to lenders' decisions to make or limit outside financing. Bolton and Scharfstein (1990) derive financial constraints based on firms' attempts to control agency costs. In their model, lenders' decisions regarding external financing are sensitive to a firm's short term performance. This gives managers incentives and addresses manager/shareholder agency costs. However, a predator knowing this relationship between a firm and its lender can take advantage of it by using price predation to lower current profits, which in turn reduces external financing and induces exit. If these contracts between firm and lender are observable, firms that are potential victims of predation will choose to make their contracts less sensitive to current performance, thus trading off higher agency costs for a lower threat of predation. The use of financial contracting by potential victims to reduce the threat of predation, and the effect of renegotiation on its effectiveness is further examined by Snyder (1996).

The deep pocket theory is also addressed by Poitevin (1989) and in a similar model by LeBlanc (1996). In the Poitevin model, there is incomplete information about the viability of the entrant. The entrant's susceptibility to predation is explained by endogenously determined financial structures, with viable entrants having to signal their high value by taking on debt rather than using equity financing. This leverage in turn provides an incentive for the equity financed incumbent to drive the leveraged entrant into bankruptcy.

ii Multiple markets and reputation The second set of asymmetric information models are reputational models of predation where the predator faces entry in multiple markets. These models attempt to demonstrate the rationality of predation by addressing the backwards induction logic of the chain store paradox in several ways. Some models examined reputation in the setting of an infinitely repeated game (Milgrom and Roberts (1982b)), where predation is a Nash equilibrium. However, use of infinitely repeated games as a response to the chain store paradox is unattractive for several reasons (Ordover and Saloner (1989: 553)), including the fact that such games have multiple equilibria, including one where accommodated entry occurs each period.

Another set of studies examined reputational models where the assumption of perfect information was relaxed as a way to avoid the logic and result of the chain store paradox. Milgrom and Roberts (1982b), Kreps and Wilson (1982) and Kreps, Milgrom, Roberts and Wilson (1982) developed models where some incumbents prefer to engage in predation rather than accommodating entry. Such preferences can result from the fact that predation is more profitable than accommodation in the single market setting, or alternatively from a narrowly irrational preference for predation when it is not. The entrant in these models does not know ex-ante what type of incumbent he is facing, strong (those with a preference for predation) or weak (those that would prefer to accommodate entry in a single market game). However, the entrant knows p, the probability the incumbent is strong.

To see how the probable existence of irrationality affects the chain store paradox result, consider a two period model where, based on expected profits, the entrant in the first market will enter. In such a game, there is no pure strategy equilibrium.[5] Kreps and Wilson (1982) examine a mixed strategy equilibrium in which the strong incumbent fights, the weak incumbent randomizes over his strategy to fight, and the second period entrant randomizes over his strategy to enter. In the mixed strategy equilibrium, the probability that the first entrant will face predation will be greater than the probability the incumbent is strong, p, as both strong incumbents and some weak incumbents will choose to predate. Kreps and Wilson show that in a model with many, but finite periods, predation can occur with a high probability as the weak incumbent will fight with a high probability even when strong or irrational incumbents are rare so that p is low. The basic predation for reputation result can be extended to the case where there are multiple types of incumbents, where an entrant is in more than one market, and where the assumption of incomplete information is not limited to the incumbent's cost (Milgrom and Roberts (1982b)). Easley, Masson and Reynolds (1985) extend the reputational model to consider multiple market entries by entrants, multiple entrants, and dynamic elements such as delaying rather than completely deterring entry.

iii Signaling The third major set of asymmetric information models are signaling models of predation. In these models, the entrant is unsure about either the incumbent's costs (Salop and Shapiro (1980), Milgrom and Roberts (1982a), Saloner (1987)) or market demand (Roberts (1986)). Entrants facing unfavorable market conditions (i.e., either a low cost incumbent or low demand conditions) are better off exiting the market than staying in. As a result, informed incumbents will want to transmit information to these entrants, through low prices, that they are facing unfavorable conditions. In a separating equilibrium, incumbent firms competing in a market with conditions unfavorable to the entrant will use low prices to signal these conditions, which results in the exit of the entrant and monopoly profits in the following period. Low prices serve as a separating signal when they are set at a level where the marginal increase in profits in the second period is greater than the profit sacrifice in the first for the strong (low cost or high demand) firm's profits but not for the weak (high cost or low demand) firm's profits.

Signaling models include models of limit pricing where lowered prices are used to deter entry. In Milgrom and Roberts's (1982a) basic model, both the incumbent and entrant can be either a high or low cost firm. Each firm knows its own costs, but not the costs of the other firm. Entrant and incumbent firms are high cost with probability p and q respectively. Moreover, both types of entrants would prefer to enter if the incumbent is a high cost type, and would prefer not to enter against a low cost entrant. Thus, with complete information, the probability of entry would be q. With incomplete information, Milgrom and Roberts show that both separating and pooling equilibria exist. In the separating limit pricing equilibrium, low cost incumbents separate themselves from high cost incumbents and deter entry. However, there is no marginal entry deterrence relative to the full information equilibrium, as the probability of entry is the probability that the incumbent is high cost, q. In the pooling equilibrium, only the low cost entrant enters. The probability of entry equals $(1 - p)$, which can be greater than, equal to, or less than q. Thus, in their model, limit pricing does not necessarily deter entry relative to the full information equilibrium.

Saloner (1987) adapted the Milgrom and Roberts limit pricing model to consider how predatory pricing can be used to induce the exit of an existing competitor. The model has three stages. In the first stage, two incumbent firms compete as Cournot duopolists. In this model Firm A has known costs, but Firm B does not know if Firm A has high or low costs. At the end of the first stage, Firm B updates its beliefs about Firm A's costs. Firm A then makes an offer to buy Firm B. In the third stage, Firm A either competes as a merged firm that faces potential entry, or competes with Firm B as a duopolist. Saloner demonstrates three effects of Firm A expanding output beyond the single period equilibrium output. First, like the Milgrom and Roberts limit pricing model, this expanded output can serve as a separating signal that the firm is a low cost firm. Under the assumptions of the model, this results in entry deterrence in the third period. In addition, even when entry is not deterred, the expansion of output will induce Firm B to reduce its output in equilibrium, and will also favorably alter the buyout price of Firm B at stage two. Thus, the output signal serves both as a limit price and as a predatory signal.

As noted above, Roberts (1986) examines a similar model where information is incomplete as to demand rather than cost. In addition, there is earlier literature on 'test market predation' (Scharfstein (1984), describing an earlier model by Salop and Shapiro (1980)) in which there could be signaling in a local or 'test' market competition that occurs prior to competition at the national level.

While these models demonstrate that rational predation can occur, both Saloner (1987) and Milgrom and Roberts (1982a) note that the welfare consequences of the limit pricing and predation outcomes are ambiguous. Thus, while these papers provide a counterargument to the assertion that predation is not rational, the fact that rational predation can increase welfare complicates the inferences one can draw for antitrust policy.

iv Other theories The theories of predation discussed in Parts i to iii all rely on asymmetric information to generate rational equilibrium predation. However, asymmetric information is not a necessary condition to generate predation in equilibrium. Cabral and Riordan (1994, 1997) have a learning curve model of equilibrium predation, in which firms' current period production costs are a function of the cumulative production. In such a learning curve environment, Cabral and Riordan show that rational predation occurs in equilibrium, where the predator expands output and lowers price in order to take further advantage of the learning curve cost reductions and to induce its rival's exit. This predation can involve, but does not require, below-cost pricing. The welfare consequences of such learning curve predation are ambiguous.

Marx and Shaffer (1999) have a complete information model of predation in intermediate goods markets. In their model, a manufacturer makes sequential purchases from two suppliers of differentiated inputs. They show that below-cost pricing of marginal units by the first supplier can facilitate rent extraction from the second, resulting in a higher joint surplus between the buyer and the first supplier. In their model, below-cost pricing does not result in exclusion, and welfare may increase or decrease.

c Empirical studies of predation

As noted in Part (a), empirical studies showing little evidence of price predation were influential in producing the consensus that predatory pricing was not an important phenomenon. Recent empirical studies have challenged the findings of this early literature and produced evidence consistent with the newer models of predation. This part reviews these empirical studies that were largely undertaken to counter the earlier literature that cast doubt on the frequency of successful predation in practice.

A study by Zerbe and Cooper (1982) reexamined and updated the litigated predatory pricing cases included in the influential Koller (1971) study. In contrast to the low rate of successful predation reported by Koller, Zerbe and Cooper found that the predator was successful, or would have been successful but for a lawsuit, in raising prices in 27 out of 40 cases. Unfortunately, neither of the articles precisely defines or describes the methodology through which a litigated case was categorized as a 'success'. Compounding the difficulties in analyzing the studies, neither the Zerbe and Cooper article, nor a later retrospective article by Zerbe and Mumford (1996) explain precisely how their methodology differs from that used by Koller.[6]

Zerbe and Mumford (1996) also cited and reexamined other episodes of predation. For example, they reexamined the gunpowder trust studied by Elzinga (1970). While Elzinga looked for below marginal cost pricing to classify cases as predation, Zerbe and Mumford used a broader criterion of predation that includes strategic pricing to drive a rival from business or to induce a rival to join a cartel. Using this broader definition, they found that five of eleven cases in which a determination could be made from the record resulted in predation. Other examples of successful predation cited include Zerbe's (1969) examination of the case of the American Sugar Refining Company, and Yamey's (1972) study of Ocean Shipping Cartels. Yamey described indirect evidence of below-cost pricing by a steamship conference in the 1880s to exclude the Mogul Steamship Company from the England/China trade. According to contemporaneous statements, the conference successfully excluded Mogul, an independent company, using loyalty rebates and below-cost pricing.[7] However, the conference was not able to exclude the larger China Shippers Mutual Steam Navigation Company, which was eventually admitted to the conference.

Other discussions of litigated cases and their frequency include Easterbrook (1981a) (examining cases and finding absence of predation); Elzinga and Mills (2001) (reexamining three cases in which the courts or the agencies failed to find firms' pricing to be predatory and concluding these cases were correctly decided); Bolton et al. (2000, 2001) (finding plaintiff success rate of 17 per cent in the ten years before the Supreme Court's *Brooke Group* decision, discussing post *Brooke* cases, and disputing evidence that recent cases show absence of predation).

One drawback of empirical studies of litigated cases is that it is unclear what inferences can be made from the results. In general, litigated cases are a highly selected sample of cases, and may not be representative, in either frequency or substance, of the larger universe of cases, including settled or dropped cases and cases never filed (see generally, Priest and Klein (1984)). Easterbrook (1981a: 316) argued that near absence of proof of predation in litigated cases is significant, as episodes of predation would be unlikely to escape detection given the existence of treble damages and competitive incentives for harmed plaintiffs to bring such cases. In contrast, Bolton et al. (2000: 2254) argue that proof of predation in litigation cases is not rare, and may be considerably higher if settled cases were taken into account.

Several studies have used regression analysis to attempt to test models of predation or their assumptions. The incentive to use predatory pricing to lower the acquisition cost of competitors was examined by Burns (1986, 1989). In the earlier article, Burns used regression analysis to examine how the acquisition prices of firms acquired by the American Tobacco Company from 1891–1906 were affected by the number of prior predatory episodes (the reputation effect) and how price wars directly affected the acquisition price of the prey. Burns found statistically significant coefficients consistent with predation reducing the cost of acquiring competitors through both reputation and direct effects. Burns estimated the effect of reputation was to reduce the acquisition costs by 25 per cent, with an additional discount of 56 per cent resulting from preying on the relatively smaller, fine cut tobacco, snuff, and smoking tobacco firms. Burns (1986: 290) noted that the estimated savings attributed to predation are also consistent merely with intensified, but lawful, price competition. Moreover, such a pattern of decline in the costs of acquiring competitors is also consistent with American Tobacco achieving scale economies or other efficiencies that result from the mergers (Lott (1999:6)). Burns (1989) examined direct evidence of predatory intent and suggested that litigation documents from the government's antitrust case against American Tobacco support the predation interpretation.

Scott Morton (1997) used regression analysis to examine pricing by ocean shipping conferences in response to entry, and found evidence consistent with the long purse theory. She examined British shipping conferences' reactions to entry over a 50-year period. Her dataset contained 47 cases, in which there were 14 price wars, resulting in 6 cases in which the entrant was driven out. Her main result was that new and smaller entrants were more likely to experience price wars, an observation consistent with the long purse theory of predation. Podolny and Scott Morton (1999) expanded this analysis to examine social characteristics of the entrants, which may serve as a proxy for the probability of future cooperativeness of the entrant. Lerner (1995) found similar evidence regarding prices of computer disk drives. Using a hedonic price regression, he found prices were relatively lower when the closest substitutes for that product were produced by thinly capitalized rivals. Weiman and Levin (1994) examined evidence of predatory behavior by the Southern Bell Company from 1894 to 1912. Using regression analysis, they found that telephone prices fell immediately prior to new entry. Moreover, prices fell further after new entry. Again, while all of these papers provide evidence consistent with the use of predatory pricing, we do not know whether these price wars would be unlawful under modern predation standards, or whether such episodes resulted in reductions in welfare.

An exception is Genesove and Mullin (2006), who provided direct evidence of predation through below-cost pricing in the sugar industry at the beginning of the twentieth century by comparing sugar prices to a direct measurement of marginal cost. Direct calculation of marginal cost is made possible in this case by the simple technology involved, and the existence of relevant testimony and contemporary audits. They found episodes of prices that were below marginal cost. In addition, they constructed competitive price-cost margins, and showed that actual margins were lower than these constructed margins. They also found that predation occurred when the cost of predation was relatively small (e.g., the episodes of predation were suspended during high demand periods), and that the episodes of predatory pricing were followed by acquisitions of competitors at lower prices.

Several authors have examined whether regulation or public ownership have an effect on the likelihood of predation. Hazlett (1995) found evidence of predation in cable television markets. Such markets are characterized by the existence of network effects and are subject to regulation by local jurisdictions. Hazlett argues that these special characteristics lower the predator's costs and raise those of the prey, making such regulated markets especially susceptible to predation. This point was made more generally by Miller and Pautler (1985). Lott (1990, 1995, 1999) presents theory and evidence on differences in the likelihood of predation by public and private firms. Lott (1990) notes that unlike private firms, public enterprises can have institutional incentives to expand output, thus making predation by such firms plausible. Lott (1995) presents evidence on below-cost dumping, showing that dumping cases predominately involve state run firms.

Lott and Opler (1996) and Lott (1999) provide a specific test of the reputational models of predation discussed in Part iii. They argue that reputational models of predation require that private firms be able to credibly commit to engage in predation. To do this, they argue that managers' compensation should not be tied to short run profits. This gives managers the incentive to expand output past the level that maximizes short run profits during the predatory episode. Further, such firms also need to prevent managers from being easily removed by shareholders during the predatory episode. Lott and Opler test these two hypotheses, and find that managers of firms accused of predation were rewarded more than managers of other firms. Moreover, they found that managers of predatory firms were not more entrenched than managers of non-predatory firms. As is the case with the evidence on predation generally, critics have noted shortcomings of the tests and evidence, and have noted that this evidence has other interpretations (Sappington and Sidak (2000)).

i Experimental evidence Experimental methods have been applied to antitrust law (see Plott (1989), Normann (2007)), and to predatory pricing in particular. Isaac and Smith (1985) examined predation in an experimental setting designed to be conducive to the observation of predatory pricing. In their experiments, predatory pricing was defined to be a price that is 'lower than would be optimal in a simple myopic (short-run) pricing strategy' and had 'the effect of preventing entry, or driving out and preventing reentry, of the prey'. Their experimental markets tailored to predatory pricing contained two firms, one large and one small. The larger firm was given a cost and 'deep pocket' resource advantage. In addition, there were sunk cost entry and reentry barriers. Variants of the experiments were conducted where the subjects did not know the demand conditions or the other seller's costs, and also where they had complete information regarding demand and cost. Despite conditions set up to be favorable to the emergence of predatory pricing, it was not observed. Harrison (1988) extended the Isaac and Smith experiments to a setting where the monopolist faced a single entrant in multiple markets. In this setting, Harrison found some evidence of predatory pricing, but the evidence is weak given that only one trial looked at multiple markets. Gomez et al. (2008) report that predation was not observed in three replications of the Harrison experiments. However, in a setting where prices were chosen after entry decisions were made and announced, predation did emerge.

A more specific experimental test of the incomplete information models of predation was performed by Jung et al. (1994). They conducted an experiment testing the incomplete information reputational equilibrium of Kreps and Wilson (1982). As noted above, entrants would prefer to enter if the monopolist is weak but not if the monopolist is strong. Marginal entry deterrence occurs when weak incumbents mimic strong ones and fight entry. In their results, Jung et al. found evidence that weak incumbents frequently fought and successfully deterred entry. Thus, while some evidence was not consistent with the particular sequential equilibrium of the Kreps and Wilson model (for example, the rate of entry increased when the experimental subjects were closer to the final period and the entrants' rate of entry was not consistent with Bayesian updating), their experiments produced strong reputational effects.

III Antitrust regulation of predation

a An economic analysis of legal rules

Economists and legal scholars have argued that the goal of legal rules, including the regulation of business conduct through the antitrust laws, is to minimize the sum of direct costs and error costs (see, e.g., Posner (2002: 563), Evans and Padilla (2005), Joskow and Klevorick (1979)). Applying this analysis to predatory pricing, error costs include the costs of false negatives or type II errors (allowing anticompetitive predatory pricing) and the costs of false positives or type I errors (wrongly condemning welfare increasing price cuts or deterring efficient price competition from occurring in the first place). Direct costs include the costs imposed on society (including litigants, consumers, and the courts) associated with the enforcement of the antitrust laws to regulate predatory pricing.

Under this framework, the optimal form and substance of a legal rule is determined by the frequency and size of the two types of error costs, as well as the costs of administering the rule. For example, if the relative cost and frequency of false positives to false negatives is high, then the optimal rule should contain both procedural and substantive safeguards that reduce the costs of false positives. As noted above,[8] the Supreme Court, in setting out a permissive rule to regulate predatory pricing, asserted that 'there is a consensus that predatory pricing schemes are rarely tried, and even more rarely successful'. More generally, Easterbrook (1984) argues that the self correcting nature of markets makes the expected costs of false positives greater than the expected costs of false negatives.

The nature of the error costs and direct costs also determines whether the optimal legal rule takes the form of an easily administered bright line rule, or a more nuanced and more difficult to administer standard. Uncertainty in the application of a nuanced standard can dramatically increase both the direct costs associated with it, raising both the frequency and cost of litigation, and the total error costs involved in enforcing such a standard. As a result, it is often the case that optimal legal rules ignore potential or speculative harms because any attempt to address them would result in an increase of direct costs far in excess of any benefit from the reduction in error costs. As Justice (then Judge) Breyer has explained in a case involving near-exclusive volume discounts:[9]

> [U]nlike economics, law is an administrative system the effects of which depend upon the content of rules and precedents only as they are applied by judges and

> juries in courts and by lawyers advising their clients. Rules that seek to embody every economic complexity and qualification may well, through the vagaries of administration, prove counterproductive, undercutting the very economic ends they seek to serve.[10]

Under these conditions, use of simple to administer rules can be preferable to a more complex standard that, in theory, would better discern between welfare increasing and welfare decreasing price cuts. This is especially true when the cost of one type of error is *de minimis*. For example, use of a rule of *per se* illegality would be rational if the conduct in question involved behavior that was almost certain to be socially undesirable, and if such conduct could be easily distinguished from other types of conduct. Naked horizontal price fixing is often argued to possess such attributes. Similarly, rules of *per se* legality or the use of safe harbors would be optimal if the relative costs of type I errors are high (Boudreaux et al. (1995), Easterbrook (1981a)). Such concerns are magnified when imperfect antitrust enforcement combined with the threat of treble damages may deter procompetitive price reductions (Crane (2005)). Indeed, the Supreme Court's concerns over the administrability of a more nuanced predation standard, in addition to concerns over the high relative costs of falsely condemning pro-competitive pricing behavior and the Court's assumption that predatory pricing is rare, led to the creation of a broad safe harbor for 'above-cost' pricing conduct in *Brooke Group*.[11]

b Predation and optimal antitrust rules

Predatory behavior can be broadly defined as behavior that excludes a rival and reduces the appropriate measure of welfare relative to the level that would be attained if such conduct was prohibited. While some have advocated using general welfare criteria (Scherer (1976) and Brodley and Hay (1981)), such a definition does not produce a workable or easily administrable test for predation. The impracticability of directly observing the welfare effects of a firm's behavior has led to a search for alternative definitions and tests for predatory behavior. This section reviews these tests for predatory pricing, which have been widely examined in detail elsewhere (McGee (1980), Zerbe and Cooper (1982), Ordover and Saloner (1992)).

i The Areeda-Turner test and cost based rules Perhaps the most influential test of predation is the cost-based test of Areeda and Turner (1975) (AT). In their seminal article, AT defined predation as selling below cost. If costs were measurable, AT would find prices above short run marginal cost lawful, and prices below short run marginal cost unlawful. Because prices would be driven to marginal cost (MC) in competitive equilibrium,

AT did not want a rule that would prevent competitive pricing by making prices above marginal cost unlawful. In contrast, prices below marginal cost are not consistent with a competitive equilibrium, and such prices would require that the predatory firm incur a profit sacrifice. Because of the difficulties of observing and measuring marginal cost, AT would use average variable cost (AVC) as a more easily observable proxy. Under the AT test, prices below AVC would be presumptively unlawful. The AT test weights heavily both the potential costs of deterring competitive price cutting, and the benefits of having a well defined, administrable standard.

Critics of the AT rule have noted that use of AVC as a proxy can be an overly permissive test, especially at output levels above q^0, the point where AVC is at its minimum. At such output levels, AVC is well below MC. As a result, such a standard allows prices that can be significantly below marginal costs. Zerbe and Cooper (1982) suggest a modified AT test where prices below average total cost (ATC) would be used for high output levels, and prices below AVC for lower output levels (see also Areeda and Turner (1978), accepting a variant of the modified AT test).

Baumol (1996) defends the use of a variant of the AVC test as the correct price floor, though he notes that AVC is not well defined. Baumol would use average avoidable costs (AAC) as the price floor, where AAC are defined to include variable costs and all fixed costs that are not sunk. Because a firm can minimize its losses by exiting whenever prices are below AAC, prices below AAC necessarily involve a profit sacrifice. AAC, and not MC, will also define the shut down point for an equally efficient rival. Thus, prices above AAC will not exclude an equally efficient rival, while prices below AAC will be exclusionary.

Others suggest modifications of the AT test that require the existence of structural preconditions as a first-stage filter (Joskow and Klevorick (1979)). The first set of factors to be examined include proxies for market power, such as the predator's market share, the size of other firms in the market, the stability of market shares, the predatory firm's profit history, and the residual elasticity of demand. The second set of factors to be examined are proxies regarding conditions of entry into the market. The third step would be to examine generally the dynamic effects of entrants on the market conditions. If the structural analysis suggests little danger of successful predation, Joskow and Klevorick would preclude plaintiffs from pursuing such cases. In cases where the first stage analysis suggests that predatory harm is possible, a price below AVC would be a sufficient but not necessary to find predation. In general, Joskow and Klevorick advocate a presumption of illegality for prices below ATC. Prices above ATC would be presumed legal unless the price cut was reversed within a reasonable period of time (for example, two years).

Bolton et al. (2000) also suggest a two tier test which would examine five elements. In the first tier, the plaintiff must prove: (1) a facilitating market structure; (2) a scheme of predation and supporting evidence; and (3) probable recoupment. Only if the plaintiff proves these three elements would the inquiry proceed to examine (4) whether price exceeded cost and (5) the absence of a business justification or efficiencies defense. While arguing that these elements are consistent with the traditional antitrust analysis of predatory pricing under *Brooke Group* (see discussion in Section IVa below), Bolton et al. would augment each stage of the traditional analysis to account for modern strategic analysis of the type reviewed in Section II(b) above. For example, the first stage analysis could incorporate reputational models of predation by creating a presumption of high entry and reentry barriers based on an incumbent's past reputation as a predator. Strategic theory would also allow the plaintiff a menu of alternatives as a basis for proving a scheme of predation. In addition, a coherent strategic theory supported by evidence would allow courts to apply a less demanding standard when assessing the probability of recoupment. With respect to the cost test, Bolton et al. would adopt Baumol's AAC benchmark, or use long run average incremental costs (see discussion of Ordover and Willig (1981) in Part iii of the Section, below).

ii 'Dynamic' predation rules Others have attempted to devise tests that would go beyond the cost based rules in an attempt to detect above-cost, but strategic, pricing. Instead of relying on the static relationship between price and cost to define predation, these authors use the intertemporal price pattern of a firm engaged in strategic pricing to devise a rule against predation. Baumol (1979) would condemn prices below average incremental cost, but also would condemn price cuts above average total cost if they were quickly reversed. This test would allow aggressive pricing by the incumbent firm, but would seek to punish attempts to recoup the sacrifice of profits by making any price cuts 'quasi permanent'. Because the potential predatory firm would be required to suffer the losses of non-compensatory price cuts or output expansions over the longer period defined by the rule, such a rule would increase the costs of predation.

Williamson (1977) also examines the intertemporal implications of predatory pricing to devise his predatory pricing rule. Williamson would condemn as predatory prices below average variable costs, but would also enjoin above-cost demand-adjusted increases in output by the incumbent in response to entry. Williamson posits that his rule, which restricts the incumbent's ability to respond to entry, would induce the incumbent to increase output and lower prices prior to entry. On the other hand, critics note that such a rule of forced accommodation may result in both the monopolist and entrant enjoying the post-entry price umbrella that would be created by the rule. Edlin (2002) proposes a rule that would prevent an incumbent from reducing prices in response to entry accompanied by a substantial price discount. Limiting the rule to 'substantial' price discounts would prevent weak entry. In addition, he argues that such a rule will better control above-cost exclusionary limit pricing, and will give better incentives for incumbents to lower their pre-entry price. Elhauge (2003) notes that these dynamic predation rules that would restrict the incumbent's ability to react to entry are likely to be futile and harmful. Specifically, incumbents' reactions to entry may be a normal and pro-competitive response when such entry will undermine an output maximizing competitive schedule of discriminatory prices. Even in the absence of competitive price discrimination, Elhauge shows that such rules can decrease both productive efficiency, and consumer welfare. Moreover, such rules are not well formulated to operate in real world markets, and would have unavoidable implementation difficulties. These difficulties include the lack of well-defined price floors and ambiguities in defining when entry or exit occurs. In addition, it is possible that these rules could enhance the credibility of a multi-market predator and may serve to increase the probability that predation or entry deterrence is successful.

iii Predation as profit sacrifice A broad definition of predatory behavior has been offered by Ordover and Willig (1981) (OW) based upon the observation of a profit sacrifice. The test is broader than the AT rule in that it considers as predatory non-compensatory output increases even if price is above costs. Specifically, under the OW definition of predation, an action is predatory if it would not be optimal but for its effect on inducing the exit of a rival. The OW rule requires that a predatory action satisfy two necessary conditions (Ordover and Saloner (1989)). The first is that the predatory firm has a profit motive in excluding the entrant – that is, the exit inducing strategy is more profitable than the optimal strategy with a viable entrant. The second is the requirement of profit sacrifice. That is, the exit inducing strategy is optimal if and only if exit is induced. Both conditions are necessary because the first condition without the second would require the incumbent to accommodate entry and ensure the viability of the rival. The second condition alone would result in competitive strategies being condemned because a more profitable strategy was viable.

OW apply this definition to the case of price predation by considering the effect of a strategy resulting in an incremental change in a firm's output from q_0 to $q_0 - \delta$. The increment of output δ involves a profit sacrifice if the reduction in output increases profits:

$$p_0 q_0 - c(q_0) < p'(q_0 - \delta) - c(q_0 - \delta) \qquad (6.1)$$

where p' is the price in the absence of the output increment. Equation (6.1) can be rewritten as:

$$p'\delta - (p' - p_0)q_0 < c(q_0) - c(q_0 - \delta) \qquad (6.1')$$

Assuming $p_0 = p' = p$ yields:

$$p\delta < (c(q_0) - c(q_0 - \delta)) \qquad (6.2)$$

Under Equation (6.2), an incremental increase in output δ is predatory if the incremental revenues $p\delta$ are less than the incremental costs of producing that increment of output. Equation (6.2) can be rewritten as:

$$p < (c(q_0) - c(q_0 - \delta))/\delta \qquad (6.2')$$

Since $p' > p_0$, $p\delta$ is an upper bound for the change in revenues, condition (6.2') yields a lower bound for a predatory price. For an arbitrary change in output, condition (6.2') would condemn prices that are less than the average cost of producing the incremental output, or average incremental cost (AIC). Condition (6.2') can be satisfied when the price of the good is greater than the AVC or marginal costs (MC).

OW also note that condition (6.2') can be used to derive conditions under which other traditional cost based predatory pricing rules would be used. If $\delta = 1$, then condition (6.2') becomes $p <$ MC, the preferred theoretical AT rule. Note that if price is less than the marginal cost of producing unit q_0, the firm can increase profits by not producing that unit. Thus, producing that marginal unit involves a profit sacrifice. If $\delta = q_0$, condition (6.2) becomes $p <$ Average Avoidable Costs (AAC) (Baumol (1996)). That is, if the price is below the firm's AAC, the firm can increase profits by shutting down. Thus, prices below MC and AAC are sufficient, but not necessary conditions to show a profit sacrifice.

Critics have questioned whether the OW standard would be administrable in practice (Easterbrook (1981b)). Moreover, the OW standard can result in the condemnation of welfare increasing conduct, as well as allowing welfare decreasing conduct (Schwartz (1989), Scheffman (1981)). To illustrate the general implications of the OW standard for predatory behavior, consider a two period model where there are two firms, an incumbent Firm *I* and an entrant Firm *E*, competing in a market with stable demand that will last two periods. Market demand in each period is given by:

$$P = M - kQ \tag{6.3}$$

where $Q = \sum_f q_f$, where $f = \{I, E\}$.

Firm f's profits in period j are given by:

$$\pi_f^j = Pq_f^j - c_f q_f^j - F_f^j \tag{6.4}$$

where c_f are Firm f's constant marginal costs, and F_f are Firm f's per-period fixed costs.

Under these conditions, action a_0^p by the incumbent Firm I in period 0 is predatory under the OW standard if (a) the exit inducing action a_0^p is more profitable than the optimal strategy with a viable entrant, and (b) when there is a profit sacrifice, so that action a_0^p is optimal if and only if exit is induced. This implies that the following necessary conditions must be satisfied (Ordover and Saloner (1989; 587):

$$\pi_0^I(a_0^p) + \pi_1^I(a_1^*|a_0^p, E\,out) > \pi_0^I(a_0^*) + \pi_1^I(a_1^*|a_0^*, E\,in) \tag{6.5}$$

$$\pi_0^I(a_0^p) + \pi_1^I(a_1^*|a_0^p, E\,viable) < \pi_0^I(a_0^*) + \pi_1^I(a_1^*|a_0^*, E\,in) \tag{6.6}$$

where a_1^* is the incumbent's optimal action in period 1 conditional upon its actions in period 0 and the entrant's viability, and a_0^* is the incumbent's optimal non-predatory strategy in period 0.

Table 6.1 lists equilibrium outcomes under different assumptions regarding the nature of the firms' interaction, as well as demand and cost parameters. Example 1 lists the equilibrium outcomes assuming that the firms are identical, and that $M = 100$, $k = 0.5$, $c_I = c_E = 10$, and $F_I = F_E = 750$. Example 2 considers a setting where Firm E has higher fixed costs. Finally, example 3 considers a setting where Firm E has higher marginal costs, but lower fixed costs than Firm I.

Example 1 shows a case where the OW definition and test correctly condemns a welfare decreasing output expansion. In the example, Firm I's optimal non-exclusionary strategy in each period is to produce 90 units in each period. This is the relevant payoff for the right hand side of both condition (6.5) and condition (6.6). Firm E's best response is to produce 45 units in both periods, which results in the entrant's profits being 262.5. The total number of units equal 135, which results in a market price of 32.5. Firm I's net profits will equal 1275 in each period, for an undiscounted two period total of 2550. Total and consumer welfare equals 9112.5 and 12,187.5 respectively.

Suppose that Firm I instead pursues an exclusionary strategy where it commits to producing 103 units in periods 1 and 2. If Firm E has already

Table 6.1 Duopoly equilibrium outcomes

	c_I, c_E	F_I, F_E		Monopoly	Cournot	Optimal First Mover (Firm E viable)	Exclusionary Output Expansion	
							First Period	Second Period
1.	10,10	750,750	P	55	40	32.5	29.25	48.5
			q_I	90	60	90	103	103
			q_E		60	45	38.5	0
			π_I	3300	1050	1275	1232.75	3215.5
			π_E		1050	262.5	-8.875	0
			AVC_I	18.3	22.5	18.3	17.28	17.28
			AVC_E		22.5	26.7	29.48	
			CW	2025	3600	4556.25	5005.6	2662.25
			TW	5325	5700	6093.75	6229.4	5867.75
2.	10,10	750,1050	P		40	33	32.5	55
			q_I		60	88	90	90
			q_E		60	46	45	0
			π_I		1050	1274	1275	3300
			π_E		1050	8	−37.5	0
			AVC_I		22.5	18.52	18.33	18.33
			AVC_E		27.5	32.82	33.33	
			CW		3600	4489	4556.25	2025
			TW		5400	5571	5793.75	5325
3.	10,14	750,300	P		44	33.5	26	38
			q_I		57.33	94	124	124
			q_E		54.67	39	24	0
			π_I		1199.33	1459	1234	2722
			π_E		1340	460.5	−12	0
			AVC_I		23.08	17.98	16.05	16.05
			AVC_E		19.49	21.69	26.5	
			CW		3136	4422.25	5476	3844
			TW		5675.33	6341.75	6698	6566

incurred its fixed costs F_E of 750, it will respond optimally by producing 38.5 units in the first period. This will result in negative net profits for Firm *E*. In the second period, Firm *E* will choose not to incur its fixed costs and would exit the market. Price falls to 29.25 in the first period, and rises to 48.5 in the second. Compared to the non-exclusionary first mover strategy, the incumbent's profits under the exclusionary commitment are 3215.5 in the first period, a profit sacrifice of 42.25 relative to the non-exclusionary first mover payoffs. However, due to the exit of Firm *E*, profits in the second period rise to 3215.5, for a two period net increase of

1898.25 over the non-exclusionary first mover payoff. Thus condition (6.5) is satisfied. Moreover, condition (6.6) is also satisfied, as the production of 103 units in the first period results in a profit sacrifice. Thus, the commitment to produce 103 units would be predatory under OW criteria (6.5) and (6.6). In addition, such a commitment would be condemned under a welfare standard, as both consumer and total welfare falls relative to the non-exclusionary first mover equilibrium.

However, the OW standard can result in the erroneous condemnation of welfare increasing output expansions (type I error), as well as the erroneous failure to condemn welfare decreasing output expansions (type II error). Row 2 of Table 6.1 illustrates a type II error. In this case, Firm *I* excludes Firm *E*, which has higher per period fixed costs, with a commitment to produce 90 units in both periods. However, this commitment is not predatory under the OW test. Here, the incumbent's commitment to produce 90 units in both periods results in higher exclusionary profits than if Firm *E* were not excluded. Thus condition (6.5) is satisfied. However, there is no profit sacrifice associated with the commitment to produce 90 units, as the best non-exclusionary output level (88 units) results in lower profits for Firm *I*. Thus, this exclusionary level of output would not be condemned as predatory under the OW test. However, relative to an equilibrium where Firm *E* is viable, both consumer and total welfare fall.

Row 3 illustrates a type I error. In this example, Firm *I* uses an output commitment to produce 124 units in each period, which would be predatory under conditions (6.1) and (6.2). Relative to the optimal first mover payoffs where 90 units are produced in both periods, a profit sacrifice is incurred in period 1, and overall profits for Firm *I* increase. However, the output expansion from 90 to 124 units results in an increase in both consumer and total welfare. Table 6.2 summarizes the outcome of the OW test, a Consumer Welfare (CW) or Total Welfare (TW) test in each of the examples listed in Table 6.1.

Note that in all cases, the equilibrium price is above the AVC of Firm *I*, and indeed is above MC. Thus an AT cost based test would not condemn any of the examples presented here. However, one advantage of the cost based tests is that they would be easier to administer than the OW test. Consider example 1, where Firm *I* and Firm *E* have equal costs. As noted above, the correct application of the OW test would find that the output expansion to 103 units was both predatory and welfare reducing relative to a non-exclusionary level of output where Firm *I* produces 90 units in each period.

An AT cost based test would only look at current prices and their relationship to the appropriate measure of cost. The OW test would also have to measure current price, cost and output. In addition, the OW test

Table 6.2 Summary

Example	*Exclusion Profitable*	*Profit Sacrifice*	*Predatory Under OW Test*	*Consumer Welfare*	*Total Welfare*	*Price > AVCI*
1	Yes	Yes	Yes	Falls	Falls	Y
2	Yes	No	No	Falls	Falls	Y
3	Yes	Yes	Yes	Rises	Rises	Y

would require the measurement of these variables for the correct but-for equilibrium output. In practice, use of the OW test will be feasible when the correct but-for output can be observed directly from historical data, e.g., when it equalled the historical non-exclusionary equilibrium output levels. However, the but-for level of non-exclusionary output may not be readily observable. Suppose, for example that in period 0, Firms *I* and *E* are Cournot duopolists. Under the Cournot equilibrium, each firm would produce 60 units, and the market price per unit would be 40. Now suppose that Firm *I* commits to producing the exclusionary level of output (103 units) in periods 1 and 2. Relative to the period 0 Cournot equilibrium, we observe an exclusionary output expansion of 43 units, an increase in Firm *I*'s profits in both period 1 and period 2, and increases in both consumer and total welfare.[12] Thus, measured relative to the observed past output levels of Firm *I*, the erroneously applied OW test would not find the expansion to be predatory because of the absence of a profit sacrifice relative to historical output levels. Moreover, because both measured total and consumer welfare rise, the erroneously applied test apparently achieves the correct result. The problems of observing the correct but-for output level will be even more acute when antitrust regulators are faced with data from real markets in which the optimal strategies are not precisely defined.

IV Antitrust law and predation

a The courts and predation

As a matter of antitrust regulation, predatory pricing is examined under Section 2 of the Sherman Act,[13] as well as under Section 13 of the Robinson-Patman Act.[14] While predatory pricing cases were not common after the passage of the Sherman Act in 1890, the number of cases increased after the passage of the Robinson-Patman Act in 1936, with the plaintiff winning the majority of cases (Koller (1971)). Early cases often focused on harm to competitors, predatory intent, and vague notions of below-cost pricing or ruinous competition, with little concern for consumer welfare, the benefits of lower prices, or protection of vigorous competition (Areeda and Hovenkamp (2002: 276), Bolton et al. (2000: 2250)). For example, in *Utah Pie*,[15] a predation case brought under the Robinson-Patman Act, the Supreme Court held that predatory intent could be inferred from the defendant's internal memoranda or from the observation of a declining price structure. The Court did not require that the plaintiff show that the predatory scheme was likely to succeed. Nor did the Court provide any coherent basis for distinguishing predatory pricing from procompetitive price competition (Boudreaux et al. (1995)).

These shortcomings were quickly addressed by the courts after the publication of the Areeda and Turner article in 1975. The lower courts rapidly adopted an average variable cost approach to defining predation. Some courts also expanded the analysis beyond the AT cost based test to include other factors, including market structure and proof of intent (see Brodley and Hay (1981), Hurwicz and Kovacic (1982), Areeda and Hovenkamp (2002: 278–9) for a listing of cases). However, even those courts that consider these other factors overwhelmingly use price-cost comparisons as the presumptive test for predation (Areeda and Hovenkamp (2002: 279)).The vast majority of the circuit courts adopt a test where prices above average total cost are lawful, those below average variable cost are presumptively illegal, and prices between ATC and AVC are presumptively legal, although the plaintiff may rebut the presumption of legality with evidence of intent or by proving that the market had structural characteristics conducive to successful predation.[16] While the AT cost based test provided a more predictable standard for separating predation than prior rules based on intent, the rule spawned litigation over both the appropriate measure of cost to be used as the price floor and whether certain costs should be included in calculating a given price floor. For example, in circuits adopting the AVC rule, much of the litigation centered on litigants' attempts to categorize certain costs as variable versus fixed.

The lower courts' evolution to cost based rules was quickly followed by Supreme Court cases in which the Court placed heavy weight on avoiding type I errors in predatory pricing cases. In *Matsushita*, the Court dismissed claims by two US television manufacturers against a group of 21 Japanese producers of televisions. The complaint alleged the defendants conspired to raise prices in Japan in order to subsidize below-cost pricing in the US. The Court concluded that summary judgment for the defendants was appropriate, noting the speculative nature of predatory pricing schemes, the structural characteristics of the market, including the absence of barriers to entry which made successful predation unlikely, and the absence of evidence relevant to the predatory pricing conspiracy. The Court noted, citing McGee (1958, 1980), Easterbrook (1981a), and Koller (1971), that there is a 'consensus among commentators that predatory pricing schemes are rarely tried, and even more rarely successful'. Noting that these observations applied to predation by a single firm, the Court observed that this would apply *a fortiori* to a predatory pricing conspiracy of the type alleged by the plaintiffs in *Matsushita*. In addition, the Court noted the high costs of false positives, commenting that such errors 'are especially costly, because they chill the very conduct the antitrust laws are designed to protect'.[17] The Court did not find it necessary to address the price-cost issue, but in a footnote noted that there would be no antitrust injury unless the firms conspired to drive the victims out of the markets by (i) pricing below the level necessary to sell their products, or (ii) some appropriate measure of cost.

The Supreme Court's decision in *Brooke Group* further advanced a predatory pricing rule that would minimize type I errors. *Brooke Group* involved an antitrust challenge to volume discounts on generic cigarettes brought under the primary line price discrimination provision of the Robinson-Patman Act. The plaintiff filed a suit, alleging among other things, that the defendant's 'discriminatory volume rebates to wholesalers violated the Robinson-Patman Act by furthering a predatory pricing scheme designed to purge competition from the economy segment of the cigarette market'.[18] After a lengthy trial, the jury returned a verdict for the plaintiff on the primary-line Robinson-Patman claim and awarded the plaintiff $49.6 million in damages, which was trebled to $148.8 million. However, the district court judge granted the defendant's motion for judgment as a matter of law and set aside the jury verdict. The Fourth Circuit Court of Appeals affirmed. The US Supreme Court granted certiorari, and also affirmed.

In its opinion, the Court held that plaintiffs who allege predatory pricing under Section 2 of the Sherman Act or under the Robinson-Patman Act must satisfy two 'not easy to establish' requirements. First, the plaintiff must prove that the alleged predatory prices are below an appropriate measure of the defendant's costs.[19] While the Court did not specify which threshold of cost applied, it rejected 'the notion that above-cost prices that are below general market levels or the costs of a firm's competitors inflict injury to competition cognizable under the antitrust laws', and stated unequivocally that 'a plaintiff seeking to establish competitive injury resulting from a rival's low prices must prove that the prices complained of are below an appropriate measure of its rival's costs'.[20]

Second, the Court held that the plaintiff must also demonstrate that the defendant had a reasonable prospect or, under Section 2 a dangerous probability, of recouping its investment in below-cost prices. The mere fact of below-cost pricing, even if combined with the (nearly always present) theoretical possibility of recovery, was insufficient, and the Court held that a case should be summarily dismissed without proof of the likelihood of 'sustained supracompetitive pricing' and recoupment. This second requirement would allow the courts, in some cases, to screen out cases without having to perform the fact intensive and costly Areeda Turner cost test (Hemphill (2001), Boudreaux et al. (1995) and Elzinga and Mills (1984)).

Applying the two requirements to the facts of the case, the Court found that, despite evidence of anticompetitive intent and evidence that the defendant's prices net of the volume discounts were below the appropriate measure of costs, the defendant was entitled to judgment as a matter of law because the plaintiff failed to demonstrate competitive injury. The Court found that the defendant faced substantial competition from rivals, and thus stood to gain only a fraction of any potential benefits that would have resulted from a predatory episode. The Court held that the evidence in the case was 'inadequate to show that in pursuing this scheme, [the defendant] had a reasonable prospect of recovering its losses from below-cost pricing through slowing the growth of generics'.[21] The Court rejected the theoretical possibility of harm as a basis for liability, noting that '[w]hen an expert opinion is not supported by sufficient facts to validate it in the eyes of the law, or when indisputable record facts contradict or otherwise render the opinion unreasonable, it cannot support a jury's verdict'.[22]

The Court adopted this test in large part to provide an administrable test for predatory pricing that would avoid the high cost of type I errors. As the Court explained:

> Low prices benefit consumers regardless of how those prices are set, and so long as they are above predatory levels, they do not threaten competition . . . We have adhered to this principle regardless of the type of antitrust claim involved. As a general rule, the exclusionary effect of prices above a relevant measure of cost either reflects the lower cost structure of the alleged predator, and so represents competition on the merits, or is beyond the practical ability of a judicial tribunal to control without courting intolerable risks of chilling legitimate price cutting. To hold that the antitrust laws protect competitors from the loss of profits due to such price competition would, in effect, render illegal any decision by a firm to cut prices in order to increase market share. The antitrust laws require no such perverse result.[23]

The Court's skepticism of predatory pricing claims expressed in its *Brooke Group* decision quickly filtered down to the lower courts. Bolton et al. (2000), Zerbe and Mumford (1996), Denger and Herfort (1994), Hemphill (2001) and Areeda and Hovenkamp (2002) all report that plaintiff success rates, low in years just prior to the Court's *Brooke Group* decision, dropped to near zero after the Court's decision.

b Challenges to the Brooke Group rule

The Court's *Brooke Group* 'hard to satisfy' rule has limited the viability of conventional, single product predatory pricing claims. However, exclusionary pricing behavior has not gone unchallenged in the courts. Litigation continues over the appropriate measure of cost. In addition, plaintiffs have shifted from conventional predatory pricing claims to claims based on market share discounts, bundled pricing of multiple products, and predatory buying (Hovenkamp (2006)). The Supreme Court has addressed the predatory buying issue, applying the *Brooke Group* rule to this activity. However, litigation over the other three issues continues in the lower courts.

i Weyerhaeuser and predatory buying The Supreme Court recently examined a case of predatory buying in *Weyerhaeuser v. Ross-Simmons Hardwood Lumber Co.*[24] Both companies operated hardwood lumber sawmills in the Pacific Northwest and purchased alder logs, the dominant species of hardwood lumber in this geographic region, as inputs. The logs were processed into hardwood finished lumber. Weyerhaeuser had become a dominant purchaser of alder logs, acquiring approximately 65 per cent of the alder logs available in the region by 2001. Because there was not a separate market for finished alder lumber, Weyerhaeuser did not have market power in the output market, having a 3 per cent market share in a national hardwood lumber market. The plaintiff/respondent Ross-Simons shut down its mill in 2001 as a result of increasing prices of alder logs and lower prices for hardwood finished lumber. Ross-Simons sued Weyerhaeuser under Section 2 of the Sherman Act, alleging that Weyerhaeuser had engaged in predatory buying, driving up the prices of alder logs in order to exclude it from the market.

At trial, a jury found Weyerhaeuser guilty of monopolization. The district court rejected Weyerhaeuser's attempts to have the court apply the *Brooke Group* test to the case. Instead, the court instructed the jury that the standard for monopolization was if Weyerhaeuser 'purchased more logs than it needed, or paid a higher price for logs than necessary, in order to prevent [Ross-Simons] from obtaining the logs they needed at a fair price'.[25] The Ninth Circuit affirmed the verdict. It also rejected the application of the *Brooke Group* test, noting that predatory buying was analytically distinct from sell-side predatory pricing because predatory buying 'does not necessarily benefit consumers or stimulate competition in the way that predatory pricing does'.[26] As a result, the Ninth Circuit concluded that 'the concerns that led the *Brooke Group* Court to establish a high standard of liability in the predatory pricing context do not carry over to this predatory bidding context with the same force'.[27]

The Supreme Court reversed. The Court noted that predatory pricing and predatory bidding claims are analytically similar, both involving the 'deliberate use of unilateral pricing measures for anticompetitive purposes' and logically requiring 'firms to incur short-term losses on the chance that they might reap supracompetitive profits in the future'.[28] The Court also noted the procompetitive benefits of aggressive bidding for inputs, and the potential costs of a standard that restrained such competition. Specifically, the Court noted that a firm's high bidding for inputs might result from a miscalculation of its input needs, as a response to increased demand for its products, or a hedge against the risk of future increases in the price of these inputs. The Court noted that 'this sort of high bidding is essential to competition and innovation on the buy side of the market'.[29] Moreover, the acquisition of more inputs will usually increase outputs, which will be a boon to consumers.

Based on the analytical similarity, and noting that 'successful monopsony predation is probably as unlikely as successful monopoly predation', the Court held that the 'two-pronged *Brooke Group* test should apply to predatory bidding'. Specifically, a predatory bidding plaintiff must prove that the predatory bidding led to a below-cost pricing of the predator's outputs. A plaintiff must also prove that the defendant has a dangerous probability of recouping the losses incurred in bidding up input prices through the exercise of monopsony power. In adopting the *Brooke Group* test, the Court rejected the open ended standard given to the jury, a standard that Hovenkamp (2006) called 'an antitrust disaster of enormous proportions'. It also rejected use of more general tests of monopolization (Lambert (2007)). In doing so, the Court again adopted an administrable standard that would avoid type I errors. The Court held that:

> As with predatory pricing, the exclusionary effect of higher bidding that does not result in below-cost pricing 'is beyond the practical ability of a judicial tribunal to control without courting intolerable risks of chilling legitimate' procompetitive conduct. Given the multitude of procompetitive ends served by higher bidding for inputs, the risk of chilling procompetitive behavior with too lax a liability standard is as serious here as it was in *Brooke Group*. Consequently, only higher bidding that leads to below-cost pricing in the relevant output market will suffice as a basis for liability for predatory bidding.[30]

Some have criticized the Court's symmetry analysis. A proper test under the Court's symmetry analysis would compare the price paid for the logs to the derived demand for the input. Instead, the Court's test compares the price and cost of the output. Moreover, the symmetry argument requires that the welfare of input suppliers be equated to the welfare of output purchasers, versus a narrower approach based on consumer welfare that the Court seems to invoke (Werden (2007), Blair and Lopatka (2008)). Moreover, the *Weyerhaeuser* case involved only monopsony in the input market and not the danger of monopoly in the relevant output market. In cases where the latter is present, predatory bidding may result in a greater incentive to engage in predation (Blair and Lopatka (2008), Hylton (2008)). This has led some to question whether the permissive rule in *Weyerhaeuser* will or should be applied to cases involving both input market monopsony and output market monopoly. Others have noted that the permissive rule should not apply in cases where excess inputs purchased are not used to expand output, as this will not result in increased output and lower prices to consumers (Blair and Lopatka (2008)). Salop (2005) proposes a similar rule, but would also not apply the permissive *Brooke Group* standard to predatory bidding that serves to raise rivals costs.

ii Loyalty discounts, market share discounts Lower courts recently have carved out several potential exceptions to the *Brooke Group* safe harbor for above-cost pricing conduct. For example, in *Concord Boat*, the Eighth Circuit suggested that an exception to the *Brooke Group* safe harbor might be appropriate when above-cost pricing is combined with an additional element or 'plus factor'.[31] In the case of *Concord Boat*, the potential plus factor was the use of market share based discounts rather than the traditional volume discounts at issue in the *Brooke Group* case. That is, instead of discount thresholds based on absolute volume, the discount triggers in *Concord Boat* were based upon the percentage share of a buyer's total purchases of products (in this case, boat engines) purchased from the defendant Brunswick. Specifically, buyers were given a 3 per cent discount for purchasing 80 per cent or more of their engines from Brunswick, a 2 per cent discount for shares between 70 and 80 per cent, and a 1 per cent discount for shares between 60 and 70 per cent. Purchasers that met these thresholds received discounts on all units purchased from Brunswick.

While the court noted that no one had argued that the defendant's market share discounts drove its prices below costs, and that the 'the decisions of the Supreme Court in *Brooke Group* and *Matsushita* illustrate the general rule that above cost discounting is not anticompetitive', it stopped short of endorsing the defendant's argument that any pricing practice that leads to above-cost prices is *per se* lawful under the antitrust laws.[32] Despite rejecting the defendant's *per se* legality argument, the Eighth Circuit reversed a jury verdict for the plaintiff. The court noted that cases in which courts previously had explicitly rejected a rule of *per se* legality for above-cost pricing all involve bundling or tying, which 'cannot exist unless two separate product markets have been linked'.[33] Because only one product, stern drive engines, was at issue here, and because there were no allegations of tying or bundling with another product, the court chose not to depart from the *Brooke Group* rule in this case. Moreover, the court found that the plaintiff's expert testimony 'was not grounded in the economic reality of the [relevant] market, for it ignored inconvenient evidence' and should have been excluded.[34] Thus, while it did not extend the above-cost safe harbor to market share discounts, the Eighth Circuit's decision to reverse the lower court is consistent with the Court's focus in *Brooke Group* on actual market facts or realties of the marketplace rather than on hypotheticals (Kobayashi (2005)).

iii The airline cases and opportunity cost A serious challenge to the *Brooke Group* rule's above-cost safe harbor is contained in the Sixth Circuit's holding in *Spirit Airlines*.[35] The Sixth Circuit held that an expansion of capacity in response to a rival's entry might be unlawful even if the price exceeded all relevant measures of cost.[36] Citing the testimony of the plaintiff's expert witness, the court reasoned that the incumbent's optimal response based on static price theory should be to lower price and output in response to entry. Thus, the observed addition of capacity was not consistent with the maximization of short term profits by the incumbent. Moreover, the court treated the addition of capacity as separate non-price conduct and, as a result, argued that there may be grounds to depart from the *Brooke Group* safe harbor. In effect, the Court adopted a 'dynamic' test of predation similar to that proposed by Williamson (1977, discussed in Section III(b)(ii)). The Sixth Circuit's creation of a potential exception to the *Brooke Group* rule based on an expansion of capacity is a significant departure from the *Brooke Group* rule. *Spirit* did not involve multiple products that were tied or bundled, and thus does not seem to fall within the existing exceptions to the *Brooke Group* rule identified by the Eighth Circuit in *Concord Boat*. Moreover, the lowering of price and the expansion of capacity in response to entry can be consistent with a rational dynamic response to entry and does not seem to rise to the level of a sufficient plus factor that would create an economically rational reason to deviate from *Brooke Group* (see Elhauge (2003) criticizing dynamic predation tests), Areeda and Hovenkamp (2006: 312) (discussing the court's confusion on this issue)). In contrast, the Tenth Circuit in *US v. AMR Corp.*[37] applied the *Brooke Group* rule despite the Justice Department's position that the *Brooke Group* rule should not govern predatory capacity expansions (Werden (2003), Areeda and Hovenkamp (2006: 304–13)).

The recent airline cases illustrate other complications that can occur under a *Brooke Group* analysis. In both *Spirit* and *AMR*, the courts considered an 'incremental' version of the *Brooke Group* cost test. Specifically, in addition to considering a test based on whether total revenues exceeded total variable costs for all flights on a given route, the courts also considered a test that compared whether the incremental profits that resulted from the addition of capacity to certain routes exceeded the incremental costs of adding this capacity (see generally, Ordover and Willig (1981), discussed in Section III(b)(iii)). Moreover, in both of these cases the courts considered measures of opportunity cost instead of accounting based measures of cost. One of the proposed cost measures used the forgone profits that resulted from the diversion of capacity (an aircraft) from another, more profitable, route as the appropriate measure of the opportunity costs of the aircraft rather than using leasing costs or other accounting measures of cost. While the *AMR* court rejected the use of such a measure of opportunity cost, the *Spirit* court accepted forgone revenues as part of the incremental costs of expanding output (Areeda and Hovenkamp (2006: 304–11)). Areeda and Hovenkamp note that use of opportunity cost can in theory send courts on 'ill-defined fishing expeditions in search of hypothetical, more profitable investments that a firm might have made'.[38] However, they argue that this criticism does not apply to the airline cases, as the shift of capacity in these cases involves identifiable shifts of aircraft from one market to another that makes calculation of the opportunity cost of forgone revenues feasible.

The airline cases also illustrate many other complications in applying the *Brooke Group*/AT cost-based test. Incremental revenue calculations must account for the fact that many passengers in hub and spoke systems will generate revenue by flying connecting segments (Elhauge (2003)). In addition, the court in *Spirit* accepted the plaintiff's analysis that separated out leisure from business travel as separate sub-markets for purposes of the incremental price-cost calculation. But use of sub-markets requires that the courts address the difficult issue of how joint and common costs are to be allocated (see Ordover and Willig (1981), Baumol (1996) for discussion of approaches to this issue generally, Werden (2003) for a discussion of the Justice Department's approach to this issue in *AMR*). Both the attempt to allocate joint and common costs between sub-markets and the attempt to use forgone profits as a measure of opportunity costs added to the number and complexity of the issues litigated in these cases. And while these developments improve the economic analysis by considering marginal revenues and costs as well as concepts such as opportunity costs, they also reduce the benefits of the *Brooke Group* rule related to the administrability of the rule and the ability to reduce the direct costs of predatory pricing litigation.

iv Multiproduct firms and bundling Another area in which the lower courts have departed from the *Brooke Group* rule is multiproduct bundling.

As noted in Part ii of this Section above, the Eighth Circuit remarked in *Concord Boat* that the *Brooke Group* safe harbor for above-cost pricing has not been applied to pricing conduct when bundling or tying is involved. An early, pre *Brooke Group* example of this is the Third Circuit's decision in *SmithKline Corp. v. Eli Lilly & Co.*[39] In that case, the Third Circuit upheld a district court's decision that Lilly violated Section 2 of the Sherman Act by offering multiproduct bundled discounts (in the form of rebates) when selling cephalosporin antibiotics to hospitals. The district court explained its holding by noting that:

> a monopolist does not receive immunity merely because it has priced the product at issue above its average cost. For the immunity is lost when it uses a pricing scheme linking the monopolistic products (Keflin and Keflex) with another competitive product (Kefzol) to deter SmithKline from entering or effectively competing in the cephalosporin market. We should be ever mindful that the gravamen of this complaint and my holding are not that the prices which Lilly separately charges for Keflin or Keflex are unreasonable from an antitrust standpoint; the nub of this case is the linkage of these latter products in a pricing scheme to deter competition in Kefzol.[40]

The lower courts also rejected application of the *Brooke Group* above-cost safe harbor in several other cases involving bundling. However, in contrast to the outcome in *SmithKline*, the courts rejected the plaintiffs' claims in these cases, largely because the plaintiffs failed to present sufficient evidence in support of their legal and economic theories (see Kobayashi (2005) for a discussion of these cases).[41] While the lower federal courts have generally followed the Supreme Court's general focus on market realities over hypotheticals, the Third Circuit's en banc holding in *LePage's v. 3M* is a notable exception. In this case, the Third Circuit upheld a jury verdict that found 3M's use of bundled rebates violated Section 2 of the Sherman Act.[42] As was the case in *Brooke Group,* the generic competitor alleged that the brand name incumbent used pricing behavior to exclude the generic competitor from the market, in part so that the brand name incumbent could diminish the effect generic competition was having on its branded product. However, in contrast to the traditional volume discounts used by the defendant in *Brooke Group,* 3M used bundled rebates. 3M's bundled rebates gave large retailers (such as Wal-Mart, K-Mart, and Target) discounts if they purchased certain volumes of various 3M products. The size of the bundled rebates increased when retailers met volume goals across six product categories, with the largest rebates going to retailers that met the volume targets in all six categories. The use of bundled rebates was challenged by LePage's, the leading manufacturer of unbranded transparent tape. LePage's alleged that the 3M's use of bundled rebates caused retailers to drop LePage's as a supplier not because of competition on the merits, but rather because of the possibility that they might fail to qualify for the largest bundled rebates.

A jury found that 3M's practices violated Section 2 of the Sherman Act. A Third Circuit panel reversed,[43] but the Third Circuit, sitting en banc, upheld the jury's verdict on the Section 2 bundling claims. As was the case in its earlier decision in *SmithKline*, the en banc Third Circuit explicitly rejected the defendant's arguments that its bundled rebates were lawful under a modified *Brooke Group* safe harbor, because the plaintiff failed to show that any of the bundle prices were below the cost of the bundle. The Third Circuit then concluded that it was sufficient for LePage's to prove that it could not compete with 3M's bundled rebates because 'they may foreclose portions of the market to a potential competitor who does not manufacture an equally diverse group of products and who therefore cannot make a comparable offer'.[44] Although the Third Circuit suggested that 3M's bundled rebates could exclude an equally efficient competitor, it did not cite any evidence that the bundled rebates would exclude such a competitor. Thus, the Third Circuit would allow a jury to find a dominant firm liable under the antitrust laws based on *the possibility* that bundled rebates, including those that yield customers discounts, could exclude an equally efficient competitor that produces a less diverse set of products. The plaintiff would not have to show that it was an equally efficient competitor, nor would it have to prove that the bundled rebates in question would have, in fact, excluded a hypothetical equally efficient competitor.

As a result, *LePage's* generated much uncertainty over the legality of using a ubiquitous practice. The Third Circuit exposed to potential antitrust liability any firm found to possess sufficient market power that chooses to offer discounts on a bundle of products that are also sold separately by firms that sell only a subset of these products. The potential for liability will result in such firms being deterred from using bundling that would have led to reduced prices for consumers and higher welfare. Thus, this decision is likely to impose the high type I error costs that led the Court to its hard-to-satisfy *Brooke Group* rule.

The Ninth Circuit recently addressed the issue of multi product price discounts in *Cascade Health Solutions v. PeaceHealth*.[45] In that case, the Ninth Circuit vacated a jury verdict for the plaintiff, explicitly rejecting the Third Circuit's approach to bundled discounts contained in *LePage's*. In *Cascade Health Solutions,* the plaintiff, which operated a hospital that offered only primary and secondary health services, successfully argued that a contract between PeaceHealth, a firm operating hospitals that provided primary, secondary, and tertiary services, and two Preferred Provider Organizations (PPOs) contained an unlawful bundled discount.[46] The bundled discounts were held to violate Section 2 of the Sherman Act despite being solicited by the PPOs. Moreover, the two affected PPOs insured approximately 15 per cent of commercial insurance patients, and the challenged discounts covered only two of 45 plans offered by 28 commercial health insurance companies in the relevant antitrust market. In a stark example of the type of result made possible by the Third Circuit's standard-free ruling in *LePage's*, the district court instructed the jury that:

> [b]undled pricing occurs when price discounts are offered for purchasing an entire line of services exclusively from one supplier. Bundled price discounts may be anti-competitive if they are offered by a monopolist and substantially foreclose portions of the market to a competitor who does not provide an equally diverse group of service and who therefore cannot make a comparable offer.[47]

The Ninth Circuit reversed, and remanded the case, holding instead that the plaintiff must prove that the bundled discount would exclude a hypothetically equally efficient competitor (HEEC).[48] The court held that:

> the primary anticompetitive danger posed by a multi-product bundled discount is that such a discount can exclude a rival is who is equally efficient at producing the competitive product simply because the rival does not sell as many products as the bundled discounter. Thus, a plaintiff who challenges a package discount as anticompetitive must prove that, when the full amount of the discounts given by the defendant is allocated to the competitive product or products, the resulting price of the competitive product or products is below the defendant's incremental cost to produce them. This requirement ensures that the only bundled discounts condemned as exclusionary are those that would exclude an equally efficient producer of the competitive product or products.[49]

However, the HEEC or 'attribution' test does not successfully differentiate between procompetitive and anticompetitive bundled discounts, and may pose a significant risk to procompetitive behavior (Kobayashi (2007), Carlton and Waldman (2008)). Because of this, academic proponents of the HEEC test would place strict limits on the use of this test by requiring that the plaintiff prove harm to competition, a probability of recoupment and an absence of competitive substitutes for the bundle (see Lambert (2005), Areeda and Hovenkamp (2006: 322)). Because the Ninth Circuit's approach in *PeaceHealth* fails to incorporate adequate limits, including a recoupment requirement, it, like the Third Circuit's approach in *LePage's*, poses a significant risk to procompetitive behavior.

V Conclusion

Areeda and Hovenkamp (2006: 323) noted that other areas of the law of monopolization are 'in much the same position as the theory of predatory pricing was in the 1970s: no shortage of theories, but a frightening inability of courts to assess them'. In the past two decades, scholarship on the economics of predatory pricing has evolved from the relatively settled consensus in which predatory pricing was thought to be irrational, rarely tried, and even more rarely successful, to a point where much less is settled. Recent theoretical work emphasizing strategic theory has shown that predation can be rational, and empirical studies have presented evidence consistent with successful predation. In this sense, the economics of predatory pricing has moved closer to other areas of monopolization.

However, the legal response to predatory pricing, a relatively administrable and permissive rule based in part on the assumption that successful predation was rare, has remained relatively intact. While the recent economic literature may have eroded this basis for the adoption of permissive standards for predatory pricing, other reasons for adopting such a rule, based on the benefits of bright line rules that would be administrable by courts, still remain. That is, the purpose of the Supreme Court's approach to predatory pricing in *Brooke Group* is not to provide an accurate and economically sophisticated measure of profit sacrifice or to accurately gauge intent. As Areeda and Hovenkamp (2006: 324) note:

> [t]he reason these tests for predatory pricing were adopted was *not* because there is widespread consensus that above-cost pricing strategies can never be anticompetitive in the long run. Rather, it is because our measurement tools are too imprecise to evaluate such strategies without creating an intolerable risk of chilling competitive behavior.

Thus, even considering the recent advances in economic theory, it is unwise to minimize or ignore this underlying purpose of the *Brooke Group* rule, or to ignore the cautionary words of then Judge Breyer from *Barry Wright*. That is, as the *Brooke Group* tests 'seek to embody every economic complexity and qualification', the risk grows that such rules 'may well, through the vagaries of administration, prove counterproductive, undercutting the very economic ends they seek to serve'.[50]

Notes

1. Professor of Law, George Mason University School of Law, 3301 Fairfax Drive, Arlington, VA 22201, bkobayas@gmu.edu.
2. *Matsushita Electric Industrial Co. v. Zenith Radio Corp.*, 475 US 574, 589 (1986).
3. *Brooke Group Ltd. v. Brown & Williamson Tobacco Corp.*, 509 US 209, 226 (1993).
4. *Standard Oil Co. v. United States*, 221 US 1 (1911). McGee does not dispute that Standard Oil obtained a monopoly in refining. The article focuses on the absence of evidence that predatory prices were used. Indeed, McGee notes that he would have preferred that predatory pricing was used, as this would have allowed consumers to benefit from the low prices. Granitz and Klein (1996) argue that Standard Oil created market power by cartelizing the transportation of oil.
5. See Kreps, Milgrom, Roberts and Wilson (1982). Suppose the weak firm fights entry to

mimic the strong incumbent. The second entrant does not learn anything, and thus will face the same expected payoff and will enter. Thus, it cannot be optimal for the weak entrant to follow a pure strategy of fighting. Nor is accommodation a pure strategy equilibrium. If all weak incumbents accommodate entry, then the second entrant will be deterred from entering if it observes predation towards the first. Assuming predation is profitable, it will now be profitable for weak incumbents to mimic strong ones.

6. As noted by Zerbe and Mumford, both the Koller study and the Zerbe and Cooper studies 'ultimately rely on subjective interpretations' (Zerbe and Mumford (1996: 958)). In the Zerbe and Cooper article, cases were coded as a 'Success' or a 'Failure' in their table of cases (Table 3 in the article) depending upon whether 'the price cut succeeds in compromising competition' (Zerbe and Cooper (1982: 655)). Zerbe and Mumford classify the 27 cases coded as a 'success' in their original paper as cases where the predator 'was successful in raising prices, or would have been successful but for the lawsuit'. See Zerbe and Mumford (1996: 958).
7. McGee (1960) also examined ocean shipping cartels and noted the exclusionary effect of the deferred rebates.
8. See the discussion accompanying notes 2 and 3 *supra*.
9. *Barry Wright Corp. v. ITT Grinnell Corp.*, 724 F.2d 227, 234 (1st Cir. 1983). For a similar view, see Hovenkamp (2005: 47, noting that 'there is relatively little disagreement about the basic proposition that often our general judicial system is not competent to apply the economic theory necessary for identifying strategic behavior as anticompetitive. This makes the development of simple antitrust rules critical. Antitrust decision making cannot consider every complexity that the market presents.')
10. See *Matsushita*, cited in note 2, at 589.
11. *Brooke Group v. Brown & Williamson Tobacco Corp.*, 509 US 209 (1993).
12. Under a two period Cournot equilibrium, undiscounted consumer and total surplus equals 7200 and 114,000 respectively. Under the exclusionary equilibrium, two period undiscounted consumer and total welfare rises to 7658 and 12,097 respectively.
13. 15 U.S.C. §2.
14. 15 U.S.C. §13.
15. *Utah Pie Co. v Continental Baking Co.*, 386 US 685 (1967).
16. Only one circuit, the Eleventh, adopted an ATC benchmark. *See* Areeda and Hovenkamp (2002) (citing *McGahee v. Northern Propane Gas Co.*, 858 F.2d. 1487 (11th Cir. 1988)). In addition, the Ninth Circuit adopted a non-cost test for predation, but allocated the burden of proving this standard based on whether prices were above average cost. *See* Areeda and Hovenkamp (2002) (citing *William Inglis & Sons Baking Co. v. ITT Continental Baking Co*, 686 F.2d 1014 (9th Cir. 1981)).
17. *Matsushita*, 475 US at 594.
18. *Brooke Group*, 509 US at 220.
19. In *Brooke Group*, the parties agreed that the appropriate measure of costs was average variable costs.
20. *Brooke Group*, 509 US at 210.
21. *Id.* at 231.
22. *Id.* at 208.
23. *Id.* at 223, citations and internal quotations omitted.
24. *Weyerhaeuser v. Ross-Simmons Hardwood Lumber Co.*, 127 S. Ct. 1069 (2007).
25. *Id.* at 1073.
26. *Id.*
27. *Id.* at 1073–4.
28. *Id.* at 1076.
29. *Id.* at 1077.
30. *Id.* at 1078, citation omitted.
31. *Concord Boat v. Brunswick Corp.*, 207 F.3d 1039 (8th Cir. 2000).
32. *Id.* at 1061–2.
33. *Id.* at 1062.

34. *Id.* at 1056.
35. *Spirit Airlines v. Northwest Airlines, Inc.*, 431 F.3d 917 (6th Cir. 2005).
36. *Id.* at 952.
37. *US v. AMR Corp.*, 355 F.3d 1109 (10th Cir. 2003).
38. Areeda and Hovenkamp (2006: 309).
39. *SmithKline Corp. v. Eli Lilly & Co.*, 575 F.2d 1056 (3d Cir. 1978).
40. *SmithKline Corp. v. Eli Lilly & Co.*, 427 F. Supp. 1089, 1129 (E.D. Pa. 1976).
41. *See Ortho Diagnostic Systems, Inc., v. Abbott Labs*, 920 F. Supp. 455 (S.D.N.Y 1996); *Virgin Atlantic Airways, Ltd. v. British Airways plc*, 69 F. Supp. 2d 571 (S.D.N.Y 1999); *Information Resources, Inc. v. Dun & Bradstreet Corp*, 359 F. Supp. 2d. 307 (S.D.N.Y. 2004).
42. *LePage's v. 3M*, 324 F.3d 141 (3d Cir. 2003).
43. *LePage's v. 3M*, 200 F.3d 365 (3d Cir. 2002).
44. *LePage's*, 324 F.3d at 177.
45. *Cascade Health Solutions v. PeaceHealth*, 502 F.3d 895 (9th Cir. 2007).
46. *McKenzie-Willamette Hospital v. PeaceHealth*, D. Or., Case No. 02-6032-HA, 2004 WL 3168282 (2004) (denial of renewed motion for directed verdict).
47. 502 F.3d at 909.
48. *Id.* at 919.
49. *Id.*
50. *Barry Wright*, 724 F.2d at 234.

References

Adelman, M. (1966), *A&P: A Study in Price-Cost Behavior and Public Policy*, Cambridge, MA: Harvard University Press.

Areeda, P. and H. Hovenkamp (2002), *Antitrust Law*, 2nd edn, New York: Aspen Publishers.

Areeda, P. and H. Hovenkamp (2006), *Antitrust Law* (2006 Supp.), New York: Aspen Publishers.

Areeda, P. and D. Turner (1975), 'Predatory Pricing and Related Practices under Section 2 of the Sherman Act', *Harvard Law Review*, 88 (4), 697–733.

Areeda, P. and D. Turner (1978), 'Williamson on Predatory Pricing', *Yale Law Journal*, 87 (7), 1337–52.

Baumol, W. (1979), 'Quasi-Permanence of Price Reductions: A Policy for Prevention of Predatory Pricing', *Yale Law Journal*, 89 (1), 1–26.

Baumol, W. (1996), 'Predation and the Logic of the Average Variable Cost Test', *Journal of Law & Economics*, 39 (1), 49–72.

Beniot, J-P. (1984), 'Financially Constrained Entry in a Game with Incomplete Information', *RAND Journal of Economics*, 15 (4), 490–99.

Blair, R. and J. Lopatka (2008), 'Predatory Buying and the Antitrust Laws', *Utah Law Review*, 2008 (2), 415–69.

Bolton, P. and D. Scharfstein (1990), 'A Theory of Predation Based on Agency Problems in Financial Contracting', *American Economic Review*, 80 (1), 93–106.

Bolton, P., J. Brodley and M. Riordan (2000), 'Predatory Pricing: Strategic Theory and Legal Policy', *Georgetown Law Journal*, 88 (8), 2239–330.

Bolton, P., J. Brodley and M. Riordan (2001), 'Predatory Pricing: Response to Critique and Further Elaboration', *Georgetown Law Journal*, 89 (8), 2495–529.

Bork, R. (1978), *The Antitrust Paradox: A Policy at War with Itself*, New York: Basic Books.

Boudreaux, D., K. Elzinga and D. Mills (1995), 'The Supreme Court's Predation Odyssey: From Fruit Pies to Cigarettes', *Supreme Court Economic Review*, 4, 57–93.

Brodley, J. and G. Hay (1981), 'Predatory Pricing: Competing Economic Theories and the Evolution of Legal Standards', *Cornell Law Review*, 66 (4), 738–803.

Burns, M. (1986), 'Predatory Pricing and the Acquisition Cost of Competitors', *Journal of Political Economy*, 94 (2), 266–96.

Burns, M. (1989), 'New Evidence on Predatory Price Cutting', *Managerial and Decision Economics*, 10 (4), 327–30.
Cabral, L. and M. Riordan (1994), 'The Learning Curve, Market Dominance, and Predatory Pricing', *Econometrica*, 62 (5), 1115–40.
Cabral, L. and M. Riordan (1997), 'The Learning Curve, Predation, Antitrust, and Welfare', *Journal of Industrial Economics*, 45 (2), 155–69.
Carlton, D. and M. Waldman (2008), 'Safe Harbors for Quantity Discounts and Bundling', mimeo, available at: http://papers.ssrn.com/sol3/papers.cfm?abstract_id=1089202.
Crane, D. (2005), 'The Paradox of Predatory Pricing', *Cornell Law Review*, 91 (1), 1–66.
Denger, M. and J. Herfort (1994), 'Predatory Pricing Claims After *Brooke Group*', *Antitrust Law Journal*, 62 (3), 541–58.
Easley, D., R. Masson and R. Reynolds (1985), 'Preying for Time', *Journal of Industrial Economics*, 33 (4), 445–60.
Easterbrook, F. (1981a), 'Predatory Strategies and Counterstrategies', *University of Chicago Law Review*, 48 (2), 263–337.
Easterbrook, F. (1981b), 'Comments on "An Economic Definition of Predatory Product Innovation"', in S.C. Salop (ed.), *Strategy, Predation, and Antitrust Analysis*, Washington, DC: Federal Trade Commission, pp. 415–46.
Easterbrook, F.H. (1984), 'The Limits of Antitrust', *Texas L. Review*, 63 (1), 1–40.
Edlin, A. (2002), 'Stopping Above-Cost Predatory Pricing', *Yale Law Journal*, 111 (4), 941–91.
Elhauge, E. (2003), 'Why Above-Cost Price Cuts to Drive out Entrants Are Not Predatory: And the Implications for Defining Costs and Market Power', *Yale Law Journal*, 112 (4), 681–827.
Elzinga, K. (1970), 'Predatory Pricing: The Case of the Gunpowder Trust', *Journal of Law & Economics*, 13 (1), 223–40.
Elzinga, K. and D. Mills (1994), 'Trumping the Areeda-Turner Test: The Recoupment Standard in *Brooke Group*', *Antitrust Law Journal*, 62 (3), 559–84.
Evans, D. and A. J. Padilla (2005), 'Designing Antitrust Rules for Assessing Unilateral Practices: A Neo-Chicago Approach', *University of Chicago Law Review*, 72 (1) 73–98.
Fudenberg, D. and J. Tirole (1986), 'A "Signal-Jamming" Theory of Predation', *RAND Journal of Economics*, 17 (3), 366–76.
Genesove, D. and W. Mullin (2006), 'Predation and its Rate of Return: The Sugar Industry: 1887–1914', *RAND Journal of Economics*, 37 (2), 47–69.
Gomez, R., J. Goeree and C. Holt (2008), 'Predatory Pricing: Rare Like a Unicorn?', in C. Plott and V. Smith (eds), *Handbook of Experimental Economics Results*, The Netherlands: North Holland, pp. 178–84.
Granitz, E. and B. Klein (1996), 'Monopolization by "Raising Rivals' Costs": The Standard Oil Case', *Journal of Law & Economics*, 39 (1), 1–47.
Harrison, G. (1988), 'Predatory Pricing in a Multiple Market Experiment: A Note', *Journal of Economic Behavior & Organization*, 9 (4), 405–17.
Hazlett, T. (1995), 'Predation in Local Cable TV Markets', *Antitrust Bulletin*, 40, 609–44.
Hemphill, C. S. (2001), 'The Role of Recoupment in Predatory Pricing Analyses', *Stanford Law Review*, 53 (6), 1581–612.
Hovenkamp, H. (2005), *The Antitrust Enterprise: Principle and Execution*, Cambridge, MA: Harvard University Press.
Hovenkamp, H. (2006), 'The Law of Exclusionary Pricing', *Competition Policy International*, 2, 21–39.
Hurwitz, J. and W. Kovacic (1982), 'Judicial Analysis of Predation: The Emerging Trends', *Vanderbilt Law Review*, 35 (1), 63–156.
Hylton, K. (2008), 'Weyerhaeuser, Predatory Bidding, and Error Costs', *Boston University School of Law Working Paper Series*, available online at: http://ssrn.com/abstract_ID=1084106.
Isaac, R.M. and V. Smith (1985), 'In Search of Predatory Pricing', *Journal of Political Economy*, 93 (2), 320–45.

Joskow, P. and A. Klevorick (1979), 'A Framework for Analyzing Predatory Pricing Policy', *Yale Law Journal*, 89 (2), 213–70.
Jung, Y. J., J. Kagel and D. Levin (1994), 'On the Existence of Predatory Pricing: An Experimental Study of Reputation and Entry Deterrence in the Chain-Store Game', *RAND Journal of Economics*, 25 (1), 72–93.
Klevorick, A. (1993), 'The Current State of the Law and Economics of Predatory Pricing', *American Economic Review Papers and Proceedings*, 83 (2), 162–7.
Kobayashi, B. (2005), 'The Economics of Loyalty Discounts and Antitrust Law in the United States', *Competition Policy International*, 1 (2), 115–48.
Kobayashi, B. (2007), 'Challenges to the *Brooke Group* Rule: Has Modern Economics Overcome the Case for Simple Antitrust Rules to Regulate Pricing Behaviour?', *Competition & Consumer Law Journal*, 15, 156–82.
Koller, R., III (1971), 'The Myth of Predatory Pricing: An Empirical Study', *Antitrust Law & Economics Review*, 4 (4), 105–23.
Kreps, D. and R. Wilson (1982), 'Reputation and Imperfect Information', *Journal of Economic Theory*, 27 (2), 253–79.
Kreps, D., P. Milgrom, J. Roberts and R.Wilson (1982), 'Rational Cooperation in the Finitely-Repeated Prisoners' Dilemma', *Journal of Economic Theory*, 27 (2), 245–52.
Lambert, T. (2005), 'Evaluating Bundled Discounts', *Minnesota Law Review*, 89 (6), 1688–757.
Lambert, T. (2007), 'Weyerhaeuser and the Search for Antitrust's Holy Grail', *Cato Supreme Court Review*, 277–312.
Leblanc, G. (1996), 'Predatory Price Wars', *Canadian Journal of Economics*, 29, (special issue 1), S293–7.
Lerner, J. (1995), 'Pricing and Financial Resources: An Analysis of the Disk Drive Industry, 1980–88', *Review of Economics and Statistics*, 77 (4), 585–98.
Lott, J., Jr. (1990), 'Predation by Public Enterprises', *Journal of Public Economics*, 43 (2), 237–51.
Lott, J., Jr. (1995), 'Are Government or Private Enterprises More Likely to Engage in Dumping? Some International Evidence', *Managerial and Decision Economics*, 16 (3), 185–204.
Lott, J., Jr. (1999), *Are Predatory Commitments Credible? Who Should the Courts Believe?*, Chicago: University of Chicago Press.
Lott, J., Jr. and T. Opler (1996), 'Testing Whether Predatory Commitments Are Credible', *Journal of Business*, 69 (3), 339–82.
Marx, L. and G. Shaffer (1999), 'Predatory Accommodation: Below-Cost Pricing without Exclusion in Intermediate Goods Markets', *RAND Journal of Economics*, 30 (1), 22–43.
McGee, J. (1958), 'Predatory Price Cutting: The Standard Oil (N.J.) Case', *Journal of Law & Economics*, 1, 137–69.
McGee, J. (1960), 'Ocean Freight Rate Conference and the American Merchant Marine', *University of Chicago Law Review*, 27 (2), 191–314.
McGee, J. (1964), 'Government Intervention in the Spanish Sugar Industry', *Journal of Law & Economics*, 7, 121–72.
McGee, J. (1980), 'Predatory Pricing Revisited,' *Journal of Law & Economics*, 23 (2), 289–330.
Milgrom, P. and J. Roberts (1982a), 'Limit Pricing and Entry Under Incomplete Information', *Econometrica*, 50 (2), 443–59.
Milgrom, P. and J. Roberts (1982b), 'Predation, Reputation, and Entry Deterrence', *Journal of Economic Theory*, 27 (2), 280–312.
Miller, J., III and P. Pautler (1985), 'Predation: The Changing View in Economics and the Law', *Journal of Law and Economics*, 28 (2), 495–502.
Normann, H. T. (2007), 'Experimental Economics for Antitrust Law and Policy', in W. Collins (ed.), *Issues in Competition Law and Policy*, Chicago: American Bar Association.
Ordover, J. (1988), 'Predatory Pricing', in P. Newman, (ed.), *The New Palgrave Dictionary of Economics and the Law*, New York: Stockton Press, pp. 77–84.

Ordover, J. and G. Saloner (1989), 'Predation, Monopolization, and Antitrust', in R. Schmalensee and R. D. Willig, (eds), *Handbook of Industrial Organization*, Amsterdam: North-Holland, pp. 538–96.
Ordover, J. and R. Willig (1981), 'An Economic Definition of Predation: Pricing and Product Innovation', *Yale Law Journal*, 91 (1), 8–53.
Plott, C. (1989), 'An Updated Review of Industrial Organization: Applications of Experimental Methods', in R. Schmalensee and R. D. Willig, (eds), *Handbook of Industrial Organization*, Amsterdam: North-Holland, pp. 1109–76.
Podolny, J. and F. Scott Morton (1999), 'Social Status, Entry and Predation: The Case of British Shipping Cartels 1879–1929', *Journal of Industrial Economics*, 47 (1), 41–67.
Poitevin, M. (1989), 'Financial Signaling and the "Deep-Pocket" Argument', *RAND Journal of Economics*, 20 (1), 26–40.
Posner, R. (2002), *Economic Analysis of Law*, 6th Edn, New York: Aspen Publishers.
Priest, G.L. and B. Klein (1984), 'The Selection of Disputes for Litigation', *Journal of Legal Studies*, 13 (1), 215–43.
Roberts, J. (1986), 'A Signaling Model of Predatory Pricing', *Oxford Economic Papers, New Series*, 38 (supp.), 75–93.
Saloner, G. (1987), 'Predation, Mergers, and Incomplete Information', *RAND Journal of Economics*, 18 (2), 165–86.
Salop, S. (2005), 'Anticompetitive Overbuying by Power Buyers', *Antitrust Law Journal*, 72 (2), 669–715.
Salop, S. and C. Shapiro (1980), 'A Guide to Test Market Predation' (unpublished mimeo).
Sappington, D. and J. G. Sidak (2000), 'Review: Are Public Enterprises the Only Credible Predators?', *University of Chicago Law Review*, 67 (1), 271–92.
Scharfstein, D. (1984), 'A Policy to Prevent Rational Test-Market Predation', *RAND Journal of Economics*, 15 (2), 229–43.
Scheffman, D. (1981), 'Comments on "An Economic Definition of Predatory Product Innovation"', in S. C. Salop (ed.), *Strategy, Predation, and Antitrust Analysis*, Washington, DC: Federal Trade Commission, pp. 397–413.
Scherer, F. (1976), 'Predatory Pricing and the Sherman Act: A Comment', *Harvard Law Review*, 89, 869–90.
Schwartz, M. (1989), 'Investments in Oligopoly: Welfare Effects and Tests for Predation', *Oxford Economic Papers, New Series*, 41 (3), 698–719.
Scott Morton, F. (1997), 'Entry and Predation: British Shipping Cartels 1879–1929', *Journal of Economics & Management Strategy*, 6 (4), 679–724.
Selten, R. (1978), 'The Chain Store Paradox', *Theory and Decision*, 9 (2), 127–59.
Snyder, C. (1996), 'Negotiation and Renegotiation of Optimal Financial Contracts Under the Threat of Predation', *Journal of Industrial Economics*, 44 (3), 325–43.
Telser, L. (1966), 'Cutthroat Competition and the Long Purse', *Journal of Law & Economics*, 9, 259–77.
Weiman, D. and R. Levin (1994), 'Preying for Monopoly? The Case of Southern Bell Telephone Company, 1894–1912', *Journal of Political Economy*, 102 (1), 103–26.
Werden, G. (2003), 'The *American Airlines* Decision: Not with a Bang but a Whimper', US Department of Justice Antitrust Division Working Paper No. EAG 03-8, available at SSRN: http://ssrn.com/abstract=446262.
Werden, G. (2007), 'Monopsony and the Sherman Act: Consumer Welfare in a New Light', *Global Competition Policy Library Article*, available at: http://www.globalcompetitionpolicy.org/index.php?id=443&action=907.
Williamson, O. (1977), 'Predatory Pricing: A Strategic and Welfare Analysis', *Yale Law Journal*, 87 (2), 284–340.
Yamey, B. (1972), 'Predatory Price Cutting: Notes and Comments', *Journal of Law & Economics*, 15 (1), 129–42.
Zerbe, R.O. (1969), 'The American Sugar Refining Company, 1887–1914: The Story of a Monopoly', *Journal of Law and Economics*, 12 (2), 339–75.

Zerbe, R., Jr. and D. Cooper (1982), 'An Empirical and Theoretical Comparison of Alternative Predation Rules', *Texas Law Review*, 61 (4), 655–715.
Zerbe, R., Jr. and M. Mumford (1996), 'Does Predatory Pricing Exist? Economic Theory and the Courts After *Brooke Group*', *Antitrust Bulletin*, 41, 949–85.

Cases

Barry Wright Corp. v. ITT Grinnell Corp., 724 F.2d 227, 234 (1st Cir. 1983).
Brooke Group Ltd. v. Brown & Williamson Tobacco Corp., 509 US 209 (1993).
Cascade Health Solutions v. PeaceHealth, 502 F.3d 895 (9th Cir. 2007).
Concord Boat v. Brunswick Corp., 207 F.3d 1039 (8th Cir. 2000).
Information Resources, Inc. v. Dun & Bradstreet Corp, 359 F. Supp. 2d. 307 (S.D.N.Y. 2004).
LePage's v. 3M, 200 F.3d 365 (3d Cir. 2002).
LePage's v. 3M, 324 F.3d 141 (3d Cir. 2003).
Matsushita Electric Industrial Co. v. Zenith Radio Corp., 475 US 574 (1986).
McGahee v. Northern Propane Gas Co., 858 F.2d. 1487 (11th Cir. 1988).
McKenzie-Willamette Hospital v. PeaceHealth, D. Or., Case No. 02-6032-HA, 2004 WL 3168282 (2004).
Ortho Diagnostic Systems, Inc., v. Abbott Labs, 920 F. Supp. 455 (S.D.N.Y 1996).
SmithKline Corp. v. Eli Lilly & Co., 575 F.2d 1056 (3d Cir. 1978).
SmithKline Corp. v. Eli Lilly & Co., 427 F. Supp. 1089, 1129 (E.D. Pa. 1976).
Spirit Airlines v. Northwest Airlines, Inc., 431 F.3d 917 (6th Cir. 2005).
Standard Oil Co. v. United States, 221 US 1 (1911).
US v. AMR Corp., 355 F.3d 1109 (10th Cir. 2003).
Utah Pie Co. v Continental Baking Co., 386 US 685 (1967).
Virgin Atlantic Airways, Ltd. v. British Airways plc, 69 F. Supp. 2d 571 (S.D.N.Y 1999).
Weyerhaeuser v. Ross-Simmons Hardwood Lumber Co., 127 S. Ct. 1069 (2007).
William Inglis & Sons Baking Co. v. ITT Continental Baking Co, 686 F.2d 1014 (9th Cir. 1981).

Statutes

15 U.S.C. §2.
15 U.S.C. §13.

7 The essential facilities doctrine

Thomas F. Cotter[1]

Introduction

According to some courts and commentators, the essential facilities doctrine sometimes requires a monopolist to provide access to a 'facility' under the monopolist's control that is deemed necessary for effective competition. Although sometimes the facility is literally a physical facility, in principle the doctrine could apply to other types of property or inputs as well including intangibles such as intellectual property. To describe the doctrine as controversial is a gross understatement; indeed, commentary on the nature of the doctrine often bears an uncanny resemblance to theological debate. Disagreement exists on almost every key issue including whether the doctrine exists at all (thus far the US Supreme Court has professed its agnosticism); what its essential characteristics are (for example, whether the monopolist must operate in two vertically related markets and whether the antitrust plaintiff must be a potential competitor of the monopolist); and whether the doctrine performs any function that cannot just as easily be performed by other, more conventional antitrust doctrines. To paraphrase the French mathematician, Laplace, is the essential facilities doctrine a hypothesis we do not need? Is it merely a relic of a bygone era of antitrust enforcement, grounded in scholastic scruples over fair dealing and just pricing, which the enlightened rationality of Hyde Park, home of the University of Chicago, and Cambridge has since convincingly dismissed as nothing more than fuzzy-headed superstition? Does the essential facilities doctrine demand too much faith in courts' abilities to regulate prices and output or to create conditions conducive to future innovation? Conversely might the essential facilities doctrine continue to play at least an occasional role in antitrust law as some sort of *deus ex machina* or doctrine 'of the gaps' to be invoked in anomalous cases? Might it potentially play an important role – perhaps more important today than ever before – in ensuring access to the essential infrastructure (the 'ground of our competing', if you will) that underlies our technologically advanced, information-based economy? Interestingly the European Community (EC) have been much less skeptical than mainstream US courts and commentators in recognizing an essential facilities-like doctrine under the rubric of 'abuse of dominant position'. In the future, this divergence between the US and European approaches may have profound implications for global commerce although it may be too early to predict the long-run impact. God, as the Modernist architect, Mies van der Rohe, once observed, is in the details.

This chapter discusses the essential facilities doctrine principally as applied, critiqued and propounded by US and EC courts and commentators. Part I provides an overview of the doctrine in the US and the EC; it also notes the doctrine's possible applications to intellectual property and some differences between the US and EC approaches. Part II discusses the economic arguments for and against the doctrine generally and with respect to various sub-issues, such as the necessity of proving two vertically-related markets. Part III concludes.

Part I Overview

Although no US Supreme Court decision ever explicitly invoked the essential facilities doctrine, advocates of the doctrine trace its lineage to a series of Supreme Court decisions decided on other grounds that might, in the alternative, support an essential facilities rationale. This Part provides a brief overview of these cases, as well as a few lower court decisions that explicitly invoked essential facilities. It also presents a brief discussion of the parallel doctrine under EC law.

US Supreme Court decisions

A case that many observers perceive as the genesis of the essential facilities doctrine is *United States v. Terminal Railroad Association*,[2] a 1912 decision of the US Supreme Court. Fourteen railroads owned stock in the Terminal Railroad Association, a company that eventually controlled all three railroad terminal facilities leading into or out of St. Louis, Missouri. In concluding that the combination violated §§ 1 and 2 of the Sherman Act, the Supreme Court noted that the association was not independent from its shareholders which consisted exclusively of competing railroads, and that the association, in addition to operating and charging for the use of terminal facilities, also set rates for the transportation of freight into and out of St. Louis.[3] The shareholders' use of the association to fix transportation prices appeared highly suspect as a form of horizontal price fixing.[4] Much of the Court's analysis, however, focused on (1) the fact that geographical and cost considerations substantially limited the number of competing terminals that could be erected in the St. Louis area and (2) the allegedly arbitrary and discriminatory nature of the prices the association charged for transportation through St. Louis.[5] In addition, the remedy the Court ordered – that the association amend its charter to permit previously excluded rail lines from membership and cease its allegedly arbitrary and discriminatory pricing practices or else face dissolution – appears to have contemplated some ongoing supervision of the association by the courts or the Interstate Commerce Commission.[6] Thus, while *Terminal Railroad* can be viewed as a garden-variety horizontal price fixing case in some respects, advocates of an essential facilities doctrine cite much of the Court's analysis, as well as the ordered remedy, as lending support to the notion that an entity controlling access to a facility to which other firms need access in order to compete has a duty to deal with these firms on reasonable and non-discriminatory terms. For this reason, *Terminal Railroad* is often cited as the first case recognizing the essential facilities doctrine even though it involved concerted rather than unilateral conduct, unlike some of the more recent cases invoking the doctrine.[7]

Another case sometimes viewed as lending support for the essential facilities doctrine is *Associated Press v. United States*,[8] in which the Supreme Court condemned the practices of the Associated Press (AP) of permitting member newspapers to block competing newspapers from membership and requiring members to supply AP exclusively with the news each member generated. As in *Terminal Railroad*, the Court did not explicitly endorse an essential facilities doctrine. While opinions differ on the merits of the outcome the Court reached, that outcome can be interpreted in a manner consistent with standard § 1 analysis of concerted refusals to deal. AP potentially wielded considerable market power, and the restraints at issue, while perhaps necessary to some degree to prevent new entrants from free-riding on the investigatory efforts of incumbent members operating within the same geographic market, may have been much broader than was necessary to achieve any procompetitive purpose.[9] Commentators nevertheless sometimes cite this decision as consistent with an essential facilities rationale. Membership in the AP being essential to competition in some newspaper markets, so the argument goes, antitrust law rightly imposed a duty upon the AP member newspapers to deal with potential competitors on reasonable and non-discriminatory terms.[10]

The principal Supreme Court decision that might be viewed as supporting the essential facilities doctrine is *Otter Tail Power Co. v. United States*.[11] Three towns that had been purchasing electric power from Otter Tail decided to establish their own, municipally-owned utility. Otter Tail allegedly retaliated by refusing to make wholesale sales of electricity to the new entities or to transmit ('wheel') electric power from other sources to these entities using Otter Tail's own power lines. The Supreme Court held that Otter Tail's refusal to deal constituted an attempt to maintain its monopoly, in violation of Sherman Act § 2. In particular, the Court affirmed the district court's finding that 'Otter Tail's refusals to sell at wholesale or to wheel were solely to prevent municipal power systems from eroding its monopolistic position',[12] and affirmed an injunction requiring Otter Tail to sell and to wheel 'at rates which are compensatory and under terms and conditions which are filed with and subject to approval by the Federal Power Commission'.[13] As in *Terminal Railroad* and *Associated Press*, however, the Court did not purport to be creating a new doctrine and did not use the term 'essential facilities', and the fact that Otter Tail was a regulated utility might suggest only a limited need for ongoing judicial oversight of the terms of the injunction. Whether *Otter Tail* lends strong support to an essential facilities doctrine therefore remains hotly debated. Compounding the debate is the fact that *Otter Tail* was a 4 to 3 decision, authored by Justice Douglas; two justices having recused themselves from participating in the case. The opinion of dissenting Justice Stewart, while concluding principally that the Federal Power Act preempted the assertion of antitrust law under the circumstances, nevertheless strongly suggests the dissenting justices' view that Otter Tail's conduct did not violate Sherman Act standards insofar as Otter Tail had 'asserted a legitimate business interest in keeping its lines free for its own power sales and in refusing to lend a hand in its own demise'.[14]

Two more recent cases pointing in opposite directions are *Aspen Skiing Co. v. Aspen Highlands Skiing Corp.*[15] and *Verizon Communications Inc. v. Law Offices of Curtis V. Trinko, LLP.*[16] In *Aspen Skiing*, the defendant Ski Co. operated skiing facilities on three of four mountains situated near Aspen, Colorado. The plaintiff Highlands operated a facility on the fourth. The two collaborated for some time in offering 'All-Aspen' passes for use on any of the four mountains. In 1978 Ski Co. refused to participate any further in the joint venture or to sell Highlands any lift tickets for Ski Co. facilities. In affirming a jury verdict for Highlands, the Supreme Court, in an opinion by Justice Stevens, stated that while there is no general duty to deal with potential competitors, a monopolist may be liable under § 2 of the Sherman Act if it lacks a legitimate business purpose for its refusal to deal. Significantly, Ski Co. offered no such purpose that the jury was required to credit; indeed, the evidence was consistent with the theory that the defendant stood to lose money in the short run, thus bolstering the inference that it expected to recoup those losses long term by reducing Highlands's ability to compete.[17] Finally, while the Court declined to pass judgment on the 'possible relevance of the "essential facilities" doctrine',[18] a broad reading of this decision along with *Terminal Railroad* and *Associated Press* might lend support to the doctrine in other cases.

Trinko, on the other hand, casts a more skeptical eye on efforts to impose § 2 liability for unilateral refusals to deal. The 1996 Telecommunications Act required incumbent local exchange carriers (LECs), such as Verizon, to provide competing LECs with access to, and operations support for the incumbents' networks. Several competing LECs complained to the

Federal Communications Commission (FCC) and state regulators that Verizon was not filling their orders for operations support in violation of the Telecommunications Act. The FCC and state regulators ordered Verizon to comply. Trinko, a customer of one of the competing LECs, AT&T, then filed a civil action against Verizon alleging that Verizon's failure to properly fill orders as mandated by the Telecommunications Act impeded competition in the market for local telephone service in violation of Sherman Act § 2. In rejecting this theory, the Supreme Court, in an opinion by Justice Scalia, perceived several problems with imposing an antitrust-based duty to share. Among these was the risk that forced sharing may reduce ex ante incentives to innovate, require courts to regulate price and output in the manner of central planners, and encourage collusion between the monopolist and potential competitors. Characterizing *Aspen* as standing 'at or near the outer boundary of § 2 liability', the Court concluded that, unlike *Aspen* and *Otter Tail*, the present case did not involve any prior course of dealing between the monopolist and the allegedly injured competitors; indeed, the duty to share imposed by the Telecommunications Act was 'something brand new'.[19] Nor did Verizon, like Ski Co., forgo any immediate benefits from which one might infer an intent to derive longer-term profits.[20] In addition, the Court emphasized that antitrust liability in the present context might provide few benefits in light of the existing regulatory oversight, and it might give rise to substantial error and administrative costs.[21] As for the essential facilities doctrine, the Court found 'no need either to recognize it here or to repudiate it here', given that the doctrine (assuming it does exist) applies only when access is otherwise unavailable.[22] In the present context, the Telecommunications Act already mandated access, and thus a necessary element of the essential facilities doctrine would have been lacking.[23]

Lower court decisions

Notwithstanding the Supreme Court's reticence on the matter, several lower court decisions in the United States have endorsed an essential facilities doctrine though they often find one or more of the requisite elements lacking on the facts presented. Hylton cites a 1952 case, *Gamco, Inc. v. Providence Fruit & Produce Bldg., Inc.*,[24] as the first lower court decision to clearly articulate an essential facilities doctrine but notes that the doctrine remained largely dormant until the 1970s.[25] Perhaps the most frequently cited listing of the doctrine's elements today derives from the Seventh Circuit's opinion in *MCI Communications Corp. v. AT&T*. The court, affirming a judgment for the antitrust plaintiff, articulated four elements: '(1) control of the essential facility by a monopolist; (2) a competitor's inability practically or reasonably to duplicate the essential facility; (3) the denial of the use of the facility to a competitor; and (4) the feasibility of providing the facility'.[26] With respect to the first two elements, courts have stated that the facility must be 'essential' in the sense that denial of access will cause the antitrust plaintiff to incur a severe, long-lasting competitive handicap.[27] At the same time, it 'need not be indispensable; it is sufficient if duplication of the facility would be economically infeasible and if denial of its use inflicts a severe handicap on potential market entrants'.[28] According to some courts, the third element, denial, requires proof that the defendant denied access on fair and reasonable terms.[29] As for the fourth element, courts continue to cite with approval the DC Circuit's statement that 'the antitrust laws do not require that an essential facility be shared if such sharing would be impractical or would inhibit the defendant's ability to serve its customers adequately'.[30] Proof that the defendant had a legitimate business justification for refusing access will suffice to defeat the claim.[31]

Several decisions also have held that, in addition to the four elements from *MCI*, a plaintiff must prove that the monopolist uses the facility to control a vertically-related market and the plaintiff is a potential competitor in either the upstream or the downstream market. For example, in *Alaska Airlines, Inc. v. United Airlines, Inc.*, the Ninth Circuit affirmed a judgment for the defendants, stating that a facility is essential only if control of the facility by an upstream monopolist entails the power permanently to eliminate competition in a downstream market.[32] Similarly, the Federal Circuit in *Intergraphic Corp. v. Intel Corp.*, vacated a preliminary injunction in favor of the antitrust plaintiff, holding that a plaintiff asserting an essential facilities claim must prove that it is in competition with the defendant either in 'the field of the facility itself or in a vertically related market that is controlled by the facility'.[33] According to Pitofsky et al., however, a few courts, including the lower court opinion in *Aspen*, have recognized the doctrine's applicability in situations involving only one market instead of two vertically-related markets.[34] In response, Marquardt and Leddy characterize the lower court's decision in *Aspen* as an aberration and quote the Areeda/Hovenkamp treatise for the proposition that the 'doctrine concerns vertical integration – in particular, the duty of a vertically integrated monopolist to share some input in a vertically integrated market . . . with someone operating in an upstream or downstream market . . . '.[35]

EC law

Article 82 of the Treaty Establishing the European Community (formerly Article 86 of the EC Treaty) states:

> Any abuse by one or more undertakings of a dominant position within the common market or in a substantial part of it shall be prohibited as incompatible with the common market in so far as it may affect trade between Member States.
>
> Such abuse may, in particular, consist in:
>
> (a) directly or indirectly imposing unfair purchase or selling prices or other unfair trading conditions;
>
> (b) limiting production, markets or technical development to the prejudice of consumers;
>
> (c) applying dissimilar conditions to equivalent transactions with other trading parties, thereby placing them at a competitive disadvantage;
>
> (d) making the conclusion of contracts subject to acceptance by the other parties of supplementary obligations which, by their nature or according to commercial usage, have no connection with the subject of such contracts.[36]

The European Court of Justice (ECJ) first applied this Article in a manner similar to the US essential facilities doctrine in its 1974 decision in *Commercial Solvents*.[37] The defendants, an American company and its Italian subsidiary, dominated the market for aminobutanol, a raw material used in the production of another chemical, ethambutol. The subsidiary also sold and used the finished product within the EC. The ECJ affirmed the European Commission's finding that there were no other significant sources of, or practical substitutes for aminobutanol.[38] The court then affirmed the conclusion that the defendants' decision to cut off the supply of aminobutanol to a former customer who competed against the Italian subsidiary in the market for ethambutol constituted an abuse of dominant position, stating:

> [A]n undertaking being in a dominant position as regards the production of raw material and therefore able to control the supply to manufacturers of derivatives, cannot, just because it decides to start manufacturing these derivatives (in competition with its former customers) act in such a way as to eliminate their competition which in the case in question, would amount to eliminating one of the principal manufacturers of ethambutol in the common market . . . [I]t follows that an undertaking which has a dominant position in the market in raw materials and which, with the object of reserving such raw material for manufacturing its own derivatives, refuses to supply a customer, which is itself a manufacturer of these derivatives, and therefore risks eliminating all competition on the part of this customer, is abusing its dominant position within the meaning of Article 86.[39]

More recently, EC courts have begun to discuss, and sometimes to apply, the doctrine in cases in which the alleged essential facility consists of intellectual property rights (IPRs). In the first of these cases, *AB Volvo v. Erik Veng (UK) Ltd*, the plaintiff, Volvo, held a registered industrial design right in the United Kingdom for the front wing automobile body panels of its '200' series of automobiles.[40] Volvo filed suit against the defendant for importing and selling infringing panels within the UK.[41] The English High Court referred to the ECJ the question whether it is 'prima facie an abuse of such dominant position for such a manufacturer to refuse to license others to supply such body panels, even where they are willing to pay a reasonable royalty for all articles sold under the licence'.[42] The ECJ held that the mere refusal to license one's IPRs does not alone constitute an abuse of dominant position, reasoning that 'the right of the proprietor of a protected design to prevent third parties from manufacturing and selling or importing, without its consent, products incorporating the design constitutes the very subject-matter of his exclusive right'.[43] The court cautioned, however, that:

> the exercise of an exclusive right by the proprietor of a registered design in respect of car body panels may be prohibited . . . if it involves, on the part of an undertaking holding a dominant position, certain abusive conduct such as the arbitrary refusal to supply spare parts to independent repairers, the fixing of prices for spare parts at an unfair level or a decision no longer to produce spare parts for a particular model even though many cars of that model are still in circulation.[44]

None of these examples of abusive conduct, however, was present in the facts offered to the court.[45]

In a subsequent case involving IPRs, the court ruled against the IPR owners. In *RTE and ITP v. Commission (Magill II)*, television broadcasters Radio Telefis Eireann (RTE), ITV and the BBC each published weekly listings of their individual television programming, in which each claimed copyright under Irish law.[46] The Commission instituted proceedings after the broadcasters refused to license Magill TV Guide Ltd to publish a comprehensive weekly programming guide that would combine all three broadcasters' listings.[47] Affirming a judgment for the Commission, the ECJ first noted that the ownership of IPRs does not necessarily confer a dominant position, but it concluded nevertheless that the Commission proved that the three broadcasters dominated the market for television listings.[48] Second, the ECJ reiterated the holding of *Volvo* that a refusal to deal does not necessarily constitute abuse, but a refusal can constitute abuse in exceptional circumstances.[49] Third, the court affirmed the judgment that the broadcasters had abused their dominant position, reasoning that: (1) the Commission had proven indispensability, given that the broadcasters were 'the only sources of the basic information on programme scheduling which is the indispensable raw material for compiling a weekly television guide'; (2) the broadcasters' refusal to deal had 'prevented the appearance of a new product, a comprehensive weekly guide to television programmes, which the appellants did not offer and for which there was a potential consumer demand'; (3) 'there was no justification for such refusal either in the activity of television broadcasting or in that of publishing television magazines'; and (4) the broadcasters had 'reserved to themselves the secondary market of weekly television guides by excluding all competition on that market . . . since they denied access to the basic information which is the raw material indispensable for the compilation of such a guide'.[50] Commentators soon picked up on the ambiguity inherent in the decision, namely, whether all four of these last-mentioned conditions (indispensability, preventing the appearance of a new product for which there is consumer demand, lack of justification, and effects in a secondary or downstream market) need to be satisfied in cases involving IPRs or otherwise, or only some subset thereof.[51]

The next major decision to discuss the essential facilities doctrine was *Oskar Bronner GmbH v. Mediaprint*.[52] *Bronner* did not involve IPRs but a distribution service for newspapers. The plaintiff, publisher of a newspaper with a small circulation in Austria, claimed that the defendants, owners and distributors of a much larger newspaper, abused their dominant position by refusing to distribute the plaintiff's newspaper by means of the defendants' early morning home-delivery service.[53] On referral from the Austrian court, the ECJ held that Bronner failed to prove that inclusion within the defendants' distribution network was indispensable given the possibility of (1) other distribution mechanisms 'such as by post and through sale in shops and at kiosks, even though they may be less advantageous' or (2) establishing an alternative home-delivery scheme.[54] The plaintiff's small circulation did not entitle it to any greater entitlement to access than anyone else:

> in order to demonstrate that the creation of such a system is not a realistic potential alternative and that access to the existing system is therefore indispensable, it is not enough to argue that it is not economically viable by reason of the small circulation of the daily newspaper or newspapers to be distributed. For such access to be capable of being regarded as indispensable, it would be necessary at the very least to establish . . . that it is not economically viable to create a second home-delivery scheme for the distribution of daily newspapers with a circulation comparable to that of the daily newspapers distributed by the existing scheme.[55]

As Bergman notes, this criterion appears to mean that 'the doctrine is applicable if a symmetric duopoly with two vertically integrated firms is not economically viable'.[56]

The recent decision in *IMS Health GmbH v. NDC Health GmbH*[57] resolved some of the open questions surrounding abuse of dominant position. IMS and its German subsidiary marketed a database said to be useful for tracking sales of pharmaceutical products in Germany.[58] A former employee of IMS set up his own competing firm, and IMS sued that firm for infringing IMS's copyright in the database.[59] The German court referred three questions to the ECJ, among them whether Article 82 should be interpreted to mean that:

> there is abusive conduct by an undertaking with a dominant position on the market where it refuses to grant a licence agreement for the use of a databank protected by copyright to an undertaking which seeks access to the same geographical and product market if . . . potential clients . . . reject any product which does not make use of the databank protected by copyright because their set-up relies on products manufactured on the basis of that databank?[60]

In answering this question, the court attempted to resolve the ambiguity of the *Magill* decision by expressly holding that:

> in order for the refusal by an undertaking which owns a copyright to give access to a product or service indispensable for carrying on a particular business to be treated as abusive, it is sufficient that three cumulative conditions be satisfied, namely, that the refusal is preventing the emergence of a new product for which there is a potential consumer demand, that it is unjustified and such as to exclude any competition on a secondary market.[61]

Elaborating on these conditions, the court stated that in *Bronner*, 'it was relevant, in order to assess whether the refusal to grant access to a product or a service indispensable for carrying on a particular business activity was an abuse, to distinguish an upstream market . . . and a (secondary) downstream market . . .'.[62] Two markets may be separate, however, even though the dominant firm does not market the relevant products or services separately.[63] Moreover, 'it is sufficient that a potential market or even hypothetical market can be identified' and 'determinative that two different stages of production may be identified and that they are interconnected, inasmuch as the upstream product is indispensable for the supply of the downstream product'.[64] In the case at hand, the court concluded that it would be a matter for the national court to determine whether the database at issue 'constitutes, upstream, an indispensable factor in the downstream supply of German regional sales data for pharmaceutical products'.[65] The court also stated that conduct would be deemed abusive 'only where the undertaking which requested the licence does not intend to limit itself essentially to duplicating the goods or services already offered on the secondary market by the owner of the intellectual property right, but intends to produce new goods or services . . . for which there is a potential consumer demand', and it would be a matter for the national court to determine if this condition, as well as the condition relating to justification in light of objective considerations, was satisfied.[66] The court therefore concluded that a firm holding both a dominant position and an IPR in an indispensable database abuses its dominant position by refusing to license another firm when the following conditions are present: (1) the firm that 'requested the licence intends to offer, on the market for the supply of the data in question, new products or services not offered by the owner of the intellectual property right and for which there is a potential consumer demand'; (2) 'the refusal is not justified by objective considerations'; and (3) the refusal reserves to the IPR owner the secondary market by excluding all competition in that market.[67]

Even after *IMS Health*, however, several questions remain.[68] A non-IPR case reflecting a rather broad reading of Article 82 is *Attheraces Ltd v. British Horseracing Board Ltd.*[69] The plaintiff, Attheraces (ATR), supplies bookmakers with information relating to horseracing.[70] To do so, ATR must obtain pre-race data from the British Horseracing Board (BHB) concerning such matters as the name and time of the race, the names and ages of the horses and so on.[71] Relations between the parties broke down, and ATR filed suit against BHB for withholding the data in violation of Article 82 and related English law.[72] The trial court entered judgment for ATR, reasoning that abuse of dominant position may occur when a seller cuts off an existing customer or refuses to grant access to an essential facility absent a legitimate business justification.[73] Significantly, the trial court held that the essential facilities doctrine could apply even in circumstances, such as were present in the case, in which the upstream seller and the downstream purchaser are not in competition with one another in the downstream market.[74] The Court of Appeal reversed the decision but only on the ground that the evidence did not support the trial court's finding that the defendants had abused their position by demanding unfair or discriminatory prices for the pre-racing data.[75] The Court of Appeal did not disturb the legal ruling that the essential facilities doctrine may apply even when there is no actual or potential competition between the plaintiff and defendant in the downstream market. As Eagles and Longdin note, in this sense the *Attheraces* ruling appears to go farther in applying the essential facilities doctrine than any of other cases discussed above.[76]

More recently, the litigation in *Microsoft v. Commission*[77] afforded the EC Court of First Instance an opportunity to elaborate further on the essential facilities doctrine in the context of software markets. Among the issues presented in this factually complex case was whether Microsoft's alleged refusal to license 'interoperability information' to potential competitors in the market for work group server operating systems amounted to an abuse of its dominant position in the client PC operating systems market.[78] In support of its position that Microsoft violated Article 82, the European Commission argued on appeal that the criteria set forth in the preceding line of EC cases do not exhaust the meaning of 'abuse of dominant position', but rather, abuses could be found under other circumstances, including those present in the *Microsoft* case (for example, 'a refusal to disclose trade secrets that has the effect of 'technologically tying' a separate product with a dominant product').[79] The Commission also contended that Microsoft's protocols were not protected by any form of IPRs.[80] The court, proceeding on the assumption that Microsoft's information *was* protected by some form of IPRs,[81] reasoned that even under the *Magill/IMS Health* standards, Microsoft had abused its dominant position. In this regard, the court first reaffirmed that a mere refusal on the part of a dominant party to license its IPRs does not constitute an abuse, but rather that exceptional circumstances must be present.[82] The court then expounded on the meaning of 'exceptional circumstances': (1) 'the refusal relates to a product or service indispensable to the exercise of a particular activity on a neighbouring market'; (2) 'the refusal is of such a kind as to exclude any effective competition on that neighbouring market'; and (3) 'the refusal prevents the appearance of a new product for which there is potential consumer demand'.[83] Exhaustively reviewing the evidence, the court agreed that Microsoft continued to hold a dominant position in the client PC operating systems market; its interoperability information was indispensable to competition in the market for work group server operating systems; a refusal to license the information entailed risk that competition in that downstream market would be eliminated; and Microsoft had indeed refused to license the information.[84] Perhaps more significantly, the court elaborated upon the 'new product' element as follows:

> The circumstance relating to the appearance of a new product, as envisaged by Magill and IMS Health . . . cannot be the only parameter which determines whether a refusal to license an intellectual property right is capable of causing prejudice to consumers within the meaning of Article 82(b) EC. As that provision states, such prejudice may arise where there is a limitation not only of production or markets, but also of technical development. It was on that last hypothesis that the Commission based its finding in the contested decision. Thus, the Commission considered that Microsoft's refusal to supply the relevant information limited technical development to the prejudice of consumers . . . The Court finds that the Commission's findings . . . are not manifestly incorrect.[85]

Finally, the court rejected Microsoft's argument that its refusal to deal was objectively justified due to the presence of IPRs, noting that the mere presence of IPRs alone is not an objective justification, and that Microsoft had not demonstrated any impairment of its ability to innovate.[86]

Part II Scholarly commentary on the essential facilities doctrine

Scholarly commentary on the essential facilities doctrine is decidedly mixed, with some scholars disapproving of the doctrine in its entirety and others supporting it in varying degrees. An initial problem the critics highlight is that forcing a monopolist to share a facility does not necessarily ensure that consumers will be any better off absent judicial oversight of the resulting prices and output. To illustrate, Areeda and Hovenkamp use a simple example of a monopolist who owns a pipeline that delivers gas to customers; competitive price and output would be $1.00 per unit and 100 units, respectively, whereas the monopoly price and output are $1.50 and 80 units. A court order requiring the monopolist to sell 20 units to the antitrust plaintiff will not alter consumer welfare; the monopolist continues to maximize profits by selling 80 units (20 to the plaintiff, 60 to other buyers) at a price of $1.50.[87] An order requiring the monopolist to sell to the plaintiff at the competitive price would avoid this problem but would give rise to the central-planner or public-utility type of problems noted by Justice Scalia in *Trinko*.[88] Courts may not be well placed to determine competitive price, and to the extent that price may vary over time, courts would need to retain some ongoing supervisory jurisdiction.[89] In a similar vein, Hylton uses an example of a firm with exclusive access to a facility that creates a competitive advantage by reducing the cost of producing some output. Requiring the firm to share access to the facility with a competitor creates an incentive for the two to set output levels no higher than before. The result may simply be a redistribution of monopoly profits or rents between the owner of the facility and the plaintiff rather than a reduction of those profits.[90] Consumers might be better off with a non-colluding competitive fringe that inhibits the monopolist from charging a full monopoly profit.[91]

A second set of problems relates to the potential for the doctrine to give rise to perverse incentives for both the potential monopolist and the potential antitrust plaintiff. For example, suppose that a court requires a monopolist to share a facility at a price below the price the monopolist would otherwise charge for access. The forced sharing reduces deadweight loss and thus increases static efficiency but simultaneously may decrease dynamic efficiency for two reasons. First, decreasing the monopolist's profit ex post may decrease the ex ante incentive to invest in creating the facility in the first place.[92] The more uncertain the payoff from the investment is initially, the greater the risk of discouraging the investment altogether.[93] To the extent governments confer IPRs precisely to encourage such investments, the application of the essential facilities doctrine to IPRs may seem particularly dubious.[94] Perhaps courts could avoid this problem by ordering access without mandating price, but as noted above, this solution leaves the monopolist with the option of continuing to sell at the monopoly price. Alternatively, courts could order the defendant to charge a price (greater than marginal cost) that compensates for the defendant's sunk costs, but this solution only worsens the problem of entrusting courts to function like public utility regulators. A second reason that forced sharing may diminish dynamic efficiency focuses on the effect on the potential antitrust plaintiff. The prospect of obtaining access to the monopolist's facility reduces the plaintiff's incentive to invest in developing its own competing facility thus perpetuating the monopolist's control over the facility and reducing the prospect of future competition.[95] To be sure, this may not be a problem in cases in which courts strictly adhere to the requirement that the facility not be susceptible of duplication by others, but some risk remains that courts will underestimate the feasibility of duplication. Moreover, future competitors may be discouraged from undertaking construction of a facility that, while infeasible before, has become feasible, if they may instead simply access the existing facility. Indeed, one of the many unsettled aspects of the doctrine is determining exactly how onerous the duplication of the facility must be in order for the doctrine to be potentially applicable. As Bergman demonstrates, a criterion that is too strict may reduce social welfare by requiring duplication under circumstances in which the social costs of duplication, including the costs to dynamic efficiency, outweigh the social benefits; at the same time, a criterion that is too lax can pose a serious threat to dynamic efficiency under conditions of uncertainty.[96]

That said, even critics of a broad essential facilities doctrine suggest some circumstances in which the problems noted in the preceding paragraphs might be of lesser consequence or may be counterbalanced by other considerations. First, in cases in which the facility is a high fixed cost, low marginal cost undertaking (that is, it has the characteristics of a natural monopoly), application of the essential facilities doctrine might seem more reasonable than in other circumstances because duplication of the facility would be socially wasteful.[97] However, ex post application of the doctrine in this and other instances may tend to reduce the ex ante incentive to invest in the initial creation of the facility. In such a case, an ex ante competitive bidding process, competing *for* the market rather than *in* the market, may be a better solution.[98] Second, if the facility belongs to a regulated monopoly (in which case it may well be a natural monopoly), a shared access rule may prevent the monopolist from evading regulation by charging a monopoly price in a related market.[99] This is Judge Easterbrook's explanation of the result in *Otter Tail*.[100] Also, if the facility owner is already subject to some form of price regulation, a judicial decree mandating compliance with such regulation may not entail much additional ongoing supervision.[101] Similarly, if the bottleneck problem can be solved by mandating access without ongoing supervision, the case for applying the doctrine may be stronger.[102] Third, there may be other instances in which application of the essential facilities doctrine might be a second-best solution. For example, if the government grants to a firm a monopoly over some asset for which there are no good substitutes, and the prospect of new entry is bleak, applying the essential facilities doctrine may increase social welfare by reducing the short-term costs of the monopoly (though, again, only if price is thereafter regulated).[103] Given the government's initial assistance, the risk of discouraging ex ante investment may be relatively small in such a case.[104] Of course, a first-best solution might be to avoid granting the monopoly in the first place.

Alternatively, in some cases, forced access may enable competitors to survive and prosper long enough to develop their own, competing facilities in the longer term.[105] In this sense, judicious application of the essential facilities doctrine could improve, rather than diminish dynamic efficiency. Areeda and Hovenkamp nevertheless remain skeptical of this rationale for the doctrine, noting both the speculative nature of the benefit to dynamic efficiency and the difficulty of distinguishing cases in which such procompetitive benefits outweigh the potential negative impact on the monopolist's ex ante incentives.[106] Another recent study however, by Beard et al., is more sanguine, noting that, in theory, forced sharing could either reduce or increase competitors' incentive to invest in new facilities in the long run, depending upon which effect – the cost saving from substituting the monopolist's facility for building one's own versus the expected profitability from new expansion – dominates.[107] Beard et al.'s empirical analysis of the local exchange telecommunications market in the wake of the 1996 Telecommunications Act suggests that some degree of forced sharing actually increased competition by enabling new entrants to gain the foothold necessary to develop their own facilities over time.[108]

If we assume that there are at least some circumstances in which application of an essential facilities doctrine would increase social welfare, the question then becomes how to develop predictable standards for applying the doctrine in such cases and avoiding its application in others. The problem, in other words, becomes the by-now-familiar one of attempting to minimize the sum total of the costs of false positives, false negatives and administrative costs.[109] It is in this regard that we encounter much of the disarray that continues to beset the doctrine. Courts and commentators, unwilling or unable to jettison the doctrine altogether but suspecting that false positives and administrative costs attributable to the doctrine are often likely to be very high, have suggested that the doctrine should apply only when a variety of stringent criteria are met – for example, only in those bottleneck situations in which an upstream monopolist controls access to a downstream market in which the monopolist also enjoys substantial market power.[110] In such a case, the monopolist's refusal to deal may eliminate or preclude horizontal competition in either the upstream or downstream market, insofar as it forces would-be competitors to enter both markets simultaneously. If the costs of entry are high enough and the perceived costs to dynamic efficiency tolerable (or on net, negative, as the Beard et al. study suggests may sometimes be the case), judicious application of the doctrine may increase social welfare under such conditions. The only question would be whether an essential facilities doctrine is necessary to achieve this result or whether garden-variety § 2 analysis suffices.

By contrast, courts and commentators less concerned about the potential costs of false positives and administrability, or viewing the risk of false negatives as being of greater concern in some contexts, might do away with many of these restrictive conditions at least in some cases. As noted above, Pitofsky et al. argue that the essential facilities doctrine can play a role even in circumstances in which there is only one relevant product market.[111] To be sure, Pitfosky et al. argue that courts should apply the doctrine only in 'rare and exceptional circumstances',[112] but they nevertheless view the doctrine as being potentially applicable whenever a monopolist refuses to make available to a competitor a facility that is both indispensable for competition and incapable of duplication, regardless of whether the competitor is also a customer of the monopolist in some other vertically-related market.[113] So understood, the essential facilities doctrine would become a tool for challenging unilateral refusals to deal that otherwise might not be actionable under Sherman Act § 2 for whatever reason.[114] In a similar vein, Frischmann and Waller argue in a recent paper that courts should deploy the essential facilities doctrine when a monopolist refuses access to certain types of 'infrastructure', regardless of the presence or absence of a vertical relationship between the plaintiff and the monopolist.[115] Citing the 'significant positive externalities . . . that open access produces', Frischmann and Waller would employ essential facilities more readily in cases in which 'the facility in question is an input which creates such substantial downstream positive externalities that a regime of open access is socially desirable'.[116] They reason that, in such cases, the social value of open access is high but likely to be undervalued by the user's willingness to pay because of the user's inability to appropriate all of the social value flowing from the use, and that, contra Areeda and Hovenkamp, the false positive and administrability risks are manageable.[117] Furthermore, Aoki and Small argue that, in some instances, the social benefits gained from mandating access to certain facilities (such as essential medicines covered by patents) may be sufficiently high as to justify constraining the monopolist from exploiting its market power either under the essential facilities doctrine or, in the case of facilities such as essential medicines that may involve IPRs, under intellectual property rules permitting the exercise of compulsory licensing.[118] Critics of these more expansive perspectives, such as Marquardt & Leddy and Temple Lang, contend that expanding the doctrine beyond the two-market scenario poses too great a risk of judicial or regulatory abuse.[119]

Applications of the essential facilities doctrine to IPRs are particularly contentious. On one hand, the whole point of much of intellectual property law is to confer exclusive rights that may enable the exercise of monopoly power as an inducement to undertake risky investments in new inventions and works of authorship.[120] To penalize the intellectual property owner ex post for exploiting the exclusivity promised ex ante may, as discussed above, have a negative impact upon dynamic efficiency. This criticism might lead some to agree with Lipsky and Sidak that 'essential facilities principles are inherently inconsistent with intellectual property protection'[121] or with Hovenkamp, Janis and Lemley that IPR owners should be subject to antitrust liability for unilateral refusals to deal only in cases in which, *inter alia*, the owners exercised their rights or attempted to exercise those rights in a manner that goes beyond the scope of the grant (for example, to leverage the rights into control over another market).[122] Most commentators, at the very least, urge extreme caution in applying the essential facilities doctrine to IPRs.[123] Yet others, including myself, argue that although there are likely cases in which the social cost of enforcing IPRs outweighs the social benefits, it is generally preferable for courts to grant necessary relief from within intellectual property law rather than from within antitrust.[124] Potential harm to future innovation may be a cognizable category of injury under US antitrust law, and regulators may consider possible harms to 'innovation markets'. The practice nevertheless remains controversial largely because of the perceived risk that if antitrust routinely takes into account such relatively speculative harms, the risk of false positives and administrative costs would skyrocket. Intellectual property law, by contrast, has at its disposal several doctrines (such as, in copyright law, the fair use doctrine and the idea/expression dichotomy) that constrain the exercise of IPRs when the risk of anticompetitive harm, while perhaps remote, outweighs the perceived incremental risk to dynamic efficiency.[125] In this regard, it may be notable that in some of the EC decisions discussed above, the property at issue was an IPR appearing to be of questionable validity. The television listings in *Magill* and the database in *IMS* were both protected by national copyrights, but arguably neither type of work falls within the core of what most people, even IP scholars, think of when one mentions the term 'copyright'. To the extent that courts find sufficient originality in even such mundane works, the tension with competition law may be difficult to resolve. Working to achieve needed reforms from within intellectual property law nevertheless may offer benefits comparable to those promised by the essential facilities doctrine without potentially distorting antitrust law in ways that may have far-reaching, unintended consequences in other contexts.

III Conclusion

The essential facilities doctrine remains controversial, and its precise application even in fora in which it is cognizable remains subject to interpretation. Although intuition may suggest that social benefits will flow from compelling a monopolist to share its property with potential competitors or customers, these benefits may be illusory if the long-run costs to dynamic efficiency are taken into account, if courts are unable to administer the terms and conditions of forced sharing at acceptable cost, or if alternative antitrust causes of action or regulatory remedies are available. Nevertheless, some scholars advance theoretical arguments for the application of the doctrine under certain circumstances, and, at least within the EC, the doctrine now appears to be firmly rooted. The coming years will provide opportunities for courts on both sides of the Atlantic (and elsewhere) to determine just how far, if at all, they are willing to require monopolists to provide access, and just how confident they are in their abilities to strike the right balance for maximizing short- and long-run social welfare.

Notes

1. Briggs and Morgan Professor of Law, University of Minnesota Law School. I thank Philip Kitzer and Nicholas Tymoczko for research assistance.
2. 224 US 383 (1912).
3. *Id.* at 406–7.
4. Under current law, the combination at issue in *Terminal Railroad* probably would be viewed as a type of joint venture. The legality of an agreement establishing a joint venture would turn on, among other things, the venture's independence from its shareholders, whether it raises too great a risk of enabling tacit price fixing, and the like. *See, e.g., Texaco, Inc. v. Dagher*, 547 US 1 (2006); Fed. Trade Comm'n & US Dep't of Justice, Antitrust Guidelines for Collaborations Among Competitors (2000), available at http://www.ftc.gov/os/2000/04/ftcdojguidelines.pdf.
5. *See Terminal Railroad*, 224 US at 407–9 (stating that the association discriminated against lines making short hauls, or hauling freight eastward through St. Louis as opposed to East St. Louis; and that its practice of rebilling for freight headed westward from East St. Louis through St. Louis served no legitimate purpose).
6. *See* Lipsky, Jr., A.B. & J.G. Sidak (1999), 'Essential facilities', *Stanford Law Review*, 51 (1187), 1195–8.
7. *See, e.g., Hecht v. Pro-Football, Inc.*, 570 F.2d 982, 992-3 (D.C. Cir. 1977); *Int'l Audiotext Network, Inc. v. Am. Tel. & Tel. Co.*, 893 F. Supp. 1207, 1219-20 (S.D.N.Y. 1994). For criticism of the interpretation of *Terminal Railroad* as the genesis of the essential facilities doctrine, *see, e.g.*, Hylton, K.N. (1991), 'Economic rents and essential

facilities', *Brigham Young University Law Review*, 1991, 1243–84 (arguing, among other things, that there was no evidence of any actual exclusion in *Terminal Railroad*).
8. 326 US 1 (1945).
9. *Compare, e.g.*, Areeda, P. and H. Hovenkamp (2004), *Antitrust Law*, 2nd edn. 2002, New York, US: Aspen Law & Business, 3A ¶¶ 770-1, *with* McGowan, D. (2004), 'Why the First Amendment cannot dictate copyright policy', *University of Pittsburgh Law Review*, 65 (281), 281–338. *Cf. Associated Press*, 326 US at 55 (Murphy, J., dissenting) (stating that 'the District Court specifically found no evidence of monopoly or domination by the Associated Press in the collection or distribution of news, the means of transmitting the news, or the access to the original sources of the news').
10. *See Associated Press*, 326 US at 13 ('Inability to buy news from the largest news agency, or any one of its multitude of members, can have most serious effects on the publication of competitive newspapers'); *id.* at 45–6 (Roberts, J., dissenting) (decrying the majority opinion as in effect turning the Associated Press into a public utility).
11. 410 US 366 (1973).
12. *Id.* at 378.
13. *Id.* at 375.
14. *Id.* at 388 (Stewart, J., dissenting).
15. 472 US 585 (1985).
16. 540 US 398 (2004).
17. *See Aspen Skiing Co.*, 472 US at 608 ('The jury may well have concluded that Ski Co. elected to forgo these short-run benefits because it was more interested in reducing competition in the Aspen market over the long run by harming its smaller competitor.'). The short-run benefits referred to were the sales of Ski Co. lift tickets to Highlands, for resale to ski customers, and the honoring of Ski Co. passes issued by Highlands which passes were backed up by an escrow account at a local bank. *See id.*; *see also id.* at 610–11.
18. *Id.* at 611 n. 44.
19. *See Trinko*, 540 US at 410.
20. *See id.* The characterization of *Aspen* as hinging on the defendant's forgoing of immediate benefits in the expectation of attaining future returns is however subject to question. As noted above, the 'short-run benefits' the Court referred to in *Aspen* included forgone sales of Ski Co. lift tickets to Highlands – *not* short-run profits from continued sales of the four-mountain pass. *See Aspen*, 472 US at 608. In *Trinko*, the Court interpreted Ski Co.'s forgone short-run benefits as including not only these lost lift ticket sales, but also the 'voluntary (*and thus presumably profitable*) course of dealing' of the entire venture. *See Trinko*, 540 US at 409 (emphasis in original). As Lopatka and Page note, there is no explicit finding in *Aspen* that Ski Co. expected to incur short-run losses from terminating its participation in the four-mountain pass venture. *See* Lopatka, J.E. and W.H. Page (2005), 'Bargaining and monopolization: in search of the 'boundary of Section 2 liability' between *Aspen* and *Trinko*', *Antitrust Law Journal*, 73 (115), 115–52. By so interpreting *Aspen*, the Court in *Trinko* arguably has raised the bar even in a case otherwise identical to *Aspen*.
21. *See Trinko*, 540 US at 411–16.
22. *Id.* at 411.
23. *See id.* at 410-11. Other Supreme Court cases that are sometimes viewed as providing support for an essential facilities doctrine include *Lorain Journal Co. v. United States*, 342 US 143 (1951) and *United States v. Griffith*, 334 US 100 (1948).
24. 194 F.2d 484 (1st Cir. 1952).
25. *See* Hylton, *supra* note 7, at 1250. *See also* Werden, G.J. (1987), 'The law and economics of the essential facilities doctrine', *St. Louis University Law Journal*, 32 (433), 433–80.
26. 708 F.2d 1081, 1132–3 (7th Cir. 1983).
27. *See, e.g.*, *Alaska Airlines, Inc. v. United Airlines, Inc.*, 948 F.2d 536, 544 & n.11 (9th Cir. 1991); *Twin Labs., Inc. v. Weider Health & Fitness*, 900 F.2d 566, 570 (2d Cir. 1990)

(stating that 'plaintiff must show more than inconvenience, or even some economic loss; he must show that an alternative to the facility is not feasible'). Presumably, as in any case litigated under Sherman Act §2, the plaintiff must also prove that the defendant possesses market power in a properly-defined market. *See Alaska Airlines*, 948 F.2d at 545 n.12; Hovenkamp, H. et al. (2005), 'Unilateral refusals to license in the US', in Shelanski, H. and F. Lévêque (eds), *Antitrust, Patents and Copyright: EU and US Perspectives*, Cheltenham, UK and Northampton, MA, US: Edward Elgar, pp. 12–55 at 19.

28. *See Hecht v. Pro-Football, Inc.*, 570 F.2d 982, 992 (D.C. Cir. 1977); *Jamsports & Enter. LLC v. Paradama Prods., Inc.*, No. 02 C 2298, 2003 WL 1873563, at *11 (N.D. Ill. Apr. 15, 2003). To be sure, the phrase 'economically infeasible' is not exactly a model of precision. *See* Areeda and Hovencamp (2004), *supra* note 9, ¶ 773b2, at 201–2 (stating that, '[a]lthough essentiality necessarily involves vexing questions of degree, some cases are clear, and it is probably wise to confine any essential facility doctrine to the clear cases', and suggesting that only facilities that are a natural monopoly, the duplication of which would be illegal, or that have been publicly subsidized can be viewed as essential); Bergman M.A. (2005), 'When should an incumbent be obliged to share its infrastructure with an entrant under the general competition rules?', *J. Ind. Comp. & Trade*, 5(8) (rejecting extreme positions that a facility is indispensable only if it 'cannot be duplicated in a physical sense', or if '*some* firm lack[s] the resources to duplicate the facility', and citing *Hecht* with approval) (emphasis in original).
29. *See Covad Comms. Co. v. BellSouth Corp.*, 299 F.3d 1272, 1286–7 (11th Cir. 2002) (citing sources), *vacated on other grounds*, 540 US 1147 (2004); *cf. Alaska Airlines*, 948 F.2d at 545 n.13 (stating that '[w]e do not reach the question of whether at some level, charging a price may be the same as an outright refusal to deal').
30. *Hecht*, *supra* note 7, 570 F.2d at 992–3; *see also Ohio Bell Tel. Co. v. CoreComm Newco, Inc.*, 214 F. Supp. 2d 810, 818 (N.D. Ohio 2002) (citing *Hecht*).
31. *See* Areeda and Hovencamp (2004), *supra* note 9, ¶ 773e (collecting cases).
32. *Alaska Airlines*, 948 F.2d at 544; *see also* Hovenkamp et al. (2005), *supra* note 27, at 19 (stating that 'withholding an essential facility is illegal only if it has the effect of foreclosing competition in the downstream market').
33. 195 F.3d 1346, 1357 (Fed. Cir. 1999).
34. See Pitofsky, R. et al. (2002), 'The essential facilities doctrine under US law', *Antitrust Law Journal* 70, 443–62.
35. Marquardt, P.D. and M. Leddy (2003), 'The essential facilities doctrine and intellectual property rights: a response to Pitofsky, Patterson, and Hooks', *Antitrust Law Journal* 70, 847-73 (quoting Areeda and Hovenkamp (2004), *supra* note 9, ¶ 771a). Areeda and Hovenkamp also argue that *Aspen* itself can be viewed as involving two markets, one for promotion of ski services and one for the services themselves: *id.* at ¶ 772c2, at 186.
36. Treaty Establishing the European Community (Nice Consolidated Version), Art. 82, *available at* http://eur-lex.europa.eu/LexUriServ/LexUriServ.do?uri=CELEX:12002E082:EN:NOT.
37. Case 6/73, [1974] ECR 223.
38. *See id.* at ¶ 16.
39. *Id.* at ¶ 25.
40. Case 238/87, [1987] ECR 6211, ¶ 3.
41. *See id.* at ¶¶ 3, 4.
42. *Id.* at ¶ 4.
43. *Id.* at ¶ 8; *see also id.* at ¶ 11.
44. *Id.* at ¶ 9.
45. *See id.* at ¶ 10.
46. Case C 241/91, [1995] ECR I-743, ¶¶ 7–9.
47. *See id.* at ¶¶ 10–11.
48. *See id.* at ¶¶ 46–7.
49. *See id.* at ¶¶ 49–50.

50. *Id.* at ¶¶ 54–6.
51. *See, e.g.*, Turney, J. (2005), 'Defining the limits of the EU essential facilities doctrine on intellectual property rights: the primacy of securing optimal innovation', *Northwestern Journal of Technology and Intellectual Property* 1-101 ('The issue of whether the requirements in *Magill* were cumulative became one of the most vexed questions in the essential facilities doctrine').
52. Case C-7/97, [1998] ECR I-7791.
53. *See id.* at ¶ 8.
54. *See id.* at ¶¶ 41–7.
55. *Id.* at ¶¶ 45–6.
56. *See* Bergman, *supra* note 28, at 8–9.
57. Case C-418/01, [2004] ECR I-05039.
58. *See id.* at ¶¶ 4-6; *see also* Temple Lang, J. (2005), 'The application of the essential facility doctrine to intellectual property rights under European competition law', in Shelanski, H. and F. Lévêque (eds), *Antitrust, Patents and Copyright: EU and US Perspectives*, Northampton, MA: Edward Elgar, 56–84 at 69, 70 (explaining the database in greater detail).
59. *See* Case C-418/01, [2004] ECR I-05039, ¶¶ 7–10.
60. *Id.* at ¶ 17. The court noted that the question was 'based on the premiss, whose validity it is for a national court to ascertain, that the use of the [database] is indispensable in order to allow a potential competitor to have access to the market in which the undertaking which owns the right occupies a dominant position'. *Id.* at ¶ 22.
61. *Id.* at ¶ 38.
62. *Id.* at ¶ 42.
63. *See id.* at ¶ 43.
64. *Id.* at ¶¶ 44–5.
65. *Id.* at ¶¶ 46–7.
66. *Id.* at ¶¶ 49–51.
67. *Id.* at ¶ 52.
68. *See* Eagles, I. and L. Longdin (2006), 'Gambling on essential facilities: withholding data as an abuse of market power in European competition law', *New Zealand Business Law Quarterly*, 12 (395), 395–415:

    > It remains uncertain, however, even after *IMS* laid down its own five-point test, whether the criteria are necessarily exhaustive. It is also not clear whether there should be a duty to supply unless the newcomer intended to produce something new (something not offered by the owner of the essential facility for which there is potential consumer demand.) The issue is largely sidestepped in both Advocate General Tizzano's opinion and the ECJ judgment by the notion that the secondary market identified may be potential or even hypothetical, where, in the words of the ECJ, 'products or services are indispensable in order to carry out a particular business and where there is an actual demand for them on the part of undertakings which seek to carry on the business for which they are indispensable'.

69. [2007] EWCA Civ 38 (CA). While the case was pending, the ECJ ruled in a separate case that the sort of pre-race data at issue in *Attheraces* did not qualify for protection under the European Database Directive. *See id.* at ¶¶ 89–92.
70. *See id.* at ¶¶ 32–5.
71. *See id.* at ¶ 47.
72. *See id.* at ¶ 87.
73. *See id.* at ¶ 108; *see also Attheraces Ltd v. British Horseracing Bd. Ltd* [2005] EWHC 3015, ¶¶ 247–52 (Ch) (Etherton, J.).
74. *See Attheraces Ltd v. British Horseracing Bd. Ltd* [2007] EWCA Civ 38, ¶ 112 (CA); *Attheraces Ltd v. British Horseracing Bd. Ltd* [2005] EWHC 3015, ¶¶ 247–52 (Ch) (Etherton, J.).
75. *See Attheraces Ltd v. British Horseracing Bd. Ltd* [2007] EWCA Civ 38, ¶ 281 (CA).

76. *See* Eagles & Longdin (2006), *supra* note 68, at 414.
77. Case T-201/04, *available at* http://curia.europa.eu/jurisp/cgi-bin/gettext.pl?lang=en&num=79929082T19040201&doc=T&ouvert=T&seance=ARRET.
78. *See id.* at ¶¶ 36–42.
79. *See id.* at ¶¶ 107, 302–9, 313, 316–17.
80. *See id.* at ¶¶ 277, 301.
81. *See id.* at ¶ 289.
82. *See id.* at ¶ 331.
83. *Id.* at ¶ 332. The court noted that 'the circumstance that the refusal prevents the appearance of a new product for which there is potential consumer demand is found only in the case-law on the exercise of an intellectual property right', *id.* at ¶ 334, i.e., not in cases such as *Bronner*.
84. *See id.* at ¶¶ 436, 561, 620, 766, 854.
85. *Id.* at ¶¶ 647–9; *see also id.* at ¶¶ 656, 664–5.
86. *See id.* at ¶¶ 697, 711.
87. *See* Areeda & Hovenkamp (2004), *supra* note 9, ¶ 771b, at 172.
88. *See Verizon Communications Inc. v. Law Offices of Curtis V. Trinko, LLP*, 540 US 398, 408 (2004). ('Enforced sharing also requires antitrust courts to act as central planners, identifying the proper price, quantity, and other terms of dealing – a role for which they are ill suited.') The English Court of Appeal in *Attheraces* made similar observations, despite applying the doctrine in that case. *See Attheraces*, [2007] EWCA Civ 38, ¶ 7 (stating that '[t]he nature of these difficult questions suggests that the problems of gaining access to essential facilities and of legal curbs on excessive and discriminatory pricing might, when negotiations between the parties fail, be solved more satisfactorily by arbitration or by a specialist body equipped with appropriate expertise and flexible powers').
89. *See, e.g.*, Areeda and Hovenkamp (2004), *supra* note 9, at ¶ 774e; Lipsky and Sidak (1999), *supra* note 6, at 1223.
90. *See* Hylton (1991), *supra* note 7, at 1252. Of course, such collusion itself is unlawful if express, but tacit agreements to collude are not necessarily illegal and can be difficult to detect. A variation on points one and two is that a successive monopoly is worse than a unitary monopoly; forced sharing, however, may facilitate the former. *See Fishman v. Estate of Wirtz*, 807 F.2d 520, 563 (7th Cir. 1986) (Easterbrook, J., dissenting).
91. *See* Hylton (1991), *supra* note 7, at 1253.
92. *See, e.g.*, Areeda and Hovenkamp (2004), *supra* note 9, ¶ 773a, at 198; Bergman, *supra* note 28, at 19–20.
93. *See* Bergman (2005), *supra* note 28, at 19–20, 22.
94. *See id.* at 22; Lipsky & Sidak (1999), *supra* note 6, at 1219; Temple Lang, *supra* note 58, at 66–7.
95. *See* Areeda and Hovenkamp (2004), *supra* note 9, ¶ 771b, at 172–3.
96. *See* Bergman (2005), *supra* note 28, at 22.
97. *See* Areeda and Hovenkamp (2004), *supra* note 9, ¶ 771c, at 173.
98. *See Fishman v. Estate of Wirtz*, *supra* note 90, at 572–3; Hylton (1991), *supra* note 7, at 1267–77.
99. *See* Areeda and Hovenkamp (2004), *supra* note 9, ¶ 771c, at 173.
100. *See Fishman v. Estate of Wirtz*, *supra* note 90, at 571–4.
101. *See* Hylton (1991), *supra* note 7, at 1275 and n.110.
102. *See* Areeda and Hovenkamp (2004), *supra* note 9, ¶ 773a, at 198 (stating that '[p]racticable remedies may be available when divestiture is appropriate, when a regulatory agency exists to control prices, or when nondiscriminatory dealing will solve the problem').
103. *See* Hylton (1991), *supra* note 7, at 1244, 1247, 1262-6, 1283 and n.130 (arguing that, by reducing the returns from investing in acquiring economically unjustifiable government-granted monopolies, such as some patents or copyrights, the essential facilities doctrine may increase social welfare). Of course, the problem, as Hylton notes, is whether courts can distinguish anticompetitive from procompetitive investments. *See id.* at 1263.

104. *See* Bergman (2005), *supra* note 28, at 22 (noting that the essential facilities doctrine may be easier to justify where the owner of the facility is or was initially a state-owned enterprise less subject to the risks of the marketplace).
105. *See* Areeda and Hovenkamp (2004), *supra* note 9, ¶ 771c, at 174.
106. *See id.* ¶ 771c, at 174; ¶ 773a, at 198. *See also* Hylton (1991), *supra* note 7, at 1279–80 (noting that requiring the AP to open its membership to newspapers that competed with existing members might have reduced the potential for collusion by eliminating the risk that a local paper might waive its right to block another local paper's membership in exchange for an agreement to fix prices, but that this risk must be balanced against the potential harm to incentives due to free-riding); McGowan (2004), *supra* note 9, at 309–13 (arguing that the result in *AP* may have contributed to the demise of competitors of AP such as UPI).
107. *See* Beard, T. R. et al. (2005), 'Mandated access and the make-or-buy decision: the case of local telecommunications competition', *Quarterly Review of Economics and Finance*, 45, 28–47.
108. *See id.*
109. *See* Beckner III, F.C. and S.C. Salop (1999), 'Decision theory and antitrust rules', *Antitrust Law Journal*, 67, 41–76; Lopatka, J.E. and W.H. Page (2001), 'Monopolization, innovation, and consumer welfare', *George Washington Law Review* 69, 367–424.
110. *See* Areeda and Hovenkamp (2004), *supra* note 9, at ¶ 771a; *Fishman v. Estate of Wirtz*, *supra* note 90 at 571-3.
111. *See* Pitofsky et al. (2002), *supra* note 34, at 458–61.
112. *Id.* at 461.
113. *See id.* at 458–61. Marquardt and Leddy hotly contest this understanding of the doctrine, arguing that, contrary to Pitofsky et al., 'courts have clearly distinguished between cases in which an incumbent exploits its legitimate competitive advantages over direct rivals in the same market and those in which the incumbent tries to leverage its advantages in one market into an adjacent market', and that '[b]y omitting the leveraging element of the essential facilities doctrine, the authors have radically expanded its scope . . .' Marquardt and Leddy (2003), *supra* note 35, at 848.
114. As noted in the text above accompanying notes 69–76, the English court's decision in *Attheraces* follows a different variation. While deferring to EC case law appearing to require the existence of two markets, the court held that the plaintiff need not prove that the monopolist competes in the second (downstream) market. Instead, the court held the plaintiff must prove only that access to the facility in question is necessary for the plaintiff to compete in that downstream market, and not capable of duplication. Text accompanying notes 69–76.
115. Frischmann, B. and S.W. Waller, 'Essential facilities, infrastructure, and open access', available at http://ssrn.com/abstract=942074. Frischmann and Waller define infrastructure as including not only such things as 'bridges, highways, ports, electrical power grids, and telephone networks', but also 'ideas, the Internet, and other assets which are vital inputs to the production of wealth at later stages of production on a basis disproportionate from their actual use'. *Id.* at 4–5.
116. *Id.* at 5, 27–8.
117. *See id.* at 35–40.
118. *See* Aoki, R. and J. Small (2004), 'Compulsory licensing of technology and the essential facilities doctrine', *Information, Economics, and Policy*, 16, 13–29. Aoki and Small focus most of their analysis, however, on the more conventional application of the essential facilities doctrine, to cases in which the owner 'is able to extend its power over the input market to another market', and like many of the other scholars noted above they caution that 'the threshold tests for compulsory licensing should be sufficiently high to ensure that the resulting static gains are large enough to outweigh . . . dynamic losses'.
119. *See* Marquardt and Leddy (2003), *supra* note 35, at 849–59; Temple Lang, *supra* note 58, at 72–3.
120. Most IPRs, of course, do not result in the owner being able to exercise market power.

Relatively few patents or copyrights are ever embodied in marketable products, let alone marketable products for which close substitutes are so scarce as to enable the owner to exercise power over price and output. Given this reality, some scholars find it puzzling that the prospect of gaining market power through investing in invention or authorship would ever motivate anyone to invent or publish. *See* Scherer, F.M. (2001), 'The innovation lottery', in R.C. Dreyfuss et al. (eds), *Expanding the Boundaries of Intellectual Property: Innovation Policy for the Knowledge Society*, Oxford and New York: Oxford University Press, 3, 19–21.

121. Lipsky & Sidak (1999), *supra* note 6, at 1219.
122. *See* Hovenkamp et al. (2005), *supra* note 27, at 35.
123. *See, e.g.*, Temple Lang (2005), *supra* note 58, at 66–7; *but see* Ritter, C. (2005), 'Refusal to deal and 'essential facilities': does intellectual property require special deference compared to tangible property?', *World Comp.* 28 (arguing that proponents of according IPRs special deference, including Lipsky & Sidak, Lang and myself, have failed to provide any hard evidence in support of our assertions).
124. *See* Cotter, T.F. (1999), 'Intellectual property and the essential facilities doctrine', *Antitrust Bulletin*, 44; Cotter, T.F. (2006), 'Evaluating the pro- and anticompetitive effects of intellectual property protection' (review of Shelanski and Lévêque, *supra* note 27), antitrustsource.com.
125. *See* Cotter, T.F. (2006), 'The procompetitive interest in intellectual property law', *William and Mary Law Review*, 48, 483-557. There is no counterpart to the fair use doctrine in patent law, though perhaps there should be, *see* O'Rourke, M.A. (2000), 'Toward a doctrine of fair use in patent law', *Columbia Law Review*, 100, 1177–249. The exercise of patent law rights can be constrained in part, however, by restrictions on patent scope, *see* Aoki & Small (2004), *supra* note 118, and (in some countries, in some rare circumstances) by compulsory licensing for matters of national emergency or by other exceptions to patent rights.

References

Aoki, R. and J. Small (2004), 'Compulsory licensing of technology and the essential facilities doctrine', *Information, Economics, and Policy*, 16, 13–29.

Areeda, P. and H. Hovenkamp (2004), *Antitrust Law*, 2nd edn, 2002, New York: Aspen Law & Business.

Beard, T. R. et al. (2005), 'Mandated access and the make-or-buy decision: the case of local telecommunications competition', *Quarterly Review of Economics and Finance*, 45, 28–47.

Beckner III, F.C. and S.C. Salop (1999), 'Decision theory and antitrust rules', *Antitrust Law Journal*, 67, 41–76.

Bergman, M.A. (2005), 'When should an incumbent be obliged to share its infrastructure with an entrant under the general competition rules?', *J. Ind. Comp. & Trade*, 5, 5–26.

Cotter, T.F. (1999), 'Intellectual property and the essential facilities doctrine', *Antitrust Bulletin*, 44, 211–50.

Cotter, T.F. (2006), 'Evaluating the pro- and anticompetitive effects of intellectual property protection' (review of Shelanksi and Lévêque, *supra* note 27), antitrustsource.com.

Cotter, T.F. (2006), 'The procompetitive interest in intellectual property law', *William and Mary Law Review*, 48, 483–557.

Eagles, I. and L. Longdin (2006), 'Gambling on essential facilities: withholding data as an abuse of market power in European competition law', *New Zealand Business Law Quarterly*, 12, 395, 395–415.

Federal Trade Commission and US Department of Justice (2000), 'Antitrust guidelines for collaboration among competitors', available at http://www.ftc.gov/os/2000/04/ftc-dojguidelines.pdf.

Frischmann, B. and S.W. Waller, 'Essential facilities, infrastructure, and open access', available at http://ssrn.com/abstract=942074.

Hovenkamp, H. et al. (2005), 'Unilateral refusals to license in the US', in H. Shelanski and F.

Lévêque (eds), *Antitrust, Patents and Copyright: EU and US Perspectives*, Cheltenham and Northampton, MA: Edward Elgar, 19, 12–55.
Hylton, K.N. (1991), 'Economic rents and essential facilities', *Brigham Young University Law Review*, 1991, 1243–84.
Lipsky, Jr., A.B. and J.G. Sidak (1999), 'Essential facilities', *Stanford Law Review*, 51, 1195–8, 1187–248.
Lopatka, J.E. and W.H. Page (2001), 'Monopolization, innovation, and consumer welfare', *George Washington Law Review*, 69, 367–424.
Lopatka, J.E. and W.H. Page (2005), 'Bargaining and monopolization: in search of the "boundary of Section 2 liability" between *Aspen* and *Trinko*', *Antitrust Law Journal*, 73 (115), 115–52.
McGowan, D. (2004), 'Why the First Amendment cannot dictate copyright policy', *University of Pittsburgh Law Review*, 65, 281–338.
Marquardt, P.D. and M. Leddy (2003), 'The essential facilities doctrine and intellectual property rights: a response to Pitofsky, Patterson, and Hooks', *Antitrust Law Journal* 70, 847, 847–73.
O'Rourke, M.A. (2000), 'Toward a doctrine of fair use in patent law', *Columbia Law Review*, 100, 1177–249.
Pitofsky, R. et al. (2002), 'The essential facilities doctrine under US law', *Antitrust Law Journal* 70, 443, 443–62.
Ritter, C. (2005), 'Refusal to deal and "essential facilities": does intellectual property require special deference compared to tangible property?', *World Comp.* 28, 281–98.
Scherer, F.M. (2001), 'The innovation lottery', in R.C. Dreyfuss et al. (eds), *Expanding the Boundaries of Intellectual Property: Innovation Policy for the Knowledge Society*, Oxford and New York: Oxford University Press, 3, 19–21.
Temple Lang, J. (2005), 'The application of the essential facility doctrine to intellectual property rights under European competition law' in Shelanski, H. and F. Lévêque (eds), *Antitrust, Patents and Copyright: EU and US Perspectives*, Cheltenham and Northampton, MA: Edward Elgar, 56–84.
Treaty Establishing the European Community (Nice Consolidated Version), Art. 82, *available at* http://eur-lex.europa.eu/LexUriServ/LexUriServ.do?uri=CELEX:12002E082:EN:NOT.
Turney, J. (2005), 'Defining the limits of the EU essential facilities doctrine on intellectual property rights: the primacy of securing optimal innovation', *Northwestern Journal of Technology and Intellectual Property*, 3, 179–202.
Werden, G.J. (1987), 'The law and economics of the essential facilities doctrine', *St. Louis University Law Journal*, 32, 433–80.

Cases

AB Volvo v. Erik Veng (UK) Ltd, Case 238/87, [1987] ECR 6211.
Alaska Airlines, Inc. v. United Airlines, Inc., 948 F.2d 536 (9th Cir. 1991).
Aspen Skiing Co. v. Aspen Highlands Skiing Corp., 472 US 585 (1985).
Associated Press v. United States, 326 US 1 (1945).
Attheraces Ltd v. British Horseracing Board Ltd [2007] EWCA Civ 38 (CA).
Attheraces Ltd v. British Horseracing Board Ltd [2005] EWHC 3015.
Commercial Solvents, Case 6/73, [1974] ECR 223.
Fishman v. Estate of Wirtz, 807 F.2d 520 (7th Cir. 1986).
Gamco, Inc. v. Providence Fruit & Produce Bldg., Inc., 194 F.2d 484 (1st Cir. 1952).
Hecht v. Pro-Football, Inc., 570 F.2d 982 (D.C. Cir. 1977).
IMS Health GmbH v. NDC Health GmbH, Case C-418/01, [2004] ECR I-05039.
Intergraphic Corp. v. Intel Corp., 195 F.3d 1346 (Fed. Cir. 1999).
Int'l Audiotext Network, Inc. v. Am. Tel. & Tel. Co., 893 F. Supp. 1207 (S.D.N.Y. 1994).
Lorain Journal Co. v. United States, 342 US 143 (1951).
MCI Communications Corp. v. AT&T, 708 F.2d 1081 (7th Cir. 1983).

Microsoft v. Commission, Case T-201/04.
Oskar Bronner GmbH v. Mediaprint, Case C-7/97, [1998] ECR I-7791.
Otter Tail Power Co. v. United States, 410 US 366 (1973).
RTE and ITP v. Commission (Magill II), Case C 241/91, [1995] ECR I-743.
Texaco, Inc. v. Dagher, 547 US 1 (2006).
Twin Labs., Inc. v. Weider Health & Fitness, 900 F.2d 566 (2d Cir. 1990).
United States v. Griffith, 334 US 100 (1948).
United States v. Terminal Railroad Association, 224 US 383 (1912).
Verizon Communications Inc. v. Law Offices of Curtis V. Trinko, LLP, 540 US 398 (2004).

8 Antitrust analysis of tying arrangements and exclusive dealing

*Alden F. Abbott and Joshua D. Wright**

I Introduction

Identifying exclusionary conduct is one of the most controversial tasks in antitrust. As evidenced by the Federal Trade Commission and Department of Justice Joint Hearings on Single Firm Conduct, antitrust jurisprudence is still in the process of identifying what conduct a firm with market power can engage in without creating the risk of antitrust liability. Two areas of significant concern involving potentially exclusionary conduct are tying (and bundling) and exclusive dealing. Both tying and exclusive dealing can potentially harm competition and generate anticompetitive effects under certain conditions that may be difficult to identify in practice. Further, both tying and exclusive dealing contracts are prevalent in markets without significant antitrust market power and have a number of procompetitive uses. The key question for antitrust policy is how to design optimal rules when the costs of false positives (finding liability for an efficient practice) significantly outweigh the costs of false negatives (failing to condemn an anticompetitive practice).

In this chapter, we consider the legal framework applied to tying, bundling and exclusive dealing arrangements and survey the relevant economic literature.

II Tying and bundling arrangements

A tying arrangement occurs when, through a contractual or technological requirement, a seller conditions the sale or lease of one product or service on the customer's agreement to take a second product or service.[1] The term 'tying' is most often used by economists when the proportion in which the customer purchases the two products is not fixed or specified at the time of purchase, as in a 'requirements tie-in' sale.[2] A bundled sale typically refers to a sale in which the products are sold only in fixed proportions (for example, one automobile and one radio; one pair of shoes and one pair of shoe laces; or a newspaper, which can be viewed as a bundle of topic-specific sections such as sports, national news, local news and entertainment). Bundling may also be referred to as a 'package tie-in'.[3] Case law in the US sometimes uses the terms 'tying' and 'bundling' interchangeably.[4]

A Legal analyses of tying and bundling

American law's treatment of tying has undergone a major transformation. At first tying was treated as an inherently anticompetitive, *per se* unlawful practice.[5] In 1947, in *International Salt Co. v. United States*, the Supreme Court stated that 'it is unreasonable, per se, to foreclose competitors from any substantial market'.[6] Then in 1949, in *Standard Oil Co. v. United States*, the Court opined that '[t]ying agreements serve hardly any purpose beyond the suppression of competition'.[7]

Since that time, however, although US courts have continued to state that tying is *per se* unlawful,[8] they have allowed many tying arrangements to escape automatic condemnation by establishing conditions that must be met before the *per se* category applies. Beginning with its landmark "*Fortner II*" decision in 1977,[9] the Supreme Court began to require substantial proof of market power in the tying product before the *per se* rule would be applied. Although the Court's 1984 *Jefferson Parish* majority opinion continued to give lip service to a *per se* analysis[10] – while reemphasizing that market power in the tying product was a requirement for *per se* illegality[11] – four of the nine Justices issued a separate opinion supporting application of a case-by-case rule of reason to tying.[12] Later that same year, the Court explained that the application of the *per se* rule to tying had evolved to incorporate a market analysis:

> [T]here is often no bright line separating *per se* from Rule of Reason analysis. *Per se* rules may require considerable inquiry into market conditions before the evidence justifies a presumption of anticompetitive conduct. For example, while the Court has spoken of a '*per se*' rule against tying arrangements, it has also recognized that tying may have procompetitive justifications that make it inappropriate to condemn without considerable market analysis.[13]

Consistent with this approach, the Supreme Court recently acknowledged that, in contrast to its 'historical distrust of tying arrangements',[14] there are '[m]any tying arrangements . . . [that] are fully consistent with a free, competitive market'.[15] Indeed, the test that lower courts use to determine whether to apply the *per se* rule to a particular alleged tie 'increasingly resembles a rule of reason inquiry'.[16] Although the elements of a *per se* tying violation have been articulated differently, courts generally require that:

> (1) two separate products or services are involved, (2) the sale or agreement to sell one is conditioned on the purchase of the other, (3) the seller has sufficient economic power in the market for the tying product to enable it to restrain trade in the market for the tied product, and (4) a not insubstantial amount of interstate commerce in the tied product is affected.[17]

For other *per se* violations, such as naked agreements to fix prices, plaintiffs are not required to define the relevant product markets or show that the defendant has market power in the tying product's market. In addition, some courts have shown a willingness to consider business justifications for the alleged tie,[18] and some courts have required proof that the tie has anticompetitive effects.[19]

The limited scope and shaky underpinnings of the *per se* rule against tying were dramatically underscored in the US Court of Appeals for the DC Circuit's landmark 2001 decision in *United States v. Microsoft Corp.*[20] That decision refused to apply the *per se* rule to 'platform software',[21] thereby creating a 'technology exception' to that rule.[22] The court reasoned that application of traditional *per se* analysis in the 'pervasively innovative' platform software industry risks condemning ties that may be welfare-enhancing and procompetitive.[23] Certain leading antitrust commentators have opined that 'the rationale [that the court] articulated for abandoning *per se* condemnation applies well beyond just the software industry', notwithstanding 'the court's protestations to the contrary'.[24]

Courts have sometimes analyzed bundling under the rubric of tying. In *United States v. Loew's, Inc.*,[25] for example, the Supreme Court found the practice of licensing feature films to television stations only in blocks (or 'bundles') containing films the stations did not want to license constituted unlawful tying in violation of Section 1 of the Sherman Act.[26] Nonetheless, in explaining its tying analysis in *Jefferson Parish*, the Supreme Court noted the fact that 'a purchaser is "forced" to buy a product he would not have otherwise bought even from another seller' does not imply an 'adverse impact on competition'.[27] This later statement suggests that bundling would not constitute unlawful tying if the purchaser simply desires to purchase less than the entire bundle of products offered for package sale at a reduced price. Rather, to prevail on an unlawful tying claim, the plaintiff would have to show an exclusionary effect on other sellers as a result of the plaintiff's thwarted desire to purchase substitutes for one or more items in the bundle from other sources.

More recently, courts have examined bundling in the context of loyalty discounts. For example, in *LePage's, Inc. v. 3M*,[28] the defendant 3M offered a 'bundled discount' on its Scotch brand tape and a variety of other products, provided the retailer met a target for purchases of private label tape from 3M as well. The en banc court affirmed the trial court's denial of judgment for defendant as a matter of law.[29] The Antitrust Modernization Committee sharply criticized *LePage's* on the grounds that it offered 'no clear standards by which firms can assess whether their bundled rebates are likely to pass antitrust muster' and is 'likely to discourage firms from offering procompetitive bundled discounts and rebates to consumers'.[30]

The Antitrust Modernization Committee proposed an alternative, three pronged standard which would require the plaintiff to demonstrate the following in order to establish a violation of Section 2 in addition to the conventional requirements: (1) after allocating all discounts and rebates attributable to the entire bundle of products to the competitive product, the defendant sold the competitive product below its incremental cost for the competitive product; (2) the defendant is likely to recoup these short-term losses; and (3) the bundled discount or rebate program has had or is likely to have an adverse effect on competition.[31]

Consistent with the evolution in legal thinking by the courts, the US federal antitrust agencies (the Department of Justice and Federal Trade Commission) in effect endorsed a structured rule of reason for intellectual property tying and bundling in the 1995 Antitrust Guidelines for the Licensing of Intellectual Property ('Antitrust-IP Guidelines').[32] The Antitrust-IP Guidelines recognize that '[c]onditioning the ability of a licensee to license one or more items of intellectual property on the licensee's purchase of another item of intellectual property or a good or a service has been held in some cases to constitute illegal tying',[33] but also state that '[a]lthough tying arrangements may result in anticompetitive effects, such arrangements can . . . result in significant efficiencies and procompetitive benefits'.[34] Pursuant to the Antitrust-IP Guidelines, the agencies consider both the anticompetitive effects and the efficiencies attributable to a tie, and would be likely to challenge a tying arrangement if: '(1) the seller has market power in the tying product', which the agencies will not presume necessarily to be conferred by a patent, copyright, or trade secret; '(2) the arrangement has an adverse effect on competition in the relevant market for the tied product; and (3) efficiency justifications for the arrangement do not outweigh the anticompetitive effects'.[35] If a package license constitutes tying,[36] the Agencies will evaluate it pursuant to the same rule of reason principles they use to analyze other tying arrangements.

In sum, US courts and federal antitrust enforcement agencies increasingly focus on the actual economic effects of particular tying and bundling arrangements in assessing their legality. The ostensible *per se* prohibition on tying remains applicable only under a limited set of conditions. There is good reason to believe that the Supreme Court will formally reject the *per se* rule and hold that the antitrust rule of reason applies to tying and bundling, if and when presented with the opportunity to do so.[37]

B Economic analysis of tying and bundling

The shift by courts and enforcers toward a more detailed fact-specific market analysis of tying and bundling arrangements is consistent with the economics literature. That literature suggests that the potential for anticompetitive harms may vary based on surrounding circumstances and that tying and bundling will often generate efficiencies. Whether tying and bundling increase or decrease consumer welfare will depend on the circumstances accompanying their use.[38] Nevertheless, many economists believe that, in general, tying and bundling are much more likely to be procompetitive than anticompetitive.[39]

1 Theories of competitive harm The early economics literature on tying identified two reasons to question whether tying and bundling are likely, as a general matter, to be useful tools for leveraging monopoly power in one market into monopoly power in a second market. First:

> tying rarely gives the producer of the tying product a monopoly position in the market for the tied product . . . A new entrant would have no difficulty in procuring in the open market the requisite cards or ink or salt to supply together with its business machines, duplicating equipment, or salt machinery.[40]

Second, a firm with a monopoly in the tying product may be unable to increase its profits by seeking to collect rents from a complementary product. Under the 'one monopoly profit argument', if the same consumers are buying both products in fixed proportions, it is the *total* price that determines consumer sales and the monopolist's pricing decisions. Consequently, a monopolist would have to lower the price on the tying product to keep the total price unchanged at the profit-maximizing level.[41] As such, the principal motives for the tie would not be exclusionary conduct aimed at monopolizing the market for the tied product in order to raise its price. Rather, the firm could be using the tie for some other purpose, such as price discrimination or reducing costs.[42]

Further analysis has demonstrated that these conclusions rely on some restrictive assumptions, for example, that the same consumers are buying both products in fixed proportions[43] and that the tied good market has a competitive, constant returns-to-scale structure. By relaxing those assumptions, some economists have identified exclusionary motives for tying, as well as strategic reasons for bundling and tying.[44]

One such line of analysis suggests that, under certain cost and demand conditions, a tying arrangement can enable a monopolist in a tying market to reduce demand for rival products in a second, imperfectly competitive tied market, thus injuring competition.[45] A commitment by the monopolist of the tying product to sell the tying and tied products only as a package enables the monopolist to commit to aggressive pricing of the tied product. If the monopolist raises its price for the tied product, the commitment to tying means that it loses not only some tied product sales, but also some sales in the profitable, monopolized tying product market.

In effect this enables the monopolist to commit itself to a low implicit price for the tied product.[46] When the market for the tied product exhibits scale economies and therefore is oligopolistic, committing to a low price may reduce competitors' sales and force them to exit.[47] Consumer harm may occur because 'when tied market rivals exit, prices may rise and the level of variety available in the market necessarily falls'.[48] While providing a potential motivation for exclusion, the analysis points out that 'the impact of this exclusion on welfare is uncertain'.[49]

Another line of analysis shows that tying may be used to preserve an insecure monopoly in the tying product.[50] Consider a firm that is a monopolist in a primary market and also sells a complementary product in a duopoly market. In addition, the primary and complementary products must be used together to provide value to consumers. The rival seller in the complementary product market can enter the primary market after incurring an entry cost. To deter the rival in the complementary product market from entering the primary market, the monopolist will tie the primary product with its version of the complementary product. By selling only the combination of products, the monopolist is committing to a low price in the complementary market, just as in the model described above. This practice can deny the rival seller in the complementary product market enough sales so that it is not worthwhile for the rival to incur the cost of entering the primary market.[51]

Yet another explanation for the monopoly tying of complementary products posits that under certain conditions the tie allows a monopolist to capture some of the producer's profits of the complementary good.[52] According to this explanation:

> the monopolist sometimes ties a product that winds up not being used by consumers . . . in order to extract surplus from, but not exclude, a rival producer. Specifically, the tying improves the monopolist's position in the pricing game that follows and serves to shift profits from the rival to the monopolist.[53]

Although 'this type of tying is frequently inefficient because, for example, consumers do not use the tied good in equilibrium',[54] this social inefficiency arguably does not justify antitrust intervention. That is because, as the authors note, the tie 'has nothing to do with harming the competitive process in the sense of creating additional market power' (rivals are not excluded and consumer do not pay a higher total price).[55]

As already indicated, tying or bundling intended to gain market share at rivals' expense need not imply consumer harm. Tying may allow for price discrimination, resulting in higher prices for some consumers than would prevail absent a tie, but lower prices for others. Even in the simplest examples, without price discrimination, tying may either raise or lower prices and raise or lower output. Non-monopolists may both gain market share and reduce prices to consumers through tying or bundling.[56] A firm that sells two complementary products has an incentive to lower the price of one to increase sales of the other. In this case, the first firm to act in this manner enjoys a huge market-share gain over its uncoordinated rivals. Moreover, those rivals do not respond by offering bundles of their own, because that would serve only to intensify the competition and leave the rivals worse off. In this scenario, bundling can reduce all prices, because consumer prices are lower when one firm that bundles competes against firms that sell single components independently than when no firms bundle.[57]

2 Procompetitive efficiencies Theoretical work in economics suggests that tying or bundling may often generate efficiencies. Economists postulate that tying and bundling can enhance consumer welfare in many ways, such as economies of joint sales, quality assurance and protection of goodwill, and cheating on a cartel price. Economies of joint sales, for example, are present throughout the economy, as in the case of shoes and shoelaces and indeed virtually every manufactured product. Quality assurance may be achieved by tying sales of products to sales of services (warranty repair) or consumables (fast-food franchisees may be required to buy critical ingredients from the franchisor). Cheating on a cartel price may be accomplished by bundling the cartelized product with valuable extras that act as a secret price discount on the cartelized product. In addition, price discrimination, such as through metering, can allow markets to be served that would not be served under a single-price monopoly. For example, light and heavy users of printers may both be served if they can buy a manufacturer's printer at a low price and its ink cartridges at a price above marginal cost.[58] Metering theories, of course, apply only when products can be purchased in variable proportions.

Some of the potential efficiencies result from joining the products in a single bundle. Empirical work on tying and bundling in competitive markets is consistent with the theory that such practices can reduce production costs. For example, consumers can purchase cold tablets that bundle active ingredients to relieve coughs, congestion and headaches at a significantly lower effective price than if the consumer purchased each of those remedies individually, because the incremental cost of adding one more active ingredient to a tablet that already is being produced is negligible.[59] Competition can cause much of the cost savings from bundling to accrue to consumers, making consumers better off than if there were no bundling.[60] Moreover, when the incremental cost of bundling separate goods is small, competition often will result in firms offering the goods both separately and in a bundle, which can improve consumer welfare.[61]

Providing choice may be costly, however. It may not be efficient to provide one of the products separately if only a few consumers prefer it. For example, such a high proportion of consumers want to buy both the left and right shoe as a bundle that the remaining customers do not justify selling them separately. Limiting the combinations of options can simplify production, which lowers costs and presumably prices to consumers.[62] Thus, although Ford Motor Company offers many options on its Ford Taurus, it offers them only in certain combinations or packages of options, so that not all possible combinations of options are available to consumers.[63] Limiting combinations of options can save fixed costs associated with a full range of product offerings and can foster product-specific cost reductions.[64]

Consistent with this reasoning, a study by two economists found that the bundling of so-called information goods, such as copyrighted music, programming, and other online content on the Internet, may prove welfare-superior to selling such goods on an individual basis.[65] The study noted that the marginal cost of adding additional units of an information good to a bundle of other information goods typically is very low, and that the demand for bundles of goods across customers can be more homogeneous than the demand for the individual components. In such circumstances, it can be more profitable to offer such goods only in a bundle. The study also found that competition between two firms that each offer sufficiently large bundles can make consumers better off,[66] and bundling by a firm facing no competition can increase total welfare but increase or decrease consumer welfare.[67]

3 Empirical evidence A full understanding of the effect of any particular tie or bundle requires a careful analysis of the circumstances surrounding the practice at issue. That likely competitive effects will be fact-dependent makes it difficult to craft statements of general application about the likely competitive effects of tying and bundling. Even an apparently benign statement such as 'offering consumers choice is better than not offering choice' may not be correct. Offering consumers more choices can be costly for firms; if the costs of providing more choice exceed the benefits to consumers, more choice can make consumers worse off.[68]

Thus, economists caution against confusing the 'theoretical possibility of harm with an empirical demonstration of such a harm'.[69] One economist has observed that the difficulty of identifying market settings in which tying and bundling might have exclusionary effects, and the fact that bundling can serve a purely efficiency-enhancing role in some market settings, 'make . . . the specification of a practical legal standard [for tying and bundling] extremely difficult'.[70]

A former chief economist of the Federal Trade Commission has argued that documented instances of anticompetitive tying are extremely rare and may not exist.[71] Other economists have made this point about vertical restraints (which include tying and bundling, among other practices) in general.[72] Noting the paucity of empirical support for the proposition that vertical restraints harm consumers (based on a literature review), they argue that one should infer that vertical restraints are likely to be benign or welfare enhancing.[73]

In short, the very limited empirical evidence that exists suggests that tying and bundling are unlikely to be anticompetitive. This supports the trend of the US courts to refuse to condemn these practices absent case-specific evidence of actual anticompetitive effects.

III Exclusive dealing

Exclusive dealing contracts involve a supplier conditioning its sale on the buyer's commitment not to purchase from the supplier's rivals.[74] While this technical definition of exclusive dealing requires the buyer to forgo all purchases from the rival supplier, some contracts involve 'partial' exclusivity, which involve the buyer committing to a fixed quantity of purchases or a percentage of its total purchases to the supplier in lieu of a 'full exclusive'. The menu of contracts implicating exclusive dealing includes more than full and partial exclusives. For instance, the economic and legal issues concerning exclusive dealing contracts are also implicated in the analysis of 'loyalty discounts' and other contracts which involve supplier commitments to discounts. For example, antitrust analysis of the competitive effects of 'all units' and other non-linear discounting schemes where the supplier commits to a discount if the retailer purchases a certain quantity or percentage of total purchases from the supplier can usefully be thought of as exclusive dealing contracts.[75] Exclusive dealing and exclusionary contracts more generally involve a broad spectrum of contracts in our modern economy. These contracts present a number of important antitrust issues requiring principled distinctions to be drawn between procompetitive exclusive dealing and arrangements that might threaten competition and harm consumers.

We begin by discussing antitrust analysis of exclusive dealing contracts with reference to a number of recent legal decisions and conclude by summarizing the economics of exclusive dealing, including possible anticompetitive effects, procompetitive explanations, and the empirical evidence.

A Legal analysis of exclusive dealing

Exclusive dealing contracts have never generated a substantial amount of suspicion under the law. Prior to the passage of the Sherman Act in 1890, and in the early days of Sherman Act jurisprudence, exclusive dealing contracts 'continued to be upheld routinely except in rare instances involving actual monopolization'.[76] Hostility to exclusive dealing increased after the passage of the Clayton Act in 1914. The first challenges to the practice under Section 3 of the Clayton Act resulted in the Supreme Court holding unlawful the arrangements in *Standard Fashion Co. v. Magrane-Houston Co.*[77] and *United Shoe Machinery Corp. v. United States.*[78] In 1949, the Court analyzed the exclusive dealing arrangements between gasoline refiners and service stations in *Standard Oil*,[79] introducing quantitative foreclosure analysis and condemning the contracts at issue because they foreclosed 49 per cent of the market. In 1951, the Court again condemned exclusive dealing contracts in *Lorain Journal Co. v. United States*[80] under Section 2 of the Sherman Act.

A decade later in *Tampa Electric Co. v. Nashville Coal Co.*,[81] the Court ushered in a new era of exclusive dealing jurisprudence in its last exclusive dealing case. The Court articulated that the plaintiff would be required to show that 'the competition foreclosed by the contract must be found to constitute a substantial share of the relevant market'.[82] The Court refused to condemn the exclusive dealing contracts at issue in that case on the grounds that the coal supply contract between Tampa Electric and Nashville Coal was found to be less than 1 per cent of the coal supplied from the Appalachian area.[83]

Since *Tampa Electric*, the evolution of antitrust jurisprudence concerning exclusive dealing has been limited to lower courts with the exception of the Supreme Court's tying decision in *Jefferson Parish* that held that a 30 per cent foreclosure would not be sufficient to support a claim. One commentator summarizes modern treatment of the foreclosure analysis in exclusive dealing cases as 'routinely sustain[ing] the legality of exclusive dealing arrangements with foreclosure percentages of 40 per cent or less'.[84]

Despite the occasional hostility to exclusive dealing and exclusionary contracts, antitrust jurisprudence has generally acknowledged that competition for contract is 'a vital form of rivalry . . . which the antitrust laws encourage rather than suppress'.[85] Acknowledging the potential consumer benefits that flow from exclusivity, modern antitrust analysis insists that plaintiffs make a prima facie showing of a number of necessary conditions for consumer harm before shifting the burden to the defendant to establish efficiency justifications for its conduct. While this showing includes foreclosure analysis, it also involves a broader inquiry into the potential for the exclusive contracts at issue to harm competition rather than merely disadvantage rivals. This analysis is fairly constant whether the arrangements are challenged under Sections 1 and 2 of the Sherman Act, or Section 3 of the Clayton Act.

The modern 'rule of reason' analysis evaluating exclusive dealing contracts focuses on a number of factors, including: the defendant's market power, the degree of foreclosure, entry conditions, the duration of the contracts at issue, whether exclusivity has the potential to raise rivals' costs, the presence of actual or likely anticompetitive effects, and business justifications. Areeda and Hovenkamp articulate the prima facie case for exclusive dealing claims as follows:

> In order to succeed in its claim of unlawful exclusive dealing a plaintiff must show the requisite agreement to deal exclusively and make a sufficient showing of power to warrant the inference that the challenged agreement threatens reduced output and higher prices in a properly defined market . . . Then it must also show foreclosure coverage sufficient to warrant an inference of injury of competition . . . depending on the existence of other factors that give significance to a given foreclosure percentage, such as contract duration, presence or absence of high entry barriers, or the existence of alternative sources or resale.[86]

A leading exclusive dealing case involving Philip Morris ('PM') and its 'Retail Leaders' program provides a useful illustration of modern antitrust analysis.[87] Retail Leaders, introduced in October 1998, involved four different 'participation levels' corresponding to both the magnitude of PM payments and the amount of advantageous display space provided to PM. At the highest two levels of Retail Leaders, PM not only made promotional payments to retailers but also granted retailers an 'industry fixture' that would occupy a specified percentage of total display space for cigarettes. At the highest level, this percentage was 100 per cent. At the mid-level of Retail Leaders, the industry fixture would occupy half of the total category of display space, specifying that PM brands were to be allocated proportionately to PM's market share (otherwise known as a 'space-to-sales' allocation). The other half of category space was to be divided between a 'prime fixture', constituting approximately 25 per cent of category space and promoting only PM brands, and a 'retailer's choice fixture', occupying the remaining 25 per cent of the space and containing competing brands and signage.[88]

Several other details of the Retail Leaders program warrant mention. First, PM paid retailers with per unit discounts known as retail display allowances ('RDAs').[89] Second, it was undisputed that Retail Leaders contracts were terminable at will without penalty upon 30 days' notice.[90] Third, under each Retail Leaders level of participation, retailers were never required to grant PM more than 'space-to-sales', or a greater percentage of shelf space than its market share.[91]

Several tobacco companies challenged Retail Leaders under both

Sections 1 and 2 of the Sherman Act. The court, after initially issuing a preliminary injunction in favor of the plaintiffs, granted PM's motion for summary judgment, dismissing the case on the grounds that PM did not have market power, and, alternatively, that the Retail Leaders program did not sufficiently foreclose rivals from the market. Specifically, the court found that Retail Leaders foreclosed only 34 per cent of the market, that plaintiffs successfully competed against PM for premium shelf space and signage and that retailers were able to terminate agreements at will.[92]

Competition between tobacco manufacturers for valuable shelf space resulted in a boon to consumers as RDAs were passed on in the form of lower prices.[93] While anticompetitive foreclosure is a viable concern, the key policy requirement is that the competitive process for distribution is left 'open', meaning that rival manufacturers have the opportunity to bid for shelf space. This condition is clearly satisfied where contracts are of short duration and easily terminable like those in the Retail Leaders program.[94] In fact, it appears that PM's prices fell relative to competitors after the implementation of Retail Leaders, suggesting that the program was procompetitive.[95]

As *RJR II* illustrates, the duration of exclusive dealing contracts is an important component of modern antitrust analysis. Exclusive dealing contracts covering shares of the market sufficient to otherwise trigger liability under a standard foreclosure analysis are routinely upheld where the contracts involve short-term commitments which allow rivals to compete for distribution.[96] *RJR II* illustrates the standard framework in modern exclusionary distribution cases, which requires a demonstration of the defendant's market power, substantial foreclosure, contracts of sufficient duration to prohibit meaningful competitive bidding by rivals and an analysis of actual or likely competitive effects.

B Economic analysis of exclusive dealing

The primary anticompetitive concern with exclusive dealing contracts is that a monopolist might be able to utilize exclusivity to fortify its market position and ultimately harm consumers. As a general matter, these concerns also extend to other contracts, such as loyalty and market-share discounts, which we discuss separately in Section III.C.

1 Theories of competitive harm The most common scenario of antitrust relevance involving exclusive dealing contracts concerns an upstream supplier, *S*, entering into an exclusive dealing contract with retailers, *R*, who in turn sell the product to final consumers. The potentially anticompetitive motivation associated with exclusive dealing contracts is clearly related to the limitation placed by that contract on R's ability to sell rival products to final consumers. The possibility of anticompetitive exclusion occurring from these types of contracts generally arises only if S is able to foreclose rival suppliers from a large enough fraction of the market to deprive those rivals of the opportunity to achieve minimum efficient scale.[97]

The well-known critique of this line of reasoning comes from the Chicago School argument that R will not have the incentive to agree to contracts that facilitate monopolization upstream because they will then suffer the consequences of facing that monopolist in their chain of distribution.[98] As a general matter, one can think of this criticism as drawing the analogy to a conspiracy among retailers, R, organized by the monopolist S to exclude S's rivals from access to distribution.[99] Like any other conspiracy, it is generally the case that each R has the incentive to deviate and remain outside the agreement by contracting with S's rivals and expanding output at the expense of rival retailers.[100] In other words, retailers have the incentive to avoid entering agreements that will ultimately harm them, and S will generally not be able to compensate retailers enough to enter into the anticompetitive exclusive contract.[101] The critique goes on to argue that observed exclusive dealing contracts must generate efficiencies rather than anticompetitive effects.

The economics literature has grown in recent years to include a series of theoretical models contemplating scenarios where S can sufficiently compensate retailers to join and remain within the conspiracy and therefore accomplish an anticompetitive purpose. These anticompetitive theories of exclusive dealing generally assume that S supplies a product that is essential to R's viability and that there are substantial economies of scale in manufacturing.

One such theory considers the case where the monopolist S adopts exclusive contracts rather than merely collecting its monopoly profit from the sale of the essential product and relies on the existence of dynamic economies of scale such as network effects.[102] Under this dynamic theory of exclusion, S's exclusive contracts prevent S's rivals or potential entrants from developing into future rivals, in order to protect future market power. Because S's rivals must operate at a cost disadvantage that drives them out and prevents entry, S is able to increase the duration and scope of its market power.[103]

A second set of models explores the possibility that coordination problems between buyers prevent the foiling of S's anticompetitive use of exclusive dealing contracts. There is a substantial industrial organization literature analyzing the conditions under which these types of coordination problems between buyers generate the possibility of anticompetitive exclusion. The seminal article of this type is by Rasmussen, Ramseyer, and Wiley ('RRW'),[104] later refined by Segal and Whinston ('SW').[105] The unifying economic logic of these models is that the potential entrant (or current rival) must attract a sufficient mass of retailers to cover its fixed costs of entry, but S's exclusive contracts with retailers prevent the potential entrant from doing so. It is then necessary to work out the conditions under which such exclusion is either not possible, possible, or probable.

A number of factors, in addition to the degree of downstream retail competition, have been identified in the exclusive dealing literature as either favoring the theoretical possibility of exclusion or rendering it less likely or impossible. Significant economies of scale in distribution militate against exclusion because, in that case, a potential entrant may need to attract only a single buyer in order to achieve minimum efficient scale. Similar logic suggests that a small number of buyers will be able to coordinate in order to support the excluded rival. Further, the exclusionary equilibrium in this model appears relatively fragile because an alternative equilibrium in which buyers reject exclusivity also exists.[106]

Recent extensions of these models focusing on the case where buyers are competitive downstream retailers rather than final consumers have produced a wide range of conflicting results under various conditions.[107] Fumagalli and Motta consider the role of retail competition in the RRW–SW framework and demonstrate that the incentives to exclude can disappear in this setting as one buyer becomes large enough to support the entry or viability of a rival.[108] Simpson and Wickelgren derive a model that produces the opposite result, arguing that downstream competition enhances the incentive to exclude as the benefits to a single buyer of resisting exclusion are minimal if all retailers are equally disadvantaged because retail competition will allow retailers to pass those costs on to consumers.[109]

The development of this literature has increased our knowledge about the potential theoretical impact of exclusive dealing contracts. However, the models generating anticompetitive exclusion generally rely on strict assumptions concerning the existence of significant economies of scale, barriers to entry, the nature of both upstream and downstream competition and, importantly, the complete absence of efficiency justifications for the contracts. Where the necessary conditions of those models are satisfied, they demonstrate that exclusive dealing contracts may harm consumers and thus are an appropriate subject for antitrust scrutiny and further analysis.

2 Procompetitive efficiencies Exclusive dealing arrangements are often efficient and result from the normal competitive process. Exclusive dealing contracts are often observed between firms lacking any meaningful market power, implying that there must be efficiency justifications for the practice. Indeed, the economics literature is replete with procompetitive explanations for exclusives and partial exclusives.[110]

The standard procompetitive account of exclusive dealing contracts involves use of exclusive dealing contracts to prevent free-riding dealers from using manufacturer-supplied investments to promote rival products.[111] For example, a manufacturer may make investments, such as purchasing display fixtures or training salespeople. Dealer free-riding on these investments involves using these investments to promote rival brands. The classic example of this type of free-riding in the antitrust context is *Ryko Manufacturing Co. v. Eden Services*,[112] where a manufacturer of car wash equipment used exclusive territories and exclusive dealing contracts to prevent its dealers from switching consumers to other brands. By facilitating dealer performance, the exclusive dealing contract allows manufacturers to collect a return on their investments and increase output.

A recent article by Benjamin Klein and Andres Lerner expands our understanding of the use of exclusive dealing by demonstrating how exclusivity minimizes free-riding in two cases where there are no manufacturer-supplied investments: first, free-riding on manufacturer-financed promotion to sell rival products, and second, free-riding in the form of failing to supply the promotion paid for by the manufacturer altogether, even in the absence of dealer switching.[113] First, because manufacturers often compensate retailers for the provision of promotional services such as premium shelf space,[114] dealers have incentives to use these additional promotional efforts to switch consumers to other products upon which the dealer earns a greater profit. Exclusive dealing can be used to prevent this type of free-riding in an analytically identical manner to the way it prevents free-riding on manufacturer-supplied investments.[115]

The second type of free-riding examined by Klein and Lerner also involves manufacturer-financed promotion. Because dealers are being compensated for promotional effort on the basis of total sales (both marginal and infra-marginal), and non-performance is costly to detect, dealers have an incentive not to supply the agreed upon promotional inputs.[116] Exclusive dealing mitigates the incentive to free-ride in this way by increasing the dealer's incentive to promote the manufacturer's product. Courts have recognized this somewhat intuitive justification for the use of exclusive dealing in *Joyce Beverages*[117] and *Roland Machinery*, noting the incentive effects of 'dedicated' or 'loyal' distribution.[118] Klein and Lerner provide an economic basis for understanding the mechanism by which dealers more actively promote the manufacturer's product in this case and consider whether *Dentsply*'s 'dealer loyalty' justification for its use of exclusive dealing was improperly rejected.[119]

Outside the expanded analysis of dealer free-riding, there are other efficient uses of exclusive dealing. One such use involves the role of exclusive dealing by individual retailers, including those without any market power, to intensify competition by manufacturers for their business and to improve purchase terms. By offering manufacturers access to the retailer's loyal customer base, a retailer is able to commit a substantial fraction of its customers' purchases to the 'favored' supplier and thereby dramatically increase each supplier's perceived elasticity of demand by making rival products highly substitutable.[120] Wright extends this analysis to explain the use of category management contracts where the particular quantity and type of shelf space devoted to the manufacturer's products is not contractually set by the retailer, but is flexibly determined over time by the category captain, a firm selected by the retailer to assist and influence decisions concerning which products in a product category are stocked, as well as how they are displayed, promoted, and priced.[121] In contrast to the case where the optimal shelf space commitments are stable, well known, easily specified by contract, and non-performance is easily detected by the manufacturer, category management contracts offer increased flexibility where such commitments are imprecise and change over time.

3 Empirical evidence As discussed, the theoretical literature focuses on the question of whether exclusive dealing contracts limit competition or are a procompetitive element of the competitive contracting process designed to solve incentive conflicts between manufacturers and retailers over the supply of promotional services. If the anticompetitive theories are correct, one expects that exclusive dealing contracts will increase prices and decrease output. Conversely, if the procompetitive theories are correct, prices should decrease and output should increase. Thus, conflicting theories generate conflicting predictions regarding the competitive effects of exclusive dealing on output and consumer welfare.

Existing empirical evidence of the impact of exclusive dealing is scarce but generally favors the view that exclusive dealing is output-enhancing. Heide et al. conducted a survey of managers responsible for distribution decisions and found that the incidence of exclusive dealing was correlated with the presence of 'free-ridable' investments.[122] Both Asker and Sass separately examine the welfare consequences of exclusive dealing in the beer market by observing the effect of exclusive dealing on total market output, as well as the output and prices of rival distributors, concluding that exclusive dealing is output increasing and does not generate foreclosure.[123]

C Loyalty discounts[124]

Loyalty discounts are a form of non-linear pricing in which the buyer's discount increases after a buyer-specific minimum threshold requirement is satisfied. One such discount is known as an 'all units' discount which applies the per unit rebate to all units purchased by the buyer if, and only if, it satisfies the threshold. A similar form of rebate is a 'market-share discount', which requires a buyer to make a specified share of its purchases from the seller in order to qualify for the discount. The relationship between loyalty discounts and exclusive dealing contracts is relatively straightforward, as the latter involves the special case where the discounts are granted if and only if the threshold commitment requires the buyer to make 100 per cent of its purchases from the supplier. We will refer to these loyalty rebate programs, such as market share discounts and all-units discounts that require less than full exclusivity, as 'partial exclusives' and reserve use of 'full exclusive' to specify 100 per cent exclusivity.

Loyalty discounts and 'partial exclusives' have generated a substantial amount of antitrust scrutiny in recent history, particularly after the *LePage's* decision, which involved a multi-market or 'bundled discount'.[125] In this Section, we will focus on single-product loyalty discounts alleged to have exclusionary effects similar to exclusive dealing.[126] Single product partial exclusives have been involved in a number of recent antitrust cases, including *FTC v. McCormick*,[127] *RJR II*,[128] *Barry Wright*,[129] *Concord Boat*,[130] and *Brooke Group*.[131]

In each of these cases, the supplier offered dealers 'loyalty discounts' in the form of partial exclusives. Many of these rebates were 'all units discounts', meaning that they were applied to all of the dealer's purchases once the minimum threshold was satisfied, including those in *Barry Wright* and *Concord Boat*, and possibly the discounts at issue in *Brooke Group*.[132] The partial exclusives in *McCormick* and *RJR II* likely did not involve an 'all units' feature, but offered increased discounts upon the commitment of a specific share of shelf space to the supplier's product. For example, in *McCormick*, which ultimately resulted in a settlement, the complaint alleged that the slotting contracts, manufacturer payments to retailers for preferred shelf space, included provisions that 'typically demand that the customer allocate the large majority of the space devoted to spice products – in some cases 90% of all shelf space devoted to packaged spices, herbs, seasonings and flavorings of the kinds offered by McCormick – to McCormick'.[133]

McCormick did not offer a procompetitive justification for these contracts, and specifically, the restrictions on distributing rival products. While Philip Morris' Retail Leaders shelf space arrangements contracts survived R.J. Reynolds's antitrust challenge in *RJR II* because the contracts were of short duration and therefore could not sufficiently foreclose rivals' access to distribution, the court did not find the contracts had any persuasive procompetitive business justification.

While partial exclusives may generate the same type of 'raising rivals' costs' concerns as full exclusives, the important question is whether these contracts are capable of producing harm to competition. As a general matter, antitrust analysis of these partial exclusives correctly proceeds by exploring whether the necessary conditions for competitive harm are satisfied, including substantial foreclosure and sufficient duration to prevent competitive bidding for distribution. Unfortunately, because the procompetitive function of partial exclusives is less well understood than that of full exclusives, courts may be tempted to conclude that partial exclusives do not have any redeeming efficiencies and more likely to find any potential anticompetitive effect sufficient to find an antitrust violation.

As discussed above, Klein and Murphy present an analysis of the procompetitive use of full and partial exclusives that may explain the prevalence of these contracts in retail settings.[134] Klein and Murphy consider the role of exclusive dealing and partial exclusives in the setting where consumers choose retailers on the basis of both average retail price and product variety. In essence, while adopting an exclusive imposes some costs on consumers in the form of preventing those consumers from satisfying their preferences for a particular brand, those costs are outweighed by the increase in consumer welfare generated by the retailer acting as a competitive bargaining agent for its customers, resulting in lower wholesale prices. This procompetitive justification extends to the case of partial exclusives, which give the retailer the flexibility to satisfy consumers with a clear preference for a rival brand. This avoids a large fraction of the consumer welfare losses associated with failing to stock a product highly demanded by some subset of consumers, while still extracting some benefits of the exclusivity in the form of increased ex ante competition for all consumers. Klein and Murphy apply this explanation to a number of partial exclusive contracts, including those in *McCormick*, the category management shelf space contract in *El Aguila Food Products v. Gruma*,[135] and the restrictive promotion contracts adopted in *Coca-Cola v. Harmar*[136] and *RJR II*.[137] Wright applies this partial exclusive analysis to the case of category management contracts where the retailer dedicates, without contractual discretion, a significant portion of its shelf space by allowing the category captain to determine or influence shelf space allocation and stocking decisions.[138]

IV Conclusion

A large number of antitrust investigations in the United States involve tying, bundling, and exclusive dealing contracts. These practices have much in common from the standpoint of economic analysis. For instance, the potential efficiencies associated with both tying and exclusive dealing, and the fact that both are prevalent in markets without significant antitrust market power, lead most commentators to believe that they are generally procompetitive and should be analyzed under some form of rule of reason analysis. Further, the anticompetitive theories applied to both tying and exclusive dealing generally involve 'raising rivals' costs' and the potential for the practice to foreclose rivals or acquire monopoly power in a second market. Despite these similarities, the legal analysis of these two practices remains remarkably divergent with the modified *per se* approach still applied to tying practices and a more sophisticated rule of reason analysis emphasizing potential consumer welfare effects applied to exclusive dealing. While developments in economic theory generally take some time to generate corresponding changes in competition policy, our analysis of these practices suggests that the adoption of a rule of reason for tying and presumptions of legality for both practices under certain conditions may be long overdue.

Notes

* A.F. Abbott is Associate Director, Bureau of Competition, Federal Trade Commission; J. D. Wright is Visiting Professor, University of Texas School of Law and Assistant Professor (on leave), George Mason University School of Law. The views expressed here are the authors' alone and are not necessarily the views of the Federal Trade Commission or any of its members. The authors thank Brandy Wagstaff for research assistance.

1. Dennis W. Carlton & Jeffrey M. Perloff, Modern Industrial Organization 319 (4th ed. 2005).
2. A 'requirements tie-in' sale occurs when a seller requires customers who purchase one product from the seller (e.g., a printer) to make all their purchases of another product from the same seller (e.g., ink cartridges). Such tying allows the seller to charge customers different amounts depending on their product usage. *Id.* at 321–2.
3. *Id.* 'Pure bundling' occurs when consumers can purchase only the entire bundle (e.g., when customers are allowed to purchase only a fixed price meal that includes all courses). 'Mixed bundling' occurs if the components also are sold separately, with a discount for purchasing the bundle (e.g., restaurant menus that include both à la carte items and complete meals). *See id.* at 324.
4. *See, e.g., United States v. Loew's, Inc.*, 371 US 38 (1962) (analyzing the licensing of feature films only in blocks (or bundles) as tying). *See also* F. Andrew Hanssen, *The Block Booking of Films Reexamined*, 43 J.L. & Econ. 395 (2000); Roy W. Kenney & Benjamin Klein, *How Block Booking Facilitated Self-Enforcing Film Contracts*, 43 J.L. & Econ. 427 (2000); Roy W. Kenney & Benjamin Klein, *The Economics of Block Booking*, 26 J.L. & Econ. 497 (1983); George J. Stigler, United States v. Loew's, Inc.*: A Note on Block-Booking*, 1963 Sup. Ct. Rev. 152 (1963).
5. Business practices merit treatment as *per se* illegal if 'their pernicious effect on competition and lack of any redeeming virtue are conclusively presumed to be unreasonable'. *N. Pac. Ry. Co. v. United States*, 356 US.1, 5 (1958).
6. 332 US 392, 396 (1947).
7. 337 US 293, 305–6 (1949).
8. ABA Section of Antitrust Law, Antitrust Law Developments 177–9 (5th ed. 2002) (hereinafter Antitrust Law Developments).
9. *United States Steel Corp. v. Fortner Enterprises*, 429 US 610 (1977).
10. 'It is far too late in the history of our antitrust jurisprudence to question the proposition that certain tying arrangements pose an unacceptable risk of stifling competition and therefore are unreasonable "*per se*".' *Jefferson Parish Hosp. Dist. No. 2 v. Hyde*, 466 US 2, 9 (1984).
11. *Id.* at 9–18.

12. *Id.* at 32–47.
13. *Nat'l Collegiate Athletic Ass'n v. Bd. of Regents*, 468 US 85, 104 n.26 (1984) (citation omitted).
14. *Illinois Tool Works Inc. v. Independent Ink, Inc.*, 126 S. Ct. 1281, 1288 (2006). *See also* Joshua D. Wright, *Missed Opportunities* in Independent Ink, 5 CATO SUP. CT. REV. 333 (2006); Bruce H. Kobayashi, *Spilled Ink or Economic Progress? The Supreme Court's Decision* in Illinois Tool Works v. Independent Ink, 53 ANTITRUST BULL. 5–33 (2008), working paper version available at SSRN: http://ssrn.com/abstract=1084475.
15. *Illinois Tool Works* , *supra* note 14, at 1292.
16. ANTITRUST LAW DEVELOPMENTS, *supra* note 8, at 178; HOVENKAMP ET AL., IP AND ANTITRUST: An Analysis of Antitrust Principles applied to Intellectual Property Law § 21.5, at 21–113 to 21–115.
17. ANTITRUST LAW DEVELOPMENTS, *supra* note 8, at 179 & n.998 (citing cases).
18. *United States v. Jerrold Elecs. Corp.*, 187 F. Supp. 545, 557–8 (E.D. Pa. 1960), *aff'd per curiam*, 365 US 567 (1961) (concluding that a tie was justified for a limited time in a new industry to assure effective functioning of complex equipment); *Mozart Co. v. Mercedes-Benz of N. Am., Inc.*, 833 F.2d 1342, 1348–51 (9th Cir. 1987) (upholding verdict for defendant because the tie may have been found to be the least expensive and most effective means of policing quality); *Dehydrating Process Co. v. A.O. Smith Corp.*, 292 F.2d 653, 655–7 (1st Cir. 1961) (affirming a judgment of a district court that directed a verdict in favor of the defendant because a tie was necessary to assure utility of two products when separate sales led to malfunctions and widespread customer dissatisfaction).
19. *Wells Real Estate, Inc. v. Greater Lowell Bd. of Realtors*, 850 F.2d 803, 815 (1st Cir. 1988) ('The tying claim must fail absent any proof of anti-competitive effects in the market for the tied product.'); *Fox Motors, Inc. v. Mazda Distribs. (Gulf), Inc.*, 806 F.2d 953, 958 (10th Cir. 1986) (declining to apply the *per se* rule to a tie that 'simply does not imply a sufficiently great likelihood of anticompetitive effect').
20. 253 F.3d 34 (D.C. Cir. 2001).
21. *Id.* at 95. In deciding a tying patent misuse claim, the US Court of Appeals for the Federal Circuit recently rejected a *per se* approach and applied tying case law to find that a package license combining alleged 'essential' with 'nonessential' patents did not constitute patent misuse because there was no separate demand for the 'nonessential' patents, and, thus, no separate product market in which competition could have been foreclosed. *US Philips Corp. v. Int'l Trade Comm'n*, 424 F.3d 1179, 1193–7 (Fed. Cir. 2005). The court rejected a *per se* approach '[i]n light of the efficiencies of package patent licensing and the important differences between product-to-patent tying arrangements and arrangements involving group licensing of patents'. *Id.* at 1193.
22. *See, e.g.*, Warren S. Grimes, *The Antitrust Tying Law Schism: A Critique of* Microsoft III *and a Response to Hylton and Salinger*, 70 ANTITRUST L.J. 199, 202 (2002) ('[C]iting the novelty of the issues and the possibility of procompetitive effects, [the DC Circuit] imposed a rule of reason to measure Microsoft's software bundling practices.'); William J. Kolasky, GE/Honeywell*: Continuing the Transatlantic Dialogue*, 23 U. PA. J. INT'L ECON. L. 513, 532 & n.66 (2002) (citing *Microsoft*, 253 F.3d at 84–97, to support a statement that technological ties 'are generally evaluated under the rule of reason').
23. *Microsoft*, 253 F.3d at 93.
24. This opinion was put forth in 2002 at the Federal Trade Commission and Department of Justice joint hearings on the intersection between intellectual property and antitrust law (hereinafter *IP-Antitrust Hearings*). Jonathan M. Jacobson & Abid Qureshi, *Did the Per Se Rule on Tying Survive* 'Microsoft'*?* (May 14, 2002, *IP-Antitrust Hearings*), http://www.ftc.gov/opp/intellect/020514jacobson2.pdf. *See also* Herbert Hovenkamp, *IP Ties and* Microsoft *Rule of Reason*, 47 ANTITRUST BULL. 369, 413 ('[W]hile developing a rule of reason for OS/application is laudable, the court's rationale for distinguishing such ties from the general run of tying arrangements cannot be supported.').
25. 371 US 38 (1962).

26. *Id.* at 41–3 (noting the blocks contained as many as 754 separate titles); *id.* at 44, 49–50 (treating block booking as tying). More recently, courts have examined bundling in the context of loyalty discounts. *See, e.g.*, *LePage's, Inc. v. 3M*, 324 F.3d 141 (3d Cir. 2003) (en banc) (involving a 'bundled discount' offered by 3M on its Scotch brand tape and a variety of other products provided the retailer met a target for purchases of private label tape from 3M as well). The en banc court affirmed the trial court's denial of judgment for the defendant as a matter of law. *But see* Brief for the United States as Amicus Curiae, *3M Co. v. LePage's Inc.*, 542 US 953 (2004) (No. 02-1865), *denying cert. to* 324 F.3d 141, *available at* http://www.usdoj.gov/atr/cases/f203900/203900.pdf (urging the Supreme Court to deny review but criticizing the Third Circuit's en banc decision for providing little guidance on how Section 2 should be applied to bundled rebates, failing to explain why 3M's conduct was unlawful, and perhaps encouraging challenges to – and therefore chilling the adoption of – procompetitive bundled rebate programs); *see also Ortho Diagnostic Sys., Inc. v. Abbott Labs., Inc.*, 920 F. Supp. 455 (S.D.N.Y. 1996) (finding 'package price' discounts that covered both competitive markets and markets in which defendant had a monopoly did not violate Section 2, because plaintiff did not show that either (1) defendant priced below its average variable cost, or (2) plaintiff was at least as efficient a producer as defendant in competitive product lines, but defendant's pricing made it unprofitable for plaintiff to continue to compete).
27. *Jefferson Parish Hosp. Dist. No. 2 v. Hyde*, 466 US 2, 16 (1984).
28. 324 F.3d 141 (3d Cir. 2003) (en banc).
29. *But see* Brief for the United States as Amicus Curiae, *LePage's*, *supra* note 26. *See also Ortho Diagnostic Sys., Inc. v. Abbott Labs., Inc.*, *supra* note 26.
30. Antitrust Modernization Commission, Report and Recommendations, 94 (April, 2007), available at http://govinfo.library.unt.edu/amc/report_recommendation/amc_final_report.pdf.
31. *Id.* at 99. Antitrust Modernization Committee Commissioner Dennis Carlton expressed concern that the first prong of the proposed 'AMC' test would fail to protect procompetitive bundling because common pricing strategies involving price discrimination, such as bundling razors and razor blades, would satisfy the first prong of the test but not threaten competitive injury. See Separate Statement of Dennis Carlton, *id.* at 398-9. Recently, the Ninth Circuit endorsed a modified version of the AMC test which embraced the first prong only but reasoned that the recoupment requirement and proof of an anticompetitive effect were either inappropriate in the bundling context or unnecessary. See *Cascade Health Solutions v. PeaceHealth*, 2007 US App. LEXIS 21075 (9th Cir. 2007).
32. US Dep't of Justice & Federal Trade Comm'n, Antitrust Guidelines for the Licensing of Intellectual Property, *available at* http://www.usdoj.gov/atr/public/guidelines/ipguide.htm (hereinafter Antitrust-IP Guidelines)
33. *Id.* § 5.3 & n.34 (citing *United States v. Paramount Pictures, Inc.*, 334 US 131, 156-8 (1948) (copyrights); *Int'l Salt Co. v. United States*, 332 US 392 (1947) (patent and related product)).
34. *Id.* § 5.3; *see infra* notes 58-67 and accompanying text (discussion of efficiencies).
35. Antitrust-IP Guidelines § 5.3 (footnotes omitted); *see also id.* § 2.2 ('[The] Agencies will not presume that a patent, copyright, or trade secret necessarily confers market power upon its owner.').
36. The Antitrust-IP Guidelines describe package licensing as 'the licensing of multiple items of intellectual property in a single license or in a group of related licenses', which 'may be a form of tying . . . if the licensing of one product is conditioned upon the acceptance of a license for another, separate product'. *Id.* § 5.3.
37. This conclusion is supported not only by the tone of the Supreme Court's decision in *Illinois Tool*, see text accompanying notes 14-15, *supra*, but by the Court's willingness (in light of economic analysis) to jettison the 95-year-old *per se* prohibition on minimum resale price maintenance in its 2007 *Leegin* holding. *See Leegin Creative Prods, Inc. v. PSKS, Inc.*, 127 S. Ct. 2705 (2007).

38. For surveys on the economic effects of bundling, *see* Bruce H. Kobayashi, *Does Economics Provide A Reliable Guide to Regulating Commodity Bundling By Firms?: A Survey of the Economic Literature*, 1 J. COMP. L. & ECON. 707 (2005); Patrick Rey, Paul Seabright & Jean Tirole, *The Activities of a Monopoly Firm in Adjacent Competitive Markets: Economic Consequences and Implications for Competition Policy* (Institut d'Economie Industrielle, Universite de Toulouse, Working Paper No. 132, 2002), *available at* http://idei.fr/doc/wp/2001/sctivities2.pdf.
39. *See, e.g.*, David Evans & Michael Salinger, *Why Do Firms Bundle and Tie? Evidence from Competitive Markets and Implications for Tying Law*, 22 YALE J. ON REG. 37 (2005).
40. RICHARD A. POSNER, ANTITRUST LAW 202 (2d ed. 2001) (footnote omitted).
41. *Id.* at 199.
42. *Id.* at 199–200; *see also* Patrick DeGraba, *Why Lever into a Zero-Profit Industry: Tying, Foreclosure, and Exclusion*, 5 J. ECON. & MGMT. STRATEGY, 433–47 (1996).
43. As early as the 1950s, Ward Bowman and others noted this limit on the theoretical conclusions discussed above. *See* Ward S. Bowman, Jr., *Tying Arrangements and the Leveraging Problem*, 67 YALE L.J. 19 (1957); Michael D. Whinston, *Tying, Foreclosure, and Exclusion*, 80 AM. ECON. REV. 837, 837–8 (1990).
44. *See* Gregory Vistnes, *Bundling and Tying: Antitrust Analysis in Markets with Intellectual Property* 3–5 (May 14, 2002, *IP-Antitrust Hearings*) (slides), http://www.ftc.gov/opp/intellect/020514vistnesppt2.pdf; *see also* Whinston, *supra* note 43, at 839; Dennis W. Carlton & Michael Waldman, *Tying, Upgrades, and Switching Costs in Durable-Goods Markets* (Nat'l Bureau of Econ. Research, Working Paper No. 11407, 2005), *available at* http://www.nber.org/papers/w11407.
45. *See generally* Whinston, *supra* note 43; Dennis W. Carlton & Michael Waldman, *The Strategic Use of Tying to Preserve and Create Market Power in Evolving Industries*, 33 RAND J. ECON. 194 (2002); José Carbajo, David de Meza & Daniel Seidmann, *A Strategic Motivation for Commodity Bundling*, 38 J. INDUS. ECON. 283 (1990).
46. For example, if (contrary to fact) a monopolist in DVD players (the tying product) committed to sell both its DVD player and a CD player (the tied product) only as a bundle for $300, a customer willing to pay $250 for a DVD player would obtain the CD player for $50, because the consumer already was willing to pay $250 for the DVD player. Thus, the commitment to bundle would set an implicit low price for the tied product, the CD player.
47. Whinston, *supra* note 43, at 839.
48. *Id.* Although originally presented in the context of goods with independent demand, this analysis can also apply to complements.
49. *Id.* at 855–6.
50. *See* Carlton & Waldman, *supra* note 45.
51. *See, e.g.*, *United States v. Microsoft Corp.*, 253 F.3d 34, 60 (D.C. Cir. 2001) ('Microsoft's effort to gain market share in one market (browsers) served to meet the threat to Microsoft's monopoly in another market (operating systems) by keeping rival browsers from gaining the critical mass of users necessary to attract developer attention away from Windows as the platform for software development.').
52. Dennis W. Carlton, Joshua S. Gans & Michael Waldman, *Why Tie a Product Consumers Do Not Use?* (August 2007) (unpublished manuscript), *available at* http://www.mbs.edu/home/jgans/papers/Carlton-Gans-Waldman-07-08-09.pdf.
53. *Id.* at 4.
54. *Id.*
55. *Id.* at 26.
56. Barry J. Nalebuff, *Competing Against Bundles*, *in* INCENTIVES, ORGANIZATION & PUBLIC ECONOMICS: PAPERS IN HONOR OF SIR JAMES MIRRLEES 323, 324 (Peter Hammond & Garth Mayles eds, 2000) (hereinafter Nalebuff, *Competing Against Bundles*). The point also holds true for tying. Tying and bundling differ in that 'bundling' refers to cases in which the tying and tied products are sold in fixed proportions, whereas 'tying'

has traditionally referred to cases in which consumers choose the quantity of the tied product they purchase. *See* CARLTON & PERLOFF, *supra* note 1, at 319. Thus, a producer can use tying to meter usage of the tying product so as to price discriminate among consumers according to their purchases of the tied product. For example, printers for personal computers often involve a technological tie between the printer and the type of ink cartridge the printer can use. Consumers who do more printing thus pay more to the producer overall than those who print less. Such a tie, however, can result in lower printer prices for consumers. *Id.* at 321.

57. Nalebuff, *Competing Against Bundles*, *supra* note 56, at 329–31.
58. CARLTON & PERLOFF, *supra* note 1, at 319–22; *see also* Marius Schwartz & Gregory J. Werden, *A Quality-Signaling Rationale for Aftermarket Tying*, 64 ANTITRUST L.J. 387 (1996); William F. Baxter & Daniel P. Kessler, *The Law and Economics of Tying Arrangements: Lessons for the Competition Policy Treatment of Intellectual Property*, in COMPETITION POLICY AND INTELLECTUAL PROPERTY RIGHTS IN THE KNOWLEDGE-BASED ECONOMY 137, 142–3 (Robert D. Anderson & Nancy T. Gallini eds, 1998) (discussing beneficial effect of tying as a 'metering' device).
59. Evans & Salinger, *supra* note 39, at 66–71.
60. *See id.* at 83 ('Tying is common in competitive markets. It results in lower costs for producers – which get passed onto consumers – or greater convenience, which benefits consumers directly.'). Even a monopolist will pass through to consumers a significant share of the cost savings from bundling. Paul Yde & Michael Vita, *Merger Efficiencies: The 'Passing-On' Fallacy*, ANTITRUST, Summer 2006, at 59 ('A monopolist that failed to expand output and reduce price in response to a cost reduction would be no less irrational than a monopolist that failed to exercise its market power.').
61. Evans & Salinger, *supra* note 39. The authors note that offering both a bundle and each component separately can involve additional fixed costs. When these fixed costs are sufficiently large, a firm may choose not to bundle and instead to offer only individual components, or may choose only to bundle and not to offer any component separately. *Id.* at 65.
62. *Id.* at 75–6.
63. *Id.* at 75–82.
64. *Id.* at 41–2.
65. *See* Yannis Bakos & Eric Brynjolfsson, *Bundling and Competition on the Internet: Aggregations Strategies for Information Goods*, 19 MARKETING SCI. 63 (2000); Yannis Bakos & Eric Brynjolfsson, *Bundling Information Goods: Prices, Profits, and Efficiency*, 45 MGMT. SCI. 1613 (1999).
66. Bakos & Brynjolfsson (2000), *supra* note 65, at 71–4 (showing that customers are able to purchase goods from competing firms selling large enough bundles at a lower effective per unit price than the price they would pay for each good if all goods are sold separately).
67. *Id.* at 72. The intuition behind this result is that bundling allows the monopolist to sell more units to customers which increases total welfare, but also allows the monopolist to charge higher average prices which extracts surplus from customers. Depending on the parameters of the model, the latter effect could be either greater or less than the former effect.
68. *Id.* at 84.
69. Dennis W. Carlton & Michael Waldman, *The Strategic Use of Tying to Preserve and Create Market Power in Evolving Industries* 31 (Nat'l Bureau of Econ. Research, Working Paper No. 6831, 1998).
70. Whinston, *supra* note 43, at 856.
71. Michael A. Salinger, *Business Justifications in Tying Arrangements* (2005), in ISSUES IN COMPETITION LAW AND POLICY (Wayne D. Collins ed., 2006).
72. *See* James C. Cooper, Luke M. Froeb, Dan O'Brien, and Michael G. Vita, *Vertical Antitrust Policy as a Problem of Inference*, 23 INT'L J. INDUS. ORG. 639 (2005).

73. *See id.*
74. Louis Kaplow and Carl Shapiro, *Antitrust*, in THE HANDBOOK OF LAW AND ECONOMICS (A. Mitchell Polinksy & Steven Shavell eds, Elsevier 2007), adopt a similar definition and provide a survey of the exclusive dealing literature discussed throughout this article. The leading antitrust treatise adopts a similar definition. PHILIP E. AREEDA & HERBERT HOVENKAMP, ANTITRUST LAW ¶ 1800a (2d ed. 2002) ('an exclusive dealing arrangement is a contract between a manufacturer and a buyer forbidding the buyer from purchasing the contracted good from any other seller, or requiring the buyer to take all of its needs in the contracted good from the manufacturer').
75. *See, e.g.*, Willard K. Tom, David A. Balto & Neil W. Averitt, *Anticompetitive Aspects of Market-Share Discounts and Other Incentives to Exclusive Dealing*, 67 ANTITRUST L.J. 615 (2000).
76. *See* Jonathan M. Jacobson, *Exclusive Dealing, 'Foreclosure,' and Consumer Harm*, 70 ANTITRUST L.J. 311, 316 (2002). Jacobson informatively traces the evolution of antitrust analysis of exclusive dealing from the pre-Sherman Act era to the present. *Id.* at 314–28.
77. 258 US 346 (1922).
78. 258 US 451 (1922).
79. *Standard Oil Co. (Cal.) v. United States*, 337 US 293 (1949).
80. 342 US 141 (1951). *See also* Kenneth L. Glazer & Abbott B. Lipsky, Jr., *Unilateral Refusals to Deal Under Section 2 of the Sherman Act*, 63 ANTITRUST L.J. 749 (1995).
81. 365 US 320 (1961). *See also* Benjamin Klein, *Exclusive Dealing as Competition for Distribution on the Merits*, 12 GEO. MASON L. REV. 119, 140–41 (2003) (discussing the economic forces motivating the long-term exclusive dealing contract in *Tampa Electric*).
82. 365 US at 328.
83. *Id.* at 330–1, 333.
84. *Id.* at 362.
85. *Menasha Corp. v. News Am. Mktg. In-Store, Inc.*, 354 F.3d 661, 663 (7th Cir. 2004). *See also Paddock Publ'ns., Inc. v. Chicago Tribune Co.*, 103 F.3d 42, 45 (7th Cir. 1996).
86. AREEDA & HOVENKAMP, *supra* note 74, at ¶ 1821.
87. *R.J. Reynolds Tobacco Co. v. Philip Morris Inc.*, 199 F. Supp. 2d 362 (M.D.N.C. 2002) (*'RJR II'*), *aff'd per curiam*, 67 F. App'x 810 (4th Cir. 2003). The analysis of *RJR* II herein relies on a previous discussion in Joshua D. Wright, *Antitrust Law and Competition for Distribution*, 23 YALE J. ON REG. 169 (2006).
88. 199 F. Supp. 2d at 370.
89. *Id.* at 369–70.
90. *Id.* at 371.
91. *Id.* at 370.
92. *Id.* at 391 ('because Retail Leaders agreements are terminable at will with thirty days notice, retail product and display space are subject to uninterrupted competitive bidding, and Plaintiffs are not substantially foreclosed from the relevant market').
93. R.J. Reynolds's economic expert conceded this point during the litigation. 199 F. Supp. 2d at 369–70. The fact that PM made significant promotional payments is consistent with the very high margins on tobacco products, giving tobacco manufacturers the incentive to pay for premium shelf space and signage that might induce incremental sales. For an economic analysis providing a procompetitive basis for understanding shelf space payments, *see* Benjamin Klein and Joshua D. Wright, *The Economics of Slotting Contracts*, 50 J.L. & ECON. 421 (2007).
94. The court made exactly such a finding. 199 F. Supp. 2d at 391. Whether short-term agreements do not have substantial anticompetitive effects as a matter of law is an open issue subject to debate across the circuits. See cases cited *infra* note 96.
95. *See* Peter Bronsteen et al., *Price Competition and Slotting Allowances*, 50 ANTITRUST BULL. 267 (2005).
96. A number of courts have held that exclusive contracts of one year or less are

presumptively lawful. *See, e.g.*, *Concord Boat Corp. v. Brunswick Corp.*, 207 F.3d 1039, 1059 (8th Cir. 2000); *CDC Techs., Inc. IDEXX Labs, Inc.*, 186 F.3d 74 (2d Cir. 1999); *Omega Envtl. Inc. v. Gilbarco, Inc.*, 127 F.3d 1157, 1163–4 (9th Cir. 1997); *Paddock Publications, Inc. v. Chicago Tribune Co.*, 103 F.3d 42, 47 (7th Cir. 1996); *Thompson Everett, Inc. v. Nat'l Cable Adver.*, 57 F.3d 1317, 1325 (4th Cir. 1995); ('the FTC and the Supreme Court concluded that even exclusive dealing contracts are lawful if limited to one year's duration'); *US Healthcare, Inc. v. Healthsource, Inc.*, 986 F.2d 589, 596 (1st Cir. 1993); *Roland Mach. Co. v. Dresser Indus.*, 749 F.2d 380, 392–5 (7th Cir. 1984). Similarly, some commentators have argued in favor of *per se* legality for such short-term contracts. *See, e.g.*, Wright, *supra* note 87.

97. This anticompetitive strategy using exclusive contracts belongs to the more general class of strategies analyzed in the raising rivals' costs literature. *See* Thomas Krattenmaker & Stephen C. Salop, *Anticompetitive Exclusion: Raising Rivals' Costs to Achieve Power Over Price*, 96 YALE L.J. 234 (1986); Stephen C. Salop & David T. Scheffman, *Raising Rivals' Costs*, 73 AM. ECON. REV. 267 (1983).
98. This line of reasoning is conventionally associated with Robert Bork. *See, e.g.*, ROBERT A. BORK, THE ANTITRUST PARADOX 309 (1978) ('A seller who wants exclusivity must give the buyer something for it. If he gives a lower price, the reason must be that the seller expects the arrangement to create efficiencies that justify the lower price. If he were to give a lower price simply to harm his rivals, he would be engaging in deliberate predation by price cutting, and that, as we have seen in Chapter 7, would be foolish and self-defeating behavior on his part').
99. This analogy is explored and used to derive the economic conditions necessary for exclusive contracts to cause anticompetitive effects, in Benjamin Klein, *supra* note 81, at 122–8.
100. *See* Elizabeth Granitz & Benjamin Klein, *Monopolization by 'Raising Rivals' Costs': The* Standard *Oil Case*, 39 J.L. & ECON. 1 (1996).
101. Douglas Bernheim and Michael Whinston, *Exclusive Dealing*, 106 J. POL. ECON. 64 (1998), formally derive this result.
102. *See* Carlton & Waldman, *supra* note 45.
103. An alternative, but related, theory of exclusion operates by driving out competing retailers and allowing S to monopolize distribution and collect its monopoly price on the distribution of rival products. *See* Whinston, *supra* note 43. This alternative theory also requires substantial economies of scope or scale in the supply of distribution services. Economies of scope in distribution may be present if, for example, S's product is essential to the economic viability of R.
104. Eric B. Rasmussen, Mark J. Ramseyer & John Shepherd Wiley, Jr., *Naked Exclusion*, 81 AM. ECON. REV. 1137 (1991).
105. Ilya R. Segal & Michael D. Whinston, *Naked Exclusion: Comment*, 90 AM. ECON. REV. 296 (2000).
106. *But see* Segal & Whinston, *supra* note 105, and MICHAEL D. WHINSTON, LECTURES ON ANTITRUST ECONOMICS (MIT Press, 2006), for arguments that the ability to make discriminatory or sequential offers to buyers increases the support for exclusion.
107. *See, e.g.*, Chiara Fumagalli & Massimo Motta, *Exclusive Dealing and Entry, When Buyers Compete*, 96 AM. ECON. REV. 785 (2006) (exclusion is not likely with downstream retail competition where potential entrant can achieve scale through distribution with a small number of retailers); John Simpson & Abraham L. Wickelgren, *Naked Exclusion, Efficient Breach, and Downstream Competition*, 97 AM. ECON. REV. 1305–20 (2007) (exclusion is possible with downstream retail competition because each individual retailer has little to gain from holding out from the exclusive and the increased benefits of upstream competition are largely passed on to final consumers); John Simpson & Abraham L. Wickelgren, *Exclusive Dealing and Entry, When Buyers Compete: Comment* (mimeo, June 2005) (same).
108. Fumagalli & Motta, *supra* note 107.
109. Simpson & Wickelgren (2007), *supra* note 107.

110. A description of other commonly accepted justifications for exclusive dealing is presented in Jacobson, *supra* note 76, at 357–60.
111. Howard Marvel, *Exclusive Dealing*, 25 J.L. & ECON. 1 (1982).
112. 823 F.2d 1215 (8th Cir. 1987). *See also* Benjamin Klein & Andres V. Lerner, *The Expanded Economics of Free-Riding: How Exclusive Dealing Prevents Free-Riding and Creates Undivided Loyalty*, 72 ANTITRUST L.J. 473, 481–3 (2007) (discussing *Ryko* as an example of this type of free-riding).
113. Klein & Lerner, *supra* note 112.
114. *See* Klein and Wright, *supra* note 93, which extends the original analysis of inadequate dealer incentives to promote and the use of vertical restraints in solving this dealer incentive problem in Benjamin Klein and Kevin M. Murphy, *Vertical Restraints as Contract Enforcement Mechanisms*, 31 J.L. & ECON. 265 (1988).
115. Klein & Lerner, *supra* note 112, at 497–502.
116. *Id.* at 502–4.
117. *Joyce Beverages v. Royal Crown Co.*, 555 F. Supp. 271, 276–7 (S.D.N.Y. 1983). *See also Hendricks Music Co. v. Steinway, Inc.*, 689 F. Supp. 1501 (N.D. Ill. 1988) ('it is perfectly legitimate and, in fact, procompetitive, for manufacturers to insist that their dealers devote undivided loyalty to their products and not use those of their competitors').
118. *Roland Mach. Co. v. Dresser Indus., Inc.*, 749 F.2d 380 (7th Cir. 1984).
119. Klein & Lerner, *supra* note 112, at 507–18. *See generally United States v. Dentsply Int'l, Inc.*, 277 F. Supp. 2d 387 (D. Del. 2003), *rev'd*, 399 F.3d 181 (3d Cir. 2005), *cert. denied*, 126 S. Ct. 1023 (2006). Klein and Lerner conclude that creating 'undivided dealer loyalty' was a plausible justification in *Dentsply*, but that 'we do not know if a more complete analysis would have found the net effect of Dentsply's exclusive dealing to be procompetitive or anticompetitive' and 'what is clear is that further analysis of the undivided loyalty rationale for exclusive dealing should have been undertaken'. Klein & Lerner, *supra* note 112, at 518.
120. *See* Benjamin Klein & Kevin M. Murphy, *Exclusive Dealing Intensifies Competition for Distribution*, 25 ANTITRUST L.J. 433 (2008). This explanation is related to, and provides the economic basis for, the argument that exclusives 'instigated' by customers should enjoy a presumption of legality. *See* Richard M. Steuer, *Customer Instigated Exclusive Dealing*, 68 ANTITRUST L.J. 239 (2000).
121. Joshua D. Wright, 'Antitrust Analysis of Category Management: *Conwood Co. v. United States Tobacco Co.*', 17 *Supreme Court Economic Review* (2009).
122. Jan B. Heide et al., *Exclusive Dealing and Business Efficiency: Evidence from Industry Practice*, 41 J.L. & ECON. 387 (1988).
123. *See* John Asker, *Diagnosing Foreclosure Due to Exclusive Dealing* (unpublished working paper, 2005); Tim R. Sass, *The Competitive Effects of Exclusive Dealing: Evidence from the US Beer Industry*, 23 INT'L J. INDUS. ORG. 203 (2005).
124. A comprehensive survey of the legal and economic issues associated with loyalty discounts appears in Bruce H. Kobayashi, *The Economics of Loyalty Discounts and Antitrust Law in the United States*, 1 COMPETITION POL'Y INT'L 115 (2005). *See also* Thomas A. Lambert, *Evaluating Bundled Discounts*, 89 MINN. L. REV. 1688 (2005).
125. The reader is referred to Kobayashi, *supra* note 124, at 137–46, for discussion of multi-product discounts.
126. *See, e.g.*, Tom, Balto & Averitt, *supra* note 75 (analyzing market share discounts as a form of de facto exclusive dealing).
127. *Federal Trade Commission v. McCormick* (FTC Dkt. No. C3939) (2000) (FTC File No. 961-0050).
128. *R.J. Reynolds Tobacco Co. v. Philip Morris Inc.*, 199 F. Supp. 2d 362 (M.D.N.C. 2002); *aff'd per curiam*, 67 F. App'x 810 (4th Cir. 2003).
129. *Barry Wright v. ITT Grinnell*, 724 F.2d 227 (1st Cir. 1983).
130. *Concord Boat Corp. v. Brunswick Corp.*, 207 F.3d 1039 (8th Cir. 2000).
131. *Brooke Group Ltd. v. Brown & Williamson Tobacco Corp.*, 509 US 209 (1993).
132. *See* Kobayashi, *supra* note 124, at Figure 1.

133. Complaint in *McCormick*, *supra* note 127, at ¶ 10. *McCormick* is analyzed in Wright, *supra* note 87, at 186–8, and Klein and Murphy, *supra* note 120.
134. Klein & Murphy, *supra* note 120.
135. *El Aguila Food Products v. Gruma Corp.*, 301 F. Supp. 2d 612 (S.D. Tex. 2003), *aff'd*, 131 F. App'x 450 (5th Cir. 2005).
136. *Coca-Cola Co. v. Harmar Bottling Co.*, 218 S.W.3d 671 (Tex. 2006), rev'g, 111 S.W.3d 287 (Tex. App. 2003).
137. *R.J. Reynolds Tobacco Co. v. Philip Morris, Inc.*, 199 F. Supp. 2d 362, 388, 390 (M.D.N.C. 2002), *aff'd per curiam*, 67 F. App'x 810 (4th Cir. 2003).
138. See Wright, *supra* note 121.

References

American Bar Association Section of Antitrust Law, *Antitrust Law Developments* (5th ed. 2002), Chicago: American Bar Association.

Antitrust Modernization Commission (2007), *Report and Recommendations*, available at http://govinfo.library.unt.edu/amc/report_recommendation/amc_final_report.pdf.

Areeda, P. and H. Hovenkamp (2002), *Antitrust Law* (2d ed.), New York: Aspen Publishers.

Asker, J. (2005), 'Diagnosing Foreclosure Due to Exclusive Dealing' (unpublished working paper), available at http:pages.stern.nyu.edu/~jasker/Paper1_ExclusiveForeclosure.pdf.

Bakos, Y. and E. Brynjolfsson (1999), 'Bundling Information Goods: Prices, Profits, and Efficiency', *Management Science*, 45 (12), 1613–30.

Bakos, Y. and E. Brynjolfsson (2000), 'Bundling and Competition on the Internet: Aggregations Strategies for Information Goods', *Marketing Science*, 19 (1), 63–82.

Baxter, W. and D. Kessler (1998), 'The Law and Economics of Tying Arrangements: Lessons for the Competition Policy Treatment of Intellectual Property', in Anderson, R. and N. Gallini (eds), *Competition Policy and Intellectual Property Rights in the Knowledge-Based Economy*, Calgary: University of Calgary Press, pp. 137–51.

Bernheim, D. and M. Whinston (1998), 'Exclusive Dealing', *Journal of Political Economy*, 106 (1), 64–103.

Bork, R. (1978), *The Antitrust Paradox*, New York: Basic Books.

Bowman, W. Jr., (1957), 'Tying Arrangements and the Leveraging Problem', *Yale Law Journal*, 67 (1), 19–36.

Bronsteen, P., D. Mills and K. Elzinga (2005), 'Price Competition and Slotting Allowances', *Antitrust Bulletin*, 50 (2), 267–81.

Carbajo, J., D. de Meza and D. Seidmann (1990), 'A Strategic Motivation for Commodity Bundling', *Journal of Industrial Economics*, 38(3), 283–98.

Carlton, D., J. Gans and M. Waldman (2007), 'Why Tie a Product Consumers Do Not Use?' (unpublished manuscript), available at http://www.mbs.edu/home/jgans/papers/Carlton-Gans-Waldman-07-08-09.pdf.

Carlton, D. and J. Perloff (2005), *Modern Industrial Organization* (4th ed), Boston: Addison Wesley.

Carlton, D. and M. Waldman (2002), 'The Strategic Use of Tying to Preserve and Create Market Power in Evolving Industries', *Rand Journal of Economics*, 33 (2), 194–220.

Carlton, D. and M. Waldman (2005), 'Tying, Upgrades, and Switching Costs in Durable-Goods Markets', *National Bureau of Economic Research, Working Paper No. 11407*, available at http://www.nber.org/papers/w11407.

Cooper, J., L. Froeb, D. O'Brien and M. Vita (2005), 'Vertical Antitrust Policy as a Problem of Inference', *International Journal of Industrial Organization*, 23 (7–8), 639–64 (2005).

DeGraba, P. (1996), 'Why Lever into a Zero-Profit Industry: Tying, Foreclosure, and Exclusion', *Journal of Economics and Management Strategy*, 5 (3), 433–47.

Evans, D. and M. Salinger (2005), 'Why Do Firms Bundle and Tie? Evidence from Competitive Markets and Implications for Tying Law', *Yale Journal on Regulation*, 22 (1), 37–89.

Federal Trade Commission and Department of Justice Joint Hearings on Competition and Intellectual Property Law and Policy in the Knowledge-Based Economy (2002).
Fumagalli, C. and M. Motta (2006), 'Exclusive Dealing and Entry, When Buyers Compete', *American Economic Review*, 96 (3), 785–95.
Glazer, K. and A. Lipsky, Jr. (1995), 'Unilateral Refusals to Deal Under Section 2 of the Sherman Act', *Antitrust Law Journal*, 63 (3), 749–800.
Granitz, E. and B. Klein (1996), 'Monopolization by "Raising Rivals' Costs": The Standard Oil Case', *Journal of Law & Economics*, 39 (1), 1–47.
Grimes, W. (2002), 'The Antitrust Tying Law Schism: A Critique of Microsoft III and a Response to Hylton and Salinger', *Antitrust Law Journal*, 70 (1), 199–229.
Hanssen, F.A. (2000), 'The Block Booking of Films Reexamined', *Journal of Law & Economics*, 43 (2), 395–426.
Heide, J., S. Dutta and M. Bergan (1998), 'Exclusive Dealing and Business Efficiency: Evidence from Industry Practice', *Journal of Law & Economics*, 41 (2), 387–408.
Hovenkamp, H. (2002), 'IP Ties and Microsoft Rule of Reason', *Antitrust Bulletin*, 47 (2–3), 369–422.
Hovenkamp, H., M. Janis and M. Lemley (2002), *IP and Antitrust*, New York: Aspen Publishers.
Jacobson, J. (2002), 'Exclusive Dealing, "Foreclosure," and Consumer Harm', *Antitrust Law Journal*, 70 (2), 311–69.
Jacobson, J. and A. Qureshi, (2002) 'Did the Per Se Rule on Tying Survive "Microsoft"?', (14 May 2002, IP-Antitrust Hearings), available at http://www.ftc.gov/opp/intellect/020514jacobson2.pdf.
Kaplow, L. and C. Shapiro (2007), 'Antitrust', in Polinksy, A. and S. Shavell (eds), *The Handbook of Law and Economics*, Amsterdam (London): North-Holland, pp. 1073–225.
Kenney, R. and B. Klein (1983), 'The Economics of Block Booking', *Journal of Law & Economics*, 26 (3), 497–540.
Kenney, R. and B. Klein (2000), 'How Block Booking Facilitated Self-Enforcing Film Contracts', *Journal of Law & Economics*, 43 (2), 427–36.
Klein, B. (2003), 'Exclusive Dealing as Competition for Distribution on the Merits', *George Mason Law Review*, 12 (1), 119–62.
Klein, B. and A. Lerner (2007), 'The Expanded Economics of Free-Riding: How Exclusive Dealing Prevents Free-Riding and Creates Undivided Loyalty', *Antitrust Law Journal*, 74 (2), 473–519.
Klein, B. and K. Murphy (1988), 'Vertical Restraints as Contract Enforcement Mechanisms', *Journal of Law & Economics*, 31 (2), 265–97.
Klein, B. and K. Murphy (2008), 'Exclusive Dealing Intensifies Competition for Distribution', *Antitrust Law Journal*, 25, 433.
Klein, B. and J. Wright (2007), 'The Economics of Slotting Contracts', *Journal of Law & Economics*, 50 (3), 421–54.
Kobayashi, B. (2005a), 'Does Economics Provide A Reliable Guide to Regulating Commodity Bundling By Firms? A Survey of the Economic Literature', *Journal of Competition Law & Economics*, 1 (4), 707–46.
Kobayashi, B. (2005b), 'The Economics of Loyalty Discounts and Antitrust Law in the United States', *Competition Policy International*, 1 (2), 115–48.
Kobayashi, B. (2008), 'Spilled Ink or Economic Progress? The Supreme Court's Decision in *Illinois Tool Works v. Independent Ink*', 53 *Antitrust Bulletin*, 5–33, working paper version available at SSRN: http://ssrn.com/abstract=1084475.
Kolasky, W. (2002), 'GE/Honeywell: Continuing the Transatlantic Dialogue', *University of Pennsylvania Journal of International Economic Law*, 23 (3), 513–37.
Krattenmaker, T. and S. Salop (1986), 'Anticompetitive Exclusion: Raising Rivals' Costs to Achieve Power Over Price', *Yale Law Journal*, 96 (2), 209–91.
Lambert, T. (2005), 'Evaluating Bundled Discounts', *Minnesota Law Review*, 89 (6), 1688–757.
Marvel, H. (1982), 'Exclusive Dealing', *Journal of Law & Economics*, 25 (1), 1–25.

Nalebuff, B. (2000) 'Competing Against Bundles', in Hammond, P. and G. Mayles (eds), *Incentives, Organization & Public Economics: Papers in Honour of Sir James Mirrlees*, New York: Oxford University Press, pp. 323–35.

Posner, R. (2001), *Antitrust Law* (2d ed), Chicago: University of Chicago Press.

Rasmussen, E., M. Ramseyer and J. Wiley, Jr. (1991), 'Naked Exclusion', *American Economic Review*, 81 (5), 1137–45.

Rey, P., P. Seabright and J. Tirole, 'The Activities of a Monopoly Firm in Adjacent Competitive Markets: Economic Consequences and Implications for Competition Policy', *Institut d'Economie Industrielle, Université de Toulouse, Working Paper No. 132*, 2002, available at http://idei.fr/doc/wp/2001/sctivities2.pdf.

Salinger, M. (2008), 'Business Justifications in Tying Arrangements', in Collins, W. (ed.), *Issues in Competition Law and Policy*, Chicago: ABA Press, pp. 1911–1928.

Salop, S. and D. Scheffman (1983), 'Raising Rivals' Costs', *American Economic Review*, 73 (2), 267–71.

Sass, T. (2005), 'The Competitive Effects of Exclusive Dealing: Evidence from the U.S. Beer Industry', *International Journal of Industrial Organization*, 23 (3–4), 203 225.

Schwartz, M. and G. Werden (1996), 'A Quality-Signaling Rationale for Aftermarket Tying', *Antitrust Law Journal*, 64 (2), 387–404.

Segal, I. and M. Whinston (2000), 'Naked Exclusion: Comment', *American Economic Review*, 90 (1), 296–309.

Simpson, J. and A. Wickelgren (2005), 'Exclusive Dealing and Entry, When Buyers Compete: Comment' (mimeo, June 2005).

Simpson, J. and A. Wickelgren (2007), 'Naked Exclusion, Efficient Breach, and Downstream Competition', *American Economic Review*, 97 (4), 1305–20.

Steuer, R. (2000), 'Customer Instigated Exclusive Dealing', *Antitrust Law Journal*, 68 (2), 239–51.

Stigler, G. (1963), '*United States v. Loew's, Inc.*: A Note on Block-Booking', *Supreme Court Review*, 1963, 152–7.

Tom, W., D. Balto and N. Averitt (2000), 'Anticompetitive Aspects of Market-Share Discounts and Other Incentives to Exclusive Dealing', *Antitrust Law Journal*, 67 (3), 615–39.

US Department of Justice and Federal Trade Commission (1995), *Antitrust Guidelines for the Licensing of Intellectual Property*, available at http://www.usdoj.gov/atr/public/guidelines/ipguide.htm.

US Department of Justice and Federal Trade Commission (2007), *Antitrust Enforcement and Intellectual Property Rights: Promoting Innovation and Competition*, available at http://www.usdoj.gov/atr/public/hearings/ip/222655.pdf.

Vistnes, G. (2002), 'Bundling and Tying: Antitrust Analysis in Markets with Intellectual Property', 3–5 (14 May 2002), available at http://www.ftc.gov/opp/intellect/ 020514vistnesppt2.pdf.

Whinston, M. (1990) 'Tying, Foreclosure, and Exclusion', *American Economic Review*, 80 (3), 837–59.

Whinston, M. (2006), *Lectures on Antitrust Economics*, Cambridge, MA: MIT Press.

Wright, J. (2006a) 'Antitrust Law and Competition for Distribution', *Yale Journal on Regulation*, 23 (2), 169–207.

Wright, J. (2006b) 'Missed Opportunities in *Independent Ink*', *Cato Supreme Court Review*, 5, 333–59.

Wright, J. (2009) 'Antitrust Analysis of Category Management: *Conwood Co. v. United States Tobacco Co.*', 17 *Supreme Court Economic Review*.

Yde, P. and M. Vita (2006), 'Merger Efficiencies: The 'Passing-On' Fallacy', *Antitrust*, Summer 2006, 59.

Cases

Brief for the United States as Amicus Curiae, *3M Co. v. LePage's Inc.*, 542 US 953 (2004) (No. 02-1865), 2004 WL 1205191.

Barry Wright v. ITT Grinnell, 724 F.2d 227 (1st Cir. 1983).
Brooke Group Ltd. v. Brown & Williamson Tobacco Corp., 509 US 209 (1993).
Cascade Health Solutions v. PeaceHealth, 2007 US App. LEXIS 21075 (9th Cir. 2007).
CDC Techs., Inc. IDEXX Labs, Inc., 186 F.3d 74 (2d Cir. 1999).
Coca-Cola Co. v. Harmar Bottling Co., 111 S.W.3d 287 (Tex. App. 2003).
Coca-Cola Co. v. Harmar Bottling Co., 218 S.W.3d 671 (Tex. 2006).
Concord Boat Corp. v. Brunswick Corp., 207 F.3d 1039 (8th Cir. 2000).
Dehydrating Process Co. v. A.O. Smith Corp., 292 F.2d 653 (1st Cir. 1961).
El Aguila Food Prods. v. Gruma Corp., 301 F. Supp. 2d 612 (S.D. Tex. 2003), aff'd, 131 F. App'x 450 (5th Cir. 2005).
F.T.C. v. McCormick (FTC Dkt. No. C3939) (2000) (FTC File No. 961-0050).
Fox Motors, Inc. v. Mazda Distribs. (Gulf), Inc., 806 F.2d 953 (10th Cir. 1986).
Hendricks Music Co. v. Steinway, Inc., 689 F. Supp. 1501 (N.D. Ill. 1988).
Illinois Tool Works Inc. v. Independent Ink, Inc., 126 S. Ct. 1281 (2006).
Int'l Salt Co. v. United States, 332 US 392 (1947).
Jefferson Parish Hosp. Dist. No. 2 v. Hyde, 466 US 2 (1984).
Joyce Beverages v. Royal Crown Co., 555 F. Supp. 271 (S.D.N.Y. 1983).
Leegin Creative Prods, Inc. v. PSKS, Inc., 127 S. Ct. 2705 (2007).
LePage's, Inc. v. 3M, 324 F.3d 141 (3d Cir. 2003).
Lorain Journal Co. v. United States, 342 US 141 (1951).
Menasha Corp. v. News Am. Mktg. In-Store, Inc., 354 F.3d 661 (7th Cir. 2004).
Mozart Co. v. Mercedes-Benz of N. Am., Inc., 833 F.2d 1342 (9th Cir. 1987).
N. Pac. Ry. Co. v. United States, 356 US 1 (1958).
Nat'l Collegiate Athletic Ass'n v. Bd. of Regents, 468 US 85 (1984).
Omega Envtl. Inc. v. Gilbarco, Inc., 127 F.3d 1157 (9th Cir. 1997).
Ortho Diagnostic Sys., Inc. v. Abbott Labs., Inc., 920 F. Supp. 455 (S.D.N.Y. 1996).
Paddock Publ'ns., Inc. v. Chicago Tribune Co., 103 F.3d 42 (7th Cir. 1996).
R.J. Reynolds Tobacco Co. v. Philip Morris Inc., 199 F. Supp. 2d 362 (M.D.N.C. 2002), aff'd per curiam, 67 F. App'x 810 (4th Cir. 2003).
Roland Mach. Co. v. Dresser Indus., Inc., 749 F.2d 380 (7th Cir. 1984).
Ryko Mfg. Co. v. Eden Servs., 823 F.2d 1215 (8th Cir. 1987).
Standard Fashion Co. v. Magrane-Houston Co., 58 US 346 (1922).
Standard Oil Co. (Cal.) v. United States, 337 US 293 (1949).
Tampa Elec. Co. v. Nashville Coal Co., 365 US 320 (1961).
Thompson Everett, Inc. v. Nat'l Cable Adver., 57 F.3d 1317 (4th Cir. 1995).
United Shoe Mach. Corp. v. United States, 258 US 451 (1922).
United States v. Dentsply Int'l, Inc., 277 F. Supp. 2d 387 (D. Del. 2003).
United States v. Dentsply Int'l, Inc., 399 F.3d 181 (3d Cir. 2005).
United States v. Jerrold Elecs. Corp., 187 F. Supp. 545 (E.D. Pa. 1960).
United States v. Loew's, Inc., 371 US 38 (1962).
United States v. Microsoft Corp., 253 F.3d 34 (D.C. Cir. 2001).
United States v. Paramount Pictures, Inc., 334 US 131 (1948).
United States Steel Corp. v. Fortner Enterprises, 429 US 610 (1977).
US Healthcare, Inc. v. Healthsource, Inc., 986 F.2d 589 (1st Cir. 1993).
US Philips Corp. v. Int'l Trade Comm'n, 424 F.3d 1179 (Fed. Cir. 2005).
Wells Real Estate, Inc. v. Greater Lowell Bd. of Realtors, 850 F.2d 803 (1st Cir. 1988).

9 Vertical restraints, competition and the rule of reason

Shubha Ghosh[1]

As a counterexample to John Maynard Keynes's pronouncement about the influence on policy of 'defunct economists', contemporary antitrust law in the United States is shaped by the living. Nowhere is this truer than in the area of vertical restraints. Starting with debates over restrictions in patent licensing[2] and continuing with the most recent debates leading up to the Supreme Court's decision in *Leegin Creative Leather Prods. v. PSKS, Inc.*,[3] the proper legal treatment of vertical restraints has been framed in terms of ongoing debates over the economics of contractual restrictions on business freedom and the structuring of competition.[4]

This chapter examines the law and economics of vertical restraints with particular attention to the Supreme Court's recent decision in *Leegin*. While the law of vertical restraints has moved towards a rule of reason, and hence greater contractual freedom under the antitrust laws, this shift requires us to rethink the meaning of competition and the role of law in shaping the rules of the marketplace. Concomitant with this shift towards contractual freedom is the centrality of intellectual property in shaping competition policy. This chapter identifies parallels between the legal analysis of vertical restraints and the theory of intellectual property, with the goal of devising a unified approach to the law and economics of distribution mechanisms. While the principal discussion is of US antitrust law, the chapter concludes with a comparison with the European Union's approach to vertical restraints, an alternative legal regime that provides greater emphasis on the competitive norm of the free movement of goods.

Vertical restraints as a possible misnomer

A vertical restraint, or vertical agreement, is a limitation on pricing, output or other marketing decisions placed in a contract between two entities in different positions in the production and distribution chain of a product or service. By contrast, a horizontal restraint is a limitation placed in a contract between two entities in the same position in the chain. For example, an agreement among manufacturers of an identical product or service is a horizontal restraint. An agreement between a manufacturer and a distributor, or a distributor and a customer, is a vertical restraint. Some commentators refer to vertical restraints as downstream or upstream restrictions, suggesting the metaphor of a product or service flowing through the stream of commerce from the manufacturer to the end user.[5]

The categories of horizontal and vertical restraints are criticized as being empty in offering legal guidance on how to structure and manage business arrangements. Professors Baxter and Kessler argue that the adjectives 'horizontal' and 'vertical' inaccurately and confusingly describe business relationships.[6] For example, they point out that horizontal restraints on price are per se illegal, but courts have, in cases, upheld such restrictions among manufacturers or suppliers. Furthermore, many cases involve agreements that are a combination of vertical and horizontal restrictions. For example, a retailer may require that manufacturers jointly agree to boycott another retailer, as occurred in the *Toys R Us* case.[7] In such situations, the distinction between horizontal and vertical is unhelpful in disposing of the case, and courts typically look at a combination of market power and harm to competition.

The spirit of the Baxter–Kessler argument is sound, but nonetheless, the usage of the words 'horizontal' and 'vertical' persists. Their proposal to replace the horizontal and vertical categories with the concepts of substitutes and complements has not taken root. Furthermore, the fight over language ignores some of the functional implications of the categories. At the heart of the distinction between horizontal and vertical arrangements is the difference between production and distribution of a product or service. Antitrust scholars concerned over competition sometimes ignore the broader question of competition over what end and through what means.[8] Most often, antitrust disputes focus on the micro, or even pico, details of the competitive process, such as how a product will be manufactured or how a service will be provided to the end user. Broader market competition over price, quantity and quality will often be in the background of the specific dispute, but the competition at issue in a particular antitrust case will often entail rivalries among players on how to structure a market and extract the relevant surplus from specific business transactions.

For example, one type of vertical restraint is a restriction on the minimum resale price at which a distributor can resell a product. This is the restraint at issue in the *Leegin* case, mentioned above and discussed in greater detail below. While minimum resale price restrictions are part of the broader competitive process by which goods are provided to consumers at the socially optimal levels of price, quantity and quality, these restrictions arise from contract negotiations between a manufacturer and retailers over how to divide the surplus earned from the marketplace. The rivalry over the surplus includes the determination of how to provide other product dimensions, such as information on product quality and maintenance, to the end user.

To see this point in another way, the issue of vertical restraints would go away if the various links in the production and distribution chain integrated into one entity that manufactured, distributed and directly sold the product to the end user. In such a situation, we are in the classic model of competition where the rivalry is between the seller and end user over the price, quantity and quality of the product. In the vertically integrated scenario, the details are determined through internal management and authority. In the vertical restraint scenario, the details are sorted out through competition among the diverse entities that constitute the production and distribution chain. The challenge to antitrust law is to devise the rules that manage competition among these diverse entities.

Characterizing the problem of vertical restraints in terms of rivalry among different entities in the production and distribution chain helps identify a common problem between the law of vertical restraints and the law of intellectual property. Intellectual property law, like vertical restraints, regulates the distribution of a product or service. Typically, the subject of intellectual property (scientific discoveries, entertainment works, information content) can be produced at positive marginal cost but distributed at zero marginal cost. The exclusivity of intellectual property rights allows the producer of the work, protected by intellectual property law, to control various aspects of the work's distribution through licensing.[9] In turn, the scope of the rights owner's exclusivity is limited by doctrines such as fair use and the first sale doctrine. In other words, intellectual property law, like vertical restraints, mimics the vertical integration of the production and distribution of a work. For intellectual property, this mimicking occurs through the creation of a legal right of exclusivity which counters the technological ease of distribution. For vertical restraints, the mimicking occurs through a contractual restriction. Therefore, it should not be surprising that many vertical restraint cases involve, either in the background or foreground, intellectual property issues.

The parallel between vertical restraints and intellectual property has implications for antitrust policy. For example, minimum resale price maintenance has been justified as a reasonable business practice allowing the manufacturer to police investments in quality and curb free-riding by retailers. But trademark law serves the same function by requiring the manufacturer to police the retailers' investment in maintaining the quality signals contained in the trademarked brand. Since minimum resale price maintenance runs the risk of serving as a mechanism for fixing the price of the product at the retail level (i.e., disguised horizontal price fixing, with all the controversies surrounding that terminology), the argument can be made that minimum resale price maintenance is a suspect means of policing the brand when trademarks are available. Consistent with this argument, the European Union treats vertical restraints on non-branded goods and services as less harmful than vertical restraints on branded goods and services under the Guidelines for Regulation 2790/99.[10]

The law of vertical restraints can be refashioned with these two insights: (1) vertical restraints arise from the competition among producers and distributors, and (2) intellectual property law also regulates the production and distribution of a product or service. The legal and economic analysis of particular types of vertical restraints can be understood in light of these two propositions.

Vertical restraints in the US: the perspective from Leegin

Since the 2007 decision by the United States Supreme Court in *Leegin*, all vertical restraints are subject to the rule of reason rather than a per se rule. Prior to this 2007 decision, vertical territorial restrictions and maximum resale price maintenance were judged by the rule of the reason, while minimum resale price maintenance was per se illegal.[11] The historic ruling in *Leegin* removed the special treatment for minimum resale price maintenance. Given the importance of this ruling, I will focus my attention on the *Leegin* decision and analyze prior case law in light of this new precedent.

The facts of *Leegin* are quite elegant in highlighting the debate over minimum resale price maintenance. Leegin sold belts under the brand name 'Brighton' which were distributed by small retailers like Kay's Kloset, located outside of Dallas, Texas. Leegin controlled the distribution of its belts through the 'Brighton Retail Pricing and Promotion Policy' which suggested prices for the designer belts. The manufacturer also created a special program to target star retailers. Kay's Kloset, because of the volume of belts it sold, was one of the stars until Leegin became disappointed with the size and atmosphere of the store. Strife between the manufacturer and retailer emerged when Kay's Kloset discounted the price of the belts in order to compete with other retailers. As a result, Leegin informed Kay's Kloset that it would no longer be a distributor of the Brighton line of belts. Kay's Kloset sued Leegin for violation of the antitrust laws, claiming that Leegin's actions violated the per se rule against minimum resale price maintenance established by the United States Supreme Court in *Dr. Miles Medical Co. v. John D. Park & Sons, Co.* in 1911.[12] The retailer won a $1.2 million judgment against Leegin, and Leegin appealed the ruling all the way to the Supreme Court. Leegin's argument on appeal was for *Dr. Miles* to be overturned in light of the rule of reason treatment the Court had applied to other vertical restraints. The

Court, in a five to four decision, ruled in favor of Leegin, holding that the per se rule in *Dr. Miles* was 'a flawed antitrust doctrine that serves the interests of lawyers . . . more than the interests of consumers'.[13] As a result, all vertical restraints are governed by the rule of reason.

The holding of *Leegin* had been predicted for a long time.[14] Shortly after *Dr. Miles* was decided, the Court had begun placing qualifications on the per se rule. In *United States v. Colgate*, a 1919 case, the Court held that suggested prices by a manufacturer did not constitute an agreement for purposes of Section 1 of the Sherman Act.[15] In a series of subsequent cases, the Court held that the per se rule did not apply if the manufacturer retained title, as would be the case in a consignment arrangement or under an intellectual property license. In 1967, the Court held, in *United States v. Arnold, Schwinn, & Co.*, that a vertical territorial restriction was per se illegal.[16] A year later, the Court held that maximum resale price maintenance was per se illegal in *Albrecht v. Herald Tribune*.[17] Then, in the 1970s, the retraction began in earnest with the Court overruling *Schwinn* in its 1977 *GTE Sylvania* decision, holding that vertical territorial restrictions had some pro-competitive benefits and therefore should be judged by the rule of reason.[18] Twenty years later, the per se rule of *Albrecht* went by the wayside in *State Oil v. Khan*, which held that the rule of reason applied to maximum resale price maintenance.[19] Against this background of changing laws, economists were questioning the per se treatment of minimum resale price maintenance, arguing that many of the pro-competitive benefits of territorial restriction applied a fortiori to minimum resale price maintenance. Practitioners and scholars knew that the shoe would eventually drop, and consistent with the decennial shift in the tide, minimum resale price maintenance went the way of maximum ten years after the *Khan* decision.

In many ways the per se rule had been chipped away. First, the limitations placed by *Colgate*, and the consignment and licensing cases removed major areas of business practice from the scrutiny of the per se prohibition. New evidentiary burdens placed on plaintiffs also effectively weakened the per se rule. In *Monsanto Co. v. Spray-Rite Service Corp.*, decided in 1984, the Court required an antitrust plaintiff raising a claim of price fixing conspiracy among manufacturer and distributors to rule out the possibility that the defendants were acting independently.[20] Four years later, the Court ruled, in *Business Electronics v. Sharp*, that an antitrust plaintiff claiming an agreement to set resale prices based on a pattern of dealer termination, must show that the manufacturer and retailer had agreed to set a specific price.[21] These two hurdles made it quite difficult for a plaintiff to prosecute an antitrust claim based on resale price maintenance. Under *Leegin,* the plaintiff must, in addition, show that the anti-competitive effects of setting minimum resale prices outweigh any pro-competitive benefits.

The Court's rejection of a per se rule in favor of the rule of reason was predicated on identifying several pro-competitive benefits from minimum resale price maintenance. At the outset, Justice Kennedy's opinion states that the rule in *Dr. Miles* was based on formalistic legal thinking as opposed to a consideration of business realities. The 1911 Court adopted a per se rule because the restriction on minimum prices was viewed as a restraint on alienation that was disfavored at common law. The 2007 Court states that equating the restriction on minimum resale prices with restraints on alienation ignored the reality that such restraints were less suspect when applied to chattels than when applied to land. Furthermore, such reliance on historic, antiquated doctrine did not take into consideration the realities of the manufacturer–dealer relationship.

Citing the economics literature extensively, the Court identifies three pro-competitive benefits to minimum resale price maintenance. First, allowing manufacturers to restrict retailers' ability to discount is an effective tool to prevent free-riding in the provision of services that might be beneficial to consumers. Second, minimum resale price maintenance is an important business tool to discipline retailers who did not meet manufacturer expectations by providing the retailers a guaranteed margin, loss of which could be threatened through termination. Finally, minimum resale price maintenance, by reducing intrabrand competition through price cutting, promotes interbrand competition that in turn encourages entry and innovation by manufacturers. Put together, the Court identifies the benefit of resale price maintenance in cementing the manufacturer–retailer relationship through curing retailer opportunism that inhibited competition at the manufacturing level.

The Court does identify two anti-competitive uses of minimum resale price maintenance as well. The first is the use of minimum resale price maintenance as a means of policing horizontal price fixing either by manufacturers or by retailers. The second is the abuse of minimum resale price maintenance by a dominant manufacturer or a dominant retailer to prevent innovation and the adoption of new distribution methods and business practices. While acknowledging these harmful uses, the Court does not see them as justifying per se condemnation. Furthermore, each of these harms could be addressed through the per se rule against horizontal price fixing or through a claim for monopolization. Since a practice may have a mix of pro-competitive and anti-competitive effects, the rule of reason is the appropriate legal standard.

In *Leegin*, the four dissenting judges express skepticism about the majority's rejection of the per se rule in an opinion authored by Justice

Breyer. Minimum resale price maintenance, the dissent points out, has led to higher prices for consumers. Congress had permitted states to legalize minimum resale price maintenance from 1937 to 1975, and 36 states did so. Retail prices in the 36 states where the practice was legal were estimated to be about 19 to 27 per cent higher than in states where it was not allowed. Minimum resale price maintenance is inconsistent with the goals and ideal of price competition. Furthermore, even if the practice does have pro-competitive benefits in promoting the entry of new manufacturers and in limiting free-riding, the dissenters do not see substantive evidence of these benefits. Instead, the dissenters point to the expansion in retailing that occurred under the per se rule against minimum resale price maintenance, as small retailers were able to compete aggressively on the basis of price and realize advantages from economies of scale. Finally, the dissent sees the change in the law as raising administrative costs and disrupting the structure of the economy:

> What about malls built on the assumption that a discount distributor will remain an anchor tenant? What about home buyers who have taken a home's distance from such mall into account? What about Americans, producers, distributors, and customers, who have understandably assumed, at least for the last thirty years, that price competition is a legally guaranteed way of life? The majority denies none of this. It simply says that these 'reliance interests [. . .] cannot justify an inefficient rule'.[22]

In contrast with the majority, the dissent does not see a problem with treating minimum resale price maintenance differently from vertical restraints. According to the dissent, the empirical evidence of anti-competitive effects and the lack of evidence of pro-competitive benefits militate against adopting the rule of reason for minimum resale price maintenance.

The contrasting majority and dissenting opinions highlight three issues central to understanding the treatment of vertical restraints in the US: (1) the difference between the rule of reason and a per se rule; (2) the use of economic theory in competition law; and (3) the meaning of competition. I address each of these issues in turn.

Rule of reason versus per se rules

The majority and dissent take diametrically opposing views on the place of the rule of reason in the analysis of agreements under the Sherman Act. Justice Kennedy's opinion states that the rule of reason is the presumed standard for challenges to anti-competitive agreements, and the per se rule is applied 'only after courts have had considerable experience with the type of restraint at issue . . . and only if courts can predict with confidence that it would be invalidated in all or almost all instances under the rule of reason'.[23] By contrast, the dissent would apply a per se rule when 'the likely anticompetitive consequences of a particular practice are so serious and the potential justifications so few (or, e.g., so difficult to prove) that courts have departed from a pure "rule of reason" approach'.[24] Justice Breyer's approach would not presume a rule of reason but would recognize that courts 'often apply' this approach.

Given such contrasting views on the appropriateness of the rule of reason, it is not surprising that there was such a split in the Court on the treatment of minimum resale price maintenance. By way of comparison, the 1997 case of *State Oil v Khan*, which ruled that maximum resale price maintenance was subject to the rule of reason, was a unanimous decision with the seven justices common to both panels agreeing on the outcome. (Justices Roberts and Alito have replaced Justices O'Connor and Rehnquist since the *Khan* decision, and we can only speculate on how these two justices would have ruled in *Leegin*. Likely, the outcome would not have been that different given the two departing justices' pro-business tendencies, but Justice O'Connor had shown a proclivity towards competition in her intellectual property jurisprudence and, therefore, may have been the swing vote that saved *Dr. Miles*.) The four dissenting justices in *Leegin*, given their votes in *Khan*, cannot be viewed as antitrust zealots. Instead, the different voting patterns can be explained by the merits of the business practice. Maximum resale price maintenance does not have 'few business justifications', to borrow the language of the *Leegin* dissent since it serves to combat monopolistic pricing by single retailers in remote geographic areas (such as the retailer in *Khan*). Even if the justification of combating monopolistic practices by retailers is questionable, maximum resale price maintenance has been used to curb price discrimination and to limit opportunistic behavior by a retailer.[25] Furthermore, maximum resale price maintenance, unlike minimum, still allows for price competition among retailers and the benefits of reduced prices to consumers. Consequently, for the dissent, maximum resale price maintenance is a potentially more reasonable business practice than minimum resale price maintenance.

Given the different burdens of persuasion the majority and dissent pose for per se rules, economic theory and norms of competition are critical in determining how a particular business practice will be treated under the antitrust laws. For the majority, the anti-competitive harms must be clear and must dominate any pro-competitive justifications in order for per se treatment to prevail. For the dissent, the pro-competitive justifications have to trump anti-competitive effects. Consequently, economic evidence as to pro-competitive effects is enough to sway the majority towards rule of reason treatment. The dissent, however, does not find the economic evidence strong enough. Two points can be gleaned from the analyses in *Leegin*: (1) economic evidence has to be garnered in an appropriate way to justify a per se rule, and (2) underlying norms of competition inform how the court views the benefits and harms of business practices. I turn to each of these two points next.

Economic theory

Economic theory plays a critical role in the majority's analysis. The citation of, and reliance on, the economics literature is perhaps the most extensive of any antitrust case. Particularly relevant to the Court's decision are articles by Mathewson & Winter (1998);[26] Klein & Murphy (1988);[27] and Deneckere, Marvel & Peck (1996).[28] So influential were the citations of economics literature that they deserved specific comment by Justice Breyer:

> Economic discussion, such as the studies the Court relies upon, can help provide answers to these questions, and in doing so, economics can, and should, inform antitrust law. But antitrust law cannot, and should not, precisely replicate economists' (sometimes conflicting) views. This is because law, unlike economics, is an administrative system the effects of which depend upon the content of rules and precedents only as they are applied by judges and juries in courts and by lawyers advising their clients.[29]

It should be pointed out that among the current nine justices, Justice Breyer is the closest to adopting the methodology of economics in his past writing and his current jurisprudence. Justice Kennedy, by contrast, is more closely identified with catholic and natural law approaches to decision-making. The irony of Justice Kennedy writing a largely economics based decision, and Justice Breyer taking a more critical stance, is perhaps a result of distance. Justice Kennedy is more willing to defer to economic expertise than Justice Breyer, who can assess the economic methodology more critically. Whatever the source of the differences, the majority and the dissent take positions that reflect differing understandings of the economics of minimum resale price maintenance.

For the majority, the economics literature serves as a source of identifiable benefits from minimum resale price maintenance. Specifically, the court cites extensively from the transaction costs economics literature identifying minimum resale price maintenance as solving an information problem arising between a manufacturer and its retailers. The problem can be stated as follows. If the manufacturer and retailers were one vertically integrated entity, this combined entity could make joint decisions about pricing the product and providing services that maximize the entity's profit. When a manufacturer and retailers are separate entities, however, decisions on pricing and provision of services must be made separately. Individual retailers are competing against each other, and one way in which such competition could occur is by retailers undercutting each other with respect to price. Such price competition can reduce profit margins and result in the underprovision of services and the exit of retailers. Manufacturers can curb such competition through vertical restraints in contracts. For example, the manufacturer could limit the territories serviced by a specific retailer and therefore curb the retailers' ability to compete for a customer base. This pro-competitive benefit of territorial restrictions explains the rule of reason treatment of territorial restrictions. In addition, a manufacturer could restrict the retailers' ability to engage in price competition by placing a floor on the resale price. If the floor is set correctly, the minimum price can ensure a profit margin to the retailer that would allow it to provide adequate services and prevent destructive exit. Furthermore, minimum resale price maintenance can create incentives for retailers to provide services to consumers by preventing a price cutting retailer from free-riding on services provided by a competitor retailer. With these economic benefits identified, the majority concludes that per se treatment against minimum resale price maintenance is unwarranted.

The dissent's response is to emphasize that there is no economic consensus about the benefits from resale price maintenance. The criticism is based on lack of empirical data. Free-riding, the underprovision of services, and destructive exit can occur in theory, but will it occur in practice? 'We do, after all, live in an economy', the dissent reminds us, 'where firms, despite *Dr. Miles'* per se rule, still sell complex technical equipment (as well as expensive perfume and alligator billfolds) to consumers.'[30] How often does free-riding actually occur, the dissent asks, and after considering the extensive record and the economics literature, the dissent answers that free-riding happens 'sometimes'.[31] More importantly, the dissent is concerned about a court's ability to distinguish between the pro-competitive and anti-competitive effects of minimum resale price maintenance. The per se rule of *Dr. Miles* provides a bright line rule for the purposes of enforcement and predictability, and the lack of any substantive economic evidence in favor of the anti-competitive harms of the per se rule warrants against moving to the rule of reason.

On the surface, the difference between the majority and dissent is largely a question of empirical evidence. But there is a substantive difference in how the two sides view the competitive process. The majority's reliance on the transaction costs economics literature results in an emphasis on the information problems that arise in the contract between the manufacturer and retailers. The information problem can be solved in part by centralized decision making through vertical integration of a manufacturer and retailers. Vertical restraints serve as a contractual substitute for vertical integration. The problem is how the law should allocate the right to set price. The majority assigns all the rights to the manufacturer to then reassign through the contract with the retailer. In effect, after the *Leegin* decision, the manufacturer has the right to set all the terms of the vertical restraints, whether based on price or territory. This right can be abrogated only when it is used in an anti-competitive fashion that outweighs the pro-competitive benefits, such as in the case of horizontal price fixing among manufacturers or among retailers.

The natural question is whether the manufacturer should have the right to set the terms of the vertical restraint, specifically the right to set minimum prices. The Coase Theorem would guide us in answering the question by consideration of transaction costs. Since the majority views the information problem as one of preventing free-riding in the provision of services, the concern is that a manufacturer is in a better position to determine what types of services should be provided (and how) as part of the product distribution to consumers. Giving a manufacturer the right to set the terms of a vertical restraint is consistent with giving it control over how a product is made and sold. Therefore, the most efficient allocation, according to the majority's thinking, is to grant the right to set price to the manufacturer which can set the terms of the agreement with retailers in a way that resolves the information problem.

The dissent, however, has a different view of the economics, starting with its description of the free-riding problem. As the dissent points out:

> '[F]ree riding' often takes place in the economy without any legal effort to stop it . . . We all benefit freely from ideas, such as that of creating the first supermarket. Dealers often take a 'free ride' on investments that others have made in building a product's name and reputation. The question is how often the 'free riding' problem is serious enough significantly to deter dealer investment.[32]

The dissent adopts an approach that is much less proprietary in its implications than the majority's approach. The dissent would unequivocally allocate the right to set a minimum price to the retailers, largely because of the benefits of open price competition. The encomium to free-riding is one to market freedom more broadly, but market freedom tempered by price competition. In contrast with the majority's decision that sees the information problems leading to free-riding as insurmountable unless the per se rule is removed, and thereby that reallocates the right to set minimum price to the manufacturer, the dissent's decision presents a world with low transaction costs in which competition between manufacturer and retailers and among retailers will prevail in the lowest price for consumers.

Both the majority and the dissent speak in terms of efficiency, but while the majority sees the prohibition against minimum resale price maintenance as clearly inefficient, the dissent is less certain, finding benefits in price competition. Different interpretations of economics theory and the weight given to empirical data explain much of the opposing conclusions. Also important are contrasting conceptions of competition, the subject of the next section.

Competitive norms

Professor Alan Meese writes convincingly about how courts have conceptualized competition in their antitrust analysis.[33] His central point is that courts tend to misunderstand non-conventional contracting and to overemphasize price competition. The *Leegin* opinion may be the remedy to the conceptual failures Professor Meese has diagnosed. The cure, arguably, is worse than the disease. The Court effectively recognizes non-standard contracting and the varied ways in which competition can occur. But the result is one that creates strong proprietary rights that ignore the benefits of traditional price competition.

The majority acknowledges that minimum resale price maintenance has the potential to benefit consumers by providing 'more options so that they can choose among low-price, low-service brands; high price-high service brands; and brands that fall in between'.[34] The majority envisions a realm of contractual freedom in which the manufacturer can use minimum resale price maintenance to promote the provision of service by retailers or, alternatively, the manufacturer can allow retailers to compete over price. The problem, of course, is that the manufacturer cannot simultaneously use both strategies for an identical product unless it effectively polices the marketplace to prevent the discounted goods from entering the market where retailers are restricted. More realistically, manufacturers of a given product will gravitate towards one regime or another, and therefore, the effect of allowing minimum resale price maintenance will vary by industry. High end, high prestige products may be marketed with little or no price competition while lower end products may be distributed through discount channels. Whatever the result, the majority sees the marketplace as one in which multiple contractual forms can flourish, providing the appropriate mix of price and quality to consumers.

The dissent adopts a more conventional view of the marketplace governed largely by price competition. Market forces, however, do not work against the provision of service and quality. In fact, they work in their favor by permitting suppliers to attract consumers through the provision of technical information and consumer services. Furthermore, territorial restrictions and other contractual terms can aid in allowing manufacturers to police the provision of service and quality by retailers. The dissent, however, does not accept the argument that minimum resale price maintenance is the most efficient or effective way to compete on the margins of quality and service. Instead, price is still the major dimension on which manufacturers and retailers do, and should, compete to ensure that consumers are provided quality goods at the minimum price. Allowing some forms of vertical restraints, such as based on territories or restrictions on maximum resale prices, would be sufficient to prevent free-riding and to realize the benefits of variety in service and price as portrayed by the majority.

An argument in the majority's favor is that competitive pressures force manufacturers to work inefficiently around the per se prohibition on minimum resale price maintenance. The majority documents the steps taken by manufacturers to adopt policies of announced prices and dealer termination that could more effectively be implemented through direct use of minimum resale price maintenance. This argument rests on the efficiency of minimum resale price maintenance compared to other contractual mechanisms, a comparison that demonstrates the lack of empirical evidence at thc heart of Justice Breyer's opinion. The fundamental question here is evaluating the role of courts in the competitive process. For the majority, the simplest answer is to minimize the role of the courts altogether by allowing contractual freedom. The irony is that the rule of reason, while making it more burdensome for a plaintiff to bring an antitrust complaint, requires a court to scrutinize a business practice more closely to gauge its pro-competitive and anti-competitive consequences. The rule of reason therefore requires more judicial scrutiny than a per se rule. Therefore, the majority's deference to contractual freedom by adopting the rule of reason invites greater scrutiny of business practices and the competitive process.

Another argument in favor of the majority's abrogation of the per se rule is that, since the decision in *Dr. Miles*, retailers have grown significantly in size and market position within the United States. Consequently, any attempt by manufacturers to limit price competition may be countered by retailers. For example, many grocery stores have store brands for staples, such as cereal and soup, which compete with the manufacturers' brands. Grocery stores can lower the price of the store brand items to put competitive pressure on the manufacturers' brands. Of course, smaller retailers, such as Kay's Kloset, the plaintiff in *Leegin*, will have a harder time competing with the manufacturers.

Recognizing non-price forms of competition through non-conventional contracting requires deeper empirical information and scrutiny of markets than the traditional use of price competition as the benchmark for assessing antitrust policy. But this observation is not a mandate that courts should uphold any policy which potentially leads to lower prices. Lower prices within a market system can come at costs of lower quality, fewer services and less innovation. However, courts and policymakers can consider some of the implications of legal rules for the structure of a particular market and resulting incentives. Using this broad template as a guideline, we can reach some conclusions about the differing conceptions of competition between the majority and the dissent.

The majority adopts a pro-manufacturer view of competition, one that countenances limitations on intra-brand competition among retailers in order to promote inter-brand competition among manufacturers. Its view of competition is analogous to the strongly proprietary view of intellectual property, also justified in terms of free-riding prevention and the promotion of new entry and new products. Just as strong intellectual property rights place the rights to define manufacturing and distribution scope within the market to the rights holder, so the majority's grant of rights to a manufacturer to set the terms of vertical restraints allows it to define the territorial scope of distribution channels for its output. In intellectual property, the strong rights are tempered in narrow ways through doctrines such as fair use and first sale, which protect the interests of users of works protected by intellectual property. In manufacturing, the rights are tempered by the standard of reasonableness to balance the pro-competitive and anti-competitive consequences of a manufacturer's contractual choices.

The dissent's defense of the per se rule against minimum resale price maintenance can be understood against this conception of the competitive process that supports the rights of manufacturers. Certainly, the dissent is not against contractual freedom, and it does not oppose the use of vertical restraints. Instead, it is concerned that the majority's decision gives manufacturers too strong a set of rights that may invite restrictions on price competition at the retail level that will hurt consumers. To borrow an analogy from intellectual property, the dissent is proposing restrictions on the rights of the manufacturer to protect the rights of the retailers much like advocates of fair use or first sale rights seek to create a balance between the intellectual property owner and users. The goal, as in the case of intellectual property, is to ensure access to, and limit control over the channels of distribution.

Which set of rights within the competitive process is most appropriate is ultimately an empirical question whose answer depends on how the legal rules play out over time in actual business practice. The empirical evidence, however, is mixed with some support that resale price maintenance, at least when administered by the state, has been an effective means of enforcing a cartel.[35] Furthermore, despite the theoretical justification for minimum resale price maintenance as a means for providing point of sale service,[36] restrictions on minimum resale prices have been used in markets, such as cookware, where point of sale service is of minimum concern.[37] In light of the conflicting empirical evidence, Justice Breyer frames the question of how to treat minimum resale price maintenance in terms of the burden of overturning an established legal precedent; meanwhile Justice Kennedy frames it in terms of identifying some cognizable pro-competitive benefit that militates against a per se prohibition. At the heart of the disagreement, however, are differing views of contract and competition. A similar contrast can be seen when we compare the new US approach to vertical restraints with the European treatment.

A comparison of the US with the EU: contrasting norms of competition

Article 81, formerly Article 85, of the Treaty of Rome governs vertical restraints under European competition law. Specifically prohibited under Article 81(1) are agreements that 'directly or indirectly fix purchase or selling prices or any other trading conditions' and that 'limit or control production, market, technical development, or investment'.[38] Exceptions are envisioned under Article 81(3) under some limited circumstances for agreements 'which contribute . . . to improving the production or distribution of goods or to promoting technical or economic progress.'[39] Pursuant to Article 81(3), the European Council has adopted several regulations that expressly create such exceptions. Regulation 17, promulgated in 1962, allows the Commission to create block exemptions from Article 81(1). Exemptions have been created for licensing of patents and know-how as well as for technology transfer. An exemption was promulgated in 1983 for exclusive distribution agreements under some clearly defined circumstances based on market share and the size of the business entities. These were in effect until 1999 when they were superseded in 2000 by Regulation 2790/99, which deals specifically with vertical agreements.

Regulation 2790/99 provides a categorically defined set of exemptions for vertical agreements based on the size of the companies and market affected by the specific agreement. The recitals acknowledge the competitive benefits of vertical agreements, particularly their ability to 'improve economic efficiency within a chain of production or distribution by facilitating better coordination between the participating undertakings'.[40] One critical efficiency highlighted is 'a reduction in the transaction and distribution costs of the parties and to an optimisation of their sales and investment levels'.[41] European competition law, like US antitrust law, recognizes the benefits of vertical restraints, particularly those that arise from removing incentives to free-ride on investments in services. But, unlike the US's adoption of an open ended balancing approach under the rule of reason, the European Union creates categorical rules for the application of the exemption. Automatically exempt are any agreements in which the supplier does not have more than 30 per cent of the market (or in the case of an exclusive supply contract, the buyer has no more than 30 per cent of the market) and if the agreement does not cover what the regulations call 'hard core' restraints, which includes fixing minimum resale prices.

The regulation also provides a general methodology for determining when a vertical agreement should be exempted. In addition to considerations of market share and business size, the following factors work in favor of an agreement: (1) the tendency of the restraint to promote inter-brand competition; (2) the use of vertical restraints on non-branded products or services is less suspect than their use on branded products or services; (3) the use of vertical restraints to control a dominant position at the retail level, such as through the imposition of a maximum resale price; (4) the use of the vertical restraint to transfer and protect know-how within a business relationship; (5) the use of a vertical restraint to protect relationship-specific investments; and (6) a vertical restraint is less suspect when it is used by an entrant providing a new product or servicing a new geographic market.

What is striking about the European approach is the contrast with the analysis in *Leegin*. While the European approach recognizes many of the pro-competitive benefits recognized by the majority in *Leegin*, Regulation 2790/99 relies more on clear rules and guidelines as opposed to a balancing test that places great weight on the pro-competitive justifications of the business practice. Justice Breyer's dissent, although he does not cite any European authorities, is very close to the European approach even if his opinion advocates maintaining a per se rule. At one point in the dissent, however, Justice Breyer states that he would propose a per se rule with a narrow exception for the entry of a new product in the marketplace, much like what we see in the European regulations.

Another contrast is the differing norms of competition in the US and the European Union that inform competition policy. The US approach focuses squarely on contractual relationships specifically and contractual freedom generally. As discussed above, the *Leegin* majority assigns rights under the contract to the manufacturer, which is given broad discretion in shaping the terms of a contract and the scheme of distribution. The emphasis in the European Union is on the consistent and free flow of goods among member states. As the European Court of Justice stated in its first opinion reviewing a vertical restraint under Article 81(1), '[T]here is no need to take account of the concrete effects of an agreement once it appears that it has as its object the prevention, restriction, or distortion of competition'.[42] The presumption is reversed under European Union law; anti-competitive effects of a vertical restraint make the restraint illegal absent an exemption. The *Leegin* majority, however, held that vertical restraint is not per se illegal, and arguably presumptively legal, once pro-competitive justifications have been shown.

Competition as defined by the free movement of goods is not surprisingly a core value in European competition law. The Treaty of Rome is essentially a free trade agreement and consequently open markets and access are fundamental norms in the structuring of markets through competition law. Justice Breyer's dissent echoes these norms with its vision of competition as well, albeit the dissenters' vision is framed in terms of price competition. The *Leegin* majority illustrates the more proprietary model of competition that is prevalent in US antitrust law and intellectual property doctrines. Competition is based on strong property rights and freedom to contract, with the terms largely determined by the party which is deemed to be the most efficient in managing the property rights. In the European Union, and in Justice Breyer's vision, competition is defined in terms of entry of new products and firms.

Given the two conflicting visions of competition on each side of the Atlantic, it is difficult to imagine some convergence in the law. The key test will be to see if the *Leegin* decision places some pressure on the European Union to create a block exemption for minimum resale price maintenance. Member states are allowed to permit some degree of minimum resale price maintenance on the sale of books in order to help publishers in promoting national culture.[43] There is also a broader debate about the benefits of minimum resale price maintenance in promoting retailing.[44] The *Leegin* decision will only fuel this debate. Whatever the result, the European solution most likely will be one that takes into account a very different model of competition and the values of market entry and price competition than evinced by the *Leegin* majority.

After the rule of reason

As Professors Kaplow and Shapiro caution, '[I]f the rule of reason is legally defined in terms of competition itself – that which promotes competition is legal, that which suppresses competition is illegal, end of story – then economics cannot directly address the legal test'.[45] The majority's decision in *Leegin* ignores this advice. Justice Kennedy's opinion absorbs the findings of transaction costs economics and transforms them into competition policy. But transaction costs economics, with all its richness and importance, does not provide a general theory of competition. As a result, the *Leegin* opinion substitutes a proprietary model of contractual freedom for a true consideration of competition norms. Justice Breyer perhaps has the better of the debate, especially when compared with the approach of European competition law.

Now that we have moved into a regime of rule of reason for all vertical restraints in the United States, the natural question is what next? Prior to the *Dr. Miles* decision in 1911, there was no common law decision that struck down a vertical restriction.[46] After *Leegin*, an illegal vertical restraint may once again become a rarity. The rule of reason mandates a consideration of both the pro-competitive and anti-competitive effects of a given agreement to determine its legality. Perhaps, as more agreements are subject to the rule of reason, courts will be able to identify specific guidelines and bright line rules for categorizing certain practices as illegal under the antitrust laws. Ideally, a categorical approach as we see in the European Union, but with different categories, will emerge. More realistically, the *Leegin* majority has created a rule of per se legality, with the pro-competitive justification of preventing free-riding serving to absolve all vertical restraints, except for those that would be actionable as horizontal restraints under Section 2. In fact, a recent speech by Commissioner Rosch of the Federal Trade Commission suggests that most vertical restraints are being challenged as monopolization cases. The result may be less competition in the form of new entry and price discounting.[47]

To end optimistically, I hope Congress, the Department of Justice and the Federal Trade Commission consider the issue of vertical restraints in the near future and consider an approach like that of the European Union. A categorical approach has the benefits, like that of a per se rule, of providing clarity and guidance to business planning while also promoting competitive entry that places a downward pressure on price. Such an approach would truly provide a rule for a competitive marketplace founded on reason rather than freedom of manufacturers to set the terms of a contract.

Notes

1. Professor of Law and Associate Director, INSITE, The University of Wisconsin Law School.
2. *E. Bement & Sons v. National Harrow Co.*, 186 US 70 (1902).
3. *Leegin Creative Leather Prods. v. PSKS, Inc.*, United States Supreme Court, slip opinion, 28 June 2007.
4. Chen, A.C.M. and K.N. Hylton (1999), 'Procompetitive theories of vertical control', *Hastings Law Journal*, **50**, 573–633.
5. Sullivan, L.A. and W.S. Grimes (2006), *The Law of Antitrust: An Integrated Handbook* (2nd edn), Minneapolis, US: Thomson-West.
6. Baxter, W.F. and D.P. Kessler (1995), 'Toward a consistent theory of the welfare analysis of agreements', *Stanford Law Review*, **47**, 615–31.
7. *Toys 'R' Us, Inc. v. Federal Trade Commission*, 221 F.3d 928 (7th Cir. 2000).
8. Kaplow, L. and C. Shapiro (2007), 'Antitrust', Harvard John M. Olin Center for Law, Economics, and Business, Discussion Paper No. 575.
9. Meurer. M. (2003), 'Vertical restraints and intellectual property law: beyond antitrust', *Minnesota Law Review*, **87**, 1871–912.

10. Fox, E.M. (2002), *Cases and Materials on the Competition Law of the European Union*, Minneapolis, US: West Group.
11. Sullivan and Grimes (2006), *supra* note 5.
12. *Dr. Miles Medical Co. v. John D. Park & Sons Co.*, 220 US 373 (1911).
13. *Leegin*, *supra* note 3.
14. Bork, R. (1978), *The Antitrust Paradox: A Policy At War With Itself*, New York: Basic Books; Hylton, K. (2003), *Antitrust Law: Economic Theory and Common Law Evolution*, Cambridge: Cambridge University Press; Posner, R.A. (2001), *Antitrust Law*, Chicago: The University of Chicago Press.
15. *United States v. Colgate & Co.*, 250 US 300 (1919).
16. *United States v. Arnold, Schwinn, & Co.*, 388 US 365 (1967).
17. *Albrecht v. Herald Co.*, 522 US 145 (1968).
18. *Continental T.V., Inc. v. GTE Sylvania Inc.*, 433 US 36 (1977).
19. *State Oil Co. v. Khan*, 522 US 3 (1997).
20. *Monsanto Co. v. Spray-Rite Service Corp.*, 465 US 752 (1984).
21. *Business Electronics Corp. v. Sharp Electronics Corp.*, 484 US 717 (1988).
22. *Leegin*, *supra* note 3.
23. *Id.*
24. *Id.*
25. Carstensen, P. and D. Hart (2003), 'Khaning the Court: how the antitrust establishment obtained an advisory opinion legalizing "maximum" price fixing', *University of Toledo Law Review*, **34**, 241–307.
26. Mathewson, F. and R. Winter (1998), 'The law and economics of resale price maintenance', *Review of Industrial Organization*, **13**, 57–75.
27. Klein, B. and K.M. Murphy (1988), 'Vertical restraints as contractual enforcement mechanisms', *Journal of Law and Economics*, **31**, 265–95.
28. Deneckere, R., H.P. Marvel and J. Peck (1996), 'Demand uncertainty, inventories, and resale price maintenance', *Quarterly Journal of Economics*, **111**, 885–911.
29. *Leegin*, *supra* note 3.
30. *Id.*
31. *Id.*
32. *Id.*
33. Meese, A.J. (2005), 'Market failure and non-standard contracting: how the ghost of perfect competition still haunts antitrust', *Journal of Competition Law and Economics*, **1** (1), 21–95.
34. *Leegin*, *supra* note 3.
35. Ornstein, S.I. and D. Hanssens (1987), 'Resale price maintenance: output increasing or restricting? The case of distilled spirits in the United States', *Journal of Industrial Economics*, **36**, 1, 1–18; Ippolito, P.M. (1991), 'Resale price maintenance: empirical evidence from litigation', *Journal of Law and Economics*, **32**, 263–95.
36. Tesler, L.G. (1960), 'Why should manufacturers want fair trade?', *Journal of Law and Economics*, **3**, 86–105.
37. Ippolito, P.M. and T.R. Overstreet, Jr. (1996), 'Resale price maintenance: an economic assessment of the Federal Trade Commission's case against Corning Glass Works', *Journal of Law and Economics*, **39**, 285–328.
38. Treaty Establishing the European Community (Treaty of Rome), Art. 81, 25 Mar 1957, 1997 OJ (C 340).
39. *Id.*
40. Commission Regulation 2790/99, 1999 OJ (L336) 21.
41. *Id.*
42. *Consten and Grundig v. Commission*, Cases 56, 58/64, (1966) ECR 299.
43. Organization for Economic Cooperation and Development (1997), 'Resale price maintenance', available at http://www.oecd.org/dataoecd/35/7/1920261.pdf.
44. Kay, J. (2007), 'The revival of price-fixing in the land of free enterprise', *Financial Times* (3 July 2007).

45. Kaplow, L. and C. Shapiro (2007), 'Antitrust', Harvard John M. Olin Center for Law, Economics, and Business, Discussion Paper No. 575.
46. Thorelli, H. (1955), *The Federal Antitrust Policy: Origination of an American Tradition*, Baltimore, US: The Johns Hopkins Press.
47. Rosch, J. T. (2007), 'Vertical restraints and Sherman Act § 2'. Available at http://www.ftc.gov/speeches/rosch/070613verticalrestraints.pdf.

References

Baxter, W.F. and D.P. Kessler (1995), 'Toward a consistent theory of the welfare analysis of agreements', *Stanford Law Review*, **47**, 615–31.

Bork, R. (1978), *The Antitrust Paradox: A Policy At War With Itself*, New York: Basic Books.

Carstensen, P. and D. Hart (2003), 'Khaning the Court: how the antitrust establishment obtained an advisory opinion legalizing "maximum" price fixing', *University of Toledo Law Review*, **34**, 241–307.

Chen, A.C.M. and K.N. Hylton (1999), 'Procompetitive theories of vertical control', *Hastings Law Journal*, **50**, 573–633.

Deneckere, R., H.P. Marvel and J. Peck (1996), 'Demand uncertainty, inventories, and resale price maintenance,' *Quarterly Journal of Economics*, 111, 885–911.

Fox, E.M. (2002), *Cases and Materials on the Competition Law of the European Union*, Minneapolis: West Group.

Hovenkamp, H., M.D. Janis and M.A. Lemley (2007), *IP and Antitrust: An Analysis of Antitrust Principles Applied to Intellectual Property Law*, New York: Aspen Law & Business.

Hovenkamp, H. (2005), *The Antitrust Enterprise: Principle and Execution*, Cambridge: Harvard University Press.

Hovenkamp, H. (2005), *Federal Antitrust Policy: The Law of Competition and Its Practice*, St. Paul: Thomson-West.

Hylton, K. (2003), *Antitrust Law: Economic Theory and Common Law Evolution*, Cambridge: Cambridge University Press.

Ippolito, P.M. (1991), 'Resale price maintenance: empirical evidence from litigation', *Journal of Law and Economics*, **32**, 263–95.

Ippolito, P.M. and T.R. Overstreet, Jr. (1996), 'Resale price maintenance: an economic assessment of the Federal Trade Commission's case against Corning Glass Works', *Journal of Law and Economics*, 39, 285–328.

Kaplow, L. and C. Shapiro (2007), 'Antitrust', Harvard John M. Olin Center for Law, Economics, and Business, Discussion Paper No. 575.

Kay, J. (2007), 'The revival of price-fixing in the land of free enterprise', *Financial Times* (3 July 2007).

Klein, B. and K.M. Murphy (1988), 'Vertical restraints as contractual enforcement mechanisms', *Journal of Law and Economics*, **31**, 265–95.

Macher, J.T. and B.D. Richman (2006), 'Transaction cost economics: an assessment of empirical research in the social sciences', Duke Law School Research Paper No. 115.

Mathewson, F. and R. Winter (1998), 'The law and economics of resale price maintenance', *Review of Industrial Organization*, **13**, 57–75.

Meese, A.J. (2005), 'Market failure and non-standard contracting: how the ghost of perfect competition still haunts antitrust', *Journal of Competition Law and Economics*, **1** (1), 21–95.

Meurer. M. (2003), 'Vertical restraints and intellectual property law: beyond antitrust', *Minnesota Law Review*, **87**, 1871–912.

Organization for Economic Cooperation and Development (1997), 'Resale price maintenance', available at http://www.oecd.org/dataoecd/35/7/1920261.pdf.

Ornstein, S.I. and D. Hanssens (1987), 'Resale price maintenance: output increasing or restricting? The case of distilled spirits in the United States', *Journal of Industrial Economics*. **36** (1), 1–18.

Posner, R.A. (2001), *Antitrust Law*, Chicago: The University of Chicago Press.
Rey, P. and J. Stiglitz (1995), 'The role of exclusive territories in producers' competition,' *RAND Journal of Economics*, **26** (3), 431–51.
Rosch, J. T. (2007), 'Vertical restraints and Sherman Act § 2'. Available at http://www.ftc.gov/speeches/rosch/070613verticalrestraints.pdf.
Sullivan, L.A. and W.S. Grimes (2006), *The Law of Antitrust: An Integrated Handbook*, (2nd edn), Minneapolis: Thomson-West.
Tesler, L.G. (1960), 'Why should manufacturers want fair trade?', *Journal of Law and Economics*, **3**, 86–105.
Thorelli, H. (1955), *The Federal Antitrust Policy: Origination of an American Tradition*, Baltimore: The Johns Hopkins Press.

Cases

Albrecht v. Herald Co., 522 US 145 (1968).
E. Bement & Sons v. National Harrow Co., 186 US 70 (1902).
Business Electronics Corp. v. Sharp Electronics Corp., 484 US 717 (1988).
Consten and Grundig v. Commission, Cases 56, 58/64, (1966) ECR 299.
Continental T.V., Inc. v. GTE Sylvania Inc., 433 US 36 (1977).
Dr. Miles Medical Co. v. John D. Park & Sons Co., 220 US 373 (1911).
Leegin Creative Leather Prods. v. PSKS, Inc., United States Supreme Court, slip opinion, 28 June 2007.
Monsanto Co. v. Spray-Rite Service Corp., 465 US 752 (1984).
State Oil Co. v. Khan, 522 US 3 (1997).
Toys 'R' Us, Inc. v. Federal Trade Commission, 221 F.3d 928 (7th Cir. 2000).
United States v. Arnold, Schwinn, & Co., 388 US 365 (1967).
United States v. Colgate & Co., 250 US 300 (1919).

10 Market concentration in the antitrust analysis of horizontal mergers

*Jonathan B. Baker**

I Introduction

This chapter examines the role of market concentration in the analysis of horizontal merger under the antitrust laws.[1] Concentration is a natural aspect of horizontal merger analysis because mergers among rivals, by their nature, reduce the number of firms participating in a market, make some firms larger than before and increase concentration within the market.

The role of concentration in merger review under the antitrust laws has changed markedly over time. During the 1960s, measures of post-merger market concentration and its increase from merger were viewed as sufficient statistics for determining whether the transaction was likely to harm competition. Over the succeeding decades, however, antitrust enforcers and courts have increasingly come to undertake a more wide-ranging economic analysis of proposed mergers. Still, the contemporary legal framework for analyzing horizontal mergers assigns a leading role to market concentration, basing a presumption of harm to competition from merger on high and increasing concentration.

This chapter evaluates the extent to which modern economic analysis supports a role for concentration in the antitrust review of horizontal mergers. It examines market definition, the predicate for measuring market shares and market concentration, and the role of market shares and concentration in the analysis of the coordinated and unilateral competitive effects of merger.[2] The central issue is when and how market shares, and market concentration statistics derived from them, form an appropriate basis for presuming harm to competition from merger.

Section II describes how concentration has been employed in the legal framework for merger analysis. Section III examines the role of market definition from an economic perspective. Section IV surveys the economic justifications for representing market concentration by the Herfindahl–Hirschman Index (HHI), a commonly-employed statistic. Section V explains the role of market concentration in the analysis of coordinated and unilateral competitive effects of merger. The final Section offers concluding thoughts about the use of market shares and market concentration as a basis for presuming harm to competition from horizontal merger.

II Market concentration in the legal framework for merger analysis

Under the primary US statute regulating mergers, Clayton Act §7, mergers are illegal if 'the effect of such acquisition may be substantially to lessen competition, or to tend to create a monopoly'.[3] In making that predictive determination with respect to horizontal acquisitions, the courts have historically assigned a leading role to one aspect of market structure: market concentration.

Modern merger law began in 1950, when Clayton Act §7, originally enacted in 1914, was amended to address what was seen as a rising tide of economic concentration in the US economy.[4] In *United States v. Philadelphia National Bank*,[5] the Supreme Court responded by setting forth a jurisprudential approach to horizontal merger analysis framed around a presumption of harm to competition created by high and increasing market concentration. This presumption is often termed the *Philadelphia National Bank* presumption or the 'structural' presumption, because it makes an inference about harm to competition from an important aspect of market structure.

During the 1960s, the Court invoked the structural presumption to prevent mergers between firms which, by modern standards, had small market shares in markets that were not concentrated.[6] At that time, the structural presumption could be invoked in almost all mergers among rivals and was in practice virtually conclusive, making all but the smallest horizontal mergers virtually illegal per se based on evidence related to market concentration.

The doctrinal framework for merger analysis developed during the 1960s has not been overruled, but the structural presumption has eroded substantially in practical significance since that time. The Supreme Court established that the presumption was rebuttable in *United States v. General Dynamics Corp.*, the Court's last major substantive merger decision.[7] The successful rebuttal in *General Dynamics* was on narrow grounds, that market concentration was measured in misleading units, in an unusual case where shares based on production differed markedly from shares based on capacity. Since *General Dynamics*, the lower courts have accepted that market shares could mislead for a wide range of reasons and have used the *General Dynamics* precedent to broaden substantially the methods by which the structural presumption can be rebutted and to make rebuttal easier.

The leading modern case, *United States v. Baker Hughes, Inc.*, a DC Circuit decision written by one future Supreme Court justice (Clarence Thomas) and joined in by another (Ruth B. Ginsburg), gives a nod to the structural presumption but does not give much practical weight to market concentration.[8] *Baker Hughes* employed and codified the doctrinal structure for horizontal merger analysis established in *Philadelphia National Bank*. According to *Baker Hughes*, the government (the usual plaintiff in a merger case) satisfies an initial burden of production by demonstrating that the merger 'will lead to undue concentration in the market for a particular product in a particular geographic area'.[9] That showing 'establishes a presumption that the transaction will substantially lessen competition' (the legal standard of the Clayton Act).[10] A burden of production then shifts to the defendants, the merging firms, to offer evidence that rebuts the presumption. 'The more compelling the [government's] prima facie case, the more evidence the defendant must present to rebut it successfully.'[11] If the defendant succeeds in its rebuttal, then the government must proffer additional evidence of anticompetitive effect. At all times the ultimate burden of persuasion remains with the government.

In practical application, though, the structural presumption was accorded little weight in *Baker Hughes*. The court described market concentration as 'a convenient starting point for a broader inquiry into future competitiveness', emphasized the variety of factors that defendants could rely upon to rebut the government's prima facie case based on market concentration, and declared that '[t]he Supreme Court has adopted a totality-of-the-circumstances approach' to evaluating horizontal mergers.[12] Using this framework, the circuit court upheld a lower court decision declining to enjoin the acquisition of a firm with a 17.5 per cent market share by a rival with a 40.8 per cent market share. It permitted the merger to proceed notwithstanding that the transaction increased concentration substantially in a market that is highly concentrated by contemporary standards.

But the structural presumption has not disappeared. A decade later, the DC Circuit – the same court that decided *Baker Hughes* – in *Federal Trade Commission v. H.J. Heinz Co.*, reversed a district court decision denying a preliminary injunction in a merger challenge and directed the district court to enjoin the merger.[13] The appeals court in *Heinz* followed the burden-shifting framework set forth in *Baker Hughes*. The court concluded that the defendants had not successfully rebutted the presumption of harm to competition created by a merger that would have combined firms with 17.4 per cent and 15.4 per cent market shares, in a market where the leading firm had a 65 per cent market share. Had the merger not been enjoined, the transaction would have created a two-firm market. The appellate panel found clear error in the district court's factual findings that the efficiencies from merger would allow the merged firm to compete more effectively against the dominant firm, thereby removing the factual underpinning to the defendants' central rebuttal argument. With no defense rebuttal, the structural presumption carried the day for the government.[14]

III The role of market definition

When courts refer to market concentration, they are concerned with the number of significant rivals and the distribution of the market shares of those firms. In order to determine market shares, it is necessary to define a market within which those shares will be measured and identify the firms that participate in that market.

A market is defined in terms of a set of products and a geographic region; accordingly, it is common to speak of the product market and the geographic market. Market definition under the enforcement agency merger guidelines turns on assessing the economic force of buyer substitution.[15] The importance of buyer substitution to antitrust analysis is evident from the following simple model of price determination in a homogeneous product industry:

$$L = \theta/\varepsilon \qquad (10.1)$$

In equation (10.1), L is the Lerner Index of price-cost margin (price less marginal cost, as a fraction of price), ε is the elasticity of market demand (defined as a positive number), and θ indexes oligopoly behavior. With perfect competition (price-taking), price equals marginal cost, so $\theta = 0$. If the industry behaves like a monopolist, choosing the joint profit-maximizing price, then the Lerner Index equals the inverse elasticity of market demand, so $\theta = 1$. Other forms of oligopoly interaction would generally be expected to lead to price to fall between the competitive and monopoly levels, so $0 \leq \theta \leq 1$.[16]

Equation (10.1) shows why buyer substitution (here summarized as the elasticity of demand) plays a critical role in determining whether firms can exercise market power. If market demand is highly elastic, it is immediately evident that the industry would not be a valuable monopoly – making antitrust enforcement unnecessary – regardless of how successful the firms are in achieving a price close to the joint profit-maximizing level (that is, regardless of how closely θ approaches one).

The antitrust analysis of horizontal mergers effectively separates the determination of ε from the analysis of how the merger would alter θ. The task of market definition is to identify a set of products and regions that would be a valuable monopoly, not undermined by buyer substitution of outside goods and services or locations. When markets are defined for merger analysis, the focus is entirely on buyer substitution. Later steps in merger review – the analyses of market concentration, competitive effects, entry and efficiencies – ask whether the merger would likely lead to higher prices by altering the oligopoly interaction (whether the merger would increase θ).

IV Measuring market concentration

Once a market is defined, the market participants are identified[17] and market shares are assigned.[18] During the 1960s and 1970s, the most commonly-employed summary statistic was the combined market share of the top four firms (often written C_4). This statistic has been replaced in common practice by the Herfindahl–Hirschman Index (HHI), defined as the sum of the squares of the market shares of the market participants.[19] (If the market shares are measured as fractions, then the HHI will lie between 0 and 1. In antitrust practice, market shares are routinely expressed as percentages (e.g., recorded as 20 rather than as 0.20), so the HHI lies between 0 and 10000.)

One traditional economic justification for using the HHI as a concentration measure views it as a measure of cartel stability.[20] Another relates it to the price elevation in static non-cooperative oligopoly models.[21] Neither of these justifications for relying on market concentration to infer competitive effects of merger ties competitive effects tightly to market concentration, however. This is not surprising, because, as will be discussed below in connection with the analysis of competitive effects of merger, a wide range of factors beyond market concentration also affect price determination in oligopoly.[22]

The empirical literature relating market structure and market power provides additional support for the concern in merger analysis with high and increasing market concentration.[23] That literature finds that increases in concentration, particularly substantial ones, may generate large increases in price – though price increases are not inevitable in concentrated markets and many factors other than concentration are also important in determining price and the competitive effects of merger.[24] The empirical literature does not provide a strong basis for choosing any particular measure of market concentration, though it is not inconsistent with the common modern antitrust practice of using the HHI to represent concentration.[25]

V Competitive effects

Contemporary horizontal merger analysis sharply distinguishes the possibility of coordinated competitive effects of merger from unilateral competitive effects. As will be seen, market shares and market concentration matter in those distinct analyses in different ways. Concentration can be informative with respect to each type of competitive effects analysis, though in each case, with the right information, competitive effects can also be understood without reference to shares and concentration.

A Coordinated competitive effects

Coordinated effects may arise through formal or informal cooperation by firms to reduce industry output and raise price. They include cartels, but they also include arrangements that would not count as agreements under Sherman Act §1. The analysis of coordinated competitive effects addresses two issues: whether the market is conducive to coordination, and whether the merger matters.

The first issue, whether the market is conducive to coordination, turns on whether the firms participating in the market can solve their 'cartel problems': reaching a consensus on the terms of coordination, deterring members from cheating on that consensus, and preventing new competition (either expansion by excluded rivals or new entries). Notwithstanding these cartel problems, coordination can and at times does succeed. Price-fixing conspiracies are regularly uncovered by antitrust enforcers, and they sometimes involve large, sophisticated firms. Moreover, empirical economic research has identified coordinated conduct in some concentrated industries and, as explained below, economic models of repeated oligopoly interaction show that higher-than-competitive coordinated pricing is often plausible even absent an express agreement on price.

Much as merger analysis examines buyer substitution separately, by devoting the market definition step to the exclusive consideration of this economic issue, it focuses on rivalry separately from entry. Accordingly, the competitive effects discussion below will address the two cartel problems that relate to rivalry among market participants – reaching consensus and deterring cheating – but not the third, entry by new competitors.[26]

Coordinating firms must reach a consensus on the terms of coordination – for example, what price each will charge or what output it will produce – without engaging in the kind of negotiations that create an unlawful agreement. Reaching consensus on the terms of coordination could be a challenge even if firms are symmetric, because each would prefer to engineer a lower industry output and higher industry price mainly through output reduction by its rivals. One way firms might solve the problem of reaching consensus is by making some coordinated outcome 'focal' (simple and obvious, or self-evident). For example, a particular coordinated price could be selected through leader-follower behavior, or a market division based on geography or historical customer relationships might be focal.

Coordination is not inevitable even if it would be profitable for all firms and the firms can identify consensus terms of coordination, because individual firms may have an incentive to cheat on those terms. They may find it more profitable to reduce price below what the terms of coordination would require if in doing so they can expand output sufficiently. To deter such conduct, a successful cartel must find a way to detect cheating rapidly and commit to punishing the cheater (perhaps merely by returning to the competitive price).

A range of familiar market features are generally thought to affect whether firms can be expected to reach consensus and deter cheating – and thus whether the market is conducive to coordination (putting aside entry issues). Product heterogeneity and complex, changing products are both thought likely to frustrate coordination by making it difficult for firms to reach terms of coordination, though these difficulties are not invariably insurmountable.[27] Features that allow a firm to expand output rapidly – perhaps a firm's own excess capacity, or vertical integration – may make cheating easy and, in consequence, frustrate coordination. Features that lead cheating firms to expect that a severe price war would result from the breakdown of a coordinated arrangement will discourage cheating, thereby facilitating coordination. These features might include excess capacity in the hands of a firm's rivals, inelastic market demand, or low marginal costs relative to market prices. Features of the market that allow firms to cheat by making extensive sales without detection facilitate coordination. These may include private or confidential transactions, or 'lumpy' sales and large buyers. They may also include unpredictable market demand, which might make it difficult for a firm experiencing a sales drought to learn that the explanation is a rival's cheating rather than a random slowdown in business.

Market concentration is also thought to help firms solve their cartel problems. With fewer firms it may be easier for firms to reach consensus on terms of coordination, in much the same way that it is easier to coordinate calendars and schedule a dinner party the fewer the people involved. It may also be easier for firms to notice rapidly that a rival is cheating when only a few firms participate in the market. The traditional rationale for challenging a merger as likely to facilitate coordination builds on this view: a reduction in the number of firms through merger, particularly when the transaction involves sizeable firms, increases the odds of industry coordination. This explanation is not entirely satisfactory because it is more of a statistical prediction than an appeal to a mechanism that would show why the merger matters. For example, it does not provide a basis for saying one possible merger in an industry presents more of a competitive threat than another, other than by reference to the size of the firms involved.

Industry coordination is understood among economists today as the product of a repeated oligopoly interaction, and is most often modeled as an infinitely-repeated oligopoly supergame (or to the same effect, as a finitely repeated interaction with uncertain termination).[28] This approach promises to offer a richer understanding of how coordination works and why a merger might matter, as suggested by the simple model set forth below.[29]

The central idea of the theoretical models is that successful coordination requires each firm participating in the market to prefer coordination to cheating. Suppose that coordinating firms reach consensus on the industry price P and on the market shares for each firm, denoted s_i for firm i.[30] For example, the industry price might be determined through leader-follower behavior, by which the leader makes a particular price focal, and the market shares might be determined through some other focal rule, such as preservation of the shares or customer relationships previously obtained. Industry output is $Q(P)$ each period, with $Q'(P) < 0$, so firm i sells the quantity s_iQ each period. Suppose further that firms have constant marginal costs, which may differ across firms, and face capacity constraints, which again may differ across firms. Let firm i have marginal cost c_i and production capacity per period of k_i. Assume $k_i \leq Q^*$, where $Q^*(P^*)$ is the industry output that would be produced were the industry to choose the joint profit-maximizing (monopoly) price P^*. Let δ represent the discount factor, which all firms share, with $0 < \delta < 1$.[31] Assume further that if a firm chooses to cheat on a coordinated arrangement, it cuts price to just under the cartel price (so the industry price remains effectively P) and in doing so is able to attract so much business as to sell to its full capacity for T periods. If the industry price does not change, aggregate industry output Q remains unchanged as well; the cheating firm steals business from its rivals without expanding the market.

With this setup, firm i earns profits from coordination of $(P - c_i)s_iQ$ each period, and the discounted present value of its stream of profits from coordination equals $[(P - c_i)s_iQ]/(1\text{-}\delta)$. If instead the firm cheats, it earns profits $[(P - c_i)k_i]$ for each of T periods, and none thereafter (as the coordinated arrangement breaks down permanently once rivals detect cheating and react), creating a stream of total profits after cheating with a discounted present value of $[(P - c_i)k_i]T[(1-\delta^T) / (1-\delta)]$.[32] Accordingly, each firm will choose to participate in the coordinated arrangement rather than cheat so long as $[(P - c_i)s_iQ]/(1 - \delta) \geq [(P - c_i)k_i]T[(1 - \delta^T)/(1 - \delta)]$. With $(1 - \delta) > 0$, this incentive constraint simplifies to:

$$s_iQ(P)/k_iT \geq (1 - \delta^T) \tag{10.2}$$

The numerator of the left hand expression in equation (10.2), $s_iQ(P)$, represents the firm's output in any period at the coordinated price P. The denominator of the same expression, k_iT, represents the total output that a firm would produce by cheating before its cheating is detected and its rivals respond by lowering price. Accordingly, the left hand expression in equation (10.2) is the ratio of the firm's single period output, if coordination succeeds, to the firm's total output while cheating. The right hand expression, $(1 - \delta^T)$, approaches zero when the discount factor approaches one for any positive T. Both sides of the equation are positive numbers. If the left hand ratio is low enough (for a given value of $(1 - \delta^T)$, then the firm will prefer cheating to continued coordination, and a coordinated arrangement will break down or fail to form in the first place. The ratio on the left hand side falls as the coordinated price P rises.

The numerator of the ratio on the left hand side of equation (10.2), output in any period during which coordination succeeds, reflects the benefit the firm obtains from continued cooperation. A firm with a larger output has more to gain from coordinated pricing than a firm that sells less. The denominator of the ratio, the output that a firm would produce by cheating while its rivals attempt to cooperate, reflects the firm's ability to expand output before its rivals catch on and cut price.[33] Thus, a firm is more likely to prefer cheating to continued coordination as its benefit from coordination declines and its ability to profit by cheating rises.

Equation (10.2) makes the familiar 'folk theorem' point that coordination will arise if every firm cares enough about the future to be deterred from cheating today by the threat of future punishment. That is, if the discount factor δ is large enough, the right hand side of equation (10.2) can be made arbitrarily small, so equation (10.2) will be satisfied for all firms. Moreover, if equation (10.2) is satisfied for all firms, so that coordination succeeds, it is likely that coordination could be stable at a range of coordinated prices; this is another common 'folk theorem' result. Moreover, if cheating can occur for a sufficiently long time without detection and punishment (that is, if T is large enough), then equation (10.2) will not hold, so no firm would find it more profitable to cooperate than to cheat.[34]

In order to understand the implications of equation (10.2) for analysis of the coordinated effects of merger, it is useful to think of the firms participating in a market arrayed in terms of their value of $s_iQ(P)/k_iT$. The firm with the lowest value of the $s_iQ(P)/k_iT$ term is hardest to convince to join the coordinated arrangement, as it benefits least from coordination relative to its ability to profit by cheating. Suppose further that all firms would find coordination more profitable than cheating for at least a small increase in price above the level that prevailed absent coordination, and picture the firms raising the coordinated price a little at a time (perhaps through leader-follower behavior). As price rises, the left hand side of equation (10.2) declines for all firms. At some coordinated price, perhaps one below the monopoly price P^*, the incentives facing the firm with the lowest value of the $s_iQ(P)/k_iT$ term will switch. Equation (10.2) will no longer be satisfied for that firm, so the firm will prefer to cheat rather than to cooperate. Under such circumstances, coordination is no longer feasible for the industry. To forestall this outcome, the firms participating in the market would be expected to stop raising price just short of the level that would induce cheating rather than cooperation from the firm with the lowest value of $s_iQ(P)/k_iT$. Doing so would preserve coordination, but the coordinating firms would not achieve the joint profit-maximizing outcome.

As this model suggests, coordination in general can be expected to be imperfect and incomplete.[35] Coordinating firms have an incentive to choose terms of coordination (here the coordinated price *P*) that increase joint profits – but to stop making coordination more effective at the point where doing so would drive a firm to cheat.[36] In the resulting coordinated equilibrium, one firm would find itself close to indifferent between cooperation and cheating, while the other market participants would find equation (10.2) readily satisfied, not a close call. The firm that is nearly indifferent between continued coordination and cheating is termed in antitrust parlance the industry 'maverick'.[37] It limits the success of coordination, preventing price from reaching the monopoly level. The industry price is the maximum price at which the maverick would find cooperation profitable, not the higher industry price the other firms would select if their views controlled. In order for the market participants to coordinate more effectively – raise price further – the maverick's incentives must change so that the constraint it imposes is relaxed. One way that could happen is through merger.

Maverick firms play an important role in merger analysis, because a merger can alter the incentives of the maverick, reducing the constraint imposed by the maverick, and thereby allow the coordinating firms to raise price closer to the monopoly level. The most direct way for a merger to do so is through an acquisition involving a maverick.

To see why, suppose firm 1 is the maverick, nearly indifferent between cooperation and cheating. Then, using equation (10.2), $s_1Q(P)/k_1T = (1 - \delta^T)$. Suppose firm 1 merges with another firm, firm 2, which is not indifferent but prefers coordination, so $s_2Q(P)/k_2T > (1 - \delta^T)$. The merged firm's market share in the coordinated consensus is assumed to equal the sum of the two firms' premerger shares, and its production capacity is the sum of the capacities of each. Then the merged firm is not indifferent, but prefers coordination to cheating – that is, that $(s_1+s_2)Q(P)/(k_1+k_2)T > (1 - \delta^T)$.[38] In short, if the firms in the industry are coordinating pre-merger and there is just one maverick, a merger involving the maverick will relax the constraint on more effective coordination, allowing the coordinating firms to raise price. Price will rise until some firm becomes indifferent between coordination and cheating. The new maverick could be the merged firm, or it could be some other firm, perhaps the one that was second most likely to cheat before the merger.

In this simple example, a merger involving non-mavericks will not affect the constraint that the maverick, firm 1, imposes on coordination. Only a merger among mavericks will relax the constraint, make coordination more effective, and lead to a higher coordinated price. This result highlights the particular danger of coordinated competitive effects that arises when mergers involve mavericks. An acquisition involving a maverick will most likely relax a constraint on coordination, leading to higher prices.[39]

Within this framework, horizontal mergers affect the likelihood and effectiveness of coordination by altering the constraints imposed by maverick producers. The straightforward story set forth above does not exhaust the ways that a merger could alter the constraint on coordination imposed by the maverick, however.[40] Stepping outside the model, an acquisition involving a non-maverick may have a variety of effects on competition. First, a merger of non-mavericks could alter the incentives of the industry maverick.[41] For example, if the merger means that the punishment facing a cheating maverick would become more severe, the maverick might be induced to accept a higher industry price without cheating.[42] But the merger of non-mavericks could instead lead the maverick to balk at charging the pre-merger price, and instead cause price to fall.[43] Second, a merger among non-mavericks could, by virtue of its efficiencies, create a new maverick firm that would prefer a lower coordinated price than before. Third, a merger involving non-mavericks could lead to higher prices by facilitating exclusion of the maverick.

Notwithstanding this range of alternatives, it is appropriate for antitrust analysis of coordinated effects to emphasize the concern arising from a merger involving a maverick. As the model above suggests, a merger involving a maverick will most likely harm competition by making coordination more effective. Accordingly, Carl Shapiro and I have proposed that if the market is conducive to coordination, then proof that an acquisition involves a likely maverick should be a sufficient basis to presume harm to competition from coordinated effects.[44]

As a practical matter, it will not always be possible to identify the effect of the merger on the constraint imposed by the maverick in a market conducive to coordination. Under such circumstances, greater concentration raises the odds that any particular merger involves a maverick. For this reason, Shapiro and I have also proposed that if the market is conducive to coordination and the likely maverick cannot reliably be identified, then high market concentration should raise a presumption that the merger involves a maverick, and, consequently, that the merger would lead to adverse coordinated effects.[45] Such a presumption would plausibly kick in at lower concentration levels if the merger narrows asymmetries among the sellers, as by reducing the differences among sellers in product attributes or seller costs or increasing the extent of multimarket contact among firms.[46]

Greater symmetry among sellers would tend to reduce the odds that a maverick firm would prefer a substantially lower coordinated price than its rivals, and thus tend to lead to higher prices by making coordination more effective.

B Unilateral competitive effects
Unilateral competitive effects of mergers arise from the loss of direct competition between the merging firms, without requiring a change in behavior by non-merging rivals. They most commonly appear in markets where firms sell differentiated products, and this industry setting will be presumed in the discussion below.[47]

Consider a differentiated product industry in which each firm sells only one product. In the pre-merger setting, firm 1 charges price P^1 and sells Q^1 units. Before the merger, firm 1 recognizes that if it raises its price by a small amount, ΔP^1, it will lose ΔQ^1 in sales (where ΔQ^1 is defined as a positive number). The gains from doing so equal $\Delta P^1(Q^1)$,[48] while the losses equal $(P^1 - C^1)\ \Delta Q^1$, where C^1 equals marginal cost and $P^1 - C^1$ represents the price-cost margin the firm would have earned on the lost sales. The firm raises price to the point where the gains from a further price increase just equal the losses, that is to where $\Delta P^1(Q^1) = (P^1 - C^1)\ \Delta Q^1$. After dividing both sides by P^1 and rearranging terms, this equation can be rewritten as $(P^1 - C^1)/P^1 = (\Delta P^1/\Delta Q^1)(Q^1/P^1)$. This latter equation can be written in the form $L^1 = 1/\eta^1$, where L^1 is the firm's Lerner Index of price-cost margin $((P^1 - C^1)/P^1)$ and η^1 is (the absolute value of) the elasticity of the residual demand facing the firm $((\Delta P^1/\Delta Q^1)(Q^1/P^1))$.[49] This equation is the first order condition for profit maximization by firm 1.

When the first firm raises price, it loses sales as some buyers switch to their second choice product (which could be no product at all, but instead a decision not to purchase from any seller). Some of those buyers may switch to the product sold by a second firm. Now suppose the first firm and the second firm agree to merge. The result is to change the merged firm's profit-maximization calculus with respect to the first product (the product formerly sold by the first firm). After the merger the direct gains from raising the price of the first product continue to equal $\Delta P^1(Q^1)$. But the net losses from raising price are no longer equal to $(P^1 - C^1)\Delta Q^1$. The reason is that some of the ΔQ^1 lost sales from the first product lead to increased purchases of the second product, allowing the merged firm to recapture some of the lost profits from raising the price of the first product in the form of increased profits on the price of the second product.[50] The increased profits on the second product can be represented as $(P^2 - C^2)\ \Delta Q^2$, with $0 < \Delta Q^2 \leq \Delta Q^1$.[51] Now the merged firm's profits from raising the price of the first product to a small amount above the pre-merger price are unambiguously positive, as $\Delta P^1(Q^1) + (P^2 - C^2)\Delta Q^2 > (P^1 - C^1)\Delta Q^1$.[52] Before the merger, the first firm declined to raise price further because the gains from doing so were not more than the losses. After the merger, the new firm recognizes that it can recapture some of those losses, so now finds it profitable to raise the price of the first product.[53]

This is not the end of the story for the merged firm, as it may also have an incentive to increase the price of the second product. The higher price for the second product may lead some of the ΔQ^1 customers who switched from the first product to the second to stick instead with the first product (increasing the profits from raising the price of the first product), or switch to a third alternative (reducing the profits from raising the price of the first product). The merged firm will choose a profit-maximizing price for both products simultaneously, taking a range of direct effects and feedbacks like these into account.[54] It will also consider price and 'repositioning' responses by third firms.[55] But one central idea underlying unilateral effects is captured in the example: a merger allows the firm to recapture some of the profits that would previously have been lost as a result of competition with its merger partner, removing a constraint on pricing and leading to higher prices.

A complementary way to understand unilateral competitive effects is to recognize that before the merger, competition from all firm 1's rivals, including competition from firm 2, contributed to determining η^1, the elasticity of the residual demand function facing firm 1. The more aggressive firm 2's competitive response to firm 1 pre-merger – the less willing firm 2 was to match firm 1's price increase or the more that firm 2 would expand output when firm 1's output contracted – the greater firm 1's loss of sales to firm 2 if firm 1 raised price pre-merger, so the more elastic firm 1's pre-merger residual demand. By merging with firm 2, however, firm 1 removed the competitive response of product 2 to a price increase on product 1.[56] In consequence, the residual demand for product 1 will become less elastic, making it profitable for the merged firm to increase the first product's price.[57]

These two complementary ways of understanding unilateral effects – that they allow the firm to recapture previously lost profits, and that they remove the competitive response of an important rival – share the idea that the merger leads to higher prices by lessening a prior competitive constraint. Nothing in either way of understanding unilateral competitive effects obviously or necessarily requires market definition or relates the magnitude of unilateral effects to market concentration.[58]

The reason is simple. In differentiated product markets, a firm's market share reflects the fraction of potential customers who select its product as their first choice. But the constraint imposed by any particular rival depends instead on the firm's customers' second choices – in particular, on the extent to which its merger partner's product is the second choice for those of its customers who would switch rather than stay loyal were the first firm to raise price. Thus, market shares are informative as to likely unilateral effects to the extent that customer second choices are distributed similarly to customer first choices.[59]

To see how concentration might matter in unilateral effects analysis, it is useful to employ a model developed by Carl Shapiro.[60] Suppose that before merger, two firms each sell a single differentiated product, that demand is linear and that the oligopoly interaction is Bertrand. Product units are defined such that the slope of each demand curve is −1, so the demand function for product 1, for example, is written $x_1 = A_1 - p_1 + \alpha_{21} p_2$. Here x represents quantity sold and p represents price, with subscripts indicating firm. The parameter α_{21} is the diversion ratio from product 2 to product 1.[61] It represents the fraction of sales lost by firm 2 when it raises the price of product 2 that are captured by product 1. Firm 1's marginal cost is denoted c_1.

Using this framework, Shapiro derives, among other things, a simple lower bound approximation formula to characterize the effect of a merger between firm 1 and firm 2 on the price of product 2.[62] Varying Shapiro's notation slightly, let $L^*_2 = [p^*_2 - p_2]/p_2$ represent the monopolist's price markup for product 2 over the pre-merger price, and let $L_1 = [p_1 - c_1]/p_1$ measure the markup for the pre-merger price of product 1 over firm 1's marginal cost.[63] Then, Shapiro shows, $L^*_2 \approx [\alpha_{21}/2][p_1/p_2]L_1$. This approximation formula implements the 'recapture of lost profits' perspective on unilateral effects, as it relates the post-merger markup for product 2 to the product of the diversion ratio (a measure of the fraction of sales recaptured through merger) and the pre-merger markup on product 1 (a measure of the magnitude of the additional profit on each recaptured sale). It is an underestimate because it ignores feedbacks that arise when the merged firm also alters the price of product 1.

Market concentration matters in this analysis if diversion ratios are related to market shares. In particular, suppose that when the price of product 2 increases, product 1 captures the fraction $s_1/(1 - s_2)$ of the sales lost by product 2. Then $\alpha_{21} = s_1/(1 - s_2)$. This representation is consistent with the idea that the second choices of the customers who switch from product 2 are distributed the same way as the first choices.[64] With this assumption, the approximation formula for the post-merger increase in the price of product 2 becomes:

$$L^*_2 \approx [1/2][s_1/(1 - s_2)][p_1/p_2]L_1 \qquad (10.3)$$

Equation (10.3) relates the price elevation resulting to merger to pre-merger market concentration. For example, if there are five identical firms pre-merger (each with 20 per cent of the market) and if each has a pre-merger Lerner Index of 40 per cent, then the estimated post-merger markup would be 5 per cent.[65]

Equation (10.3) shows that high concentration generally raises a serious threat of unilateral competitive effects. For example, equation (10.3) implies that in a differentiated product industry in which all firms price at about the same level and have 40 per cent margins, a merger between a firm with 50 per cent of the market and a firm with 20 per cent of the market would lead to an increase in the price (that is, a value of L*) of about 8 per cent for one product and 12.5 per cent for the other. The products would have to be in very different market segments, appealing to different groups of customers, in order to make it plausible that a substantial number of customers switching away from their first-choice product would not shift to the merger partner's product and that the price effects of merger would be much smaller than is suggested by application of equation (10.3).[66] Put differently, errors in measuring the diversion ratios that arise from using market shares as a rough proxy for them are unlikely to be large enough to make implausible the inference that prices will rise non-trivially following this merger when market shares are so high, absent additional information showing that switchers from each merging firm would rarely prefer the product sold by the other firm.

In some cases, it may be easy to exploit this implication of high concentration for unilateral effects. When Whirlpool acquired Maytag in 2006, for example, Whirlpool accounted for about half the US market in both residential washing machines and residential dryers, while Maytag had about one-fifth of each. Those high shares, combined with the observations that both Whirlpool and Maytag had storied American brand names and both specialized in lower-end, top-loading washing machines (while new rivals from abroad specialized in high-end, front-loading machines), should have provided a reasonable basis for presuming that the merger would lead to adverse unilateral competitive effects.[67]

Another example comes from the Federal Trade Commission's (FTC) investigation of General Electric's proposed acquisition of AgfaNDT in 2003. In the US, both firms supplied ultrasonic non-destructive testing (NDT) equipment, used by quality control and safety engineers to inspect materials without damaging them. The FTC reported that in each of three markets:

> the merging parties were the two largest firms, and the combined firm would have had a market share of greater than 70% in each of the markets. Documents

> and testimonial evidence indicated that the rivalry between GE and Agfa was particularly close, and that, for a wide variety of industry participants, the products of the two firms were their first and second choices.[68]

Equation (10.3) suggests, based on market concentration alone, that the GE/Agfa merger would have led to substantial price elevation in one or both firm's products, unless the firms were distant rivals serving different groups of customers (thus calling into question the likelihood that the products of the two firms were first and second choices for a substantial group of customers).[69] Additional information cited by the FTC, from documents and testimony, made it clear to the agency that this implication of the market shares was not misleading. The Commission obtained a consent order requiring divestiture of GE's NDT business.

If market concentration is lower, more information about the distribution of customer second choices would be required before inferring diversion ratios and potentially identifying harm to competition from merger based on market shares. Suppose, for example, that the merging firms each have market shares of 10 per cent, pre-merger margins are 40 per cent for each, and the pre-merger prices of each are similar. Equation (10.3) would imply a post-merger price increase slightly more than 2 per cent for each. Now there would be more concern about the possibility of errors in measuring the diversion ratios that arise from using market shares as a rough proxy for them, and thus more concern about whether the inference that prices will rise non-trivially following the merger could be mistaken. Accordingly, the lower the merging firms' market shares, the greater the need to analyze additional information about diversion ratios before inferring harm to competition from merger and the weaker the presumption of harm to competition from unilateral effects based on market shares. Uncertainty about the market definition could similarly weaken the presumption of harm to competition from high merging firm shares in a unilateral effects case.[70]

If the available information permits informed and reasonably precise estimates of diversion ratios or the change in residual demand elasticities resulting from merger, then presumptions of harm to competition can be based on this information, without need for defining markets or measuring concentration.[71] Under such circumstances, there would be no need to define markets in order to determine the likely unilateral competitive effects of merger.[72] Alternatively, presumptions of harm to competition in unilateral effects cases can reasonably be based on market shares, through application of equation (10.3), consistent with a 'default' assumption that the diversion ratios between the products sold by the merging firms are proportional to their market shares, though the strength of that presumption should vary with the magnitude of the market shares.[73]

VI Conclusion

Both the economic and legal literatures relating market concentration to the competitive effects of merger are framed around the question of whether market share statistics provide a good basis for presuming harm to competition from merger. The general issue is a decision theory problem of determining whether error and enforcement costs are minimized by conditioning liability (or, with a presumption, a higher probability of liability) on a limited factual showing, here related to market shares. From this perspective, it makes sense for enforcers and courts to rely upon a presumption of harm to competition based on market concentration and market shares if harm to competition from merger is correlated with concentration and shares, if shares can be observed inexpensively (relative to alternative ways of identifying competitive problems), and if it would be expensive for a firm contemplating an anticompetitive merger to manipulate market concentration and share measurements in order to avoid enforcement.[74]

The analysis in this chapter makes the case for a qualified use of market share statistics as a basis for presuming harm to competition from merger.[75] It explains when and why market shares and market concentration provide a good signal of harm to competition from merger. When better evidence is available – in a coordinated effects case, about the identity of the maverick and the effect of merger on its behavior; and in a unilateral effects case, about diversion ratios and gross margins or the effect of the merger on each firm's residual demand elasticity – then market concentration statistics are unlikely to contribute much. But in the many cases in which such evidence is weak or lacking, inferences from evidence on market structure may be appropriate. This evidence is not perfectly correlated with harm to competition (in part because shares and concentration relate to the underlying economic theory differently in a coordinated case from a unilateral one); shares and concentration are not always easy to measure (particularly because market definition can be difficult); and shares and concentration are not free from manipulation by the merging firms (through the contest over market definition) – but shares and concentration can nevertheless be useful in predicting adverse competitive effects of merger.

In both coordinated and unilateral effects cases, as indicated above, there is a sensible basis for inferring harm to competition from market concentration or market shares. An important challenge for antitrust law in the future – one that is both legal and economic – is to specify the deference that should be accorded to a presumption based on concentration and shares in a legal standard or jury instruction. The goal should be to allocate burdens of production and persuasion in ways that give presumptions based on market concentration and market shares an appropriate weight in light of the modern understanding of the role concentration can play in the analysis of the competitive effects of horizontal mergers.

Notes

* Washington College of Law, American University, Washington, DC.

1. Mergers of rivals are termed 'horizontal'. Mergers involving sellers of complements, particularly between firms and their suppliers or distributors, are termed 'vertical'. Mergers involving unrelated firms are termed 'conglomerate'.
2. This chapter does not address important economic issues in horizontal merger analysis not directly related to market concentration, such as entry and efficiencies.
3. 15 U.S.C. §18 (Clayton Act §7).
4. *See Brown Shoe Co. v. United States*, 370 US 294 (1962) (recounting legislative history).
5. *United States v. Philadephia Nat'l Bank*, 374 US 321 (1963).
6. *United States v. Von's Grocery Co.*, 384 US 270 (1966) (the merging firms together controlled 7.5 per cent of market sales; and the largest firm in the market had an 8 per cent share); *United States v. Pabst Brewing Co.*, 384 US 546 (1966) (in one market, the merged firm accounted for 4.49 per cent of the sales).
7. 415 US 486 (1974). During 1975, the Court issued three substantive decisions in bank merger cases, but *General Dynamics* is generally viewed as the last major Supreme Court decision interpreting Clayton Act §7.
8. *United States v. Baker Hughes, Inc.*, 908 F.2d 981 (D.C. Cir. 1990).
9. *Id.* at 982.
10. *Id.*
11. *Id.* at 991.
12. *Id.* at 984.
13. 246 F.3d 708 (2001).
14. For a detailed analysis of the case, see Jonathan B. Baker, *Efficiencies and High Concentration: Heinz Proposes to Acquire Beech-Nut* (2001), in John E. Kwoka, Jr. & Lawrence J. White, eds., *The Antitrust Revolution* 150 (4th. ed. 2004).
15. US Department of Justice and Federal Trade Commission, *Horizontal Merger Guidelines* (1992, revised 1997), *available at* http://www.usdoj.gov/atr/public/guidelines/hmg.htm. In non-merger contexts, the US courts may also define markets with reference to supply substitution. This alternative is criticized in Jonathan B. Baker, *Market Definition: An Analytical Overview*, 74 ANTITRUST L.J. 129 (2007), which provides a detailed discussion of a wide range of conceptual and practical issues that arise in defining markets.
16. In a more fully specified model, marginal cost might depend on output and exogenous cost-shift variables like factor prices; demand (and hence the demand elasticity) might depend on output and exogenous demand-shift variables like income; and oligopoly conduct might depend on marginal cost, demand and the exogenous variables in the model. Some theories of oligopoly, for example, suggest that oligopoly conduct may depend on market concentration or unanticipated declines in demand.
17. Under the Merger Guidelines, market participants include firms currently selling the products in the locations in the market, and also 'uncommitted' entrants that could do so quickly and with little sunk (unrecoverable) costs of entry. Uncommitted entrants are assigned market shares equal to the capacity they could profitably divert into the market in the event price was to rise a small amount.
18. Market shares may be measured in various units, most commonly sales revenues, sales units or production capacity. The analysis of the merger usually does not turn on the units in which market shares are measured, but *General Dynamics* was one such case. For further discussion of measurement units, see Gregory J. Werden, *Assigning Market Shares*, 70 ANTITRUST L.J. 67 (2002).
19. The HHI was introduced in the 1982 Department of Justice Merger Guidelines. It is

the most prominent member of a class of single-dimensional concentration indices that satisfy certain plausible mathematical properties. David Encaoua & Alexis Jacquemin, *Degree of Monopoly, Indices of Concentration and Threat of Entry*, 21 INT'L ECON. REV. 87 (1980). Concentration from mergers is also sometimes described in terms of the number of significant firms participating in the market. Thus a merger in a market with four such firms might be described as reducing the number of significant rivals from four to three.

20. George Stigler, *A Theory of Oligopoly*, 72 J. POL. ECON. 44 (1964). A simplified sketch of Stigler's idea supposes that every buyer purchases one unit, industry customers arrive independently, and the probability that a customer would patronize a given firm after a cartel has formed equals the firm's market share (a measure of its past success in attracting customers). Under the assumption that no firm is cheating, the distribution of any firm's customer arrivals during a period can be characterized as binomial with probability equal to its market share s of the n industry customers. The expected sales for any firm equal ns, and the variance of firm sales equals $ns\ (1-s)$. In this framework, a firm will learn that some rival is cheating only by experiencing a surprising sales drought, basing that conclusion on statistical inference. Thus, the scope for secret cheating, and the instability of a cartel, grows larger as the variance of each firm's sales grows. The average variance of firm sales across the industry equals $[1/n]\ \Sigma\ ns(1 - s) = (1\text{-}\Sigma s^2) =$ (1-HHI). This observation suggests that the stability of an industry cartel is inversely related to the HHI. When the HHI is high, it is difficult for firms to cheat without detection, deterring cheating and making the cartel stable.

There are a number of difficulties with the argument as presented here. For example, it does not explicitly model a firm's decision to cheat rather than cooperate, or how a firm would respond if it believes that a rival has cheated; uncertainty about inferring n is not modeled; and it is not obvious why cartel stability would turn on the average variance in sales rather than the smallest sales variance. Contemporary theoretical models of cartel stability address some of these issues by working instead within a repeated game setting. *E.g.* Edward J. Green & Robert H. Porter, *Noncooperative Collusion Under Imperfect Price Information*, 52 ECONOMETRICA 87 (1984).

An alternative argument relating the HHI to cartel stability, not suggested by Stigler, assumes that a firm's gains from cheating decrease as its market share rises (perhaps because it has more to lose from the cartel breaking down) and that the likelihood that its cheating would be detected by rivals rises with its market share (perhaps because rivals can more easily learn whether larger firms are cheating). Then each firm's expected gains from cheating rise with $s(1 - s)$. Assuming that each firm's decision to cheat is independent, then the odds that some firm will cheat would be related to $\Sigma\ s(1 - s) = (1 - \text{HHI})$.

21. In general, in such models, the index of oligopoly conduct θ from equation (10.1) can be thought of as proportional to the HHI. In particular, when the firms have constant (though differing) marginal costs and reach a Cournot equilibrium, then each firm's price-cost margin equals its market share divided by the industry demand elasticity. Accordingly, if L in equation (10.1) is understood as the average output-weighted industry margin, then, L = HHI/ε. Keith Cowling & Michael Waterson, *Price-Cost Margins and Market Structure*, 43 ECONOMICA 267 (1976). *See also* Robert E. Dansby & Robert D. Willig, *Industry Performance Gradient Indexes*, 69 *Am. Econ. Rev.* 249 (1979) (relating changes in aggregate surplus to the HHI in Cournot equilibirum).

22. Market concentration may be the product of prior strategic decisions by firms, such as investments in advertising, which also affect prices. *See generally*, John Sutton, SUNK COSTS AND MARKET STRUCTURE (1991). For a recent theoretical analysis suggesting that higher fixed costs lead simultaneously to higher prices and greater market concentration, while higher costs of stimulating buyer willingness to pay (endogenous sunk costs) raise concentration while reducing prices, see Nelson Sá, 'Sunk Costs, Market Structure and Welfare: A General Equilibrium Interpretation' (Working Paper, Nov. 29, 2007). For an empirical study highlighting the importance of accounting for the

endogeneity of concentration in assessing the relationship between price and concentration, see William N. Evans, Luke M. Froeb & Gregory J. Werden, *Endogeneity in the Concentration-Price Relationship: Causes, Consequences, and Cures*, 41 J. INDUS. ECON. 431 (1993).

23. Industry profitability is not a good measure of market power, however, and there is little basis, theoretical or empirical, for relating industry profitability to market concentration. Harold Demsetz, *Two Systems of Belief About Monopoly*, in INDUSTRIAL CONCENTRATION: THE NEW LEARNING (H.J. Goldschmid, H.M. Mann & J.F. Weston, eds. 1974) (theoretical critique); Richard Schmalensee, *Inter-Industry Studies of Structure and Performance*, *in* 2 HANDBOOK OF INDUSTRIAL ORGANIZATION 976 (R. Schmalensee & R. Willig, eds. 1989) (Stylized Fact 4.5) (empirical survey).
24. Schmalensee, *supra* note 23, at 988 (Stylized Fact 5.1); Leonard Weiss, *Conclusions*, *in* CONCENTRATION AND PRICE 266–84 (Leonard Weiss, ed. 1989) (empirical survey). For other within-industry examples relating concentration and prices, *see, e.g.*, Timothy F. Bresnahan & Valerie Y. Suslow, *Oligopoly Pricing with Capacity Constraints*, 15/16 ANNALES D'ECONOMIE ET DE STATISTIQUE 267 (1989); Jonathan B. Baker, *Econometric Analysis in* FTC v. Staples, 18 J. PUB. POL'Y & MARKETING 11 (1999).
25. The empirical literature relating market structure to innovation suggests a similar conclusion. *See* Jonathan B. Baker, *Beyond Schumpeter vs. Arrow: How Antitrust Fosters Innovation*, 74 ANTITRUST L.J. 575 (2007).
26. Supply expansion by market participants that are not part of the coordinated arrangement would be considered as part of the analysis of competitive effects, but is not discussed further here.
27. Firms might reach consensus with heterogeneous, complex, or changing products through information exchange or the adoption of focal rules to simplify the coordination task. The latter approach might involve, for example, adopting a common set of product definitions, or, even if product definitions differ, adopting a common practice of quoting prices as discounts off book.
28. From the perspective of these models, the value of θ from equation (10.1) that is observed in any period is a snapshot – a realization during that period of the outcome of a repeated interaction.
29. For a non-technical discussion of the issues considered below, *see generally* Jonathan B. Baker, *Mavericks, Mergers, and Exclusion: Proving Coordinated Competitive Effects Under the Antitrust Laws*, 77 N.Y.U. L.REV. 135 (2002). For more extensive discussion of the family of repeated game models of coordination and their application to antitrust, with citations to the underlying economics literature, *see generally* Louis Kaplow & Carl Shapiro, *Antitrust* §§3.2–3.3 (oligopoly theory and collusion) & §4.2 (oligopoly theory and coordinated effects of merger) in 2 HANDBOOK OF L. & ECON. (A. Mitchell Polinsky & Steven Shavell, eds. 2007); Massimo Motta, COMPETITION POLICY: THEORY AND PRACTICE §§ 4.25, 4.3 (collusion) (2004); Kai-Uwe Kuhn, *The Coordinated Effects of Mergers*, in Paolo Buccirossi, ed., *Handbook of Antitrust Economics* (2008).
30. Side payments, such as payments to a high cost firm not to produce, are ruled out by assumption. In consequence, the coordinating firms may not be able to reach the joint profit-maximizing outcome.
31. The discount factor can be expressed as $\delta = 1/(1+r)$, where r is the interest rate between two periods of time.
32. The value of T is assumed identical for all firms.
33. If $T = 1$, then k_i, which was previously defined as the firm's production capacity, can be reinterpreted as the additional amount the firm can sell without detection if it decides to cheat.
34. As T grows large, the left hand side of equation (10.2) can be made arbitrarily small, while the right hand side approaches unity (as $0 < \delta < 1$).
35. Coordinating firms are unlikely to achieve an outcome that maximizes their joint profits for a number of reasons, some of which are not captured by the model. First, they may not be able to punish cheating as strongly as would be necessary. In addition, they may

not be able to allocate joint profits in a manner satisfactory to all because they may be unable to make side payments. Third, they may need to reduce the coordinated price below the joint profit-maximizing level or tolerate occasional price wars in order to deter cheating in an environment of uncertainty. Fourth, they may have difficulty identifying the joint profit-maximizing outcome when coordinating over multiple products or markets without communicating.

36. Cheating is rarely the cause of cartel breakups because colluding firms develop organizational methods to detect and deter it. Margaret C. Levenstein & Valerie Y. Suslow, *What Determines Cartel Success?* 44 J. ECON. LIT. 43, 75–9 (2006). Rather, breakups more commonly result from the desire of some members to renegotiate the terms of the coordinated outcome following unexpected shocks to demand or other forms of instability in the economic environment, or from the inability of the cartel to deter or accommodate entry. Although renegotiation is not permitted within the model set forth in the text, equation (10.2) suggests one reason why it might take place. Suppose that in the coordinated arrangement, the output shares (that is, the market shares s_i) are allocated in the same way as capacity shares (k_i/Q); this is a possible focal rule for determining market shares. Then firms would have an incentive to expand capacity in order to be awarded a higher market share. The maverick could place itself in a particularly strong bargaining position by doing so, as a higher capacity could threaten to tip its incentives from cooperation to cheating, and thus allow the maverick to impose substantial costs on the other firms if they do not award it a higher market share.
37. *See* US DoJ & FTC (1992) Horizontal Merger Guidelines §2.12. In an oligopoly, the common industry setting leading to antitrust scrutiny of horizontal mergers, if firms are able to coordinate it is likely that some firm, and most likely a single firm, will find itself just willing to participate in the coordinated arrangement, nearly indifferent between cooperating and cheating. Put differently, in oligopoly markets where it is plausible that firms are coordinating imperfectly pre-merger, it is possible to imagine multiple mavericks but that is unlikely unless the maverick firms are nearly identical. Accordingly, the remainder of this discussion will presume that there is just one maverick.
38. The proof turns on showing that $(s_1+s_2)Q(P)/(k_1+k_2)T > s_1Q(P)/k_1T$. This is true if and only if $(s_1+s_2)/(k_1+k_2) > s_1/k_1$, which is equivalent to $(s_1+s_2)k_1 > s_1(k_1+k_2)$ or $s_2k_1 > s_1k_2$. The last equation holds if and only if $s_2/k_2 > s_1/k_1$, which is equivalent to $s_2Q(P)/k_2T > s_1Q(P)/k_1T$. The last inequality holds by virtue of the initial assumption that firm 2 prefers coordination while firm 1 is indifferent between coordination and cheating.
39. A merger involving a maverick could in theory instead benefit competition. This unusual outcome could occur if the merger generates large cost savings, so that it enhances the maverick's incentive to keep the coordinated price low, thereby causing the industry price to decline. Such a merger would not be profitable for the merger partners unless the cost savings are very large, however.
40. These other possibilities are discussed in more detail in Baker (2002), *Mavericks* at 182–8. *See also* Kuhn, *supra* note 29, at §3.43.
41. This possibility raises obvious difficulties of proof.
42. Remarkably, therefore, it is possible that a merger conferring efficiencies on the merging firms could lead to *higher* industry prices.
43. For example, a merger of non-mavericks could lead the industry maverick to act more competitively than before if buyer responses to the merger reduce the maverick's demand and make that demand more elastic.
44. Jonathan B. Baker & Carl Shapiro, *Reinvigorating Horizontal Merger Enforcement*, in HOW THE CHICAGO SCHOOL OVERSHOT THE MARK: THE EFFECT OF CONSERVATIVE ECONOMIC ANALYSIS ON U.S. ANTITRUST (Robert Pitofsky, ed. 2008). This presumption would be rebuttable, as by showing that the presumption was improperly invoked (*e.g.* the market was not properly defined or not conducive to coordination), that the merger would not alter the prospects for industry coordination (*e.g.* because the maverick would have no less incentive to constrain coordination after the merger than before),

that entry or expansion would likely undermine or counteract any harm to competition, or that efficiencies from merger would make the deal pro-competitive on balance.

45. *Id*. This presumption would be rebuttable.
46. *See* Andrew R. Dick, *Coordinated Interaction: Pre-Merger Constraints and Post-Merger Effects*, 12 GEO. MASON. L. REV. 65, 72–6 (2003). On the significance of multimarket contact for coordination, see B. Douglas Bernheim & Michael D. Whinston, *Multimarket Contact and Collusive Behavior*, 21 RAND J. Econ. 1 (1990); William N. Evans & Ioannis N. Kessides, *Living By the 'Golden Rule': Multimarket Contact in the U.S. Airline Industry*, 109 Q. J. Econ. 341 (1994); *but cf.* David Genesove & Wallace P. Mullin, *Rules, Communication, and Collusion: Narrative Evidence from the Sugar Institute Case*, 91 Am. Econ. Rev. 379, 391–3 (2001) (colluding sugar refiners chose not to exploit multimarket contact to enhance punishment of cheaters).
47. Unilateral effects may also arise in bidding and auction markets, in markets with relatively homogeneous goods where firms compete by choosing production levels and capacities, and in a market with a dominant firm and competitive fringe. The analysis of unilateral effects in bidding and auction markets is similar in spirit to the analysis in differentiated product markets. A variety of economic models of unilateral effects of merger are analyzed in Gregory J. Werden & Luke M. Froeb, *Unilateral Competitive Effects of Horizontal Mergers*, in Paolo Buccirossi, ed., *Handbook of Antitrust Economics* (2008), working paper available at http://ssrn.com/abstract=927913.
48. The gains are technically $\Delta P^1(Q^1 - \Delta Q^1) = \Delta P^1(Q^1) - \Delta P^1\Delta Q^1$, but the $\Delta P^1\Delta Q^1$ term, the product of two small numbers, is second order in magnitude and can be ignored.
49. A firm's residual demand function describes how its quantity sold responds to changes in its price, after taking into account the competitive responses of rivals. It differs from the more familiar structural demand function, which describes how a firm's quantity sold responds to changes in its price holding constant the prices charged by rivals. For further discussion, see generally Jonathan B. Baker & Timothy F. Bresnahan, *Estimating the Residual Demand Curve Facing a Single Firm*, 6 INT'L J. INDUS. ORG. 283 (1988).
50. Note that firm 2's product does not have to be the best substitute for firm 1's product – perhaps more of the lost sales go to some third firm's product. What matters is that a significant group of firm 1's customers would respond to a higher price for firm 1's product by switching to firm 2's product. For those customers, firm 2's product is their second choice at pre-merger prices. Accordingly, a merger between sellers of differentiated products may harm competition even when most of the customers switching away from firm 1's product select the products of non-merging firms or do without the product entirely, and even when some third product is the second choice for more of firm 1's customers than is the product sold by firm 2.
51. That is, the increased profits equal the price-cost margin on the second product, which could be different from the price-cost margin on the first product, times the increase in second product sales (which will be a portion of the lost sales on the first product).
52. In this representation, sources of incremental profits from a small price rise are placed on the left hand side of the equation, while sources of incremental losses are placed on the right.
53. An alternative intuition arising from the same model arises from observing that after the merger, output expansion by the first firm leads it to cannibalize some of the sales that would otherwise have gone to its merger partner. From this perspective, the merger can be thought of as lowering the marginal revenue obtained from selling the first product or, equivalently, as raising that product's marginal cost (properly understood as incorporating an opportunity cost). Accordingly, the acquisition gives the merged firm an incentive to reduce output of the first product. The marginal cost perspective is emphasized in Joseph Farrell & Carl Shapiro, 'Antitrust Evaluation of Horizontal Mergers: An Economic Alternative to Market Definition' (2008).
54. The mathematics of the profit-maximization calculus for the merged firm are treated in, for example, Werden & Froeb, *supra* note 47 for various assumptions about the structure of buyer preferences and the interaction among sellers.

55. Firms may reposition products by altering their physical or non-physical attributes. Rival repositioning could counteract or deter the exercise of market power by the merged firm, so must be accounted for in a full analysis of the unilateral competitive effects of merger. For a model of repositioning, see Amit Gandhi, Luke Froeb, Steven Tschantz, & Gregory J. Werden, *Post-Merger Product Repositioning*, J. INDUS. ECON, 56 (1), 49–67.
56. Following the merger, firm 1 likely has an incentive to raise the price of both products. The merged firm has an incentive to raise the price of the first product because it knows that the acquisition will allow it to recapture some of the lost profits through increased sales of the second product. But it similarly has an incentive to raise the price of the second product – making the pricing response of the second product less aggressive than it would have been pre-merger.
57. This idea is implemented empirically in Jonathan B. Baker & Timothy F. Bresnahan, *The Gains from Merger or Collusion in Product Differentiated Industries*, 33 J. INDUS. ECON. 427 (1985). This method offers a way of approximating the post-merger incentive to raise price based on the assumption that the merged firm reduces output of both products by the same percentage. (However, it does not provide an exact solution to the merged firm's joint profit maximization problem.) One advantage of this approach over simulation methodologies based on using margin data and diversion ratios is that it does not require knowledge of the oligopoly solution concept or reliable estimates of the level of marginal cost. (Information about oligopoly conduct is instead inferred empirically from the past reactions of the non-merging firms.) Farrell & Shapiro, *supra* note 53, propose a diagnostic test that identifies unilateral effects without estimating their magnitude. Their approach relies upon margin data and diversion ratios, but makes no assumption as to oligopoly conduct.
58. Farrell & Shapiro, *supra* note 53. Baker & Bresnahan, *Estimating the Residual Demand Curve*, *supra* note 49, and Baker & Bresnahan, *The Gains from Merger or Collusion*, *supra* note 57, provide examples involving the US brewing industry during the 1970s that demonstrate that market shares can perform poorly in identifying market power and unilateral competitive effects of merger among sellers of differentiated products.
59. This point is recognized in the Merger Guidelines. US DoJ & FTC (2006) Horizontal Merger Guidelines §2.211. *See also* Robert D. Willig, *Merger Analysis, Industrial Organization Theory, and Merger Guidelines* (1991), BROOKINGS PAPERS ON ECON. ACTIVITY (MICROECONOMICS) 28, 299–305 (showing the relationship between market shares and diversion ratios in a logit demand system).
60. *See generally* Carl Shapiro, *Unilateral Effects Calculations* (Sept. 2007), *available at* http://faculty.haas.berkeley.edu/shapiro/unilateral.pdf. See also Carl Shaprio, *Mergers with Differentiated Products*, 10 ANTITRUST 23 (1996).
61. Diversion ratios are related to demand elasticities. For example, $\alpha_{21} = [\varepsilon_{21}/(-\varepsilon_{11})][x_2/x_1]$, where ε_{21} is the cross elasticity of demand from product 2 to product 1, ε_{11} is the own elasticity of demand for product 1, and the x's are quantities for the two products.
62. Shapiro also derives the equations for an exact solution of the model. The approximation formula is simpler to apply.
63. Note that L_1 is a conventionally-defined Lerner Index, with the price after markup as the denominator, while the denominator of L^*_2 is instead the price before markup.
64. The expression $(1-s_2)$ appears in the denominator because customers switching away from product 2 do not choose product 2. The assumption that $\alpha_{21} = s_1/(1 - s_2)$ ignores the possibility that some customers switch out of the market altogether, making the aggregate diversion ratio (total diversion to other products in the market as a fraction of total sales lost by product 2) less than unity. If the aggregate diversion ratio is less than unity, the approach set forth here would lead to an over-estimate of the (lower bound approximation to the) post-merger price increase.
65. If the firms are symmetric, and diversion ratios are related to market shares as indicated in the text (*e.g.*, $\alpha_{21} = [s_1/(1 - s_2)]$), then all diversion ratios reduce to $\alpha = 1/(n - 1)$, where n is the number of firms pre-merger. Shapiro provides an exact formula for the

price increase resulting from merger for the symmetric linear Bertrand case: $L^* = [1/2]\,[\alpha/(1 - \alpha)]L$. With diversion ratios related to market shares, this reduces to $L^* = [1/2(n - 2)]L$. For the example in the text, where $n = 5$ and $L = 0.4$, then $L^* = 6.7$ per cent, which is slightly higher than the 5 per cent figure given by the lower bound approximation used in the text.

66. The Merger Guidelines note that one way to tell whether diversion ratios are related to market shares is to analyze the information about consumers' actual first and second product choices 'provided by marketing surveys, information from bidding structures, or normal course of business documents from industry participants'. US DoJ & FTC (2006) Horizontal Merger Guidelines §2.211 n.22. The analysis of buyer substitution undertaken when defining the market may provide information that suggests or rules out this possibility, without need for further investigation.
67. The Department of Justice nevertheless declined to challenge this merger, citing in justification for its decision expansion by recent entrants, the presence of large wholesale buyers, and cost-savings from merger. *US Department of Justice Antitrust Division Statement on the Closing of its Investigation of Whirlpool's Acquisition of Maytag* (US Department of Justice, March 29, 2006), *available at* http://www.usdoj.gov/atr/public/press_releases/2006/215326.pdf. For criticism of the Justice Department's decision not to challenge the transaction, see Baker & Shapiro, *supra* note 44.
68. US Department of Justice and Federal Trade Commission (2006), *Commentary on the Horizontal Merger Guidelines* 28, *available at* http://www.usdoj.gov/atr/public/guidelines/215247.htm. The Commission also found that the remaining fringe manufacturers would not have been able to constrain a unilateral price increase by the merged firm. See also *Analysis of Agreement Containing Consent Orders to Aid Public Comment, In re General Electric* (Dec. 18, 2003) (File No. 0310097, Docket No. C-4103), *available at* http://www.ftc.gov/os/caselist/0310097/0310097anal031218.pdf.
69. This interpretation of the FTC's findings is plausible, although the FTC's discussion of the case does not specify the market shares of the individual firms, their pre-merger prices, or pre-merger price-cost margins.
70. Suppose, for example, that two markets are plausible, with concentration high in the first and low in the second. Then it may be difficult to infer diversion ratios from market shares with confidence, and appropriate to examine additional evidence about buyer substitution before shifting a burden of production to defendant to rebut a presumption of harm to competition.
71. See Baker & Shapiro, *supra* note 44.
72. Jonathan B. Baker, *Product Differentiation Through Space and Time: Some Antitrust Policy Issues*, 42 Antitrust Bulletin 177, 182-90 (1997). Even if market definition and concentration are not used in the economic analysis of unilateral effects, however, they can be useful as a way of describing those effects in litigation. *See generally*, Jonathan B. Baker, *Stepping Out in an Old Brown Shoe: In Qualified Praise of Submarkets*, 68 Antitrust L.J. 203, 209–17 (2000).
73. Baker & Shapiro, *supra* note 44. The presumption of harm to competition in unilateral effects cases would be rebuttable. If based on market shares, it might be rebutted, for example, by showing that the market was not defined properly, that the market shares were not measured correctly, or that the market shares misled as to the likelihood of unilateral effects (as by presenting evidence of diversion ratios and price-cost margins). If based on diversion ratios and price-cost margins, it could be rebutted, for example, by showing that the diversion ratio between the merging firms' products is lower than claimed, or that the margin on the product to which sales are diverted is lower than claimed by the government. Either way, it could also be rebutted with evidence that rival repositioning, entry, or efficiencies from merger would prevent or counteract the harm to competition.
74. *See* Jonathan B. Baker, *Per Se Rules in the Antitrust Analysis of Horizontal Restraints*, 36 Antitrust Bull. 733, 740 n.29 (1991).
75. For a discussion of the appropriate role for concentration in the merger guidelines,

see Jonathan B. Baker & Steven C. Salop, *Should Concentration be Dropped from the Merger Guidelines?* in ABA Antitrust Section Task Force Report, PERSPECTIVES ON FUNDAMENTAL ANTITRUST THEORY (July 2001) at 339–54.

References

Analysis of Agreement Containing Consent Orders to Aid Public Comment, In re General Electric (Dec. 18, 2003) (File No. 0310097, Docket No. C-4103), available at http://www.ftc.gov/os/caselist/0310097/0310097anal031218.pdf.

Baker, J. (1991), Per Se Rules in the Antitrust Analysis of Horizontal Restraints, *Antitrust Bulletin*, 36 (4), 733–43.

Baker, J. (1997), Product Differentiation Through Space and Time: Some Antitrust Policy Issues, *Antitrust Bulletin*, 42 (1), 177–96.

Baker, J. (1999), Econometric Analysis in *FTC v. Staples*, *Journal of Public Policy & Marketing*, 18, 11.

Baker, J. (2000), Stepping Out in an Old Brown Shoe: In Qualified Praise of Submarkets, *Antitrust Law Journal*, 68 (1), 203–18.

Baker, J. (2001), 'Efficiencies and High Concentration: Heinz Proposes to Acquire Beech-Nut', in Kwoka, J. Jr. and L. White (eds), (2004), *The Antitrust Revolution* (4th ed.), New York, Oxford University Press, pp. 150–69.

Baker, J. (2002), Mavericks, Mergers, and Exclusion: Proving Coordinated Competitive Effects Under the Antitrust Laws, *New York University Law Review*, 77 (1), 135–203.

Baker, J. (2007), Beyond *Schumpeter vs. Arrow:* How Antitrust Fosters Innovation, *Antitrust Law Journal*, 74 (3), 575–602.

Baker, J. (2007), Market Definition: An Analytical Overview, *Antitrust Law Journal*, 74 (1), 129–73.

Baker, J. and T. Bresnahan (1985), The Gains from Merger or Collusion in Product Differentiated Industries, *Journal of Industrial Economics*, 33 (4), 427–44.

Baker, J. and T. Bresnahan (1988), Estimating the Residual Demand Curve Facing a Single Firm, *International Journal of Industrial Organization*, 6 (2), 283–300.

Baker, J. and S. Salop (2001), 'Should Concentration be Dropped from the Merger Guidelines?' in *ABA Antitrust Section Task Force Report, Perspectives on Fundamental Antitrust Theory*, pp. 338–53, available at http://www.abanet.org/ftp/fundamentaltheory.pdf.

Baker, J. and C. Shapiro (2008), 'Reinvigorating Horizontal Merger Enforcement', in R. Pitofsky (ed.), *How the Chicago School Overshot the Mark: The Effect of Conservative Economic Analysis on U.S. Antitrust*, New York, Oxford University Press USA, pp. 235–91.

Bernheim, B. and M. Whinston (1990), Multimarket Contact and Collusive Behavior, *RAND Journal of Economics*, 21 (1), 1–26.

Bresnahan, T. and V. Suslow (1989), Oligopoly Pricing with Capacity Constraints, *Annales D'Economie et de Statistique*, 15/16, 267–89.

Cowling, K. and M. Waterson (1976), Price-Cost Margins and Market Structure, *Economica*, 43 (171), 267–74.

Dansby, R. and R. Willig (1979), Industry Performance Gradient Indexes, *American Economic Review*, 69 (3), 249–60.

Demsetz, H. (1974), 'Two Systems of Belief About Monopoly', in Goldschmid, H., H. Mann and J. Weston (eds), *Industrial Concentration: The New Learning*, Boston, Little, Brown & Co., pp. 164–84.

Dick, A. (2003), Coordinated Interaction: Pre-Merger Constraints and Post-Merger Effects, *George Mason Law Review*, 12 (1) 65–88.

Encaoua, D. and A. Jacquemin (1980), Degree of Monopoly, Indices of Concentration and Threat of Entry, *International Economic Review*, 21 (1), 87–105.

Evans, W. and I. Kessides (1994), Living By the 'Golden Rule': Multimarket Contact in the U.S. Airline Industry, *Quarterly Journal of Economics*, 109 (2), 341–66.

Evans, W., L. Froeb and G. Werden (1993), Endogeneity in the Concentration Price Relationship: Causes, Consequences, and Cures, *Journal of Industrial Economics*, 41 (4), 431–38.

Farrell, J. and C. Shapiro (2008), 'Antitrust Evaluation of Horizontal Mergers: An Economic Alternative to Market Definition', available at http://faculty.haas.berkeley.edu/shapiro/alternative.pdf.

Gandhi, A., L. Froeb, S. Tschantz and G. Werden (2008), Post-Merger Product Repositioning, *Journal of Industrial Economics*, 56 (1), 49–67.

Genesove, D. and W. Mullin (2001), Rules, Communication, and Collusion: Narrative Evidence from the Sugar Institute Case, *American Economic Review*, 91 (3), 379–98.

Green, E. and R. Porter (1984), Noncooperative Collusion Under Imperfect Price Information, *Econometrica*, 52 (1), 87–100.

Kaplow, L. and C. Shapiro (2007), 'Antitrust', in Polinsky, A.M. and S. Shavell (eds) *Handbook of Law & Economics*, Amsterdam, North-Holland, pp. 1073–225.

Kuhn, K-U. (2008), 'The Coordinated Effects of Mergers', in Paolo Buccirossi ed. *Handbook of Antitrust Economics*, Cambridge, MA, MIT Press, pp. 105–44.

Levenstein, M. and V. Suslow (2006), What Determines Cartel Success?, *Journal of Economic Literature*, 44 (1), 43–95.

Motta, M. (2004), *Competition Policy: Theory and Practice*, Cambridge, Cambridge University Press.

Sá, N. (2007), 'Sunk Costs, Market Structure and Welfare: A General Equilibrium Interpretation', Working Paper, 29 November.

Schmalensee, R. (1989), 'Inter-Industry Studies of Structure and Performance', in R. Schmalensee & R. Willig (eds), *Handbook of Industrial Organization*, Amsterdam, North-Holland, pp. 951–1009.

Shapiro, C. (1996), Mergers with Differentiated Products, *Antitrust*, 10 (2), 23–30.

Shapiro, C. (Sept. 2007), Unilateral Effects Calculations, available at http://faculty.haas.berkeley.edu/shapiro/unilateral.pdf.

Stigler, G. (1964), A Theory of Oligopoly, *Journal of Political Economy*, 72 (1) 44–61.

Sutton, J. (1991), *Sunk Costs and Market Structure*, Cambridge MA, MIT press.

United States Department of Justice and Federal Trade Commission (1992, revised 1997), Horizontal Merger Guidelines, available at http://www.usdoj.gov/atr/public/guidelines/hmg.htm.

United States Department of Justice and Federal Trade Commission (2006), Commentary on the Horizontal Merger Guidelines 28 (2006), available at http://www.usdoj.gov/atr/public/guidelines/215247.htm.

United States Department of Justice Antitrust Division, (2006, March) Statement on the Closing of its Investigation of Whirlpool's Acquisition of Maytag (US Department of Justice, March 29, 2006), available at http://www.usdoj.gov/atr/public/press_releases/2006/215326.pdf.

Weiss, L. (1989), 'Conclusions', in L. Weiss (ed.), *Concentration and Price*, Cambridge, MA, MIT Press.

Werden, G. (2002), Assigning Market Shares, *Antitrust Law Journal*, 70 (1), 67–104.

Werden, G. and L. Froeb (2008), Unilateral Competitive Effects of Horizontal Mergers, in P. Buccirossi ed. *Handbook of Antitrust Economics*, Cambridge, MA, MIT Press.

Willig, R. (1991), Merger Analysis, Industrial Organization Theory, and Merger Guidelines, *Brookings Papers on Economic Activity (Microeconomics)*, 28, 281–312.

Cases

Brown Shoe Co. v. United States, 370 US 294 (1962).

F.T.C. v. H.J. Heinz Co., 246 F.3d 708 (D.C. Cir. 2001).

United States v. Baker Hughes, Inc., 908 F.2d 981 (D.C. Cir. 1990).

United States v. Gen. Dynamics Corp., 415 US 486 (1974).

United States v. Pabst Brewing Co., 384 US 546 (1966).

United States v. Philadephia Nat'l Bank, 374 US 321 (1963).
United States v. Von's Grocery Co., 384 US 270 (1966).

Statute

15 U.S.C. §18 (Clayton Act §7).

11 Patent litigation, licensing, nonobviousness, and antitrust

Michael J. Meurer[1]

I Introduction

In early work on optimal patent design Nordhaus (1969) focused on selection of an optimal patent life, chosen to strike an appropriate balance between the need to stimulate research and the desire to avoid monopolistic production of the invention. More recently, the scope (Gilbert and Shapiro (1990) and Klemperer (1990)) and timing (Scotchmer and Green (1990)) of the patent grant have also been studied as instruments of patent policy. I investigate the same trade-off analyzed by Nordhaus but I consider the instruments of patent validity and antitrust policy, and take patent scope, timing, and life as given. The motivation for this choice is that it is more representative of American patent policy than the use of patent life as an instrument, and it allows me to explore the interaction of patent litigation, output restriction, and the incentive to innovate, more easily than if I considered patent scope or timing. In addition, the model developed below captures many of the salient policy issues associated with chemical or pharmaceutical product innovation.

A patent system in which all patents are valid and have a fixed term is a crude method of promoting research. A patent is desirable in cases in which it raises research expenditure in projects where investment would be too small (relative to the social optimum), but it can also lead to excessive research investment. The performance of the patent system could be improved by making the reward to the innovator a continuous choice variable controlled by a regulator. Varying the life of the patent would be one method of achieving this result. An alternative method of making the reward continuous is to link the probability of a patent grant to the nature of the research. Such a system could induce the choice of any level of research expenditure between the levels of expenditure induced by the no-patent and certain-patent alternatives, while producing less expected deadweight loss than the certain patent system. Actually, in the US patent system, uncertainty about the validity of the patent grant enters at the litigation stage rather than the patent approval stage.[2] Hence my analysis is complicated by the possibility of patent litigation and settlement.

The purpose of this chapter is to characterize an optimal patent policy using the probability of patent validity as the policy instrument. The optimal policy is then compared to the practice of American patent law. In addition, policy issues concerning the intersection of patent and antitrust law are considered.

I study an environment in which inventors of new products sometimes license their patents to avoid a trial on the issue of patent validity.[3] This model stands in contrast to models of cost reducing process inventions in which patentees may license their patents to improve the technology held by their rivals (see Gallini and Winter (1985), and Katz and Shapiro (1985) and (1987)). Both factors are undoubtedly important in explaining why process innovations are licensed, but with a model of new product innovation, it is possible to study licensing motivated solely by the threat of litigation.[4]

Whether trial occurs in equilibrium depends on the magnitude of the joint profit from a patent license. Antitrust law treats patent licenses deferentially, allowing restraints in license agreements that tend to restrict output to the monopoly level. But like cartel members, the parties producing the patented product have an incentive to cheat on the terms of the license and raise their output. Inefficiencies associated with contract formation and enforcement depress industry licensing profits. If licensing causes industry profits to fall below the monopoly level, then trial may occur in equilibrium because joint trial costs may be less than the drop in expected joint profit. The litigation or licensing activities have two implications for the efficiency of the patent system: they may reduce the deadweight loss associated with the patent monopoly (but trial imposes a new social cost), and they affect the payoffs to the winner and loser of the research contest, thereby influencing the choice of research expenditure.

My characterization of the optimal probability of validity yields several noteworthy results. First, a strong antitrust policy should be complemented with a strong patent policy (in the sense of a relatively high probability of validity), and conversely, a weak antitrust policy should be complemented with a weak patent policy. Second, I show that an optimal patent policy may lead to trial in equilibrium. This is possible because a high probability of validity (which would render the threat of trial not credible) may cause overinvestment in research, while a small probability of validity (which leads to licensing) may cause underinvestment. Thus, the sacrifice of trial costs may be necessary to get the 'right' level of research. Third, patent litigation has greater social value when antitrust policy is weak; this is true because the social value to a patent challenge grows relative to the social value of settlement as settlement grows more effective at imposing output restriction. Patent challengers can be encouraged to challenge weak patents, for example, by fee-shifting or through policies that give challengers more control over the timing and location of patent lawsuits.

Finally, I compare the *nonobviousness* standard of US patent law with an optimal patent policy. The nonobviousness standard is legalese for a requirement that the innovative process display some quantum of inventiveness. Roughly speaking, the more surprising or more difficult an innovation was to achieve, the more likely it is to satisfy nonobviousness. In the model below, I interpret the elasticity of the probability of successful innovation with respect to research investment as a measure of the obviousness of the innovative process. I show that the optimal probability of validity is inversely related to obviousness.

What is the intuition for this result? Other things being equal, the optimal probability of validity is low for a research technology such that the probability of success is relatively insensitive to research investment. Such a technology leads to excessive private research because firms race to get a patent. A low probability of validity reduces the rents to the winner of the patent race and thereby diminishes investment. Similarly, the optimal probability of validity is high when the research outcome is relatively sensitive to effort, because private investment tends to be too low relative to the social optimum since the patentee does not appropriate the full social value of the innovation.

In contrast, I show that the value of the innovation is not monotonically related to the optimal probability of validity. To see why, consider two unrelated new product innovations that result from the same kind of research technology, but the second has greater demand than the first. If the probability of validity is the same in both cases, then the socially optimal and the equilibrium levels of research are both higher in the second case. But it is unclear whether the optimal or equilibrium investment rises faster. It may be necessary to raise or lower the probability of validity to maintain equality between· the social optimum and the private equilibrium.

II A model of research, patent licensing, and litigation

I study a two-player, five-stage, complete information model of innovation. Briefly, the stages are: (1) simultaneous choice of research investment, (2) a decision whether to infringe a patent, (3) a settlement offer, (4) acceptance or rejection of the offer, and (5) a decision whether to continue to trial after settlement rejection. In stage (1) a pair of identical firms make simultaneous investments in research at a cost of x_i. The probability that firm i will get a patent is given by $p_i(x_1, x_2)$. If neither firm is successful, then there is no further action. If one of the firms obtains a patent (the patent system does not allow a patent grant to more than one inventor), then the firms continue to stage 2.

Stages (2) through (5) model patent litigation. At stage (2) the loser of the research contest chooses whether or not to compete in the market created by the patented invention. Entry into the new market requires the loser to make an irreversible investment in production or marketing. This investment makes the loser liable for patent infringement. For convenience I assume the cost of entry is zero. The only viable defense to a patent infringement suit in the model is a showing of patent invalidity due to nonobviousness. The infringer can prove invalidity with a probability α. This probability is commonly known.

Given infringement at stage (2) the winner of the research contest makes a settlement demand to the infringer at stage (3). A settlement agreement might specify royalty terms under which the infringer is allowed to continue production. It might also contain other output restrictions. I am not concerned about the details of the settlement agreement and simply suppose that it leaves a profit of Z to the infringer.

At stage (4) the infringer accepts or rejects the settlement demand. The game ends with acceptance. Rejection leads to stage (5). At stage (5) the patentee either brings an infringement suit or drops the case. If the case goes to trial then the patent is upheld with probability $1 - \alpha$ or invalidated with probability α. Both parties incur a trial cost of T.

After settlement or trial, production takes place in accordance with policies specified by patent law, antitrust law or the licensing contract. Industry profit is given by V_1, V, or $2V_0$ when production occurs under monopoly, under duopoly with a license, or under duopoly given patent invalidity, respectively. I assume that $V_0 > T$ and $V \in [2V_0, V_1]$ where the magnitude of industry profit under a settlement license depends on two factors. The first is the application of antitrust law to patent licenses. Antitrust law is more tolerant of contract terms that restrict output in the context of patent licenses than in other contractual settings. The range of V accommodates a range of antitrust regimes that differ in permissiveness toward patent licenses.[5] Second, even though antitrust law tolerates output restrictions facilitated by patent licenses, the normal temptations to cheat that face any cartel create transaction costs that erode industry profit under a settlement license. The likely result is that duopoly licensing profits are less than monopoly profits. I define S_0, S, and S_1 to be the social value of production of the new product corresponding to industry profit levels $2V_0$, V, and V_1, where $S_0 \geq S \geq S_1$.

A The settlement of patent litigation[6]

The subgame perfect Nash equilibrium is found by working backwards from the end of the game. Equilibrium of stages (2) through (5) may result in trial, no entry, or two different types of licensing agreements. In one type of license the patentee does not have a credible threat of bringing an infringement suit; the license is merely a collusive device for raising industry profit. In the other type of license both parties could get positive expected payoffs from trial, and the license is a bona fide settlement of litigation.

At stage (5) the patentee will not go to trial unless the expected payoff is higher than the alternative of sharing the market with the infringing entrant. Since the patent is invalidated with probability *a*, trial has a higher expected payoff to the patentee if:

$$(1 - \alpha) V_1 + \alpha V - T \geq V_0 \qquad (11.1)$$

If condition (1) fails then the loser of the patent contest would infringe at stage (2). The patentee would offer a license giving a profit of $Z = V_0$ to the infringer. The purpose of the license is not to avoid trial, but to use the 'ancillary' output restrictions available in a patent license to raise industry profit. The infringer would accept the license and the profit to the patentee would be $W^C = V - V_0$, the profit to the infringer would be $L^C = V_0$, and the social value of the innovation gross of research expenditures would be $\Sigma^C = S$. (The C indicates *collusive* settlement; W indicates *winner* of the patent contest; L indicate *loser*; and Σ^C represents the gross *social* value of the innovation accounting for trial outcomes and costs.)

Now suppose that the patentee has a credible threat of going to trial, i.e., condition (1) is satisfied. The next issue is whether the loser of the patent contest has a credible threat of going to trial. This is equivalent to condition (2) which states that an infringer gets a non-negative expected profit from trial.

$$\alpha V_0 - T \geq 0 \qquad (11.2)$$

If this condition is not satisfied, then the loser of the research contest will not enter at stage 2.[7] The result is a profit to the patentee of $W^N = V_1$ a profit to its competitor of $L^N = 0$, and a social value of the innovation of $\Sigma^N = S_1$. (The N represents *no* entry.) When conditions (1) and (2) are satisfied entry occurs and settlement emerges as the bargaining outcome when it maximizes joint profit, thus the condition:

$$V + 2T \geq 2\alpha V_0 + (1 - \alpha) V_1 \qquad (11.3)$$

must be satisfied for settlement. The payoffs to the patentee and its rival and the social value in the case of a settlement license are:

$$W^S = V - \alpha V_0 + T,$$
$$L^S = \alpha V_0 - T,$$
and
$$\Sigma^S = S \tag{11.4}$$

To distinguish this case from collusive settlement I will call it regular settlement. Finally, when both conditions (1) and (2) are satisfied, but condition (3) fails to hold, the parties go to trial to test patent validity. The payoffs are:

$$W^T = (1 - \alpha) V_1 + \alpha V_0 - T,$$
$$L^T = \alpha V_0 - T,$$
and
$$\Sigma^T = \alpha S_0 + (1 - \alpha) S_1 - 2T \tag{11.5}$$

Since the parameter α which represents the probability of patent invalidity is central to the normative analysis below, it is worthwhile to note the relationship between α and the various litigation outcomes. For patents with a small probability of invalidity condition (2) fails and the loser of the patent race does not enter. For large values of α condition (1) fails and the parties agree to a collusive patent license. For intermediate values of α both parties have a credible threat and either trial or settlement may occur. Inspection of conditions (1), (2), and (3) shows that trial does not occur for any value of α unless the following condition is satisfied:

$$V_1 T < V_0 (V_1 - V) \tag{11.6}$$

Thus, if the cost of trial is sufficiently low, then intermediate values of α may lead to trial. The rival is willing to go to trial because α is large enough to make the expected value of trial larger than the cost. The patentee favors trial over settlement because licensing causes a dissipation of the rents attributable to the patent ($V_1 - V$). Notice, in particular, that trial never occurs if $V = V_1$.[8]

Inspection of conditions (1), (2), and (3) also shows that settlement does not occur for any value of α unless the following condition is satified:

$$V_1 T \leq V_0 (V_1 - V_0) \tag{11.7}$$

I assume that (7) always holds.

B Investment in research

The first stage of the model incorporates the familiar contest to win a new product patent.[9] Two firms simultaneously choose x_i, a research expenditure; if no firm successfully invents a new product there is no further action; if some firm is successful it receives a patent; only one patent is granted. The firms make their investment decisions knowing that the government's patent policy implies a certain probability of invalidity α, and foreseeing the equilibrium outcome of the litigation process, and the implied payoffs to the winner and loser of the patent contest.

The expected profit of research to firm i is:

$$\pi_i = p_i(x_i, x_j)W + p_j(x_i, x_j)L - x_i, j \neq i \tag{11.8}$$

This expression states that firm i wins the patent contest with probability p_i and earns the expected payoff W. Firm j wins with probability p_j and firm earns L. Firm i incurs the cost x_i from its research investment. The precise values of W and L are determined by the choice of α and which equilibrium outcome arises in stages (2) through (5).

Restrictions are imposed on the functions p_1 and p_2 such that the research technology leads to a unique symmetric Nash equilibrium. These conditions are given in the Appendix to this chapter. Let $x = f(W, L)$ be the equilibrium expenditure by each firm as a function of the payoffs to the winner and loser of the patent contest. Natural restrictions on the technology (which are also given in the Appendix) imply:

$$\partial f/\partial W > 0 > \partial f/\partial L \tag{11.9}$$

So the equilibrium investment increases in the payoff to the winner and decreases in the payoff to the loser.

The amount of research investment stimulated by a patent contest may be greater or less than the socially optimal amount. Problems arise because the private and social value of innovation generally diverge, and because competitors race to be the first to complete an innovation in order to secure the patent. The result can be investment that is either too small or too large (compared to the social optimum), usually accompanied by inefficient duplication of research efforts.

III Optimal patent policy

The optimal patent policy controls the equilibrium research effort indirectly by fixing the probability of invalidity a, which determines the contest payoffs W and L, which in turn determine equilibrium investment x^*. The probability of invalidity also determines the social value of the innovation gross of research costs, Thus, the problem of the social planner is to search the feasible set of (x^*, Σ) pairs to maximize expected social welfare.

The social planner's problem is to choose $a \in [0,1]$ to maximize expected social welfare, which is given by:

$$ESW = 2p(x^*)\Sigma - 2x^* \tag{11.10}$$

where $p(x^*) \equiv p_1(x^*, x^*) = p_2(x^*, x^*)$. Recall x^* depends on W and L, while W, L and Σ depend on α through expressions (4) and (5). The welfare measure is constructed by taking the probability that one of the two firms obtains a patentable innovation multiplied by the gross social value of the innovation minus the research costs. The optimal policy is partially characterized in the following two propositions.

Proposition 1. Collusive settlement, regular settlement, trial, and no entry all occur as the equilibrium litigation outcome of an optimal policy for certain environments.

Proposition 2. The litigation outcomes can be ranked in terms of the research investment that they induce. The ranking of the outcomes from lowest to highest investment is: collusive settlement, regular settlement, trial, and no entry.

Proof. Examples in the Appendix prove Proposition 1. To prove Proposition 2, take a fixed environment and suppose that condition (6) holds. From conditions (1), (2), and (3) it follows that the equilibrium litigation outcomes are ordered in terms of α. When $\alpha < T/V_0$ the loser of the patent contest does not infringe. When $T/V_0 \leq \alpha < [V_1 - V - 2T]/[V_1 - 2V_0]$ trial occurs. When $[V_1 - V - 2T]/[V_1 - 2V_0] \leq \alpha \leq [V_1 - V_0 - T]/[V_1 - V_0]$ regular settlement occurs. When $[V_1 - V_0 - T]/[V_1 - V_0] < \alpha$ collusive settlement occurs. If condition (6) does not hold then trial does not occur for any α. The ordering of the other three outcomes remains the same with the boundary between no entry and regular settlement occurring at $\alpha = T/V_0$. This ranking in terms of α can be related to the equilibrium research investment x^*. From the payoff expressions W and L contained in Section IIA, one can see that W is decreasing in α and L is increasing in α. From condition (9) it follows that x^* varies inversely with α. Therefore we have the ranking in the proposition. QED.

The optimization problem for the social planner is illustrated in Figure 11.1. A representative level curve for the social welfare function is shown with the constraint set. Expected social welfare rises with Σ, and rises then falls in x^*. The constraint set is determined by the equilibrium outcomes of the litigation settlement subgame. The figure shows the set is

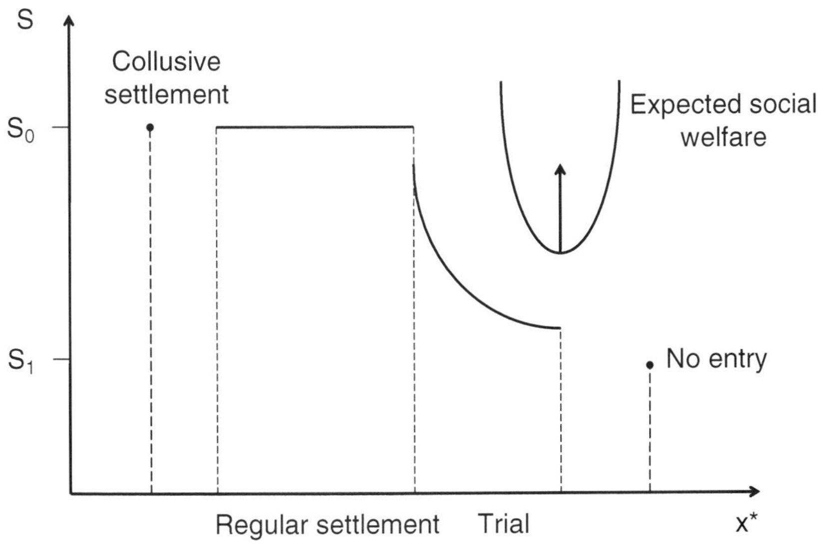

Figure 11.1 *The social planner's problem*

not connected. The isolated points arise from the no entry and collusive settlement outcomes. Recall that payoffs are not sensitive to the probability of infringement for these outcomes because one of the players does not have a credible threat of going to trial. The lowest level of investment is achieved through collusive settlement because the patent is probably invalid, and payoffs for the winner and the loser of the patent contest are relatively close. The highest level of investment is achieved when the patent is probably valid and the loser of the contest does not enter. This is a winner-take-all scenario which induces heated research competition. The segment of the constraint set corresponding to equilibrium trial only exists when condition (6) is satisfied. This segment is downward sloping because a smaller value of α raises the value of a patent and equilibrium investment, but it also increases the probability of monopoly deadweight loss. Trial yields a higher investment than regular settlement simply because it arises from smaller values of α than settlement. The social optimum occurs at the tangency of one of the level curves with the constraint set (or else there is a corner solution).

The social planner faces a trade-off between a strong research incentive and a small deadweight loss. A patent that is certainly valid (or $\alpha < T/V_0$) induces the no entry outcome and tends to be optimal when the firms underinvest in research relative to the social optimum. Even though the deadweight loss is maximized, this policy may be optimal if the firms only appropriate a small portion of the social value of the innovation. A patent that is certainly invalid (or $1 - \alpha < T/[V_1 - V_0]$) induces collusive settlement. The patentee does not have a credible threat of going to trial but can use a settlement license to raise industry profit. Despite the collusive nature of settlement this policy tends to be optimal when the social planner wants to discourage investment.[10] Research investment may exceed the social optimum when the race to win the patent is the dominant factor affecting investment.

Regular settlement or trial offer intermediate levels of research incentive. Assume condition (6) is violated so that an equilibrium trial is not possible. The social planner may prefer regular settlement over collusion because it induces higher investment with the same deadweight loss. At the same time regular settlement induces lower investment than no entry and alleviates deadweight loss. If condition (6) holds, the social planner may prefer trial over the alternatives because it induces a level of investment that is intermediate between that induced by settlement on the one hand and no entry on the other. Getting this intermediate level of investment may be worth the sacrifice in trial costs. Furthermore, the gross social value of trial may be higher than no entry despite trial costs, because the possibility of invalidity may diminish the deadweight loss.

IV Antitrust and patent policy

Ideally antitrust and patent policy should be coordinated to maximize expected social welfare. Antitrust policy towards settlement directly affects the output restrictions and deadweight loss attributable to licenses. It also affects the profitability of licensing and thus the incentives for research investment and the likelihood of settlement compared to trial. In this chapter I take antitrust policy as fixed and study the optimal choice of patent validity probabilities. Nevertheless it is possible to learn something about the interaction of the policies by determining the optimal response of patent validity probabilities to exogenous changes in antitrust policy.[11]

The variables S and V capture the effect of antitrust policy. Social value, S, and industry profit, V, from licensing move in the opposite direction as antitrust policy changes. A stringent policy limits the ability of a licensor to introduce ancillary contract terms that restrict output. This corresponds to a relatively high value of S and low value of V. A permissive policy has the opposite effect, leading to a low value of S and high value of V.

A change in antitrust policy affects the settlement payoffs, but does not affect the trial or no entry payoffs.[12] The absence of settlement licenses means that payoffs are unaffected given trial or no entry. When settlement occurs, the payoff to the winner of the patent contest grows and the social value of the innovation shrinks when antitrust policy is relaxed.

The reverse is true when antitrust policy is tightened. Because of the structure of the bargaining, the payoff to the loser of the patent contest is not affected by the antitrust policy.[13] In addition to payoffs, a change in policy also shifts the boundary between trial and regular settlement. As the policy is relaxed trial becomes less likely. I will only consider marginal changes in antitrust policy and therefore ignore movement of this boundary.

The optimal probability of invalidity responds to antitrust policy only in the regular settlement case. Obviously, the optimal probability does not respond to a marginal in antitrust policy if the optimum induces trial or no entry in the litigation subgame. Antitrust policy has no effect. Furthermore, the optimal probability does not respond in the case of collusive settlement. The reason is simply that the optimal probability is indeterminate for collusive settlement. Any value α such that $1 - \alpha > T/[V_1 - V_0]$ yields a collusive settlement. If the optimum induces regular settlement, then an exogenous change in antitrust policy provokes an offsetting change in patent policy. Specifically, if antitrust policy is relaxed, then the optimal probability of invalidity rises; if antitrust policy is tightened, then the optimal probability of invalidity falls. As a result, patent and antitrust policy must have offsetting effects on the profit of the winner of the patent contest.

Let me explain this result assuming a marginal tightening of antitrust policy. A tighter policy reduces deadweight loss from licensing. The social planner should respond by choosing higher research investment, because the marginal social value of investment has risen. The planner should notice that the tighter policy erodes the private incentive for investment, because industry licensing profits fall. Therefore, achieving higher investment requires a more secure patent and a lower probability of invalidity. I prove this result in the following proposition.

Proposition 3. When the optimal policy calls for regular settlement, the optimal probability of invalidity should be chosen to counteract the effect of changes in antitrust policy on the profitability of licenses.

Proof. Altering the antitrust policy moves V and S in the opposite direction. The first order condition for the social planner choosing x is given by $Sp'(x) = 1$. From this expression we find that $dx/dS = -p'(x)/Sp''(x)$. Since the assumptions in the Appendix imply $p'' < 0 < p'$, $dx/dS > 0$. Thus the optimal policy requires an increase in equilibrium investment when antitrust policy is made more stringent so that S rises. But the effect of a stricter policy is to decrease V. This does not affect the profit of the loser of the patent contest from a settlement; it does reduce the settlement profit of the winner. Hence if α is unchanged x would fall. The optimal policy dictates that α must fall enough to more than offset the effect of V. Thus α must fall when the antitrust policy becomes more stringent. Similarly α must rise when the policy becomes more lax. QED.

V Nonobviousness standard

The critical hurdle in pursuit of a patent is Section 103 of US patent law – nonobviousness.[14] The standard as interpreted in *Graham v. John Deere Co.*, 383 US 1 (1966), calls for three determinations: (1) the scope and content of the prior art, (2) the level of ordinary skill in the inventor's art, and (3) the difference between the prior art and the claimed invention. If the difference is nonobvious to a person of ordinary skill in the art then Section 103 is satisfied.

Direct application of the test begets arcane technical issues that trouble judges and juries. To augment the test judges have fashioned various non-technical subtests.[15] Roughly speaking the subtests fall into two categories. One category emphasizes the process of invention, e.g., failure by others, long-felt unmet nearly simultaneous independent invention (which works against the inventor), skepticism of experts, unexpected results, or movement of skilled researchers in a different direction. The other category emphasizes commercial aspects of the development of the invention, e.g., commercial success, immediate copying, or extensive licensing of the patent. There are no precise guidelines for integration of the subtests into the traditional three-part test. It is clear, however, that passing one or more of these subtests bolsters the inventor's claim of nonobviousness. The effect of the subtests is to make the probability that the courts find an invention nonobvious depend on the attribute measured in the subtest. For example, the greater the commercial success of an invention the higher the probability of patent validity.

My goal here is to connect the optimal probability of validity in the model to these subtests of nonobviousness. I do that by examining the comparative statics of α^*. I find that the optimal probability of validity is monotonic in certain parameters relating to the invention process, but not in parameters relating to commercial success. To obtain these results I restrict attention to the following research technology:[16]

$$p_i = \theta x_i (x_1 + x_2)^{\gamma - 1}, \quad \text{where} \quad 0 < \gamma < 1 \tag{11.11}$$

This functional form has some useful properties. Notice that the probability that one of the firms is successful is $\theta(x_1 + x_2)\gamma$. Thus the variable γ measures the elasticity of the probability of successful invention with respect to total investment expenditure. A small value of γ implies the probability of invention is not very sensitive to investment. Conversely, for large values of γ the probability of success is very sensitive to investment. The scaling factor θ can be used to account for the intrinsic difficulty of achieving an innovation. It could also account for the patent approval decision by the Patent Office. An exogenous change in the approval rate would shift θ.

The following proposition makes use of the functional form in (11) to provide a simple characterization of the optimal policy when it induces regular settlement.

Proposition 4. When the optimal policy induces regular settlement for the technology given in (11), the probability of invalidity, α^*, solves:

$$2\gamma S = (1 + \gamma) V - \alpha V_0 + 2T \tag{11.12}$$

Proof. The relevant expressions for social and private payoffs are found in (4). Since Σ^S is independent of α, the first order condition from (10) gives $\gamma\theta(2x)\gamma^{-1}S = 1$. From (8) the private equilibrium value of x satisfies $\theta[(\gamma + 1)W^S + (\gamma - 1)L^S](2x)\gamma^{-1} = 2$. Combining these terms and substituting for W^S and L^S yields (12) which gives the unique maximum. QED.

The key result expressed in equation (12) is that the probability of invalidity α^* is inversely related to γ. In other words, the optimal policy is more favorable to the patentee when the elasticity of research technology is close to one. The reason is that equilibrium research investment tends to be too low relative to the social optimum for large values of γ and too high for small values of γ.[17] For example, suppose γ is close to zero, then it is easy to see why there tends to be excessive investment. Since the probability that one of the firms will innovate, $\theta(2x^*)\gamma$, becomes close to the constant θ, regardless of the total investment, the social planner wants to discourage research.[18] In contrast, the firms want to win the patent race and thus overinvest. To reduce the firms' investment incentive sufficiently the probability of invalidity must be high. When γ is close to one, the equilibrium investment tends to be too low because the appropriability problem dominates, and the optimal probability of invalidity must be small.

This result supports the use of subtests based on attributes of the research process, but it does not clearly support any of the extant subtests. For example, the subtests relying on failure of others or long-felt unmet need could be associated with the model through θ. The failure of others might be attributable to a low value of θ. But from (12) we see that the optimal probability of invalidity is independent of θ.[19] At any rate the available subtests are not clearly linked to the elasticity of the research technology. My result suggests a dichotomy between the serendipitous invention versus the Edisonian invention. When γ is small it makes sense to say that a successful inventor was lucky. When γ is large it makes sense to say that a successful inventor 'perspired'; that the additional investment induced by a patent could have made the difference between success and failure.[20]

Besides linking the nonobviousness standard to the elasticity of the research technology, expression (12) yields two other interesting comparative static results: first, α^* is decreasing in terms of the positive externality generated by the innovation, and second, the effect of the value of the innovation on α^* is ambiguous. It is evident from (12) that α^* is falling in S. For fixed licensing profit, V, a relatively high value of S indicates that the innovation generates substantial social benefits, for example spillovers to other areas of research, that are not captured by an innovator. It would be straightforward and desirable to create subtest based on spill-over benefits created by an invention.

In contrast, the subtest based on the commercial success of an innovation is not supported by this analysis. Condition (12) can be used to study the effect of the value of the innovation on the optimal probability of validity. Here value refers to the commercial significance of the innovation, measured, for example, by the intercept of linear demand curve. An upward shift in demand raises V_0, V, and S. Examples can be adduced in which α^* either rises or falls. The ambiguous effect of the value of the innovation on the probability of invalidity arises because both the socially optimal investment, and the private equilibrium investment rise with the value of the innovation. It may be the case that the equilibrium investment rises too fast relative to the social optimum, and an increase in the probability of invalidity would be required. Or conversely, the equilibrium investment may rise too slowly which requires a decrease in the probability of invalidity.[21]

VI Conclusion

In this chapter I undertake a normative analysis of new product innovation in a model in which the government chooses the optimal probability of patent validity. The major goals of the chapter are to explicate the role of antitrust policy and costly litigation in the patent system, and to determine the optimal implementation of the nonobviousness standard of patentability. I find that, in a model with complete information, equilibrium patent trials occur for certain probabilities of validity because of asymmetric stakes in the litigation created by the patent licensing process. But trials vanish from equilibrium in this model if the antitrust policy governing licensing is too lenient. An optimal policy might result in trial, because the intermediate probabilities of patent validity which lead to intermediate levels of research effort also give rise to trial. It may be the case that weak patents which lead to settlement result in too little research, and strong patents which lead to unchallenged monopoly result in too much research; consequently, equilibrium trials are tolerated under the optimal policy.

The nonobviousness standard is intended to limit patent grants to inventions that represent a significant advance over previous technology. To implement this standard the courts have relied on various tests related to the research process as well as tests related to commercial success of the inventions. I assume a particular constant elasticity research process and show that the optimal probability of validity increases in that elasticity. In contrast, the linkage between commercial success and nonobviousness may be undesirable, since the optimal probability of validity is not monotonic in the commercial value of the innovation.

Notes

1. Professor of Law, Michaels Faculty Scholar, Boston University School of Law. Thanks to Ed Prescott, Herb Mohring, Bob Marshall, and Paul Joskow for helpful comments. Previous versions of this chapter were distributed as: 'Designing an Optimal System of Patent Litigation' (July 1987), 'Optimal Patent Litigation' (December 1992), and 'Patent Litigation, Licensing, and the Nonobviousness Standard' (July 1995).
2. In theory the Patent Office makes the same type of determination of validity that courts make. Patent applications are frequently rejected, but persistent applicants can reapply and usually succeed. See, *Duplan Corp. v. Deering Miliken, Inc.*, 444 F.Supp. 648, 750 (D.S.C. 1977). In note 19, I discuss random patent approval.
3. A survey of patent licensors revealed that 27 per cent of licenses covered products for which there is no close substitute. See Caves, Crookell and Killing (1983).
4. I am ignoring the possibility that the patentee licenses competing manufacturers to mitigate the impact of the hold-up problem on purchasers. This theory is explored by Shepard (1987) and Farell and Gallini (1988).
5. There are settlement cases concerning sham process patents, and a case involving the novelty of a drug, in which antitrust charges have been sustained against the licensor and licensees. Hence it may be the case that the factors that determine the probability of validity also determine the joint settlement profit. I disregard this possibility and assume that V is constant. See Priest (1977), for a discussion of patent licenses used to facilitate cartels.
6. For a more general treatment of the settlement of patent litigation, see Meurer (1989).
7. The loser of the patent contest does not have a credible threat unless there is some barrier to entry to production and sales besides the patent. There would be no profits and no incentive to go to trial otherwise. If more than two firms can compete after the patent is invalidated then V_0 could be reinterpreted as per firm profit for a market with n firms. Obviously, V_0 would be smaller and credibility would be a bigger problem for the loser of the patent contest.

   I also assume there are only two active firms at the litigation and research stages. Multiple potential infringers create modeling problems associated with the public good nature of patent litigation and multilateral bargaining. Assuming one potential infringer avoids these complications.
8. A payment by the patentee in exchange for a promise by its rival to withdraw from the market and never challenge the patent's validity would eliminate equilibrium trials. So would a promise by the patentee to exit the market or a merger between the firms.

More subtle means of achieving the same effect are possible through restraints in license agreements. If these tactics are precluded by antitrust law, then equilibrium trials are a possibility.

9. For a review, see Reinganum (1984).
10. The use of weak or insignificant patents to cartelize an industry through licensing has been successfully attacked under the antitrust laws. See Priest (1977). In the setting of this model it would be difficult for the government to win a case because it would require a showing that the license was not in settlement of a bona fide dispute. If the antitrust authorities could distinguish and prohibit collusive settlement licenses, then the payoffs would change so that $W^C = L^C = V_0$ and $\Sigma^C = S_0$ The analysis of the optimal policy would not change significantly.
11. For other work studying the patent and antitrust interface, see Kaplow (1984), Chang (1995), and Green and Scotchmer (1995).
12. Antitrust policy can affect the litigation and no entry payoffs. The payoff to the monopolist, V_1 can be affected especially by Section 2 of the Sherman Act, whereby limits are placed on the ability of monopolists to exploit their market power. I only consider antitrust policy toward settlement licenses.
13. If the licensing surplus were shared equally the result in the proposition is not significantly affected. An increase in V would raise the payoffs to the winner and loser equally. For typical research technologies this will lead to greater research investment ex ante, and the same proof applies.
14. Non-obviousness 'appears to be the predominant ground in court decisions of invalidity'. Kitti (1979) at p. 56.
15. See Merges (1988).
16. The parameter θ must be chosen to ensure that the probabilities p_1 and p_2 are well defined.
17. From (8) the private equilibrium investment is $(1/2)[(\theta/2)(W + \gamma (W + L) - L)]^{1/(1-\gamma)}$. From (10) the socially optimal investment is $(1/2)[\gamma\theta S]^{1/(1-\gamma)}$. So private investment is too high if and only if $\gamma < [W - L]/[2S - W - L]$.
18. The equilibrium probability that one of the firms will get a patent is given by $\theta [(\theta /2)(W + \gamma (W + L) - L)]^{1/(1-\gamma)}$. This has a limit of θ as γ goes to zero.
19. The variable θ is determined in part by the rate of patent approval in the Patent Office. The fact that α^* is independent of θ means that exogenous changes in the behavior of the Patent Office should not influence the probability of validity. Assuming a large random element to patent approval by the Patent Office is reasonable because of the limited information and resources available for processing applications, and because of the ex parte nature of the proceedings. Nevertheless, it would be valuable in future work to allow both the Patent Office and the courts to control the probability of validity.
20. Implementing a subtest based on the elasticity of the research technology would be complicated. One approach would rely on statistical measures of the elasticity derived from other research projects in the same area of technology.
21. This conclusion differs from Kitch (1977) who advocates a weak standard of nonobviousness and believes that commercial success should be used to infer nonobviousness. His claims cannot be evaluated in the context of this model since he addresses a research process of cumulative innovation that has no counterpart in this model. Merges (1988) dissents from Kitch and reaches conclusions complementary to mine.

References

Caves, R., H. Crookell and J. Killing (1983). 'The Imperfect Market for Technology Licenses', *Oxford Bulletin of Economics and Statistics*, 45(3), 249–67.

Chang, H. (1995). 'Patent Scope, Antitrust Policy, and Cumulative Innovation', *RAND Journal of Economics*, 26(1), 34–57.

Farrell, J. and N. Gallini (1988). 'Second Sourcing as a Means of Commitment: Monopoly Incentives to Attract Competition', *Quarterly Journal of Economics*, 103(4), 673–94.

Friedman, J. (1977). *Oligopoly and the Theory of Games*, North-Holland Publishing: Amsterdam.
Gallini, N. and R. Winter (1985). 'Licensing in the Theory of Innovation', *RAND Journal of Economics*, 16(2), 237–52.
Gilbert, R. and C. Shapiro (1990). 'Optimal Patent Length and Breadth', *RAND Journal of Economics*, 21(1), 106–12.
Green, J. and S. Scotchmer (1995). 'On the Division of Profit in Sequential Innovation', *RAND Journal of Economics*, 26(1), 20–33.
Kaplow, L. (1984). 'The Patent-Antitrust Intersection: A Reappraisal', *Harvard Law Review*, 97(8), 1813–92.
Katz, M. and C. Shapiro (1985). 'On the Licensing of Innovations', *RAND Journal of Economics*, 16(4), 504–20.
Katz, M. and C. Shapiro (1987). 'R&D Rivalry with Licensing or Imitation', *American Economic Review*, 77(3), 402–20.
Kitch, E. (1977), 'The Nature and Function of the Patent System', *Journal of Law and Economics*, 20(2), 265–90.
Kitti, C. (1979). 'Patent Invalidity Studies: A Survey', *Idea*, 20(4), 55–76.
Klemperer, P. (1990). 'How Broad Should the Scope of Patent Protection Be?', *RAND Journal of Economics*, 21(1), 113–30.
Merges, R. (1988). 'Commercial Success and Patent Standards: Economic Perspectives on Innovation', *California Law Review*, 76(4), 803–76.
Meurer, M. (1989). 'The Settlement of Patent Litigation', *RAND Journal of Economics*, 20(1), 77–91.
Nordhaus, W. (1969). *Invention, Growth, and Welfare*, MIT Press: Cambridge.
Priest, G. (1977). 'Cartels and Patent License Arrangements', *Journal of Law and Economics*, 20(2), 309–77.
Reinganum, J. (1984). 'Practical Implications of Game Theoretic Models of R&D', *American Economic Review Papers and Proceedings*, 74(2), 61–6.
Scotchmer, S. and J. Green (1990). 'Novelty and Disclosure in Patent Law', *RAND Journal of Economics*, 21 (1), 131–46.
Shepard, A. (1987). 'Licensing to Enhance Demand for New Technologies', *RAND Journal of Economics*, 18(3), 360–68.

Cases

Duplan Corp. v. Deering Miliken, Inc., 444 F.Supp. 648, 750 (D.S.C. 1977).
Graham v. John Deere Co., 383 US 1 (1966).

Statutes

15 U.S.C. §2.
35 U.S.C. §103.

Appendix

The model features a typical patent contest in which $p_i(x_1, x_2)$ is the probability that firm i receives a patent on a new product invention. I assume that (1) the probabilities p_1 and p_2 are twice continuously differentiable, non-negative and their sum is less than or equal to one, (2) the technology available to firms 1 and 2 is identical, thus, $p_1(x_1, x_2) = p_2(x_2, x_1)$ for any values of x_1 and x_2, (3) the probability of success is strictly increasing in own investment and strictly decreasing in the other firm's investment, and (4) $\partial^2 p_i/\partial x_1 \partial x_2 < 0$ at $x_1 = x_2$. Assumption (4) rules out large spillovers and requires that the marginal gain in the probability of a patent from own investment is declining as the other firm's investment increases. One last assumption (5) is used to assure the second order conditions are satisfied: for $W \geq L \geq 0$, I assume $W\partial^2 p_1/\partial x_1 \partial x_1 + L\,\partial^2 p_1/\partial x_2 \partial x_2 < 0$.

I first show that a unique equilibrium pair (x_1, x_2) exists for the patent contest with payoffs given in expression (8) in the main text. From Theorem 7.1 in Friedman (1977) I have existence. I limit the choice of x_1, and x_2 to some interval making the strategy set compact. This can be done without loss of generality since a choice of $x_1 > V_1$ would be unprofitable given any x_2 and could not be part of a Nash equilibrium. Furthermore, the payoff functions are strictly quasiconcave by (5), so existence is assured.

The equilibrium in research expenditures is unique if the best reply mappings are contractions according to Theorem 7.7 in Friedman (1977). Showing that the absolute values of the slopes of the reaction functions are less than one is sufficient to show uniqueness. The reaction functions are given implicitly by:

$$\begin{aligned} &Wp_1^1 + Lp_2^1 = 1 \\ &\textit{and} \\ &Lp_1^2 + Wp_2^2 = 1 \end{aligned} \qquad (11.\text{A}1)$$

Applying the implicit function theorem to the first order conditions gives a slope of:

$$-\frac{Wp_1^{12} + Lp_1^{12}}{Wp_1^{11} + Lp_1^{22}} \qquad (11.\text{A}2)$$

Thus, the reaction function is a contraction if:

$$|Wp_1^{11} + Lp_1^{22}| > |(W + L)p_1^{12}| \qquad (11.\text{A}3)$$

This inequality does not follow from the assumptions on p and is assumed to hold guaranteeing uniqueness.

Using the implicit function theorem and (A1) one can write $x_1 = f_1(W,L)$ and $x_2 = f_2(W,L)$. (A3) assures the implicit function theorem can be used. By symmetry $x_1 = x_2 = f(W,L)$. Expression (9) in the main text holds through application of the implicit function theorem to (A1) through the use of assumptions (4) and (5).

Finally, I use the research technology in expression (11) in the text to provide four examples in which each of the litigation outcomes is part of the socially optimal patent policy. Suppose $\gamma = 1/2$, $V_0 = 1$, $V = 3$, $V_1 = 4$, $S_0 = 10$, $S = 8$, $S_1 = 6$, and $T = 0$. Then $\alpha^* = 0.384$ and trial occurs in equilibrium. Expected social welfare under the optimal policy is approximately 2.54 per cent higher than in the best settlement outcome, approximately 24.62 per cent higher than in the case of no entry and approximately 32.92 per cent higher than in the case of collusive settlement. The choice of $T = 0$ is not required; there is sufficient continuity in the problem that trial still occurs in the optimal policy for sufficiently small T.

In the next example the only change from above is $S = 9.5$ and $S_1 = 9$.

Then $\alpha^* = 0$ and no entry is socially optimal. In this case for $T = 0$ trial is the same as no entry, but for any $T > 0$, trial is strictly worse. Expected social welfare under the optimal policy is approximately 32.72 per cent higher than in the best regular settlement outcome, and approximately 74.55 per cent higher than in the case of collusive settlement.

For the third example let $\gamma = 1/2$, $T = 0$, $V_0 = 1$, $V = V_1 = 3$, $S_0 = 5$, and $S = S_1 = 4$. Then $\alpha^* = 0.25$ and regular settlement is socially optimal. Trial is no longer a feasible outcome. Expected social welfare under the optimal policy is approximately 1.59 per cent higher than in the case of no entry, and approximately 16.36 per cent higher than in the case of collusive settlement.

For the final example use the values above except $V = V_1 = 5$, $S_0 = 6$, and $S = S_1 = 5$. Then $\alpha^* = 1$ and collusive settlement is socially optimal. Here trial is not feasible, and the best regular settlement is equivalent to collusive settlement. Expected social welfare under the optimal policy is 32 per cent higher than in the case of no entry.

Index